W9-CAJ-848

The Vest-Pocket MBA

SECOND EDITION

Jae K. Shim, Ph.D.
Joel G. Siegel, Ph.D., CPA
Abraham J. Simon, Ph.D., CPA

PRENTICE HALL
Paramus, New Jersey 07652

Library of Congress Cataloging-in-Publication Data

Shim, Jae K.
    The vest-pocket MBA / Jae Shim, Joel Siegel,
Abraham Simon.—2nd ed.
        Includes index.
        ISBN 0-13-460312-5 (C)—ISBN 0-13-460304-4 (P)
        1. Managerial accounting.   2. Business enterprises—
Finance.   I. Siegel, Joel G.   II. Simon, Abraham J.   III. Title.
HF5635.S55295   1997   96-40269
658.15—dc21   CIP

Printed in the United States of America

10 9 8 7 6 5 4 3 (C)

10 9 8 7 6 5   (P)

ISBN 0-13-460312-5

9 780134 603124   90000

ATTENTION: CORPORATIONS AND SCHOOLS

Prentice Hall books are available at quantity discounts with bulk purchase for educational, business, or sales promotional use. For information · please write to: Prentice Hall Special Sales, 240 Frisch Court, Paramus, New Jersey 07652. Please supply: title of book, ISBN number, quantity, how the book will be used, date needed.

PRENTICE HALL
Paramus, NJ 07652

On the World Wide Web at http://www.phdirect.com

Dedication

TO OUR WIVES
CHUNG, ROBERTA, AND MARILYN

For the love, patience, and
assistance they have given us

TO THE MEMORY OF OUR FATHERS
We miss them so much

Acknowledgments

We wish to specially thank our editors at Prentice-Hall for their invaluable input in the preparation of the manuscript. Bette Schwartzberg, Ellen Coleman, and Sybil Grace provided encouragement and outstanding editorial comments and suggestions that were of immeasurable benefit. Their efforts are greatly appreciated. Patricia Virga, our developmental editor, did an excellent job of going over the entire manuscript to assure technical accuracy and appropriate writing style. Her earnest and helpful efforts are greatly recognized. Thanks also to Cathy Johnson and Jackie Boggi-Roulette our production editors, for their help in the production process.

About the Authors

JAE K. SHIM, Ph.D., is Professor of Business Administration at California State University, Long Beach. He received his M.B.A. (Business Economics) and Ph.D. (Operations Research) degrees from the University of California at Berkeley. Dr. Shim, a management consultant, has published numerous articles in such journals as *Financial Management, Econometrica, Decision Sciences, Management Science, Long Range Planning, OMEGA*, and *Journal of Operational Research Society*. He has over 35 college and professional books to his credit, including *Handbook of Financial Analysis, Forecasting and Modeling, The Vest Pocket CFO*, and *The Vest Pocket CPA*. Dr. Shim is the recipient of the 1982 *Credit Research Foundation* award for his article on financial modeling.

JOEL G. SIEGEL, Ph.D., CPA, is a professor of accounting and finance at Queens College of the City University of New York and a financial consultant to management. He is the author of 50 published and about-to-be-published books and over 200 articles. Dr. Siegel's articles have appeared in professional journals, including *The Financial Executive, The Financial Analysts Journal, The CPA Journal, The National Public Accountant, Credit and Financial Management*, and the *International Journal of Management*. He has served as consultant and/or advisor to numerous organizations, including the AICPA, Citicorp, and ITT. He was affiliated with Coopers and Lybrand, CPAs, and Arthur Andersen, CPAs. In 1972 Dr. Siegel was the recipient of the Outstanding Educator of America award. He is listed in *Who's Where Among Writers* and in *Who's Who in the World.*

ABRAHAM J. SIMON, Ph.D., CPA, is professor of accounting and information systems at Queens College of the City University of New York. He has served as consultant to several organizations and the City of New York. He has authored professional books for the AICPA and the Council on Municipal Performance. Dr. Simon's articles have appeared in many journals, including the *International Journal of Accounting Education and Research,* the *National Public Accountant*, and *Credit and Financial Management*. Professor Simon has practiced extensively as a CPA.

About the Contributors

STEPHEN W. HARTMAN, Ph.D., is a financial consultant and advisor to companies and a professor of management at the Graduate School of Business at New York Institute of Technology. He has authored several books and has written numerous articles in professional business journals.

JOYCE O. MOY, J.D., is a practicing attorney and an adjunct professor of law at Queens College of the City University of New York. She is a consultant to companies on legal matters. She has been a partner in a law firm, as well as a legal editor for Matthew Bender and Company and Research Institute of America.

Contents

Contents

Contents

Introduction

Here is a handy pocket problem-solver for today's busy executive. It's a working guide to help you quickly pinpoint

- What to look for
- What to watch out for
- What to do
- How to do it

in the complex world of business. You'll find ratios, formulas, guidelines, and rules of thumb to help you analyze and evaluate any business-related problem. Throughout, you'll find this book practical, quick, and useful.

Uses for this book are as varied as the topics presented. Part I (Chapters 1, 2, and 3) takes you through accounting principles and guidelines for evaluating a company's financial health. You'll learn techniques for analyzing another company's financial position should you wish to invest, extend credit, or compare. We present internal accounting applications to help you evaluate your own company's performance, profitability, marketing effectiveness, and budgeting process. You'll learn how to highlight problem areas with variance analysis.

Part II (Chapters 4, 5, and 6) takes a look at financial and economic measures for decision making. Through breakeven and sensitivity analysis, you'll be able to move your company toward greater profits. For investment purposes, this part presents guidelines for evaluating proposals, whether they be short or long term, for profit potential and risk-return comparisons. You'll learn management and financing techniques to ensure the best possible strategies for maximizing and acquiring cash.

Part III (Chapters 7 and 8) takes you through the seemingly complex world of quantitative analysis. You'll use statistics for forecasting and validity testing. Decision theories include linear programming, learning curve theory, and queuing models; these are presented concisely and comprehensively to help you use such sophisticated techniques with relative ease. And, you'll learn how computer applications facilitate the many complex procedures.

Part IV (Chapters 9, 10, 11, and 12) takes you through the world of management and marketing. You will learn various management techniques, production operations management, the marketing process of planning and distribution, and how to price and promote products. These management and marketing techniques and processes have been presented in an extremely understandable and practical format to make them as useful a possible. The statutory and case law affecting business operations and decisions are also presented. Legal requirements must be known to protect the business entity.

Part V (Chapters 13 and 14) covers the economic issues of interest to business managers because they have a significant impact upon corporate success or failure. Attention should be given to the changing economic environment as well as economic indices and statistics in making financial and investment decisions. Many companies are multinational so business managers must understand the opportunities and difficulties associated with international trade. Some relevant issues of concern to business people are exchange rates, foreign restrictions and limitations, political risk, import/export relationships and foreign prices.

This book has been designed in question-and-answer format in order to address the pertinent issues that come up during the course of business. The questions are typical of those asked by persons like yourself. The answers are clear, concise, and to the point. In short, this is a veritable cookbook of guidelines, illustrations, and "how-to's" for you, the modern decision maker. Keep it handy for easy reference throughout your busy day.

Jae K. Shim   Joel G. Siegel   Abraham J. Simon

ACCOUNTING TOOLS
AND GUIDELINES

1

How to Evaluate a Company's Financial Position: Part I

Financial analysis of other companies is important if you are

- An investor who needs to formulate portfolio decisions
- A creditor who must make sure he gets paid
- An auditor who needs to appraise her client's financial astuteness
- A financial manager who wants to evaluate and improve areas of inadequacy and improvement
- A marketing manager who wants to establish product line strategies

Here are your guidelines for conducting a financial analysis.

1 THE INCOME STATEMENT ANALYSIS

1.1.1 Evaluating Earnings Quality

What are the importance of earnings quality?

Earnings quality refers to realistic earnings, or monies earned after various factors have been taken into account. The following factors will have a bearing on the earnings quality of the company:

- The P/E ratio (market price per share divided by earnings per share) used in equity financing decisions. A low P/E ratio means lower earnings quality.

- Effective interest rate in credit decisions. Compensating balance requirements and the cost of borrowing will be higher when earnings quality is lower.
- Availability of future financing sources. Poor earnings quality may put fewer funds at the company's disposal.
- The bond rating. Poor earnings quality means a lower bond rating, and this may lower the market price of bonds.

WARNING: Beware the "high accounting risk" company. Many fall under this category, including:

- "Glamour" companies, known for profitability growth
- Companies in the public eye
- Companies with problems getting adequate financing
- Companies whose management might previously have been dishonest

How do accounting policies affect earnings quality?

You should compare the company's accounting policies with industry standards. If the firm's policies are more liberal, earnings quality is likely to be lower. Realistic policies as determined by industry standards can be found in American Institute of Certified Public Accountants (AICPA) industry audit guides, AICPA statements of position, and CPA firm publications.

WHAT TO DO: Compare reported earnings based on the most realistic accounting principles with the principles used by the firm. If realistic policies would have resulted in less profit, then the earnings quality would be lower. For example, the deferred method of accounting for investment tax credit is more realistic than the flow-through method. The deferred method amortizes the tax credit against tax expense over the life of the asset. The flow-through method reduces tax expense in full for credit in the year of acquisition, thus, companies using this method would have lower earnings quality.

What constitutes accurate revenue recognition?

Revenue recognition means recording revenues when earned, either at the time of sale or rendering of services. Make sure that revenue is being recognized only when warranted. For example, a company might record credit sales without adequate provision for bad debts even if the risk of not collecting is high. Revenue should not be recognized when material services have not yet been performed, for example, if a correspondence school claims revenue before the student has begun work. On the other hand, revenue recognition may be deferred unjustifiably, in which case consider net income to be improperly understated.

How do I interpret over- or underaccrued expenses?

Underaccrued or overaccrued expenses, that is, those that are recorded too low or too high, result in poor earnings quality. For example, a warranty provision that does not adequately address problems with product quality would result in an underaccrued expense. WHAT TO DO: Adjust net income based on realistic normal charges.

EXAMPLE 1.1

Bad debts were recorded at $12,000. The analyst finds this to be an overestimated expense, and believes bad debts should have been estimated to be $9,000. Net income, hence, should be increased by $3,000.

What about accounting changes?

An accounting change is appropriate if it is made to conform to a new Financial Accounting Standards Board (FASB) statement, AICPA industry audit guide, or Internal Revenue Service (IRS) regulation. An unwarranted accounting change, either in principle (method) or estimate, detracts from earnings quality. Often, these changes can mislead earnings growth estimates. WARNING: If a firm makes many accounting changes, you will not be able to use current period earnings as a reliable base for predicting future earnings.

How should I interpret income smoothing?

Income smoothing occurs when earnings are reported artificially, and it results in lower earnings quality. Why? Because net income does not portray economic results as they are, but rather as management wants them shown. WARNING TO CREDIT AND LOAN OFFICERS: A weak relationship between sales and net income may be a sign of income smoothing.

EXAMPLE 1.2

Company J's ratio of net income to sales for the period 19X1 to 19X4 is given as follows:

19X1	19X2	19X3	19X4
0.10	0.05	0.18	0.02

The trend shows a weak relationship between net income and sales. This may mean possible income smoothing.

What do discretionary costs tell me?

Management can alter at will such discretionary costs as advertising, repairs, research, and training. Ask yourself, "Does the amount of discretionary costs for this period conform to previous trends, industry norms, future expectations?" Remember, an unjustified decrease in discretionary costs means lower earnings quality. Why? Because management is depriving its business of required expenditures. SUGGESTION: Take particular note of decreasing trends in these ratios: discretionary costs to sales and discretionary costs to assets.

FOR CREDIT AND LOAN OFFICERS: Use index numbers to compare discretionary costs with base year amounts. Example 1.3 shows how to do it.

EXAMPLE 1.3

The relationship between research and sales for 19X1 to 19X3 is given as follows:

	19X1	19X2	19X3
Sales	$120,000	$150,000	$80,000
Research	12,000	18,000	6,000
Ratio of research to sales	0.10	0.12	0.075

*19X1 is the base year.

Since 19X1 is the most typical year, it is assigned an index number 100. In 19X2, the index number is 150 ($18,000/$12,000). In 19X3, the index number is 50 ($6,000/$12,000).

A negative trend is indicated here. Research is lower than in previous years, but it should have been increased to ensure future success.

EXAMPLE 1.4

Company F gives the following information regarding its fixed assets:

	19X1	19X2
Fixed assets	$6,000	$6,300
Less accumulated depreciation	(3,300)	(3,700)
Book value	2,700	2,600
Repairs	400	300
Replacement cost of fixed assets	8,000	8,900

	19X1	19X2
CPI value of fixed assets	8,600	9,400
Sales	47,000	55,000
Working capital	4,000	3,400
Cash	1,000	930
Debt-to-equity ratio	0.42	0.68
Downtime of fixed assets in terms of available capacity	2.1%	5.3%

The following observations point to inadequate maintenance of capital:

- The ratio of repairs to gross fixed assets went from 0.067 ($400/$6,000) in 19X1 to 0.048 ($300/$6,300) in 19X2. For the same period, there was a reduction of repairs to sales from 0.0085 ($400/$47,000) to 0.0055 ($300/$55,000).

- From 19X1 to 19X2 there was a widening difference between replacement cost and book value as well as between CPI value and book value. These trends reflect growing obsolescence of assets. NOTE TO MARKETING MANAGERS: Production problems may be in store; these can adversely affect future sales.

- Increased downtime indicates growing equipment problems.

- There were minimal purchases of fixed assets in 19X2 ($300). In this year, the ratio of new acquisitions to the gross fixed asset base was 0.05 ($300/$6,000). There will be a problem replacing the assets when required owing to the firm's weakening cash and working capital position. In turn, the higher replacement cost will hurt liquidity. A high debt-to-equity ratio means the company will have a problem getting adequate financing, particularly when there is a tight money market.

Here are some other signposts to look for regarding discretionary costs:

- *Cost-reduction program.* A cost-control program lowers earnings quality when material cutbacks in discretionary costs occur.

- *Proper reductions in discretionary costs.* A decline in discretionary costs is not *always* unwarranted. A reduction may be required when the prior corporate policy was inadequate.

- *Boost in discretionary costs.* A material boost in discretionary costs will likely enhance future earnings.

- *Income management.* If discretionary costs fluctuate relative to revenue, income smoothing may be occurring.

How do I measure cash flow?

Net income is better in quality when backed up by cash because it can be used to pay debt, expand, etc. WHAT TO DO: Look at the trend in cash flow from operations to net income.

EXAMPLE 1.5

A partial income statement of Company H is given as follows:

Sales		$1,600,000
Less cost of sales		(600,000)
Gross margin		$1,000,000
Less operating expenses		
Wages	$150,000	
Rent	220,000	
Utilities	40,000	
Depreciation	70,000	
Amortization expense	50,000	
Total operating expenses		(530,000)
Income before other revenue and expenses		$ 470,000
Interest expense	$ 60,000	
Less amortization of deferred income	(20,000)	
Total other revenue and expense		(40,000)
Net income		**$ 430,000**

The ratio of cash flow from operations to net income is computed as follows:

Cash flow from operations

Net income		$430,000
Add noncash expenses:		
Depreciation	$ 70,000	
Amortization expense	50,000	
Total noncash expenses		120,000

Less noncash revenue:

Amortization of deferred income	(20,000)
Cash flow from operations	**$ 530,000**

$$\frac{\text{Cash flow from operations}}{\text{Net income}} = \frac{\$530,000}{\$430,000} = 1.23$$

Cash revenue and expenses are more factual than estimated revenue and expenses. For example, salary expenses are more certain than depreciation, and thus are more reliable.

Now do I analyze taxable income?

In general, taxable income is lower than net income because firms use more conservative policies for tax reporting. However, if book income greatly exceeds taxable income, the earnings quality may be lower. WHAT TO LOOK FOR: A widening disparity between the two is reflected in a trend toward increasing the deferred income tax credit account.

EXAMPLE 1.6

ABC Company furnishes the following information:

	19X1	19X2	19X3
Deferred income tax credit	$200	$230	$350
Sales	12,000	13,500	14,200
Net income	3,000	3,200	2,600
Deferred income tax credit to sales	0.017	0.017	0.025
Deferred income tax credit to net income	0.067	0.072	0.135

The increase in the deferred account in base dollars was 115 ($230/$200) for 19X2 and 175 for 19X3 ($350/$200). The increase in deferred income tax credit to both sales and net income indicates a widening difference between book income and taxable income.

Take note of these special circumstances:

Foreign earnings. Many businesses earn profits in low-tax foreign countries. Such profits are often not repatriated back to the United States because they would be subject to U.S. taxes. If you consider net income as funds available to stockholders, then net income that includes foreign profits would be overstated.

Effective tax rate. The effective tax rate relates tax expense to before-tax income. A reduction in the effective tax rate arising from a onetime source (such as an investment tax credit for a major plant expansion) causes overstated earnings from the point of view of the investment analyst. These tax benefits will not continue in future years.

Domestic International Sales Corporation (DISC). Net income is overstated when DISC tax deferrals exist.

1.1.2 Using Accounting Estimates

How does uncertainty in accounting estimates affect earnings quality?

The more subjective the estimates used to determine earnings are, the more uncertain are the results. For example, a ship builder uses a percentage-of-completion accounting method because of its long-term activities. There would be a significant amount of uncertainty associated with the earnings, especially if a great amount of estimates is involved. WHAT TO DO: You should compare estimated and actual losses over the years. A significant difference points to lower earnings quality. WARNING: Material gains and losses on the disposition of assets may imply that improper estimates were used to compute depreciation. REMEMBER THIS: The greater the percent of assets involving many accounting estimates is, the more uncertain the reported results will be.

EXAMPLE 1.7

Company S's provision for expense warranties came to $80,000 in 19X1 and $120,000 in 19X2 .Actual warranty costs were $110,000 in 19X1 and $180,000 in 19X2. The unfavorable difference in 19X1 was $30,000, or 37.5% of the original estimate ($30,000/$80,000). In 19X2, the unfavorable difference grew to $60,000, or 50% of the estimate ($60,000/$120,000). You cannot rely on this company's estimation process.

Additionally, earnings for 19X1 and 19X2 are overstated by virtue of the underestimated expense provisions.

You should distinguish between revenue and expense items that are cash related versus those that are based on estimates. CREDIT AND LOAN OFFICERS: Pay attention to trends indicated from these ratios:

- Cash expenses to total revenue
- Estimated expenses to total revenue
- Cash revenue to total revenue
- Estimated revenue to total revenue
- Cash expenses to net income
- Estimated expenses to net income
- Cash revenue to net income
- Estimated revenue to net income

Trends should always be compared over the years within the same company, with competing companies, and with industry norms. The following example shows some of these ratios.

EXAMPLE 1.8

Company A provides the following information for the period 19X1 and 19X2,

	19X1	19X2
Cash and near-cash revenue	$ 80,000	$ 95,000
Noncash revenue	160,000	210,000
Total revenue	**$240,000**	**$305,000**
Cash and near-cash expenses	$ 30,000	$ 70,000
Noncash expenses	80,000	140,000
Total expenses	**$110,000**	**$210,000**
Net income	**$130,000**	**$ 95,000**
Estimated revenue to total revenue	0.67	0.69
Estimated revenue to net income	1.23	2.21
Estimated expenses to total expenses	0.73	0.67
Estimated expenses to total revenue	0.33	0.46
Estimated expenses to net income	0.62	1.47

You can see that there is greater uncertainty regarding the net income for 19X2 because of higher ratios in nearly every category—the only ratio that decreased was estimated expenses to total expenses.

What is residual income and how do I measure its effects?

Residual income can be calculated using the following formula:

Net income – (cost of capital × total assets)
= residual income

The higher the ratio of residual income to net income, the better the earnings quality. Why? Because the company is earning a sufficient amount to cover its minimum rate of return on assets. This measure tells the real earnings of the business. FOR ECONOMISTS: You would like to know what a company really earns after taking into account the minimum return on assets (cost of capital). Example 1.9 tells you how to find out.

EXAMPLE 1.9

A company's cost of capital is 12%, its net income is $800,000, and its assets total $4,000,000. Residual income is calculated as follows:

Net income	$800,000
Less cost of capital times total assets (12% × $4,000,000)	(480,000)
Residual income	$320,000
Ratio of residual income to net income ($320,000/$800,000).	0.40

Persons preparing and using the financial statement must determine the cost of capital based on data in the annual report. The cost of capital considers the cost of various financing instruments and their weights (percentages) in the capital structure. For example, the cost of debt is interest and the cost of stock is dividends. The weights of debt and stock in the capital structure depend on the ratio of each in dollars to the total debt and equity.

The cost of financing may depend on current market prices rather than book value. Cost of capital determination is of interest to you if you are a

- *Financial manager* who wants to determine the best mixture of new financing that lowers overall cost of financing
- *Managerial accountant* who needs to compute the discount rate for capital budgeting decisions
- *Creditor or investment analyst* who needs to ascertain

the riskiness of the company on the basis of the rate change in the cost of capital

1.1.3 Analyzing Acquisitions

What accounting methods are used for business combinations?

Two methods of accounting used for business combinations are pooling and purchase. You must carefully evaluate pooling because it can portray artificial earnings growth. Here, the purchaser recognizes the earnings of the acquired business for an entire year, even though the acquisition was made some time during the year. WHAT YOU SHOULD DO: Eliminate that part of the reported results that includes the profit of the acquired firm before the date of acquisition.

Bring forth the net assets of the acquired company at book value, *not* market value. Since book value is typically less, the understated assets (e.g., fixed assets) will result in understated expenses (e.g., depreciation). The result is overstated earnings. You should adjust the net assets of the acquired business from book value to market value and also adjust the expenses to determine a realistic earnings figure comparable to what the earnings would have been using the purchase method.

Bringing forth net assets at book value will suppress such asset valuations. Thus, upon the sale of those assets, earnings will be overstated. You should adjust net income downward to account for the difference between the reported and probable gain if the asset valuation was based on market value.

The purchase method is more realistic than pooling. Here, net income of the acquired business is recognized from the date of acquisition to year-end. Market value shows the worth of the assets better than outdated historical cost. Take note of the reasonableness of the market value used.

WARNING: Even under purchase, weak companies may still show strong operating results by buying very profitable businesses. Hence, you should look at the trend and dollar effect upon profitability of purchase transactions.

CHECKLIST OF QUESTIONS REGARDING ACQUISITIONS

- Is earnings growth illusory?
- In pooling, is book value of acquired assets significantly understated relative to market value?
- In pooling, were there onetime gains on the sale of low-cost basis assets?

- In purchase, were the fair values assigned to assets realistic?
- In purchase, were equity securities issued at an unusually high price?

How do I handle construction contracts?

TO LOAN OFFICERS AND CREDITORS: Watch closely if the company classifies period costs as construction costs so as not to lower reported results. Also note whether cost overruns on contracts are occurring but are not being recognized in the statements.

Does income from discontinued operations affect earnings quality?

Income from discontinued operations is typically of a onetime nature and should be ignored when forecasting future earnings. Also, a discontinued operation implies that the business is in a state of decline or that a poor management decision is responsible for the company's entering the discontinued line of business. REMEMBER: Income from continuing operations is the most representative earnings figure applying to the company's current operating performance.

What are signs of unreliable earnings?

Look for these signs of unreliable earnings:

- Poor internal control (This implies possible undetected accounting errors.)
- Material error corrections relating to prior years
- A history of income smoothing as evidenced by accounting and financial publications (e.g., brokerage reports)
- Liberal accounting policies
- Skyrocketing audit fees owing to problems in the company's accounting system
- High turnover rate in using CPA firms

What does the audit report mean?

FOR INVESTMENT AND CREDIT ANALYSTS: Consider carefully the audit report for a company; in particular, remember that earnings quality is highest if the firm has received an unqualified opinion. With a qualified opinion, the CPA states that "except for" (a limitation placed on the scope of the audit) or "subject to" (an uncertainty, like a lawsuit), the financial statements present financial position and operating results fairly. A disclaimer means the CPA cannot render an opinion, which generally occurs when he or she did not conduct the necessary audit procedures. An adverse opinion means the CPA believes the statements do not conform to generally accepted accounting principles (GAAP).

NOTE: A material event occurring after year-end but before the issuance of the audit report (for example, a catastrophe loss) may be disclosed in the audit report.

1.2 APPRAISING THE FINANCIAL STRUCTURE

1.2.1 Evaluating Earnings Stability

How do I compute growth rate?

A company's growth rate equals

$$\frac{\text{Net income} - \text{dividends}}{\text{Common stock equity}}$$

A high ratio indicates a company's ability to generate internal funds and a minimal reliance on external sources. WHAT TO DO: Compare the company's growth rate with those of major competitors and with industry norms.

How do I define stability of earnings?

Stable earnings, that is, those that remain relatively constant, are of higher quality because you can project future earnings more readily. Less instability is also associated with corporate operations. You should compute the following ratios:

- One-time gains and losses to net income
- One-time gains and losses to sales

How Do I Measure Earnings Stability? A lack of stability indicates riskiness associated with the business. WHAT TO DO: Evaluate trends in earnings stability by examining a long interval of time, say ten years. The more vacillation in earnings, the lower the earnings quality. You can use the following measures:

- *Average net income.* The computation of average net income for a ten-year period smooths out erratic income statement elements and cyclical impacts on the business. Average net income therefore is a good indicator of earning power.
- *Average pessimistic earnings.* This represents the average earnings based on the worst possible situation with

the business. FOR CREDIT AND LOAN OFFICERS: To measure risk, use the minimum earnings figure in cases where the business is very risky.

Standard Deviation (SD) in Earnings

$$SD = \sqrt{\frac{\sum(y - \overline{y})^2}{n}}$$

where

y = net income for period t
$\overline{y}$ = average earnings
n = number of years

A high standard deviation indicates low earnings quality.

Coefficient of Variation (CV) in Earnings

$$CV = \frac{SD}{\overline{y}}$$

This is useful in appraising relative earnings instability. A high coefficient means high risk.

Instability Index (I) of Earnings

$$I = \sqrt{\frac{\sum(y - \overline{y}^T)^2}{n}}$$

where

y^T = trend earnings for period t, computed as follows:
$y^T = a + bt$

where

a = dollar intercept
b = slope of trend line
t = time period

Trend earnings are best determined with a computer. The instability index shows the variation between actual and trend earnings. A high index points to low earnings quality.

Beta. Beta, which may be determined by computer, is equal to

$$r_{jt} = a_j + \beta_j r_{mt} + E_{jt}$$

where

r_{jt} = return on security j for period t
a_j = constant
β_j = Beta for security j
r_{mt} = return on a market index (like Dow Jones)
E_{jt} = error term

Beta measures the riskiness of a stock. A high beta shows that the company's stock price fluctuates more than the market index. For example, a beta of 1.7 means that the company's stock price can increase or decrease 70 percent faster than the market. A beta of 0.6 means that the company's stock price can increase or decrease 60 percent less than the market. Various financial services (e.g., Standard & Poor's) will provide beta values for specific companies.

Over a number of years, a company's stock may have a positive beta during some periods and a negative beta during others.

EXAMPLE 1.10

Company P shows the following earnings trend:

19X0	$80,000
19X1	75,000
19X2	70,000

The standard deviation in earnings is computed as follows:

$$SD = \sqrt{\frac{\Sigma(y - \bar{y})^2}{n}}$$

$$y = \frac{\Sigma y}{n} = \frac{\$80,000 + \$75,000 + \$70,000}{3}$$

$$= \frac{\$225,000}{3} = \$75,000$$

Year	$(y - \bar{y})$	$(y - \bar{y})^2$
19X0	$ + 5,000	$25,000,000
19X2	0	0
19X3	$ - 5,000	$25,000,000
Total		$50,000,000

$$SD = \sqrt{\frac{\$50,000,000}{3}} = \sqrt{16,666,666}$$

$$= \$4,082.48 \text{ (rounded)}$$

The coefficient of variation in earnings is computed as follows:

$$CV = \frac{SD}{\bar{y}} = \frac{\$4,082.48}{\$75,000} = 5.4\%$$

What is the significance of gross profit percentage?

IMPORTANT FOR MANAGEMENT EXECUTIVES: A high gross profit percentage (gross profit divided by sales) reflects positive earnings quality. Usually it means the business can control its manufacturing costs, a task sometimes difficult to achieve. NOTE: Operating expenses are easier to control because they are internal and can be subject to cost control programs.

What is operating leverage?

Operating leverage refers to the extent that fixed costs are contained in the company's cost structure. Use these ratios to measure operating leverage:

- Fixed cost to total cost
- Percent change in operating income to the percent change in sales volume
- Net income to fixed costs

An increase in the first two or a decrease in the third indicates higher fixed costs. These may cause earnings to vacillate, thereby suggesting lower earnings quality.

ATTENTION FINANCIAL MANAGERS: The company's cost structure affects earnings as volume changes. Companies with high operating leverage will have high risk because fixed cost cannot be lowered when revenue declines.

A high ratio of variable cost to total cost shows earnings indicate stability. Variable costs may be adjusted more easily than fixed cost during a decline in product demand. MARKETING MANAGERS REMEMBER: The cost makeup of products affects product line profitability.

What are the advantages of original sales generating further revenue?

When a company can obtain additional revenue from its initial sale, this means greater earnings stability. For example, the sale of a TV may lead to further business (such as a service contract, tubes, etc.). FOR MARKETING MANAGERS: When setting policy, note trends as reflected in the following ratios:

- Replacement and maintenance revenue to new sales
- Replacement and maintenance revenue to total revenue
- Replacement and maintenance revenue to net income

Rising trends point to better earnings quality.

How do I recognize an opportunist market?

Short-term schemes (such as single government contracts) increase profit temporarily and thus are of poor earnings quality. FOR MARKETING MANAGERS: Be sure to compute the following ratios:

- Short-lived income to total revenue
- Short-lived income to net income

How do I evaluate the product line?

In terms of marketing strategy, companies whose product line demand is relatively constant are minimally affected by the business cycle. Companies with product lines that relate closely to gross national product show more fluctuation in earnings. SUGGESTION: To stabilize operations, products should be added that have different seasonal peaks. The following factors should be considered when evaluating the product line.

Nature of the Product. Certain products enhance earnings stability by performing well in recessionary as well as growth periods. Such products include necessity items and retail trade.

MARKETING MANAGERS: The product mix selection is vital. Some products detract from earnings stability. These include novelty goods, high-priced items, excluding those that appeal to a select marketing (e.g., Rolls Royces), heavy goods, and raw materials. Higher earnings quality would be associated with new, similar products that can be developed easily from the company's basic manufacturing operations or new products that produce supplementary demand instead of eating into existing product lines.

Variances in the Product Line. Volume, price, and cost may vary throughout a company's product line. The more variability in these elements, the greater the earnings vacillation.

SUGGESTION TO THE MANAGEMENT EXECUTIVE: You should evaluate the fluctuation in quantity, selling price, and cost for each major product. Try charting graphs. Also, compute the standard deviation by product. MARKETING MANAGERS: You may wish to compute sales mix, cost, and quantity variances.

Product Line Diversification. A single-product firm possesses less earnings stability because it is more susceptible to earnings vacillation and runs higher risk of product obsolescence.

ADVICE FOR MARKETING MANAGERS: Diversification in the product line coupled with negatively correlated products is best.

In appraising the product line, you should determine the correlation coefficient between products (refer to Section 7.6). SUGGESTION: Use a computer-determined correlation matrix. Also, measure product demand elasticity as follows:

$$\frac{\text{Percent change in quantity}}{\text{Percent change in price}}$$

If the ratio exceeds 1, this indicates elastic demand. Poor earnings quality occurs when products are positively correlated with elastic product demand.

EXAMPLE 1.11

The correlation matrix of Company I's product line is given as follows:

Product	A	B	C	D	E	F
A	1.00	0.13	−0.02	−0.01	−0.07	0.22
B	0.13	1.00	−0.02	−0.07	0.00	0.00
C	−0.02	−0.02	1.00	0.01	0.48	0.13
D	−0.01	−0.07	0.01	1.00	0.01	−0.02
E	−0.07	0.00	0.48	0.01	1.00	0.45
F	0.22	0.00	0.13	−0.02	0.45	1.00

Of course, perfect correlation exists with the same product. For example, the correlation between Product A and Product A is 1.00. High positive correlation exists between Products E and C (0.48) and E and F (0.45). Since these products are closely tied to each other, risk is indicated.

Low negative correlation exists between Products A and D (−0.01) and Products A and C (−0.02).

No correlation exists between Products B and E (0.00) and Products B and F (0.00).

It would have been better for Company I if it had some products that had significant negative correlations (e.g., −0.60). Unfortunately, it does not.

Unusual Product Demand. Extraordinary product demand coupled with skyrocketing prices detracts from earnings quality. MARKETING MANAGERS TAKE NOTE: This causes an unusual situation that is not likely to be repeated.

Consumer Taste. A company with a product line vulnerable to rapid shifts in consumer taste has lower earnings stability.

Product Introduction. A company that introduces new products to replace old ones has better earnings stability. FINANCIAL MANAGERS: Examine the number of patented products being introduced to the total product line.

Product Mix. MARKETING MANAGERS: You should determine the degree to which the product line can be considered growth, mature, declining, and/or developing. You should also evaluate the risk in the life cycle. Prefer mature and growth products to declining or developing ones.

1.2.2   Recognizing Revenue Stability

How does product demand affect revenue stability?

Product demand susceptible to outside forces detracts from revenue stability. WARNING TO MARKETING MANAGERS: Export sales to a foreign country may disappear as that country develops its own manufacturing capability.

When a company sells to diversified industries that are susceptible to contrasting cyclical factors, greater revenue stability results. HINT: To reduce the effects of economic cycles, the company should enter noncyclical or countercyclical business lines. ANOTHER SUGGESTION: Geographic diversification reduces vulnerability to economic downturns.

What about costs of raw materials?

Vulnerability in raw material cost causes earnings vacillation. FINANCIAL ACCOUNTANTS: Look at trade publications to appraise cost instability.

A company without alternative raw material sources experiences greater uncertainty regarding future earnings. Dependence on potentially unreliable supply sources (e.g., oil) increases risk. HINT TO MANAGEMENT EXECUTIVES: To curtail a company's price and supply risk of raw materials, you should vertically integrate.

How do I assess risk and uncertainty?

Net income is affected by both controllable (e.g., management decisions) and uncontrollable (e.g., shortage in money supply) factors. The more uncontrollable the factors influencing operations, the greater the uncertainty in earnings. Be sure to appraise the degree of influence uncontrollable factors have over operations.

Riskiness can be measured by the degree of frequency with which abnormal events occur. If uncertainties are great, net income will be less predictable.

There is a trade-off between risk and return. The higher the risk, the greater should be the return (see also Section 5.3).

Corporate Risk. WARNING TO MANAGEMENT EXECUTIVES: Corporate risks are plentiful. For example, a company may be overly dependent on a select few employees or there may be a militant union.

Political Risk. Political risk applies to fund reputation, exchange shifts, local customs, and regulations.

Operations in politically unstable foreign countries point to poor earnings quality. FINANCIAL MANAGERS: You should ascertain the profit and assets for each foreign country considered to be high risk. Examine these relevant ratios:

- Questionable foreign revenue to total revenue
- Questionable foreign profit to total profit
- Export revenue to total revenue
- Export profit to total profit
- Total assets in each questionable foreign country to total assets
- Total assets in foreign countries to total assets

Companies that depend on government contracts and subsidies may have lower earnings stability because governmental spending is susceptible to hostile events and the whims of legislators. FINANCIAL ACCOUNTANTS: Compute the percent of profit derived from government contract work and the extent to which the work is nonrepetitive.

MANAGEMENT EXECUTIVES: Appraise the strictness of governmental regulation. What is the level of current and potential governmental interference? FINANCIAL MANAGERS: Here you should review current and proposed laws and regulations of governmental agencies. Make note of legislative hearings and information from trade publications. Know the impact of current and contemplated tax legislation. Stringent environmental and safety regulations may also be involved (e.g., pollution control devices for equipment). Also, be familiar with the attitudes of the regulatory agency; rate increases may take too long.

CHECKLIST OF
POLITICAL FACTORS TO CONSIDER
IN APPRAISING EARNINGS QUALITY

- Operations in foreign trouble spots
- Regulatory environment
- Environmental and safety legislation
- IRS areas of attack, such as tax shelters

1.2.3   Determining Quality of Earnings

What is the significance of adequate insurance?

If assets are insured improperly, there will not be adequate compensation for losses. A company having a high-risk product line without proper insurance risks uncertainty. SUGGESTION TO MANAGEMENT EXECUTIVES: Where companies within an industry have difficulty obtaining insurance, try pooling your risks by setting up mutual insurance companies. This way, equity interests are retained and insurance premiums are paid.

WARNING SIGNS TO FINANCIAL MANAGERS

- A declining trend in the ratio of insurance expense to fixed assets
- Repeated drops by insurance companies
- Significantly rising insurance rates
- Unusual losses that point out inadequate coverage

What is a segmental disclosure?

Segmental disclosure relates to specific business-line performance, and is required when a company obtains 10 percent or more of its revenue or profit from an industry, product line, geographic area, single customer, or domestic government contract. MANAGEMENT EXECUTIVES: This disclosure helps management executives in appraising risk and corporate earning power. For example, if a high percent of revenue is obtained from "problem" foreign areas, this indicates high risk.

Of what importance is management?

Management quality affects investors' confidence in the firm. Look for these tipoffs to poor management:

- Past mismanagement of corporate affairs
- Previous bankruptcy
- Exaggerations in the annual report
- Inability to adjust to changing times

What do employee relations tell me about the company?

Poor employee relations lower earnings stability. Take note of these indicators:

- Number and duration of prior strikes
- Extent of union militancy

- Expiration date of union contracts
- Employee turnover

Should I take note of interest rates?

FOR FINANCIAL MANAGERS: Interest depends on the prime rate, magnitude of financing, and type of financing. Interest on short-term debt changes with the prime rate, and this changes with the business cycle. Interest on long-term debt has greater stability.

How do I evaluate the type of industry?

In appraising earnings quality, you should take into account whether the industry is growing or declining. Earnings have superior value if they come from a healthy, expanding industry. For example, a firm in a technological industry has greater uncertainty owing to possible obsolescence.

Companies in a staple industry have more earnings stability by virtue of inelastic product demand.

Since labor-intensive businesses have a higher percentage of viable cost within the total cost structure, they have more stability than capital-intensive ones.

FOR MARKETING MANAGERS: Consider the degree of competition by looking at the ease of entry, price wars, and lower-cost imports from foreign markets.

CHECKLIST OF INDUSTRY CHARACTERISTICS BEARING UPON EARNINGS QUALITY

- Technological
- Labor- or capital-intensive
- Staple
- Competition
- Regulation
- Industry cycle

1.2.4 Measuring External Forces

What should I know about inflationary measures?

Consider inflation-adjusted profits a superior indicator than net income when gauging either management performance or amount of funds available to meet cash requirements. NOTE TO INVESTORS AND CREDITORS: Examine the inflation footnote. This tells you what net income would be on a Consumer Price Index (CPI)-adjusted and replacement-cost basis.

Net income is overstated to the extent that it includes

inflationary earnings. Why? Because the profits arise from price levels and replacement costs, not operational performance. WHAT TO DO: To see the effect of inflation on net income, you should compare:

- CPI-adjusted net income to net income
- Replacement cost net income to net income
- Monetary assets to monetary liabilities

If net income is reported significantly higher than the inflation figure would indicate, consider earnings quality to be poor. The greater the difference, the poorer the earnings quality. A high ratio of monetary assets to monetary liabilities is not advantageous because of the resulting net purchasing power loss.

1.3 WAYS TO COUNTERACT INFLATION

FOR FINANCIAL MANAGERS, MARKETING MANAGERS, AND FINANCIAL ACCOUNTANTS: You can combat the adverse effects of inflation in the following ways.

Selling Price. Selling prices may be increased at short intervals to improve profit margins. Price catalogues and sales literature should be changed quickly. Keep price quotations for only a short time.

Selling prices should be on a next-in, first-out (NIFO) basis in order to keep replacement costs as the basis for new selling prices.

When a long interval exists between the time an order is received and the merchandise shipped, you should increase prices up to the time of shipment. As work is being done, progress payments should be received.

For long-term contracts, there should be a "cost plus" provision tied to the price index.

Cost Control. You should find cheaper ways of performing operations. Avoid product components that have excessive price increases. Try to enter into long-term purchase agreements.

If inflation is expected to worsen, engage in futures contracts to obtain raw materials at present prices.

Get competitive bids from insurance companies and change carriers periodically when it is cost beneficial.

Marketing. Deemphasize products significantly impacted by inflation and emphasize those that are inflation resistant.

Avoid projects with long payback periods. Do not introduce unprofitable products unless design changes can ultimately make the product profitable.

Labor Aspects. Automated companies utilizing minimal labor do better during inflation. Tie wage increases to improved productivity.

Financial Consideration. In inflation, a business with a net monetary position (monetary assets minus monetary liabilities) will incur a loss in purchasing power. Therefore, you should hold a minimum in cash and receivables.

Debt results in increased purchasing power since you will be paying creditors back in cheaper dollars. However, debt should not be excessive.

Real estate is a good investment during inflation. You can also borrow from insurance companies against the cash surrender value of life insurance; these loans are likely to be available at lower interest than the prevailing rate.

During inflationary periods, dividends should be cut back to retain earning power and required cash flow. Do not pay dividends that exceed inflation-adjusted net income.

Asset Management. Efficient asset management reduces cost and risk. For instance, cash management should accelerate cash inflow and defer cash outflow.

Put projects into self-contained economic units. Why? The ultimate success would not be contingent on completion of the entire project. This assists in controlling escalating costs.

HINT: To minimize risk, try joint ventures.

Accounting Aspects. With regard to taxes, companies dependent on depreciation are in a worse position than those depending on research and development. Depreciation is charged gradually, and thus the tax saving comes ratably. Research and development is expensed immediately; thus a full tax deduction is possible.

SUGGESTION: During inflationary periods, use the last-in, first-out (LIFO) inventory method to achieve maximum tax savings.

1.4 WHAT IS THE IMPACT OF FOREIGN OPERATIONS?

When the dollar is devalued, foreign assets and income in countries with strong currency are worth more dollars, provided foreign liabilities do not exceed the value.

When foreign assets are appropriately balanced against foreign liabilities, the company is better protected from changes in exchange rates; this tends to stabilize earnings. WHAT TO DO: You should evaluate the company's exposed position for each foreign country in which a major operation is located.

FOR INVESTMENT ANALYSTS: When evaluating foreign operations, consider the following:

- The degree of intercountry transactions
- Varying year-ends of foreign subsidiaries
- Foreign restitutions on fund transfer
- The foreign country's tax structure

WARNING: Beware of erratic foreign exchange rates. The magnitude of vacillation in the exchange rate is measured by its percent change over time and/or its standard deviation.

According to FASB Statement 52, foreign currency gains and losses are reported as a separate item in stockholders' equity. Look at the trend in the ratio of foreign exchange gains and losses to net income to evaluate the degree of stability.

A forward exchange contract applies to an agreement to buy or sell identifiable foreign currency when the delivery of such currency occurs at a later time. It is used to hedge against exchange risks easing from foreign currency transactions. FINANCIAL MANAGERS: Consider such a contract positively because the company is attempting to minimize its foreign currency exposure.

WARNING TO INVESTMENT ANALYSTS: You should frown upon forward exchange contracts used for purposes of speculation. Why? It indicates that management likes to take risks.

Multinational companies having material foreign operations face uncertainties regarding the repatriation of funds and local customs and regulations. The inability of a U.S. company to fire employees in Japan, for instance, makes labor a fixed cost.

Operations in politically and economically unstable foreign regions indicate poor quality of earnings. The potential for change in government, with its concurrent negative effects, must be considered. The analyst should determine the earnings derived and assets in each questionable foreign country. Useful ratios here are:

1. Questionable foreign revenue to total revenue
2. Questionable foreign earnings to net income
3. Total export revenue to total revenue
4. Total export earnings to net income
5. Total assets in "questionable" foreign countries to total assets
6. Total assets in foreign countries to total assets

Illustration

An example of a useful disclosure with regard to foreign exposure is that made by G Company in its 19X9 annual report. The company disclosed that of total export sales of $316,336,000 through foreign military contracts with the U.S. government in 19X8, $301,198,000 was made to the Middle East. This is a significant percentage, 95.2%. In 19X9, such export sales to the Middle East dropped to $54,265,000, of total export sales of $73,186,000. This percentage is materially less, 74.1%. It is significant to note that the tremendous decline in total export sales from 19X8 to 19X9 of 76.9% ($243,150,000 divided by $316,336,000) was due to the decline in business to the Middle East.

2

How to Evaluate a Company's Financial Position: Part II

2.1 BALANCE SHEET ANALYSIS

This chapter continues where Chapter 1 left off. In the sections to follow, you will learn how to complete your analysis of a company's financial health.

2.1.1 Examining the Balance Sheet

How are assets evaluated?

If assets are overstated, net income is likewise overstated because a loss has not been reflected. Similarly, when liabilities are understated, net income is overstated because an expense provision has not been made.

FOR CREDIT AND LOAN OFFICERS: To adjust for overstated assets and understated liabilities, you should use realistic rather than reported values for balance sheet analysis. Example 2.1 shows you how.

EXAMPLE 2.1

Company X reports total assets of $7,000,000, total liabilities of $2,000,000, and stockholders' equity of $5,000,000. Specific accounts are given as follows:

Long-term investments
(lower of book or market) $600,000

Goodwill	200,000
Deferred pension credit	300,000

NOTES

Investments have a market value of $900,000.

With regard to acquired companies, superior earnings have not been generated.

The present value of future pension benefits exceeds pension fund assets by $400,000.

Restated total assets are as follows:

Reported total assets	$7,000,000
Increase on investments	300,000
Decrease in goodwill	(200,000)
Realistic total assets	**$7,100,000**

Restated total liabilities are given as follows:

Reported total liabilities	$2,000,000
Increase in pension deficiency	400,000
Realistic total liabilities	**$2,400,000**

Asset quality depends on the degree of certainty of their cash realization with regard to amount and timing. A decline in inventory turnover, for instance, suggests future inventory write-offs.

SUGGESTION: Segregate assets by risk category. For example, receivables have a higher probability of realization than deferred charges. The more dollars in a high-risk category, the lower the earnings quality. FOR THE INVESTMENT ANALYST: Check trends in the following ratios:

- High-risk assets to total assets
- High-risk assets to sales

EXAMPLE 2.2

Company Y reports total assets of $8,000,000 and sales of $10,000,000.

High-risk items

Deferred charges	$300,000
Receivables from very financially troubled companies	200,000
Inventory of technological items that are obsolete	100,000
Total high-risk assets	**$600,000**

Relevant ratios

High-risk assets to total assets

($600,000/$8,000,000)   0.075

High-risk assets to sales

($600,000/$10,000,000)   0.06

Risk should be evaluated within each major asset category. NOTE: Ratios are relative only in comparison to other companies.

EXAMPLE 2.3

Company Z reports receivables of $3,000,000. Included are the following high-risk receivables:

Notes receivable resulting from an extension of unpaid balances from delinquent customers	$200,000
Advances to politically unstable foreign countries	300,000

You can thus conclude that $500,000 of the $3,000,000 in receivables, or 16.7%, are of poor quality.

NOTE: Single-purpose or specialized assets are of lower quality than multipurpose ones. Assets without separable value cannot be sold easily and thus would have high risk associated with them. An example: work-in-process inventory.

CHECKLIST OF FACTORS TO CONSIDER WHEN ANALYZING THE BALANCE SHEET

- The impact of changing political, economic, industry, and corporate conditions on the balance sheet
- Percent of high-risk assets to total assets
- Multipurpose or single-purpose assets
- Effect of government policies on asset realization

2.1.2 Evaluating Operations

What should I look for in the cash account?

FOR FINANCIAL MANAGERS: You should determine whether part of the cash account is restricted and unavailable for use. Examples of this would be a compensating balance required for a bank loan or cash held in a politically unstable country.

EXAMPLE 2.4

Company Z reports cash of $3,000,000.

NOTES

The company has a $10,000,000 bank loan that requires a 5% compensating balance.

Cash amounting to $200,000 has been expropriated by the foreign government.

Thus, of the cash balance $300,000,000, $700,000, or 23.3% is not available for use.

How do I appraise receivables risk?

INVESTMENT ANALYSTS: You can appraise receivables risk by examining the nature of the receivable balance. For example, a high-risk receivable would be one due from a country experiencing severe financial problems.

Companies that depend on one or two customers are more vulnerable than those with many equally important accounts.

Since fair-trade laws protect consumers, receivables from another company are safer than those from consumers.

NOTE: Factoring accounts receivable, a higher-cost financing alternative, may mean the company has liquidity difficulties.

When sales are lagging, the business might boost receivables by shipping unneeded merchandise to customers, sometimes giving generous credit terms. This is a game because the merchandise may well be returned. CREDIT AND LOAN OFFICERS: Be sure to note the following "red flags":

- A significant increase in revenue in the last quarter of the present year
- A significant amount of sales returns in the first quarter of the following year
- A material decline in sales for the first quarter of the following year

Four Indicators of Receivable Risk. You can determine realization risk in receivables by calculating the following four ratios:

- *Annual credit sales to average accounts receivable.*

Accounts Receivable Turnover =
$$\frac{\text{annual credit sales}}{\text{average accounts receivable}}$$

If sales vary greatly throughout the year, average accounts receivable should be computed as a weighted average based on a monthly or quarterly accounts receivable balance.

• *Days in collection period.*

$$\text{Collection period} = \frac{365}{\text{accounts receivable turnover}}$$

The longer receivables are past due, the higher the risk of not collecting. A longer collection period may be justified, however, when credit terms have been liberalized, for example, with new product introduction or as a competitive reaction.

• *Accounts receivable to total assets.*
• *Accounts receivable to sales.* A larger receivable balance compared to the prior year may point to realization risk.

EXAMPLE 2.5

Company A shows the following financial data:

	12/31/X1	*12/31/X2*
Sales	$420,000	$530,000
Total assets	610,000	670,000
Accounts receivable	60,000	100,000

(On Jan. 1, 19X1, accounts receivable were $50,000.)

Accounts receivable turnover	7.64	6.63
Collection period	47.78 days	55.05 days
Accounts receivable to total assets	0.098	0.149
Accounts receivable to sales	0.143	0.189

Note that all ratios deteriorated in 19X2. Thus, there is a higher realization risk in accounts receivable in 19X2.

Bad Debts. An unjustified lowering of bad debts overstates earnings. This occurs, for example, when bad debts are reduced even while sales are made to riskier customers and/or actual bad debts are increasing.

Be sure to examine the following ratios:

• Bad debts to accounts receivable
• Bad debts to sales

Here are some items to note:

• Overstatement of bad debts sets up an accounting cushion, and this results in understatement of net income.

- When there is a substantial bad debts provision in the current period owing to inadequate provisions in earlier periods, the trend in net income has been distorted.

EXAMPLE 2.6

Company B presents the following financial data:

	19X1	19X2
Sales	$90,000	$120,000
Accounts receivable	28,000	39,000
Bad debts	3,000	3,500
(Sales are being made to more marginal customers.)		
Ratio of bad debts to sales	0.033	0.029
Ratio of bad debts to accounts receivable	0.107	0.09

Because the company is selling to riskier customers, bad debts should be going up. Instead, they are going down as they relate to sales and accounts receivable. By understating bad debts, net income and accounts receivable are overstated, and net income should be reduced for the increased earnings. If you conclude that the realistic ratio of bad debt to sales in 19X2 should be 3.2%, then bad debts should be $3,840 (3.2% × $120,000) rather than $3,500. Thus, reported earnings should be reduced by another $340.

Sales Returns. A large number of sales returns indicates a quality problem with the merchandise. When there is increasing liability for returns and a significant reduction in the ratio of sales returns to sales, this indicates an inadequate quality provision and net income has been overstated.

Loans Receivable. ATTENTION LOAN OFFICERS: Take note of the following indicators, which point to high realization risk in the loan portfolio:

- An inadequate loss provision
- Interest not received on loans or interest rate downwardly adjusted

You should determine

- The trend in the loan loss provision to total outstanding loans
- The market value of collateral to the loan balance
- The difference over time of the loan loss provision to the eventual loan loss amount
- The ratios of loans receivable to total assets and loans receivable to stockholders' equity

What significance does inventory play?

At the plant, wholesaler, or retailer, an inventory buildup reflects a realization problem. Take note when inventory rises at a faster rate than sales.

EXAMPLE 2.7

Finished goods increased by 60% while total inventory increased by 45%. Sales went up by only 15%.

A future production slowdown may be possible since there is a decline in raw materials coupled with an increase in work-in-process and finished goods.

EXAMPLE 2.8

Company C shows the following inventory components:

	19X1	*19X2*
Raw materials	$100,000	$90,000
Work-in-process	60,000	110,000
Finished goods	15,000	30,000

Over the year, raw materials went down by 10% ($10,000/$100,000), work-in-process went up by 83.3% ($50,000/$60,000), and finished goods increased by 100% ($15,000/$15,000). The inconsistent trend between raw materials compared to work-in-process and finished goods indicates a production slowdown. It also indicates a high probability of obsolescence in inventory due to the buildup.

REMEMBER THIS: When the increase in sales significantly exceeds the increase in inventory, good management is indicated.

EXAMPLE 2.9

Company D shows the following inventory:

	19X1	*19X2*
Sales	$300,000	$400,000
Inventory	50,000	60,000

Sales went up by 33.3% while inventory increased by 20%. This means good inventory management.

A turnover rate should be computed for each inventory category by department. To compute:

$$\text{Inventory turnover} = \frac{\text{cost of sales}}{\text{average inventory}}$$

Also, determine the number of days inventory is held:

$$\text{Age of inventory} = \frac{365}{\text{inventory turnover}}$$

Poor turnover may suggest potential obsolescence, perhaps from problems with the product line or advertising. IMPORTANT FOR FINANCIAL MANAGERS: A high turnover rate may point to insufficient inventory balances, and this can cause a loss in business. There are cases, however, where proper justification exists for a low turnover rate, for example, when prices of raw materials are expected to rise.

When a company uses its "natural year-end," the turnover rate may be very high because the inventory level will be quite low at that time.

EXAMPLE 2.10

The following data are given for Company E:

	19X1	19X2
Finished goods	$11,000	$17,000
Cost of sales	73,000	85,000
(As of Jan. 1, 19X1. finished goods total $8,000)		
Inventory turnover	7.7	6.1
Age of inventory	47.4 days	59.8 days

The deteriorating ratios point to higher realization risk in inventory.

Higher realization risk in inventory exists when merchandise is subject to fluctuation in price or with fad, specialized, and perishable items. Low realization risk applies to standardized, staple, and necessity merchandise. Raw materials are of lower risk than finished goods owing to their universal and multiple uses.

Inventory secured to creditors under loan agreements has higher realization risk as does inadequate insurance coverage for inventory.

Since inventory is reported at the lower of book or market value, the amount shown in the financial statements could be significantly less than the inventory is worth. For credit decision-making purposes, you should always use market value.

During a rapid inflationary period, first-in-first-out (FIFO) may cause exaggerated earnings because older costs are being matched against current revenue.

CHECKLIST OF INVENTORY RISK

- Buildup at plant, wholesaler, or retailer
- Comparing the trend in raw materials to work-in-process to finished goods
- A high ratio of work-in-process to total inventory
- Inventory that fluctuates widely in price
- Inventory used as collateral
- Inadequately insured inventory
- Inventory prone to political risk

CHECKLIST OF WARNING SIGNS FOR EVALUATING INVENTORY

- Unusual costs reflected in inventory
- A change in inventory policy that boosts earnings
- Fourth-quarter adjustments that significantly affect inventory valuation
- Inventory valuation dependent on internal cost records
- Sudden inventory write-offs

2.1.3 Assessing Accounting Practices

What do increased prepaid expenses mean?

A significant increase in prepaid expenses may point to capitalization of items that were expensed in prior years.

How do I assess a company's investments?

Investments in equity securities are taken at cost or market value, whichever is lower. An investment portfolio having a market value exceeding cost constitutes an undervalued asset.

NOTE TO INVESTMENT ANALYSTS: If, in the prior period, an unjustified change occurred from current to noncurrent classification, you should adjust earnings downward for unrealized losses on noncurrent investments (shown as a reduction to stockholders' equity).

Higher realization risk in the investment portfolio is indicated when the ratio of revenue (dividend income, interest income) to the carrying value of investments declines. You should also note that debt securities may be reported at cost even if they are higher than market value, provided the decline is considered temporary. HINT: See if there is a subsequent event disclosure concerning unrealized losses that have occurred in the securities portfolio. If so, you should adjust the investment account downward.

EXAMPLE 2.11

Company F reports the following information:

	19X1	*19X2*
Investments	$40,000	$45,000
Income from investments	5,000	4,000

The 19X2 annual report footnote titled "Subsequent Events" reported a decline of $7,000 in the portfolio.

Income to investments decreased from 12.5% ($5,000/ $40,000) in 19X1 to 8.9% ($4,000/$45,000) in 19X2, thereby pointing to a higher realization risk in the portfolio. Post-balance-sheet disclosure indicates that the 19X2 investment amount of $45,000 is overstated by $7,000.

Higher realization risk in the investment portfolio exists with volatile securities, even though such securities may be more profitable in a bull market. WHAT TO LOOK FOR: The portfolio should be diversified by industry, economic sector, and geographic location. Be sure to appraise the extent of diversification and stability associated with the portfolio. Less realization risk exists with negatively or non-correlated securities than with positively correlated ones. A vacillating trend of market value to their cost over a period of time indicates instability in the portfolio. Realization risk can also be measured by computing the standard deviation in the rate of return.

CHECKLIST FOR APPRAISING THE INVESTMENT ACCOUNT

- A portfolio having a market value exceeding cost
- Trend in investment income to investments
- Subsequent event disclosure indicating a decline in market value of securities
- Purchasing securities of another company in order to gain a controlling interest when the other company has negative attributes (e.g., high risk)

How are fixed assets analyzed?

Failure to replace or maintain old assets, especially within technological companies, will result in operational deficiency and breakdown.

MANAGEMENT EXECUTIVES: You should determine the following:

- Age and condition of each major asset category
- Replacement cost compared to historical cost of the asset base

- Trend in fixed asset acquisitions to total gross assets
- Rate of return on fixed assets measured by net income to fixed assets and sales to fixed assets
- Disclosure in the footnotes of inactive and inefficient assets (e.g., references to downtime)

INVESTMENT ANALYSTS: You should determine earnings trend. Make sure fixed assets were written down at the proper time.

Here's a good sign: An appropriation of retained earnings for future capital expansion.

EXAMPLE 2.12

Company F reports the following information regarding fixed assets:

	19X1	19X2
Fixed assets	$120,000	$100,000
Repairs and maintenance	7,000	3,500
Replacement cost	200,000	230,000

Note an inadequate maintenance of fixed assets as reflected by the decline in repairs and maintenance to fixed assets from 5.8% to 3.5%, the widening difference between replacement and historical cost from $80,000 to $130,000, and the reduction in fixed assets.

If you believe that repairs and maintenance to fixed assets should realistically be 5% in 19X2, you would reduce earnings by an additional 1.5%, which amounts to $1,500 (1.5% × $100,000).

CHECKLIST OF FACTORS TO CONSIDER WITH FIXED ASSETS

- Repairs and maintenance to fixed assets
- Fixed asset acquisitions to total gross assets
- Net income to fixed assets
- Machinery output levels
- Specialized assets
- Equipment subject to governmental pollution requirements

Depreciation. Use the depreciation method that most realistically reflects the decline in service potential of the asset and that results in the best earnings quality.

FINANCIAL ACCOUNTANTS: In appraising the adequacy of the company's depreciation rate, you should compare it to industry standards and to the rate used for tax purposes.

INVESTMENT ANALYSTS: You should examine the trend in depreciation expense to fixed assets and depreciation expense to sales. Lower trends imply insufficiency in depreciation reflective of asset obsolescence.

EXAMPLE 2.13

Company G reports the following:

	19X1	19X2
Fixed assets	$520,000	$600,000
Sales	630,000	740,000
Net income	120,000	125,000
Depreciation expense per books	18,000	20,000
Depreciation expense per tax return	22,000	25,000
Depreciation expense to fixed assets	0.035	0.033
Depreciation expense to sales	0.029	0.027

The reduction in these ratios implies insufficiency in depreciation reflective of asset obsolescence.

The percent increase in fixed assets was 15.4%, but the percent increase in depreciation was only 11.1%, another sign of inadequate depreciation.

You conclude that tax depreciation is more representative, and a downward adjustment to 19X2 net income of $5,000 is warranted.

Lower earnings quality is indicated when a reduction in depreciation emanates from an unjustified change in the life or salvage value of fixed assets. In this situation, you should reduce net income by the reduction in depreciation expense.

CHECKLIST OF POOR DEPRECIATION POLICY

- Does not accurately reflect the decline in service potential of the asset
- The book depreciation rate is materially less than the tax depreciation rate
- Declining trend in depreciation expense to sales
- Moderate increase in depreciation expense coupled with a sizable increase in capital expansion

What about intangibles?

CREDIT AND LOAN OFFICERS: Intangibles are usually overstated when estimating their future income-generating capability. For instance, corporate goodwill might be overstated in a recessionary period.

You should carefully scrutinize realization risk as indicated by the following ratios:

- Intangible assets to total assets
- Intangible assets to stockholders' equity
- Change in intangibles to the change in net income (a material amount of the change coming from capitalization rather than expensing is a warning sign)

SPECIAL NOTE TO THE INVESTMENT ANALYST: Accounting Principles Board (APB) Opinion 17 allows for a 40-year period to amortize intangibles. Some companies ignore reality and use the maximum amortization period. Absurdly, intangibles placed on the books before the effective date of the Opinion (1970) do not have to be amortized at all.

EXAMPLE 2.14

Company I reports the following information:

	19X1	*19X2*
Intangible assets	$60,000	$200,000
Total assets	610,000	630,000
Sales	700,000	725,000
Net income	90,000	130,000
Intangible assets to total assets	0.098	0.317
Intangible assets to sales	0.086	0.276

Higher asset realization risk is indicated by the increasing ratios. Also, the 233% increase in intangibles coupled with the 44% increase in profit may show that net income is overstated. Why? Because of the failure to reflect items that should have been expensed rather than capitalized.

In some instances, intangibles may be considerably undervalued. Patents may be recorded at amounts significantly less than present value of related future cash flows. NOTE: Patented items have less worth when they can be easily infringed upon by minor change or when they apply to a technological item. Also consider the financial capability of the business to defend the patent in court and take a look at patent expiration dates as well as new patents being issued.

Goodwill is only reported when a company buys another at a cost greater than fair market value of the acquired firm's net assets. FINANCIAL MANAGERS: Evaluate the reported value of goodwill by ascertaining whether the acquired company indeed has superior earning power. If not, goodwill is really of no value.

CHECKLIST FOR APPRAISING
THE RISKINESS OF INTANGIBLES

- Ratio of intangible assets to total assets
- Ratio of intangible assets to net income
- Specific suspected intangible (e.g., goodwill) to total assets
- Ratio of change in intangibles to change in net income

What is the significance of deferred charges?

ATTENTION CREDIT AND LOAN OFFICERS: Watch the deferred charges closely. Why? These depend to a large extent on estimates of future probabilities rather than other assets. The probability that expectations will fail to be achieved is relatively high. Or, the company may defer a cost with no future benefit in order not to charge it against earnings. No cash realization can be applied to deferred charges, and consequently they cannot be used to meet creditor obligations. Dubious deferred charges include moving, start-up and plant rearrangement costs.

WARNING: A company may try to boost earnings by deferring costs that were expensed in previous years.

There are instances in which an increase in deferred charges is appropriate, for example, deferring start-up costs when beginning a lucrative new operation.

CREDIT AND LOAN OFFICERS: In gauging the realization risk in deferred charges, you should determine the following trends:

- Deferred costs to sales
- Deferred costs to net income
- Deferred costs (e.g., deferred advertising) to total expenditures (e.g., total advertising)

Remember, rising trends point to higher realization risk.

The higher the ratio of intangible assets and deferred charges to total assets, the greater the asset risk.

CHECKLIST OF PROBLEMS WITH
DEFERRED CHARGES

- Deferral of costs expensed in prior years
- Deferral of costs for book purposes that are expensed for tax purposes
- Increasing trend in deferred charges to total expenditures
- Sudden write-off of deferred charges

What do estimated liabilities show?

CAUTION FOR THE INVESTMENT ANALYST: Incorrectly estimated liabilities for future costs and losses may impair the significance of net income. WHAT TO DO: You should exclude arbitrary adjustments to estimated liabilities when ascertaining corporate earning power. If you conclude that estimated liabilities are being used to smooth earnings, add back the amounts credited to earnings. For instance, net income obtained by recouping previous year reserves may be invalid.

CREDIT AND LOAN OFFICERS: Be on guard: A firm with an unrealistically low provision for future costs has lower earnings quality. For instance, it is illogical for a business to lower its warranty provision when there are product deficiencies.

There may be an overprovision of an estimated liability when management wants to reduce excessive earnings. This also sets up an accounting cushion.

Lower earnings quality exists when more operating expenses and losses are charged to reserve accounts compared with the amounts charged in prior periods.

CHECKLIST OF QUESTIONS CONCERNING ESTIMATED LIABILITIES

- Are reserve provisions properly stated?
- Has an accounting cushion been set up?
- Were reserve estimates modified?
- Was there an estimated liability established to offset a significant extraordinary gain?

2.2 LIQUIDITY

What is liquidity?

Liquidity refers to the company's ability to convert non-cash assets to cash or to obtain cash to meet maturing obligations. CREDIT AND LOAN OFFICERS: You must appraise the current amount of liquid assets as well as future flows. A potential problem is indicated when expected cash outflows exceed inflows.

In appraising a seasonal business, year-end financial data may not be representative. Thus, use quarterly or monthly averages to level out seasonal effects.

SUGGESTION: In financing seasonal requirements, employ short-term credit to meet short-term cash problems. Seasonal firms also require open lines of credit.

How do I determine cash adequacy?

You can appraise cash adequacy by examining the following trends:

- Cash flow generated from operations (net income plus noncash expenses minus noncash revenue)
- Cash flow generated from operations less cash payments needed to pay debt on principal, dividends, and capital expenditures
- Cash flow generated from operations before interest expense

EXAMPLE 2.15

Company B reports the following information for the year ended December 31, 19X1:

Net income	$750,000
Depreciation	30,000
Amortization expense	15,000
Interest expense paid in cash	140,000
Amortization of a deferred credit	7,000
Gain on sale of fixed assets	20,000
Payments on debt principal	300,000
Dividends	90,000
Capital expenditures	280,000
Cash flow provided from operations	
Net income	$750,000
Adjustments	
Depreciation	30,000
Amortization expense	15,000
Amortization of a deferred credit	(7,000)
Gain on sale of fixed asset	(20,000)
Cash flow provided from operations	
	$768,000

The cash flow provided from operations prior to interest expense is $908,000 ($768,000 plus $140,000), a sufficient cash flow from operations to satisfy interest expense.

Cash flow provided from operations less cash payments needed for debt on principal, dividends and capital expenditures is computed as follows:

Cash flow provided from operations		$768,000
Less		
Payments on debt principal	$300,000	
Dividends	90,000	
Capital expenditures	280,000	(670,000)
Residual cash provided from operations		**98,000**

ATTENTION: Not much cash is left over!

FINANCIAL MANAGERS: You should evaluate the trend in sales to cash. A high ratio indicates inadequate cash, and this may lead to future financial difficulties. A low ratio points to excess cash where there is a return foregone on the excessive balance.

EXAMPLE 2.16

Company G reports the following information:

	19X1	*19X2*
Cash	$700,000	$600,000
Sales	7,000,000	8,000,000
Cash turnover	10	13.3

Cash inadequacy is apparent in 19X2, and this will lead to difficulties in liquidity.

CHECKLIST OF MEASURES FOR GAUGING CASH ADEQUACY

- Amount and timing of cash flows
- Ability to delay cash payments
- Ability to get financing
- Closeness to cash of assets and liabilities
- Cash flow generated from operations
- Cash flow generated from operations less cash payments for debt principal, dividends, and capital expenditures

How do I examine current liabilities?

CREDIT AND LOAN OFFICERS: Examine the trend in current liabilities to total liabilities, current liabilities to stockholders' equity, and current liabilities to revenue. Higher trends may point to liquidity difficulties. BAD SIGN: Delays in paying creditors.

When evaluating current liabilities, you should ascertain whether they are "patient" (e.g., supplier with a long-standing relationship) or "pressing" (e.g., bank loan payable, taxes). Then examine the trend in pressing liabilities to patient liabilities. An increasing trend points to greater liquidity risk.

How do I appraise financial flexibility?

FINANCIAL MANAGERS AND FINANCIAL ACCOUNTANTS: In appraising a company's financial flexibility, you should evaluate how quickly assets can be converted to cash, the capability of getting additional financing, the extent of nonoperating assets, and the ability to change operating and investing activities.

WARNING TO MANAGEMENT EXECUTIVES: Excessive financial flexibility may reduce the rate of return. For instance, holding cash enhances liquidity but reduces the rate of return. Open lines of credit will ensure that funds are available when required, but remember there is usually a cost associated with this.

CHECKLIST FOR EXAMINING
FINANCIAL FLEXIBILITY

- Nearness of assets to cash
- Salability of assets
- Open credit lines
- Length of payback period
- Ability to modify policies in changing times

How do I undertake a funds flow evaluation?

CREDITORS AND INVESTORS: Here are 14 measures to use in appraising a company's funds flow status:

- *Current and acid-test ratios.*
- *Accounts receivable and inventory turnover.*
- *Working capital.* Substantial working capital is required if the business is not capable of borrowing on short notice. Working capital should be related to other financial statement accounts like revenue and total assets.
- *Revenue to current assets.* A high rate of turnover implies inadequate working capital. A low turnover means excessive current assets.
- *Working capital provided from operations to net income.* Greater liquidity exists when earnings are backed up by liquid funds.

- *Working capital provided from operations to total liabilities.* This shows the extent to which internally obtained working capital can meet liabilities.
- *Cash plus marketable securities to current liabilities.* This shows the cash immediately available to meet short-term debt.
- *Cost of sales, operating expenses, and taxes to average current assets.* This reveals the adequacy of current assets to meet ongoing business expenses.
- *Quick assets (cash plus receivables plus marketable securities) to year's cash expenses.* This shows the ability to meet expenses with highly liquid assets.
- *Sales to accounts payable.* This tells you whether the business can partly finance without incurring cost. When less trade credit is available, creditors think more negatively.
- *Net income to sales.* A declining profit margin means possible losses.
- *Fixed assets to current liabilities and current liabilities to noncurrent liabilities.* These ratios show possible precarious financing policies. Financing fixed assets with current debt may produce a problem. Why? The debt is due before the proceeds from the fixed assets are realized.
- *Accounts payable to average daily purchase.* Here you see the number of days required for the business to pay creditors.
- *Liquidity index.* This shows the number of days current assets are away from cash.

EXAMPLE 2.17

	Amount	× Days from Cash	= Total
Cash	$ 40,000	—	—
Accounts receivable	90.000	25	$2,250,000
Inventory	120.000	30	3.600.000
	$250,000		$5,850,000

$$\text{Index} = \frac{\$5,850,000}{\$250,000} = 23.4 \text{ days}$$

What are important asset characteristics?

OF VITAL CONCERN TO FINANCIAL MANAGERS: A business that can sell assets without adversely affecting earnings of other assets has a financial advantage, particularly when the assets are not overly interdependent. For instance, the sale of a marketable security will not negatively affect other marketable securities. CAUTION: Certain assets may be so closely related that the disposition of one significantly affects others (e.g., the sale of a machine in a production network).

ATTENTION: Price characteristics of assets also relate to their marketability. Wide price fluctuation may prevent the business from selling assets when it is in financial difficulty.

Long-term assets (like machinery) are riskier than short-term assets (like inventory) because it will be more difficult to dispose of them.

What about availability and cost of financing?

Availability of funds is required for a business to grow. External considerations (like money supply) and internal considerations (like bank relationships) will affect the availability and cost of financing.

FINANCIAL MANAGERS: Take note of restrictions on the firm's ability to borrow and its ability to get financing at reasonable interest rates.

TO THE INVESTMENT ANALYST: What is the mixture of commercial paper and bank loans? Commercial paper costs less and can be used only by highly creditworthy businesses.

CREDIT AND LOAN OFFICERS BEWARE: The following red flags may appear in the debt footnote:

- Compensating balances have increased
- The effective interest rate has increased
- The weighted average debt for the year exceeds the year-end debt balance
- Loan acceleration clauses are in effect (failure to satisfy a current installment on debt may make the loan due immediately)
- There has been a near violation of loan restriction requirements

CHECKLIST FOR EVALUATING A COMPANY'S FINANCING

- External and internal constraints on the business
- Ability to issue commercial paper
- Loan compliance requirements to actual financial position
- Collateral value of property to the principal balance of a loan

2.3 SOLVENCY

What is solvency?

Solvency is appraised to determine whether the business can meet long-term obligations when due. CREDIT AND LOAN OFFICERS: You should be concerned with long-term funds flow. Pay particular attention to

- Long-term funds available to meet long-term debt
- Long-term financial and operating status of the business
- The magnitude of long-term debt in the capital structure
- Realizability of noncurrent assets
- Earning power of the company

How do I measure financial solvency?

Here are nine ways to measure financial solvency. Where possible, use market value of assets rather than book value in computing these figures.

- *Ratio of long-term debt to stockholders' equity.* A high ratio points to riskiness.
- *Ratio of cash flow from operations to long-term debt.* This measures the sufficiency of funds to satisfy noncurrent obligation.
- *Ratio of net income, before interest and taxes, to interest.* This indicates the number of times interest expense is met and shows the extent of profit decline the company can handle.
- *Ratio of cash flow from operations plus interest to interest.* This ratio is superior because it reflects actual cash available to satisfy interest. Remember, cash flow rather than profits is used to pay interest.
- *Ratio of net income, before fixed charges and taxes, to fixed charges.* This ratio evaluates a company's ability to meet fixed costs. A low ratio presents a problem.
- *Ratio of cash flow provided from operations plus fixed charges to fixed charges.* This is an excellent indicator because cash is needed to satisfy fixed costs.
- *Ratio of noncurrent assets to noncurrent liabilities.* Long-term obligations are ultimately paid from noncurrent assets. A high ratio points to greater protection from long-term creditors.
- *Ratio of retained earnings to total assets.* The trend here shows the company's earning capability over the years.

- J. Wilcox's gambler's ruin prediction formula. This shows a firm's liquidation value and hence is useful to appraise solvency. Liquidation value equals cash and marketable securities at market value plus inventory, accounts receivable, and prepaid expenses at 70 percent of the reported amount plus other assets at 50 percent minus current liabilities minus long-term liabilities.

What are unrecorded assets?

Unrecorded assets constitute resources of the business anticipated to have future benefit. They include tax loss carry-forward benefits or purchase commitments in which the business buys an item at a price materially below the going price.

What are unrecorded liabilities?

Unrecorded liabilities are not shown in the balance sheet, but they require future payment or rendering of services. Such liabilities include:

- Unfunded past service pension expense
- Excess of vested benefits over pension fund assets
- Operating lease commitments
- Lawsuits

NOTE TO CREDIT AND LOAN OFFICERS: FASB Statement 47 requires disclosure of long-term obligations. You should examine commitments under unconditional purchase obligations and future payments on long-term debt.

FINANCIAL ACCOUNTANTS: You can determine whether unrecorded liabilities are significant by comparing them to total liabilities and/or total assets.

How do I appraise noncurrent liabilities?

FOR CREDIT AND LOAN OFFICERS: You should evaluate carefully the deferred tax credit account. Deferred taxes applicable to depreciation may never be due when fixed assets are bought repeatedly. Hence, the account may not be payable for a long period of time. If the deferred tax account reverses, it is properly a long-term liability.

Even though the deferred investment tax credit account is reported as a liability, later tax payment may not be required. The deferred investment tax credit account is simply amortized against income tax expense. Therefore, you need consider no adverse impact on solvency.

WHAT TO DO: In appraising estimated liability accounts, you should examine their source and sufficiency of amount. For instance, estimated liabilities for litigation can ultimately mandate material payments.

Preferred stocks with a maturity date or sinking fund requirements are more like debt than equity, and will require future cash payment. On the other hand, reported liabilities need not really be such, such as, for example, convertible bonds with attractive conversion features.

Are consolidated financial statements truly representative?

A financially poor subsidiary may be combined with a healthy one, thereby resulting in a satisfactory net consolidated position. Analysis of the consolidated financial statements may point to financial difficulties within an individual subsidiary.

REMEMBER THIS: Liabilities shown in the consolidated balance sheet are not a lien on total assets. A creditor of a given subsidiary cannot be paid from the assets of that subsidiary unless the parent guarantees its debt. Hence, when evaluating a consolidated statement, you should concentrate on the financial capability and individual financial statements of the given subsidiary.

NOTE TO CREDIT AND LOAN OFFICERS REGARDING PENSION PLANS: In case of corporate liquidation, up to 30 percent of the company's net worth may be used to meet pension fund deficiency.

In defined-benefit pension plans, identified assets must comprise more than 5 percent of net assets available for benefits. Determine the extent to which such assets can be realized and their proportion to total assets. INVESTMENT ANALYSTS: You should view negatively a situation in which a significant percentage of available net assets are invested in financially deficient companies.

CHECKLIST FOR LOOKING AT CONSOLIDATED STATEMENTS

- Restrictions on the remission of earnings by the subsidiary to the parent
- Ascertaining whether a tax provision should be provided in the undistributed foreign subsidiary's earnings
- Change in year-end of subsidiary
- Parent guarantee for subsidiary loans

CHECKLIST FOR LOOKING AT PENSION PLANS

- Changes in actuarial assumptions affecting earnings
- The amount of unfunded past service cost
- The variance between pension fund net assets and vested benefits

- Present value of vested and nonvested benefits
- Asset quality in the pension fund

Should I examine the Statements of Cash flows?

A comparison of statements over several years can depict the present and future direction of the business; it can reveal operating, investing, and financing activities and allow better planning for future investing and financing needs; and it can highlight unusual items as well as distorted relationships.

The statement of cash flows allows you to predict future cash flows on the basis of present asset and liability structure as well as planned acquisitions and financial mix. INVESTMENT ANALYSTS: You can appraise growth potential by taking into account the balance of cash and cash equivalents. CREDIT AND LOAN OFFICERS: Pay attention to the source and uses of cash.

Sources of Cash. Cash flow provided from operating activities are the best source because they result internally without the cost associated with financing in external markets. The higher the ratio of cash provided from operations to net income, the better. Also, look at the ratio of cash provided from operations to total sources of funds. You should prefer a high ratio. Check cash provided from operations to total net cash inflow from investing and financing activities. A higher ratio is better.

CREDITORS AND INVESTORS: You should also evaluate external financing sources. To what extent is financing being done with long-term debt versus equity securities? What is the risk involved in financing? What is the cost of financing? Will the fund sources be available even in times of tight money?

SOME GOOD SIGNS: Conversion of bonds and preferred stock to common stock is looked upon favorably.

This is presented in the section showing significant noncash investing and financing activities section at the bottom of the statement of cash flows.

Sale of fixed assets brings a negative implication because the firm is viewed in a state of contraction. The reduction in such assets without adequate replacement adversely affects earning power.

Uses of Cash. In looking at the use of cash, you should note the assets acquired and how they were financed. Are the assets risky (e.g., specialized) or nonrisky (e.g., multipurpose)? WHAT TO DO: Evaluate the assets in terms of uncertainty and expected return. The type of assets bought indicates future direction of the company. Is the business moving into new product lines?

By not acquiring new assets, management may not be optimistic about the future. Is the industry in a downturn? Remember, improper maintenance of capital will negatively affect future earning power because of the possibility of equipment breakdown.

Investments in other companies might be beneficial if they result in diversification, either horizontally or vertically.

An upward trend in intangibles may be favorable. An increase in patents may point to the company's introducing "solid" products for future profit growth.

A reduction in long-term debt may imply less risk because it means less future cash payment. However, if matured low-interest, long-term debt has been replaced with high-interest, long-term debt, the firm has lost a financial advantage.

INVESTMENT ANALYSTS: Examine the dividend trend to see if it is stable or variable, increasing or decreasing. Are dividends sufficient for stockholder needs? Does cash flow from operations adequately meet the dividends?

CAUTION: Acquisition of treasury stock may be prompted by a desire to boost earnings per share.

2.4 BUSINESS FAILURE

When must bankruptcy be reported?

AICPA Statement on Auditing Standards No. 34, titled "The Auditor's Considerations When a Question Arises About an Entity's Continued Existence," requires the auditor to recognize and report on possible business failure. When the company is expected to go out of business, assets must be on a liquidation basis. A lack in going concern may be indicated by operating losses, deficiency in working capital and rejection of trade credit. If a business does fail and the auditor has not mentioned problems concerning the continuity of the business, a liability suit could be instituted.

How can I predict bankruptcy?

E. Altman's "Z-score" is a useful measure of predicting bankruptcy in the short run. Z-score equals

$$
\begin{aligned}
&\left(\frac{\text{Working capital}}{\text{Total assets}} \times 1.2 \right) \\
+\ &\left(\frac{\text{Retained earnings}}{\text{Total assets}} \times 1.4 \right) \\
+\ &\left(\frac{\text{Operating income}}{\text{Total assets}} \times 3.3 \right)
\end{aligned}
$$

$$+ \left(\frac{\text{Market value of common and preferred stock}}{\text{Total liabilities}} \times .06 \right)$$

$$+ \left(\frac{\text{Sales}}{\text{Total assets}} \times 1 \right)$$

Score	Probability of Failure
1.8 or less	Very high
1.81 to 2.7	High
2.8 to 2.9	Possible
3.0 or higher	Very low

Use the Z-score in forecasting failure and in telling management whether it should make cutbacks to retain needed funds.

ATTENTION CREDIT AND LOAN OFFICERS: In appraising an entity's susceptibility to failure, you should examine the trend in these ratios:

- Working capital to total assets
- Debt to equity
- Total liabilities to total assets
- Fixed assets to stockholders' equity
- Net income to total assets
- Cash flow from operations to total liabilities
- Net income plus interest to interest

FOR MANAGEMENT EXECUTIVES: Here are other indicators of possible failure:

- Material drop in market price of stock
- Material decline in cash flow from operations and in earnings
- Presence in an industry with a high probability of failure
- Young and/or small company
- Material contraction in dividends

Look to these financial and operating deficiencies to indicate financial distress:

- Inability to get further financing
- Inability to meet past-due obligations
- Poor financial reporting system
- Movement into business areas unrelated to the firm's basic business
- Failure to keep up to date
- Failure to control costs

- High degree of competition

SUGGESTION TO FINANCIAL MANAGERS: You can take the following steps to prevent failure:

- Have open lines of credit with banks
- Get rid of unprofitable product lines and divisions
- Improve asset management
- Engage in a cost-reduction program

3

Internal Accounting Applications for Your Company

In this chapter you will find measures and guidelines for internally evaluating your company's performance. There are discussions of

- Divisional and departmental performance analysis
- Selling price formulation and strategy
- Product-line evaluation techniques
- Budgeting process and budget types
- Variance analysis for highlighting and correcting problem performance areas

As a management executive, your goals should be many. Among them include profitability, high market share, product leadership, personnel development, productivity, and employee satisfaction. The guidelines set forth in this chapter will help you to realize your company's potential in all these areas.

3.1 HOW TO ANALYZE DIVISIONAL AND DEPARTMENTAL PERFORMANCE

What criteria are used for measuring performance?

In evaluating how well a business segment is doing, use the following criteria:

- Budgeted versus actual cost
- Profitability—in order to arrive at the profit of a division, prices for internal transfers may have to be established
- Return of investment
- Residual income

FOR MANAGERIAL ACCOUNTANTS: You can evaluate administrative functions by preparing performance reports. Look at such dollar indicators as executive salaries and service department costs as well as nondollar measures like number of files handled, phone calls taken, and invoices processed. NOTE: It's more difficult for you to evaluate the performance of a marketing department than a manufacturing department. Why? The former depends more on external factors, which are more difficult to control than internal ones.

When evaluating a division manager, you should look at controllable profit; that is, controllable revenue less controllable costs. REMEMBER: The manager should not be held accountable for factors (costs, for example) beyond his or her control.

What is the cost center approach?

The cost center approach is an efficiency evaluation in which budgeted cost is compared to actual cost. A cost center is most often the smallest segment of activity or area of responsibility for which costs are accumulated. This approach is typically used by departments rather than divisions. Departmental profit is difficult to derive because of problems with revenue and cost allocations.

What is divisional profit?

Divisional profit equals a division's revenue less direct and indirect costs. Since it is possible to determine divisional earnings, profit is the most often used method of evaluation. The divisional profit concept allows for decentralization, as each division is treated as a separate business entity with responsibility for making its own profit.

How do I use transfer pricing?

In determining divisional profit, a transfer price may be necessary. This is the price charged among divisions for the transfer of an assembled product or service. MANAGERIAL ACCOUNTANTS: Possible transfer prices include:

- *Actual cost plus profit markup.* This allows cost inefficiencies to be passed on from the selling division to the buying division.

- *Negotiated market price.* This equals the outside market price less the amount saved (e.g., for transportation, salesperson salaries, and commissions) by working from within the organization. The negotiated market value for services may be based on a per-hour rate or a flat rate. If a negotiated price cannot be agreed upon, the transfer price would be established arbitrarily by a higher authority. This is the best price to use, because it reflects the true value of the item.

- *Budgeted cost plus profit markup.* This should be used when a negotiated market price is not available, say for a new product. Here, the selling division has an incentive to control its cost since credit will be applied on the basis of budgeted cost only.

EXAMPLE 3.1

Division A wants to transfer an assembled item to Division B. Division A can sell the item to an outside company for $100. Cost savings of transferring the item internally are $20 (i.e., shipping costs, insurance on delivery, sales commission). Thus, the transfer price should be $80.

SUGGESTION: Do not use a temporarily high or low market price. Rather, use the average market price for the given period.

RULE OF THUMB: The maximum transfer price is the price that the buying division can purchase the item for outside. Do not allow the selling division to charge a higher price. In fact, if the buying division can get the item from the outside for less than inside, you probably should consider the selling division quite inefficient.

EXAMPLE 3.2

The selling division wants to charge $50 for an internal transfer. The buying division can acquire the same item from outside for $45. The transfer price should be $45.

SOMETHING TO THINK ABOUT: If the buying division can get the item at less than the selling division price, should the buying division be forced to buy inside (at the outside price, of course), or should it be permitted to buy outside? The answer depends on what would be best for overall corporate profitability.

EXAMPLE 3.3

The selling division wants to charge $70 for 100 assembled units. Current statistics for the selling division follow:

Units sold	10,000
Variable cost per unit	$50
Fixed cost	$100,000

Therefore, the selling division's fixed cost per unit is currently

$10 ($100,000/10,000)

Idle capacity (underutilization of facilities) exists. The buying division can buy the item outside for $55, so this should be the maximum transfer price. The buying division should buy from inside because it would be best for overall corporate profitability. Here's evidence:

Savings to selling division (variable cost × units): $50 × 100	$5,000
Cost to buying division (outside price × units): $55 × 100	$5,500
Disadvantage to company for buying division to go outside:	$500

CONCLUSION: There is no saving in fixed cost to the selling division if the buying division goes outside. Why? When idle capacity exists, fixed cost remains constant regardless of units produced.

How is divisional profit determined?

Now that you understand transfer pricing, you can determine the divisional profit.

EXAMPLE 3.4

XYZ Corporation has two production divisions (assembling and finishing) and one service division (maintenance). The assembling division assembles 800 units, 200 of which are sold to an outside concern for $40 each. The other 600 units are transferred to the finishing division, which in turn sells the units at $80 each. The negotiated market value is $35 each. The maintenance division earns revenue of $3,000 rendering services to the public. This division also renders repair services to the assembling division at a fair market value of $6,000 and to the finishing division at a fair market value of $8,000. The costs applicable to the divisions are

	Assembling	Finishing	Maintenance
Direct	$4,000	$5,000	$4,300
Indirect (allocated)	6,000	7,000	5,000

MANAGERIAL ACCOUNTANTS: You can now determine the profit of each division as shown in Schedule A on page 61. The total profit of XYZ Corporation equals the aggregate of its divisions, or $27,700 ($13,000 + $7,000 + $7,700), excluding nonallocated central costs. This is verified as follows:

Revenue to outside ($8,000 + $48,000 + $3,000)		$59,000
Less costs		
Direct ($4,000 + $5,000 + $4,300)	$13,300	
Indirect ($6,000 + $7,000 + $5,000)	18,000	
Total costs		(31,300)
Profit (before nonallocated costs)		$27,700

NOTE: Certain corporate costs are not allocated to any division. Examples of these include interest expense on corporate debt and the president's salary.

How to measure return on investment (ROI)?

Return on investment equals net income divided by total assets.

This performance measure is superior to profit because it accounts not only for earnings, but also the assets to get those earnings.

EXAMPLE 3.5

Compare the following data for Divisions X and Y:

	Division X	*Division Y*
Net income	$ 100	$ 1,000
Assets	$1,000	$100,000
Return on investment	10%	1%

Division X is clearly the better division. Why? It earns a higher rate on assets employed.

MANAGERIAL ACCOUNTANTS: In deriving ROI for a division, you would assign revenue, expenses, and assets, including direct and indirect, for each division. Those belonging to the corporation are allocated to each division by some predetermined basis.

In using ROI you should value total assets at replacement cost or CPI-adjusted value. If you use book value or gross cost, ROI goes up artificially over time because total assets (the denominator) decrease.

When is residual income used to evaluate divisional performance?

Refer to Section 1.1 for a description of residual income.

SCHEDULE A

Assembling (A)		Finishing (F)		Maintenance (M)	
Revenue 200 × $40	$8,000	Revenue: 600 × $80	$48,000	Revenue	$3,000
Transfer price (F): 600 × $35	21,000			Transfer price (A)	6,000
Total revenue	$29,000			Transfer price (F)	8,000
				Total revenue	$17,000
Costs		Costs		Costs	
Direct	$ 4,000	Direct	$ 5,000	Direct	$ 4,300
Indirect	6,000	Indirect	7,000	Indirect	5,000
Transfer price (M)	6,000	Transfer price (A)	21,000	Total costs	$ 9,300
Total costs	$16,000	Transfer price (M)	8,000	Profit	$ 7,700
Profit	$13,000	Total costs	$41,000		
		Profit	$ 7,000		

INTERNAL AUDITORS: Consider the following advantages of residual income as a measure of divisional performance:

- It incorporates risk. The riskier the division, the higher the minimum required rate of return assigned to it.
- It uses different rates of return for different types of assets.
- It assigns different rates of return to different divisions depending on risk.
- It is expressed in dollars rather than as a percent. This leads to goal consistency between the corporation and the division.

WARNING: Since the assignment of risk is subjective, residual income will always have this basic limitation.

How should I weigh controllability?

When evaluating a divisional manager, you should look at the controllable profit for which he or she is responsible. WARNING: If you allocate uncontrollable costs to the manager, you'll breed resentment.

2 CONTRIBUTION MARGIN ANALYSIS

What is the contribution margin?

The contribution margin equals sales less variable costs. A detailed contribution margin income statement has the following components:

Sales
Less: Variable cost of sales
Manufacturing contribution margin
Less: Variable selling and administrative expenses
Contribution margin
Less: Fixed costs
Net income

EXAMPLE 3.6

The selling price of an item is $6; unit sales total 520,000; beginning inventory is 40,000; ending inventory is 60,000; unit variable manufacturing cost is $4; variable selling cost per unit is $1.20; fixed manufacturing overhead totals $200,000, and selling and administrative expenses come to $80,000.

With this information, the units produced for the period can be calculated as follows:

Sales	520,000
Ending inventory	60,000
Merchandise needed	580,000
Less beginning inventory	(40,000)
Production	**540,000**

The contribution margin income statement would be as follows:

Sales (520,000 × $6)		$3,120,000
Less variable cost of sales		
Beginning inventory (40,000 × $4)	$ 160,000	
Variable cost of goods manufactured (540,000 × $4)	2,160,000	
Variable cost of goods available	2,320,000	
Less ending inventory (60,000 × $4)	(240,000)	
Total		(2,080,000)
Manufacturing contribution margin		$1,040,000
Less variable selling and administrative expenses (520,000 × $1.20)		(624,000)
Contribution margin		$416,000
Less fixed costs		
Overhead	200,000	
Selling and administrative	80,000	
Total		(280,000)
Net income		**$ 136,000**

MANAGEMENT EXECUTIVES: Use contribution margin analysis to appraise the performance of your manager and program. CAUTION: This approach is acceptable only for internal reporting!

When should I sell a product below normal selling price?

A company should accept an order at below-normal selling price when idle capacity exists (since fixed cost remains constant), as long as there is a contribution margin on that order.

EXAMPLE 3.7

Ten thousand units are currently sold at $30 per unit. Variable cost per unit is $18, and fixed costs total $100,000. Therefore, the fixed cost per unit equals $10 ($100,000/10,000). Idle capacity exists. A prospective customer is willing to buy 100 units at a selling price of only $20 per unit.

Ignoring market considerations (for example, unfavorable reaction by customers paying $30 per unit), you should recommend the sale of the additional 100 units. Why? Because it results in a positive additional (marginal) profitability of $200, as indicated in the following example:

Sales (100 × $20)	$2,000
Less variable cost (100 × $18)	(1,800)
Contribution margin	200
Less fixed cost	0[a]
Net income	**$ 200**

[a]Because of idle capacity, there is no additional fixed cost. If the order were to increase fixed cost by $50, say, because it required a special tool, it is still financially advantageous to sell the item at $20. The additional profit is now $150, as illustrated in this example:

Sales (100 × $20)	$2,000
Less variable cost (100 × $18)	(1,800)
Contribution margin	200
Less fixed cost	(50)
Net income	**$ 150**

EXAMPLE 3.8

Financial data for T Corporation are given as follows:

	Per Unit
Selling price	$5.40
Direct material	1.50
Direct labor	1.70
Variable overhead	0.40
Fixed overhead ($100,000/40,000 units)	2.50

Selling and administrative expenses are fixed except for sales commissions, which are 12% of the selling price. Idle capacity exists.

An additional order has been received for 600 units from a prospective customer at a selling price of $4.50. You should accept the order because, since fixed costs stay the same at idle capacity, a net profit results, as illustrated in this example:

Sales (600 × $4.50)	$2,700
Less variable manufacturing costs (600 × $3.60ª)	(2,160)
Manufacturing contribution margin	$ 540
Less variable selling and administrative expenses (12% × $2,700)	(324)
Contribution margin	$ 216
Less fixed cost	(0)
Net income	**$ 216**

ªVariable manufacturing cost equals variable manufacturing cost per unit times number of units produced.

EXAMPLE 3.9

The marketing manager had decided that for Product A he wants a markup of 30% over cost. Particulars concerning a unit of Product A are given as follows:

Direct material	$ 4,000
Direct labor	10,000
Overhead	2,500
Total cost	$16,500
Markup on cost (30%)	4,950
Selling price	**$21,450**

Total direct labor for the year equals $1,200,000. Total overhead for the year equals 25% of direct labor ($300,000), of which 40% is fixed and 60% is variable. The customer offers to buy a unit of Product A for $18,000. Idle capacity exists. You should accept the extra order because it provides a marginal profit, as indicated in this example:

Selling price		$18,000
Less variable costs		
Direct material	$4,000	

Direct Labor	10,000	
Variable overhead ($10,000 × 15%)a	1,500	(15,500)
Contribution margin		$2,500
Less fixed overhead		(0)
Net income		**$ 2,500**

aVariable overhead equals 15% of direct labor, calculated as follows:

$$\frac{\text{Variable overhead}}{\text{Direct labor}} = \frac{60\% \times \$300,000}{\$1,200,000}$$

$$= \frac{\$180,000}{\$1,200,000} = 15\% \text{ of direct labor}$$

MANAGEMENT EXECUTIVES: You can employ contribution analysis to see the optimum way of utilizing capacity.

EXAMPLE 3.10

A company produces a raw metal that can either be sold at this stage or can be processed further and sold as an alloy. Information on the raw metal and alloy are given as follows:

	Raw Metal	Alloy
Selling price	$150	$230
Variable cost	80	110

Total fixed cost is $300,000; either the raw metal, the alloy, or both can be manufactured; 800,000 hours of capacity are available; unlimited demand exists for both the raw metal and the alloy; two hours are required to make one ton of raw metal; and three hours are needed to produce one ton of alloy.

The contribution margin per hour is computed as follows:

	Raw Metal	Alloy
Selling price	$150	$230
Less variable cost	(80)	(110)
Contribution margin	70	120
Hours per ton	2	3
Contribution margin per hour	$ 35	$ 40

You should produce only the alloy, because it results in a higher contribution margin per hour. Fixed costs do not enter into the calculation because they are constant regardless of whether the raw metal or the alloy is manufactured.

FOR MANAGERIAL ACCOUNTANTS: Use contribution margin analysis to determine the bid price on a contract.

EXAMPLE 3.11

Travis Company has received an order for 6,000 units. The management executive wants to know the minimum bid price that would produce a $14,000 increase in profit. The current income statement follows:

Income Statement

Sales (30,000 units × $20)		$600,000
Less cost of sales		
Direct material	$60,000	
Direct labor	150,000	
Variable overhead (150,000 × 40%)	60,000	
Fixed overhead	80,000	(350,000)
Gross margin		$ 250,000
Less selling and administrative expenses		
Variable (includes transportation costs of $0.20 per unit)	15,000	
Fixed	85,000	(100,000)
Net income		**$ 150,000**

If the contract is taken, the cost patterns for the extra order will remain the same, with these exceptions:

• Transportation costs will be paid by the customer
• Special tools costing $6,000 will be required for just this order and will not be reusable
• Direct labor time for each unit under the order will be 10% longer

WHAT TO DO: Derive the bid price in this manner:

Current Cost Per Unit

Selling price	$20	($600,000/30,000)
Direct material	2	($60,000/30,000)

Direct labor	5	($150,000/30,000)
Variable overhead	40%	of direct labor cost ($60,000/$150,000)
Variable selling and administrative expense	$0.50	($15,000/30,000)

See Schedule B on pages 70-71.

The contract price for the 6,000 units should be $80,000 ($680,000 - $600,000), or $13.33 per unit ($80,000/6,000).

The contract price per unit of $13.33 is less than the $20 current selling price per unit. Remember, by accepting the order, total fixed cost will remain the same except for the $6,000 cost of special tools.

MANAGEMENT EXECUTIVES: The contribution margin income statement approach can be used to evaluate the performance of department managers as well as their divisions.

EXAMPLE 3.12

Let's assume a three-division company. Relevant data are displayed in Schedule C on pages 72-73.

You can conclude from Schedule C that Division X shows highest profit.

3.3 PRICING TOOLS

What pricing method should I use?

Product pricing is a matter of concern to management executives, accountants, and marketing managers. Use either of the following two methodologies:

- *Absorption costing approach.* Here, pricing equals total cost plus profit markup. This approach covers all costs and should be employed when pricing new products and current business.

- *Contribution margin approach.* When a new order comes in and the prospective customer will buy only at a lower price, you should use the contribution margin approach, particularly when idle capacity exists. Here, the price is set at the variable cost plus profit markup. Remember, at idle capacity, fixed cost is constant. The order should only be accepted when selling price is greater than variable cost.

How do I analyze pricing policies if I am a managerial accountant?

Analyze the impact that economies of scale have on the costs and required production time. Evaluate the degree to which increased worker experience (i.e., the learning curve) will lower the per-unit cost with increased production.

You should determine different prices based on the segment involved, whether manufacturer, wholesaler, retailer, or consumer. The price to each segment will differ depending on the applicable marketing costs, such as advertising and distribution.

What price methods should I use if I am a marketing manager?

When you establish a price, take the following factors into account:

- Return on sales
- Share of market
- Age categorization
- Economic breakdown
- Regional location
- Social aspects
- Ethnic wants

Also, consider the customer's perception of prestige—higher may suggest a "quality" image to the consumer.

When you want to attract further business for other products or service contracts, you should prefer contribution margin pricing over full costing. However, do not use this approach if you think selling at a lower price will bring a negative reaction from existing customers.

CAUTION: When you decide to increase the price, do so only to the point that it does not cause a disproportionate decrease in volume. For instance, a 14-percent price increase may result in a 20-percent reduction in volume, thereby effecting overall lower earnings.

Set target rates of return for products that depend on risk, stage in the life cycle, and whether the initial sale generates subsequent business for other products or services. Ask to what extent the product line is affected by the learning curve (see Section 8.4).

SCHEDULE B

INCOME STATEMENT

| | 30,000 | 36,000 | |
	Current	Projected	Computed last
Sales	$600,000	$680,000[d]	
Cost of sales			
Direct material	$ 60,000	$ 72,000	($2 × 36,000)
Direct labor	150,000	183,000	($150,000 + [6,000 × $5.50[a]])
Variable overhead	60,000	73,200	($183,000 × 40%)
Fixed overhead	80,000	86,000	($80,000 + $6,000)
Total	$350,000	$414,200	

70

Variable selling and administrative costs	$ 15,000	$ 16,800	($15,000 + [6,000 × $0.30])[b]
Fixed selling and administrative costs	85,000	85,000	
Total	$100,000	$101,800	
Net income	$150,000	$164,000[c]	

[a] $5 × 1.10 = $5.50

[b] $0.50 – $0.20 = $0.30

[c] $150,000 + $14,000 = $164,000

[d] Net income + selling and administrative expenses + cost of sales = sales

$164,000 + $101,800 + $414,200 = $680,000

71

SCHEDULE C

	Total	DIVISIONS		
		X	Y	Z
Sales	$500,000	$300,000	$150,000	$ 50,000
Less variable manufacturing costs[a]	(200,000)	(100,000)	(70,000)	(30,000)
Manufacturing contribution margin	$300,000	$200,000	$ 80,000	$ 20,000
Less variable selling and administrative expenses[b]	(60,000)	(25,000)	(30,000)	(5,000)
Contribution margin	$240,000	$175,000	$ 50,000	$ 15,000
Less controllable fixed costs[c]	(40,000)	(20,000)	(18,000)	(2,000)
Short-run performance margin[d]	$200,000	$155,000	$ 32,000	$ 13,000
Less uncontrollable fixed costs[e]	(60,000)	(50,000)	(9,000)	(1,000)
Segment margin[f]	$140,000	$105,000	$ 23,000	$ 12,000
Joint fixed costs[g]	30,000			
Net income	$110,000			

aVariable manufacturing costs equal direct material, direct labor, and variable overhead. The variable manufacturing costs are derived by multiplying the variable manufacturing cost per unit by the number of units produced.

bVariable selling and administrative costs equal variable selling and administrative cost per unit times number of units sold.

cControllable fixed costs are controllable by the division manager, if, for instance, he or she is responsible for advertising.

dShort-run performance margin equals the profitability figure used to evaluate the division manager's performance.

eUncontrollable fixed costs equal costs for which the division manager has no responsibility, such as property taxes and insurance.

fSegment margin is the profitability figure used to evaluate divisional performance. This is the last earnings figure shown for each division. The segment margin of all divisions is equal to the total segment margin of the company.

gJoint fixed costs are not allocated to divisions because it is not rational to do so since they do not apply to them. These might include professional fees, president's salary, and interest expense on corporate debt.

73

3.4 EVALUATING THE PRODUCT LINE

*What factors do I consider when evaluating
a product line?*

IF YOU'RE A MANAGEMENT EXECUTIVE:
Appraise introduction of a new product according to its synergistic effects, that is, how the new product fits into the whole product line.

IF YOU'RE A FINANCIAL MANAGER: Decide whether to discontinue products that show losses. In making your decision, consider the following factors:

- Eliminating a product would reduce volume and sales commissions but would necessitate higher base salaries for salespeople
- Fixed costs must still be recovered

You may still keep products that show a net loss based on full costing but that show a contribution margin.

Inventory stockouts should be recorded along with lost sales. Back-order costs should likewise be determined (see also Section 8.5).

SUGGESTION: Finance risky product lines with less risky funding, thereby reducing overall business risk. For example, a fad item should be financed with equity.

IF YOU'RE A MARKETING MANAGER: You can appraise the riskiness of product lines by computing the probability distribution in price, volume, and cost for products (see also Section 8.3).

How should I prepare marketing analysis reports?

To make your reports clear, you should express them not only in dollars but in percentages, ratios, and graphs. You should also provide reasons for any problems along with appropriate recommendations.

3.5 HOW TO MEASURE MARKETING EFFECTIVENESS

How do I measure marketing effectiveness?

Here's what you can do within your job function:

- *Management executives:* Examine product warranty complaints and their disposition.
- *Managerial accountants:* Determine revenue, cost, and earnings by product line, customer, industry segment, geographic area, distribution channel, type of marketing effort, and average order size.

- *Financial managers:* Prepare new product evaluations in terms of risk and profitability.

- *Marketing managers:* Appraise strengths and weaknesses of the competition as well as promotional effectiveness. Evaluate revenue, marketing costs, and profits before, during, and after promotion efforts. Also, know your competitor's reaction. Identify advertising costs by media, including newspaper, journal, direct mail, television, and radio.

How do I measure the effectiveness of the sales force?

GUIDE FOR MANAGERIAL ACCOUNTANTS: Gauge sales force effectiveness by looking at income generated by salespeople, call frequency, sales incentives, sales personnel costs (e.g., salary, auto, hotel), and dollar value of orders obtained per hour spent.

FINANCIAL MANAGERS: To gauge performance of your marketing employees, compute the following ratios:

- Revenue and/or net income per employee
- Marketing costs to sales

By doing so, you derive a proper selling price, identify poor marketing activities, and establish a proper discount.

FOR MARKETING MANAGERS: In determining salesperson profitability, subtract variable product costs and selling expenses from sales. Also, determine the profitability by type of sales solicitation (phone, mail, or personal visit). Find out the break-even point for each salesperson.

Establish an optimal commission plan for salespeople by incorporating the following strategies:

- Give a higher commission for original business than for repeat business.

- Vary commission rates depending on the territory and type of product being sold (e.g., a slow-moving item could have a higher commission).

- Base the commission on the product's profitability rather than on the selling price.

- Use a graduated commission rate on product sales that exceed the established quota.

SUGGESTION: Do not evaluate sales performance on actual sales generated but rather on profitability.

What financial measures should I use to evaluate success?

Financial measures of marketing success include

- Market share

- Sales
- Trend in inventory at wholesalers and retailers
- Profit margin

IF YOU'RE A MANAGEMENT EXECUTIVE: Look at marketing costs in terms of physical distribution, including inventory management, order processing, packaging, warehousing, shipping vehicle, and customer services.

IF YOU'RE A FINANCIAL MANAGER: Evaluate marketing costs according to the means of distribution, whether retailer, direct mail, or wholesaler. Examine the trend in the percentage of marketing cost to revenue as a basis for ascertaining the selling price.

3.6 BUDGETING TECHNIQUES

What is a budget?

A budget is a plan that quantifies the company's goals in terms of specific financial and operating objectives. Follow these steps in the budgeting process:

- Establish goals
- Develop strategies
- Formulate plans of action
- Evaluate the market
- Look at economic and political conditions
- Analyze competition
- Identify the life cycle of the product
- Appraise the company's financial strength
- Take corrective action

How do I formulate a budget?

Budgets may cover a long- or short-term period. The first step is to estimate future sales, and then production costs are based upon them.

A flexible budget employs budgeted figures at different capacity levels. Choose the best expected (normal) capacity level (100 percent) and assign pessimistic (80-percent), optimistic (110-percent), and full (150-percent) capacity levels.

MANAGEMENT EXECUTIVES: You can then see how the company's performance is at varying capacity levels. Fixed costs remain constant as long as the firm operates below full capacity.

What types of budgets must I prepare?

Many types of budgets should be prepared, including production, cash, sales, costs, profit, purchases, and forecasted financial statements.

Production Budgets. This type of budget tells how many units will be produced and their cost for a given period. If you're a financial manager, this budget will help you to find out your cash needs. MANAGERIAL ACCOUNTANTS: You need this budget for proper planning.

EXAMPLE 3.13

A company has a sales budget of 30,000 finished units. Beginning inventory is 6,000 units, and the expected ending inventory is 18,000 units. The cost per unit is $8. Budgeted production cost is estimated as follows:

Budgeted sales	30,000
Desired ending inventory	18,000
Need	48,000
Beginning inventory	(6,000)
Budgeted production	42,000
Budget cost of production (42,000 × $8)	**$336,000**

Assume three pieces of raw material are needed to produce one unit. There are 65,000 pieces on hand at the beginning of the period. Desired ending inventory is 80,000 pieces. Budgeted purchases of needed pieces are as follows:

Needed for production (42,000 × 3)	126,000
Desired ending inventory	80,000
Need	206,000
Beginning inventory	(65,000)
Budgeted purchases	141,000

If each piece costs $1.50, the budgeted cost of purchases is $211,500 (141,000 × $1.50).

Cash Budgets. In preparing a cash budget, start with beginning cash, add cash receipts, and subtract cash payments to arrive at ending cash. Cash receipts include anything that yields cash, like borrowing money or selling assets. CAUTION: Cash receipts are not necessarily the same as revenue (e.g., credit sales). Cash payments consist of cash disbursements, like buying assets or paying off debt. Not all expenses are cash payments (for example, depreciation).

OF SPECIAL NOTE: In many cases, cash collections will have to be predicted when a cash discount is given for early collection.

EXAMPLE 3.14

A company sells on terms of 3%/10 days, net/30 days. The following collection pattern has been observed:

- 60% of credit sales are collected within the discount period
- 30% are collected at the end of 30 days
- The balance is collected at the end of 60 days
- At the end of any month, 25% of sales on which cash discounts will be taken are still uncollected

Estimated sales are

	Oct.	Nov.	Dec.
Cash sales	$ 50,000	$40,000	$ 80,000
Credit sales	100,000	90,000	120,000

September credit sales are $110,000 and August credit sales are $85,000.

Schedule D is a table of collections on sales.

INTERNAL AUDITORS: To appraise performance of managers and programs, make a comparison between budgeted and actual revenue, cost, and time.

Zero-Base Budgeting (ZBB). With ZBB, each year's expected expenditure must be justified. Existing and new programs must have value and contribute to overall objectives of the firm. Each project is reexamined at the beginning of the period. When a project does not meet established criteria, it is dropped.

STEPS FOR FINANCIAL MANAGERS IN USING ZBB

- Appraise the activity of a division, department, or operation
- Analyze each activity from a cost-benefit perspective
- Formulate a decision package that accomplishes the specified goal
- Rank the decision packages in order of priority
- Assign limited funds to competing activities on the basis of merit

What should the decision package include?

The decision package describes the activity to be per-

SCHEDULE D

Month	Collections on Current Month's Sales		Collections from Previous Month's Sales		Collections from Credit Sales Made Two Months Ago[d]	Total
	Cash	Credit[a]	Discount[b]	No Discount[c]		
October	$50,000	$43,650	$16,005	$33,000	$ 8,500	$151,155
November	40,000	39,285	14,550	30,000	11000	134,835
December	80,000	52,380	13,095	27,000	10,000	182,475

[a] $0.6 \times 0.97 \times 0.75 \times$ current sales

[b] $0.6 \times 0.97 \times 0.25 \times$ credit sales from previous month

[c] $0.3 \times$ credit sales from previous month

[d] $0.1 \times$ credit sales from two months ago

formed and consists of various ways in time and money to meet the objective. The manager indicates a recommended path as well as alternative possibilities. Then upper management decides which path to fund, assuming it wishes to accept the activity.

A decision package may be rejected, accepted at a minimal funding level, accepted at the minimal funding level plus an increment, or approved at the requested funding level.

3.7 HIGHLIGHTING PROBLEM AREAS WITH VARIANCE ANALYSIS

What is variance analysis?

Variance analysis is a comparison between standard and actual performance. If you are a managerial accountant, financial manager, production manager, or are in marketing, variance analysis will be useful to you.

Use variance analysis to

- Control costs
- "Red flag" present and prospective problems (this way, you can follow the "management by exception" principle)
- Identify responsibility so you know whom to "call on the carpet"
- Formulate corporate objectives
- Aid in decision making
- Provide a vehicle for better communication within the organization

You should prepare performance reports that focus on the difference between budgeted and actual figures. Look at these items:

- Production (cost, quantity, and quality), to gauge the foremen's performance
- Sales and market share, to evaluate marketing managers
- Profit, to appraise overall operations
- Return on investment, to evaluate asset utilization

How do marketing managers compute sales variances?

EXAMPLE 3.15

Budgeted sales for 19X1

Product A: 8,000 units at $5.50 per unit	$ 44,000
Product B: 24,000 units at $7.50 per unit	180,000
Expected sales revenue	**$224,000**

Actual sales for the year

Product A: 6,000 units at $6.00 per unit	$ 36,000
Product B: 28,000 units at $7.00 per unit	196,000
Actual sales revenue	**$232,000**

A positive sales variance of $8,000 is composed of sales price and volume variances. The sales price variance equals actual selling price versus (minus) budgeted selling price times actual units sold.

Product A ($6.00 vs. $5.50 × 6,000)	$ 3,000 F[a]
Product B ($7.00 vs. $7.50 × 28,000)	14,000 U[b]
Sales price variance	$11,000 U

[a]Favorable.
[b]Unfavorable.

The sales volume variance equals actual quantity versus budgeted quantity times budgeted selling price.

Product A (6,000 vs. 8,000 × $5.50)	$11,000 U
Product B (28,000 vs. 24,000 × $7.50)	30,000 F
Sales volume variance	$19,000 F

Proof

Sales price variance	$11,000 U
Sales volume variance	19,000 F
Sales variance	$ 8,000 F

How do I apply standards and cost variances?

When actual cost exceeds standard cost, variance is unfavorable. Be sure to determine the reason behind the variance in order to facilitate appropriate corrective action.

Set standards according to their application as follows:

Job Function	*Situation*	*Standard*
Financial managers	Cost reduction	Stringent

Managerial accountants	Inventory valuation	Fair
Marketing managers	Pricing decision	Realistic
Buyers	Expensive purchases	Perfection

When should I do a variance analysis?

Standard prices (material price, wage rate) are determined at the beginning of the period.

Variance analysis can be performed by year, quarter, month, day, or hour depending on the importance of identifying a problem quickly.

MANAGERIAL ACCOUNTANTS: Because you do not know the number of units produced or services rendered until the end of the period, you cannot arrive at such variances until then.

How do I interpret a variance analysis?

Immaterial variance percentages (i.e., variance divided by standard cost) not exceeding 5 percent need not be investigated further unless they occur consistently and show a potential problem.

MANAGERIAL ACCOUNTANTS SHOULD DO THIS: When a product is made or a service is rendered, you need to compute these three measures:

- Actual cost equals actual price times actual quantity, where actual quantity equals actual quantity per unit of work times actual units of work produced.
- Standard cost equals standard price times standard quantity, where standard quantity equals standard quantity per unit of work times actual units of work produced.
- Control variance equals actual cost minus standard cost.

Control variance consists of the following components:

- Price (rate, cost) variance (standard price versus actual price times actual quantity)
- Quantity (usage, efficiency) variance (standard quantity versus actual quantity times standard price)

Compute these for both material and labor.

Material Variances. MANAGERIAL ACCOUNTANTS: The material price variance permits you to appraise the purchasing department function and examine the effect of raw material cost changes on overall corporate earnings. The material quantity variance is the responsibility of the production supervisor.

EXAMPLE 3.16

The standard cost of one unit of output (product or service) was $15: three pieces at $5 per piece. During the period, 8,000 units were produced. Actual cost was $14 per unit: two pieces at $7 per piece.

Material control variance

Standard quantity times standard price (24,000 × $5)	$120,000
Actual quantity times actual price (16,000 × $7)	112,000
	$ 8,000 F

Material price variance

Standard price versus actual price times actual quantity ($5 vs. $7 × 16,000)	$ 32,000 U

Material quantity variance

Standard quantity versus actual quantity times standard price (24,000 vs. 16,000 × $5)	$ 40,000 F

MANAGEMENT EXECUTIVES: You cannot control material price variances when higher prices arise from inflation or shortage situations or when rush orders are required by the customer who will bear the ultimate cost increase.

Look for possible causes of unfavorable material variances.

CHECKLIST OF UNFAVORABLE MATERIAL VARIANCE

Cause	Responsible Entity
Unnecessarily high prices paid	Purchasing
Purchased material differed from specifications	Purchasing
Inspection did not reveal defective goods	Receiving
Workers' incompetency	Foremen
Poor supervision	Foremen
Deficient mix in material	Production manager
Immediate delivery of materials by plane	Traffic

Unfavorable quantity variance	Foremen
Forced acquisitions	Purchasing
Unanticipated change in production volume	Sales manager

SOLUTIONS FOR MANAGEMENT EXECUTIVES: By examining the nature and degree of the material price variance, you may decide to

- Increase prices
- Substitute cheaper materials
- Change a production method or specification
- Implement a cost-reduction plan

Labor Variances. The standard labor rate should be based on the contracted hourly wage rate. Where wage rates are set by union contract, the labor rate variance will typically be minimal. Labor efficiency standards are normally established by engineers on the basis of an analysis of the manufacturing operation. Determine labor variance exactly as you would material variance.

EXAMPLE 3.17

The standard cost for labor is four hours times $9 per hour, or $36 per unit.
   During the period, 7,000 units were manufactured.
   The actual cost is six hours times $8 per hour, or $48 per unit.

Labor control variance

Standard quantity times standard price (28,000 × $9)	$252,000
Actual quantity times actual price (42,000 × $8)	336,000
	$ 84,000 U

Labor price variance

Standard price versus actual price times actual quantity ($9 vs. $8 × 42,000)	$ 42,000 F

Labor quantity variance

Standard quantity versus actual quantity × standard price (28,000 vs. 42,000 × $9)	$126,000 U

INTERNAL AUDITORS: Examine reasons for an unfavorable labor price variance. Some examples are

Cause	*Responsible entity*
Use of overqualified or an excessive number of workers	Production manager or union contract
Improper work assignments from poor job descriptions	Personnel
Overtime	Production planning

NOTE: An unfavorable labor price variance may be unavoidable when experienced workers are in short supply.

Determine reasons for an unfavorable labor efficiency variance, including

Cause	*Responsible entity*
Improper supervision	Factory foremen
Deficient machinery	Maintenance
Poor-quality material	Purchasing
Inadequate material supply	Purchasing

Overhead Variances. The overhead variance consists of the controllable and volume variances. The necessary computations are

- Overhead control variance equals actual overhead versus standard overhead (standard hours times standard overhead rate)
- Controllable variance equals actual overhead versus budget adjusted to standard hours. Note: Budget adjusted to standard hours equals fixed overhead plus variable overhead (standard hours times standard variable overhead rate)
- Volume variance equals standard overhead versus budget adjusted to standard hours

EXAMPLE 3.18

The following information is provided by Company M:

Budgeted overhead (includes fixed overhead of $7,500 and variable overhead of $10,000)	$17,500
Budgeted hours	10,000
Actual overhead	$ 8,000

Actual units produced		800
Standard hours per unit of production		5

Preliminary calculations

Budgeted fixed overhead ($7,500/10,000 hr)		$0.75
Budgeted variable overhead ($10,000/10,000 hr)		1.00
Total budgeted overhead ($17,500/10,000 hr)		$1.75
Standard hours (800 units × 5 hr per unit)		4,000 hr

Overhead control variance

Actual overhead		$ 8,000
Standard overhead		
Standard hours	4,000 hr	
Standard overhead rate	$1.75	(7,000)
		$ 1,000 U

Controllable variance

Actual overhead		$ 8,000
Budget adjusted to standard hours		
Fixed overhead	$7,500	
Variable overhead (standard hours × standard variable overhead rate—4,000 × $1)	4,000	11,500
		3,500 **F**

Volume variance

Standard overhead		$ 7,000
Budget adjusted to standard hours		11,500
		$ 4,500 U

Factory foremen have responsibility for the controllable variance and thus influence actual overhead incurred. The volume variance looks at plant utilization and thus is controllable by management executives and production managers.

MANAGEMENT EXECUTIVES: Variable overhead variance data are useful in formulating output level and output mix decisions. They also help in appraising decisions regarding variable inputs. WARNING: Fixed overhead variance data do not generate useful information for operating decisions, but they do furnish information regarding decision-making astuteness when buying some combination of fixed plant size and variable production inputs.

A consistently unfavorable overhead volume variance may arise from purchasing the wrong size plant, deficient scheduling, insufficient orders, material shortages, equipment failure, long operating time, or poorly trained employees. Idle capacity may indicate long-run operating planning problems.

Raw Material Costs. Examine the variability in raw material costs. MANAGERIAL ACCOUNTANTS: Look at price instability as discussed in trade publications. HINT TO MANAGEMENT EXECUTIVES: Emphasize vertical integration to reduce the price and supply risk of raw materials.

Variances for Selling Expenses. Cost variances for the selling function may pertain to the territory, product, or personnel. MARKETING MANAGERS: Evaluate your sales force within a territory, including time spent and expenses incurred.

EXAMPLE 3.19

Company O provided the following sales data:

Standard cost	$240,000
Standard salesperson days	2,000
Standard rate per salesperson day	$ 120
Actual cost	$238,000
Actual salesperson days	1,700
Actual rate per salesperson day	$ 140

Total cost variance

Actual cost	$238,000
Standard cost	240,000
	$ 2,000 F

Categorize the total favorable variance of $2,000 into salesperson days and salesperson costs.

Variance in salesperson days

Actual days versus standard days times

standard rate per day
(1,700 vs. 2,000 × $120) $36,000 F

Since less days than expected were required to handle the sales territory, the variance is favorable.

Variance in salesperson costs

Actual rate versus standard rate times
actual days ($140 vs. $120 × 1,700) $34,000 U

Because the actual rate per day exceeded the standard rate per day, the variance is unfavorable.

PART II

FINANCIAL AND ECONOMIC MEASURES

4
Break-even, Operating Leverage, and Discounting Analysis

Break-even analysis lies at the heart of your company's success. Whether you're a management executive, managerial accountant, financial manager, or financial analyst, understanding this technique is a must.

As its basis, break-even analysis draws upon contribution margin analysis, discussed in Section 3.2. Operating leverage (see Section 1.2.1) follows directly from break-even analysis. The third component, present and future value analysis, completes the spectrum of analytic techniques found in this chapter. Together, they will help you keep your company afloat and turn a profit.

4.1 BREAK-EVEN ANALYSIS

What is break-even analysis?

Break-even analysis, also known as cost-volume-profit analysis, is used to determine the sales volume at which a company is able to cover all its costs without making or losing money.

What are the uses of break-even analysis?

Use break-even analysis to organize your thinking on important broad features of your business. It is especially pertinent when beginning a new activity, such as starting a new business, expanding an already existing business, or introducing a new product or service.

Many managers within a company will find uses for break-even analysis. It answers these important questions:

- *Management executives:* Have the company's break-even possibilities been improving, or have they been deteriorating over time? What will be the impact of major labor negotiations?

- *Marketing managers:* Will a major marketing campaign generate sufficient sales to justify the cost of the campaign? Would introduction of a new product add or detract from the company's profitability?

- *Production managers:* Would modernization of production facilities pay for itself?

If you are an accountant, providing data for the break-even analysis will be your responsibility. If you are a financial analyst or investor, you might want to know about efforts a company makes to reduce its break-even point.

NOTE: Break-even analysis has its limitations. Refer to Section 4.3 for a discussion of them.

CHECKLIST OF USES
FOR BREAK-EVEN ANALYSIS

- Evaluating the start of a new business
- Evaluating the profitability of a new product line or service
- Evaluating the profitability of investing in a major capital expansion

What are the key factors in break-even analysis?

The break-even point depends on three factors:

- The product's selling price
- The variable costs of production, selling, and administration
- The fixed costs of production, selling, and administration

The stability of the selling price during a given income period depends on several factors, including the general market conditions and the behavior of the economy overall.

Break-even analysis, if used properly, will enable an in-depth evaluation of production and administrative activities. WHAT TO DO: You need to forecast production, selling, and administrative costs and then exclude those that are fixed or variable.

How do I determine the break-even point?

HERE'S WHAT TO DO: First, separate variable from fixed costs. Use this example as a guide:

EXAMPLE 4.1

Company A produces a single product that has very elastic demand. Assume a stable market price over the income period. The product sells for $100 per unit. The variable cost per unit is $20 (this includes variable production, marketing, and administrative costs). Fixed cost is $1,000,000. At normal capacity, 100,000 units can be produced during this income period using a single production shift.

The contribution margin income statement, assuming normal capacity, is given as follows:

	Amount	% of Sales
Sales (100,000 units × $100 per unit)	$10,000,000	100%
Less variable costs (100,000 units × $20 per unit)	(2,000,000)	(20)
Contribution margin	8,000,000	80
Less fixed costs	(1,000,000)	(10)
Operating income	**$7,000,000**	**70**

At 80% capacity, the income statement would appear as follows:

	Amount	% of Sales
Sales (0.80 × 100,000 units × $100 per unit)	$8,000,000	100
Less variable costs (0.80 × 100,000 units × $20 per unit)	(1,600,000)	(20)
Contribution margin	6,400,000	80
Less fixed costs	(1,000,000)	(12.5)
Operating income	**$5,400,000**	**67.5**

REMEMBER THIS: With fixed selling price and per-unit variable cost, as sales volume drops below normal capacity, variable costs to sales remain constant, as do contribution margins to sales. At break-even, sales equals variable costs plus fixed costs, and net income equals zero. Also, break-even contribution margin equals fixed cost:

$$S_b = Vc_b + FC, \text{ and}$$
$$CM_b = FC$$

where

S_b = Sales volume at break-even
VC_b = Total variable cost at break-even
FC = Total fixed costs

CM_b = Contribution margin at break-even

Contribution margin, whether at break-even or otherwise, relates to sales as follows:

$$CM = a \times S$$
where
a = the constant ratio of contribution margin to sales.

Substituting for contribution margin in the above formulas, you can derive these:

$$a \times S_b = FC$$

$$S_b = \frac{FC}{a}$$

EXAMPLE 4.2

The break-even sales volume for Company A described in the preceding example is calculated as follows:

$$S_b = \frac{\$1,000,000}{0.80}$$
$$S_b = \$1,250,000$$

ANOTHER WAY: You can express these formulas in more conventional ways as follows:

$$a = \frac{CM}{S}$$
$$CM = S - VC$$
$$a = \frac{S - VC}{S}$$
$$S_b = \frac{FC}{\frac{S - VC}{S}}$$

How do I express break-even in physical units?

To express break-even in units rather than dollars, you need to relate dollar sales to volume. With a single-product company, this can be expressed as follows:

$$S = P \times Q$$
where
P = unit selling price
Q = sales volume in physical units

You also need to express total variable cost (VC) per unit or average variable cost (AVC). The relation between the two is expressed as follows:

$$VC = AVC \times Q$$

At break-even, this formula becomes

$$CM_b = (P \times Q_b) + (AVC \times Q_b)$$

where

Q_b = break-even sales in physical units.

The conventional formula for break-even sales volume in physical units is given as follows:

$$Q_b = \frac{FC}{P - AVC}$$

Again, using Company A from the previous examples, break-even sales volume in physical units is computed as follows:

$$Q_b = \frac{\$1,000,000}{\$100 - \$20}$$

$$Q_b = \frac{\$1,000,000}{\$80}$$

$$Q_b = 12,500 \text{ units}$$

Break-even sales volume in dollars relates to break-even sales volume in physical units as follows:

$$S_b = P \times Q_b$$
$$S_b = \$100 \times 12,500$$
$$S_b = \$1,250,000$$

CONCLUSION: If each unit sold provides a unit contribution margin of $80, then 12,500 units sold will be necessary to generate enough variable profits to cover fixed costs of $1,000,000.

Proof	Average	Physical Units[a]	Total
Sales	$100	12,500	$1,250,000
Less variable costs	(20)	(12,500)	(250,000)
Contribution margin	80	12,500	$1,000,000
Less fixed costs	(80)	(12,500)	(1,000,000)
Operating income	0		$ 0

[a]Break-even sales volume.

Can I express break-even graphically?

Graphs are usually quite helpful in illustrating break-even. Here's an example:

EXAMPLE 4.3

Figure 4.1 shows break-even sales in dollars. To the left, sales volume is below break-even, shown as a loss. Above break-even, each sales volume shows a profit.

REMEMBER: Profit divided by loss equals sales minus total costs.

Figure 4.1 shows four dollar amounts:

Amount	Significance
$1,000,000	Total fixed costs; dollar amount that contribution margin must achieve for break-even
$1,250,000	Break-even sales volume at which contribution margin will equal total fixed costs
$1,333,333	Dollar value of contribution margin when it covers both total fixed costs and total variable costs
$1,666,667	Dollar sales volume at which contribution margin covers total costs

FIGURE 4.1: BREAK-EVEN IN TERMS OF CONTRIBUTION MARGIN

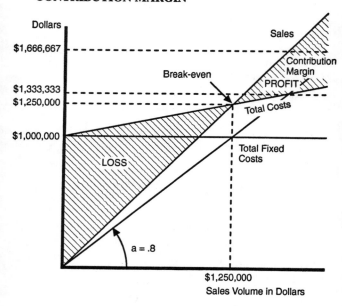

Here's how to calculate $1,666,667 and $1,333,333: Remember,

$$S = \frac{FC}{a - b}$$

For this formula to be useful, a must be greater than b. In the given analysis, $a = 80\%$ and $b = 20\%$. Thus, the sales volume at which contribution margin just covers costs is

$$S = \frac{\$1,000,000}{0.8 - 0.2} = \$1,666,667$$

To calculate contribution margin at this sales volume,

$$CM = 0.8 \times \$1,666,667 = \$1,333,333$$

CALCULATE FOR YOURSELF: When contribution margin is $1,333,333, then total costs also equal this figure.

Figure 4.2 shows break-even sales volume in physical units. The dollar amounts are the same as for Figure 4.1. One new amount, $250,000, represents the total variable cost at break-even sales volume of 12,500 units. NOTE: At break-even, sales of $1,250,000 less $250,000 of total variable costs equals the contribution margin, $1,000,000.

FIGURE 4.2: BREAK-EVEN IN PHYSICAL UNITS FOR THE SINGLE-PRODUCT FIRM

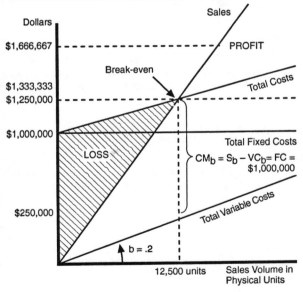

4.2 SENSITIVITY ANALYSIS: CHANGES IN BREAK-EVEN

How do changes in selling price affect break-even?

So far, break-even analysis has assumed a constant selling price. If it changes, then somewhat different formulas for break-even would be applied. Recall this formula from Section 4.1:

$$a = \frac{CM}{S} = \frac{P - AVC}{P}$$

You can see that a is dependent on the selling price and the unit variable cost. If the unit selling price changes, then a would change as follows:

$$\Delta a = \left(\frac{AVC}{P}\right) \times \left(\frac{\Delta P}{P + \Delta P}\right)$$

where

Δa = change in the ratio of contribution margin to sales

ΔP = change in the unit selling price

EXAMPLE 4.4

Using the same information for Company A given in Section 4.1, consider now a change in selling price from $100 to $80. The ratio of contribution margin to dollar sales is computed as follows:

$$a = \left(\frac{\$20}{\$100}\right) \times \left(\frac{-\$20}{(\$100 + [-\$20])}\right) = -0.05$$

CONCLUSION: The decreased selling price has reduced the ratio of contribution margin to dollar sales from 80% to 75%.

Proof	*Amount*	*% of Sales*
Sales (100,000 units × $80 per unit)	$8,000,000	100.0
Less variable costs (100,000 units × $20 per unit)	(2,000,000)	(25.0)
Contribution margin	6,000,000	75.0
Less fixed costs	(1,000,000)	(12.5)
Operating income	**$5,000,000**	**62.5**

Now calculate the new break-even sales volume as follows:

$$S_b = \frac{\$1,000,000}{0.75} = \$1,333,333$$

$$Q_b = \frac{\$1,000,000}{\$80 - \$20} = 16,667 \text{ units}$$

NOTE: The new break-even sales volume in physical units (16,667) times the new unit selling price ($80) results in a new break-even dollar sales volume ($1,333,333). This agrees with the preceding calculations.

This is a form of sensitivity analysis; that is, the sensitivity of a company's break-even sales volume to changes in the selling price. In this example, the selling price dropped by 20 percent, which required an increase in break-even dollar sales volume from $1,250,000 to $1,333,333, or 6.67 percent. The required increase in break-even sales volume of physical units would be 4,167 units (12,500 to 16,667), or 33.3 percent.

How can a change in unit selling price affect the break-even sales volume?

Recall the discussion in Section 3.7 comparing standard and actual amounts. Now make a similar comparison between old and new actual amounts, referred to as variations (not variances). Three relevant variations are described as follows:

Price Variation. Price variation refers to the loss in sales revenue on the original physical break-even sales volume resulting from lower selling price. *Formula:* Price variation equals the new price minus the old price times the old physical break-even sales volume.

Quantity Variation. This refers to the gain in sales revenue resulting from the required increase in the physical break-even sales volume at the new unit selling price.

Cost Variation. Cost variation refers to the rise in total variable costs owing to the required increase in physical break-even sales volume. *Formula:* Cost variation equals new physical break-even sales volume minus old physical break-even sales volume times unit variable cost.

EXAMPLE 4.5

Using the preceding formulas, calculations for Company A are given as follows:

Price variation = ($80 − $100) × 12,500 = −$250,000

Quantity variation = (16,667 − 12,500) × $80 = $333,333

Cost variation = (16,667 − 12,500) × $20 = $83,333

Analysis combining the three is shown as follows:

	Amount	% of Old Break-even Sales
Favorable quantity variation	$333,333	26.67
Less unfavorable price variation	(250,000)	(20.00)
Net rise in break-even dollar sales	83,333	6.67
Less unfavorable cost variation	(83,333)	(6.67)
Break-even	$ 0	0

$333,333/$1,250,000 = [a]26.67
$250,000/$1,250,000 = 20%
$83,333/$1,250,000 = 6.67

How can a change in unit variable cost affect break-even?

To determine the change in unit variable cost, use this formula:

$$\Delta a = \frac{-(\Delta AVC)}{P}$$

where

ΔAVC = the change in the unit variable cost and P is assumed unchanged

EXAMPLE 4.6

For Company A, there has been a rise in unit variable cost from $20 to $30. Calculations for the change in a (or the ratio of CM to S) is shown as follows:

$$\Delta a = \frac{-\$10}{\$100} = -0.10$$

A decline in the value is demonstrated as follows:

	Amount	% of Sales
Sales (100,000 units × $100)	$10,000,000	100
Less variable costs (100,000 units × $30 per unit)	(3,000,000)	(30)
Contribution margin	7,000,000	70
Less fixed costs	(1,000,000)	(10)
Operating income	$ 6,000,000	(60)

The new break-even dollar sales volume can be calculated as follows:

$$S_b = \frac{\$1,000,000}{0.7} = \$1,428,571$$

The rise in unit variable costs will have a greater impact on the break-even sales volume. Why? Because the fall in the unit selling price changes only the value of a, whereas the rise in unit variable cost has a greater effect.

How do changes in total fixed costs affect break-even?

You can compute the impact of a change in total fixed costs on break-even by using the following formula:

$$\Delta S_b = \frac{\Delta FC}{a}$$

where

ΔS_b = the change in dollar break-even sales volume

ΔFC = the change in total fixed costs, and a is assumed unchanged

EXAMPLE 4.7

For Company A, total fixed costs rose from $1,000,000 to $1,500,000. The impact in terms of new break-even dollar sales is computed as follows:

$$\Delta S_b = \frac{\$500,000}{0.8} = \$625,000$$

As a result of the $500,000 increase in total fixed costs, the break-even dollar sales rises from $1,250,000 to $1,875,000.

How can I summarize these changes?

Remember these simple rules:

• A rise in the unit selling price will lower the break-even sales volume, whether in dollars or in physical units, and vice versa

• A rise in the unit variable cost will increase the break-even sales volume, and vice versa

• A rise in total fixed costs will increase the break-even sales volume, and vice versa

EXAMPLE 4.8

Changes between break-even dollar sales, unit selling price, unit variable cost, and total fixed costs are shown in the three tables on pages 102-104.

BREAK-EVEN DOLLAR SALES IN RELATION TO CHANGES IN UNIT SELLING PRICE

(1) Unit Selling Price (P)	(2) Unit Variable Cost (AVC)	(3) Unit Contribution Margin (P - AVC)	(4) Ratio of Unit Contribution Margin to Unit Selling Price $\left(\dfrac{P - AVC}{P}\right)$	(5) Total Fixed Costs (FC)	(6) Break-even Dollar Sales (S_b)
$ 20	$20	$ 0	0	$1,000,000	Undefined
40	20	20	0.50	1,000,000	$2,000,000
60	20	40	0.67	1,000,000	1,500,000
80	20	60	0.75	1,000,000	1,333,333
100	20	80	0.80	1,000,000	1,250,000
120	20	100	0.83	1,000,000	1,200,000

BREAK-EVEN DOLLAR SALES IN RELATION TO CHANGES IN AVERAGE VARIABLE COST

(1) Unit Selling Price (P)	(2) Unit Variable Cost (AVC)	(3) Unit Contribution Margin (P – AVC)	(4) Ratio of Unit Contribution Margin to Unit Selling Price $\left(\dfrac{P - AVC}{P}\right)$	(5) Total Fixed Costs (FC)	(6) Break-even Dollar Sales (S_b)
$100	$ 5	$95	0.95	$1,000,000	$1,052,632
$100	10	90	0.90	$1,000,000	$1,111,111
$100	15	85	0.85	$1,000,000	$1,176,471
$100	20	80	0.80	$1,000,000	$1,250,000
$100	25	75	0.75	$1,000,000	$1,333,333
$100	30	70	0.70	$1,000,000	$1,428,571

BREAK-EVEN DOLLAR SALES IN RELATION TO CHANGES IN TOTAL FIXED COSTS

(1) Unit Selling Price (P)	(2) Unit Variable Cost (AVC)	(3) Unit Contribution Margin (P – AVC)	(4) Ratio of Unit Contribution Margin to Unit Selling Price $\left(\dfrac{P - AVC}{P}\right)$	(5) Total Fixed Costs (FC)	(6) Break-even Dollar Sales (S_b)
$100	$20	$80	0.80	$ 400,000	$ 500,000
100	20	80	0.80	600,000	750,000
100	20	80	0.80	800,000	1,000,000
100	20	80	0.80	1,000,000	1,250,000
100	20	80	0.80	1,200,000	1,500,000

You can make these observations:

- The lower the unit selling price (1), the lower the unit contribution margin (3)
- The ratio of unit contribution margin to unit selling price (4) falls as the unit selling price drops
- The break-even dollar sales (6) is a result of dividing the unit contribution margin ratio (4) into the total fixed costs (5)

Figure 4.3 shows an inverse linear relation between break-even dollar sales and different values of the unit selling price. The lower limit is equal to the total fixed costs, shown with broken lines in the figure. The lower the unit selling price, the lower the unit contribution margin ratio and the higher the break-even dollar sales volume. As the unit selling price falls and approaches the constant unit variable cost, the contribution margin ratio approaches zero and the break-even dollar sales volume will become impossibly high. There is no upper limit to break-even sales.

In Figure 4.4, there is a direct but nonlinear relation between break-even dollar sales and the different values of the unit variable cost. Figure 4.5 also shows a direct linear relation between the break-even dollar sales and the different values of total fixed costs.

FIGURE 4.3: BREAK-EVEN DOLLAR SALES IN RELATION TO CHANGES IN UNIT SELLING PRICE

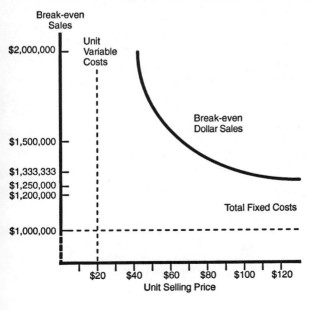

FIGURE 4.4: BREAK-EVEN DOLLAR SALES IN RELATION TO CHANGES IN AVERAGE VARIABLE COST

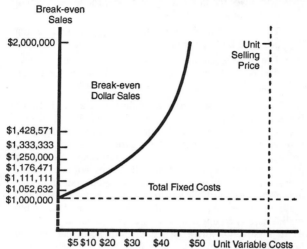

FIGURE 4.5: BREAK-EVEN DOLLAR SALES IN RELATION TO CHANGES IN TOTAL FIXED COSTS

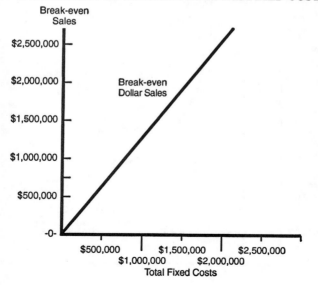

4.3 FROM BREAK-EVEN TO TARGET PROFITS

How can I determine desired profit levels?

The objective of your business is not simply to break even but to make a profit. Break-even analysis can be easily extended to focus on a target level of profits. A simple modification of the break-even formula will help you compute target profits:

$$S_d = \frac{FC + \pi_d}{\dfrac{S - VC}{S}}$$

where

S_d = the desired or target level of dollar sales, and

π_d = the desired or target level of profits

What is the relation between operating leverage and break-even?

The measure of operating leverage used with break-even analysis is called degree of operating leverage (DOL), defined as follows:

$$DOL = \frac{\text{percent change in operating income}}{\text{percent change in sales}}$$

The relationship between degree of operating leverage, and dollar sales volume, and break-even is stated as follows:

$$DOL = 1 + \frac{S_b}{S - S_b}$$

EXAMPLE 4.9

The relationship between degree of operating leverage and dollar sales volume as well as break-even dollar sales is shown in the following table, and also in Figure 4.6.

DEGREE OF OPERATING LEVERAGE RELATED TO DOLLAR SALES VOLUME FOR TWO LEVELS OF BREAK-EVEN DOLLAR SALES

Dollar Sales (S)	Break-Even Dollar Sales (SI_b)	(DOL_1)	Break-Even Dollar Sales (S_b)	(DOL_2)
0	$625,000	0	$1,250,000	0
$ 500,000	625,000	4	1,250,000	$-1/2$
625,000	625,000	Undefined	1,250,000	-1
666,667	625,000	16	1,250,000	$-1\,1/7$
750,000	625,000	6	1,250,000	$-1\,1/2$
833,333	625,000	4	1,250,000	-2
1,000,000	625,000	$2\,2/3$	1,250,000	-4
1,250,000	625,000	2	1,250,000	Undefined

1,333,333	625,000		1,250,000	16
1,500,000	625,000		1,250,000	6
1,666,667	625,000		1,250,000	4
2,000,000	625,000		1,250,000	2 $\frac{2}{3}$
2,500,000	625,000		1,250,000	2
2,666,667	625,000	1 $\frac{15}{17}$	1,250,000	1 $\frac{15}{17}$
3,000,000	625,000	1 $\frac{5}{7}$	1,250,000	1 $\frac{5}{7}$
3,333,333	625,000	1 $\frac{6}{10}$	1,250,000	1 $\frac{6}{10}$
4,000,000	625,000	1 $\frac{5}{11}$	1,250,000	1 $\frac{5}{11}$
5,000,000	625,000	1 $\frac{1}{3}$	1,250,000	1 $\frac{1}{3}$
5,333,333	625,000	1 $\frac{15}{113}$	1,250,000	1 $\frac{15}{49}$
6,000,000	625,000	1 $\frac{15}{129}$	1,250,000	1 $\frac{5}{19}$
6,666,667	625,000	1 $\frac{9}{87}$	1,250,000	1 $\frac{3}{13}$
8,000,000	625,000	1 $\frac{5}{59}$	1,250,000	1 $\frac{5}{27}$
$10,000,000	625,000	1 $\frac{1}{15}$	1,250,000	1 $\frac{1}{7}$

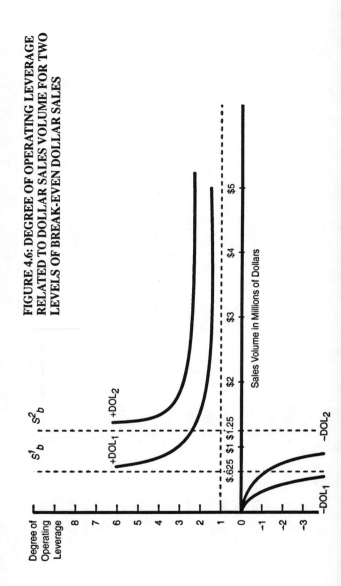

FIGURE 4.6: DEGREE OF OPERATING LEVERAGE RELATED TO DOLLAR SALES VOLUME FOR TWO LEVELS OF BREAK-EVEN DOLLAR SALES

CONCLUSIONS: If you double the break-even dollar sales volume, you must double your actual dollar sale volume in order to maintain the same level of responsiveness of profits to changes in dollar sales volume.

The previous example assumes two different levels of break-even dollar sales. Another break-even dollar sales volume can result from a change in either the unit selling price, the unit variable cost, or the total fixed costs.

EXAMPLE 4.10

From the previous example, assume the break-even dollar sales volume of $625,000 is basically the result of a change in total fixed costs from $1,000,000 to $500,000. The responsiveness of profits in relation to operating income and to changes in dollar sales volume is shown on page 112.

Assumptions: $I = S - VC - FC$ and $VC = (0.2) \times S$; two levels of fixed costs (FC) = $500,000 and $1,000,000.

As dollar sales rise from $750,000 to $833,333, operating income also rises from $100,000 to $166,667, assuming break-even dollar sales level equals $625,000. The percent change in operating income (66.67 percent) equals the ratio of the change in operating income ($66,667) to the old operating income ($110,000). The percent change in sales (11.11) equals the ratio of the increase in sales ($83,333) to the old level ($750,000). When break-even sales volume doubles to $1,250,000, the dollar sales volume also must double in order to yield the same percent changes in operating income and sales. The degree of operating leverage shows that the percent change in income is 6 times the percent change in sales when break-even dollar sales total $625,000 and actual sales increase from $750,000 to $833,333. If actual sales rise from $1,500,000 to $1,666,667, the same degree of operating leverage holds for break-even dollar sales ($1,250,000).

What happens when a fixed capacity exists that limits sales volume, and break-even sales increase because of declining selling prices or increasing unit variable cost? REMEMBER THIS: As the unit selling price or unit variable cost changes, break-even dollar sales and the degree of operating leverage will also vary. Example 4.11 shows the relation between DOL and break-even dollar sales (BE$S) for a given capacity sales volume.

CHANGES IN BREAK-EVEN DOLLAR SALES AND THE RESPONSIVENESS OF PROFITS TO CHANGES IN DOLLAR SALES VOLUME

Dollar Sales (S)	Break-Even Dollar Sales (S_b)	Operating Income (I)	Change in Operating Income (ΔI)	Percent Change in I	Percent Change in S	Degree of Operating Leverage (DOL)
$ 750,000	$ 625 000	$100,000				
833,333	625,000	166,667	66,667	66.67	11.11	6
1,500000	1,250,000	200,000				
1,666,667	1,250,000	333,333	$133,333	66.67	11.11	6

EXAMPLE 4.11

DOL IN RELATION TO BE$S

Break-Even Sales (BE$S)	Capacity Sales	Profit-Generating Sales	Degree of Operating Leverage
$0.3	$6.0	$5.7	1.05
1.0	6.0	5.0	1.20
2.0	6.0	4.0	1.50
3.0	6.0	3.0	2.0
4.0	6.0	2.0	3.0
5.0	6.0	1.0	6.0
6.0	6.0	0.0	Undefined

OBSERVATIONS: Degree of operating leverage begins at a minimum value of 1.05 and increases as break-even sales increase. The relation, which is not linear, is shown in Figure 4.7. The increase in break-even sales or the responsiveness of profits to sales leads to an ever larger increase in the degree of operating leverage. The given percent changes in sales lead to larger percent changes in profits at higher break-even levels. CONCLUSION: The responsiveness of profits to sales is a double-edged sword. Why? The higher break-even levels operate regardless of a rise or fall in sales.

FIGURE 4.7: OPERATING LEVERAGE AND CAPACITY

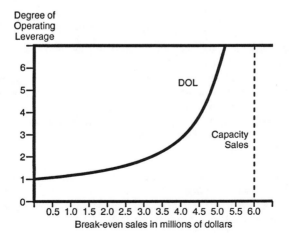

What are the limitations of break-even analysis?

In its simplest form, break-even analysis makes a number of assumptions about which you must be very clear. One such assumption treats the unit selling price as a constant. This, in turn, rests on two further assumptions: (1) the elasticity of demand must be very high for the unit selling price to remain constant as sales volume expands and (2) the selling price must remain relatively stable over the income period. In truth, neither is likely to hold in actual practice, and this makes forecasting the unit selling price much more difficult.

The second major assumption holds that unit variable costs are also constant and that fixed and variable costs have been properly separated, identified, and quantified. However, separating out variable from fixed costs is an ongoing problem.

Once you have determined the unit variable cost, make certain it remains constant over the income period. If it does not, then you must compute a series of breakdown calculations incorporating the most probable unit variable costs.

Likewise, examine the likelihood that total fixed costs will remain constant. Do this at every level of your analysis. If you find factors that will cause fixed costs to vary, then you must compute a series of break-even analyses using the most probable values of total fixed costs.

A RULE FOR MANAGEMENT EXECUTIVES: One of your major objectives should be to keep a tight grip on your company's break-even volume. This means constant efforts to keep break-even from increasing as a result of adverse conditions that lower unit selling price and raise unit variable costs and total fixed costs.

CHECKLIST OF QUESTIONS CONCERNING BREAK-EVEN ANALYSIS

- Is demand sufficiently elastic that rises in sales volume would have no appreciable effect on unit selling price?
- Is unit selling price expected to be relatively stable over the income period to which the break-even analysis applies?
- Have costs been measured properly? Have historical costs been adjusted appropriately to reflect future costs during the income period or income periods under study?
- Are total fixed costs expected to remain constant over the income period under study?
- Does the break-even analysis assume organizational slack, that is, are costs assumed to have been appropriately minimized?

- Is unit variable cost assumed to be constant?
- Is the probable range of break-even volumes estimated in terms of a particular future period or periods?
- Does the break-even analysis provide probability estimates as to whether or not break-even can be achieved?

4.4 PRESENT AND FUTURE VALUE: WHEN YOU RECEIVE THE MONEY

You will often find that today's and tomorrow's dollars are treated the same when, in fact, they are not. This section explores the relation between present and future values of money.

In this section you will learn present and future (also called compound) values in terms of loans, leases, and bonds. You will also find applications to such items as accumulation of a sinking fund, calculation of sales growth, and present value of a fund-raising campaign for a nonprofit organization.

What is the importance of present and compound value calculations?

If you are a management executive, planner, financial or investment analyst, or investor, present and compound value calculations lie at the very heart of your decisions.

Use present and compound value techniques when estimating the present values of items reported in a statement of financial condition. BE AWARE: Every statement is composed of present values of asset, liability, and ownership interest. In reality, accountants do not report most items appearing on the statement in terms of present values, but rather on historical costs or some modification thereof. The longer an item appears on a statement, the less likely it is that these cost values relate to present values. You must be aware of this limitation in order to use the statement properly.

Present and compound value techniques are essential for planning purposes, particularly when estimating

- Present values used in investment and capital budget decisions
- Effects of inflation on organizational activities
- Present values of loans, bonds, annual installments to a sinking fund, and so on

How do I calculate the relation between today's and tomorrow's values over one period?

Use this formula:

$$FV = (1 + i) \times PV$$

where
   FV = future value at the end of the period
   PV = present or today's value
   i = interest rate

The difference between PV and FV is calculated as follows:

$$IA = FV - PV$$

or

$$IA = i \times PV$$

where
   IA = the dollar interest amount earned on the loan by the lender

If you know the future value rather than the present value of the loan, then you can calculate the present value as follows:

$$PV = \left(\frac{FV}{1 + i} \right)$$

EXAMPLE 4.12

Company B borrows $500,000 for one year at 12% interest. The company is obligated to pay off its loan plus interest at the end of the one-year borrowing period. How much must the company pay? Use the formula to calculate the value of the loan at maturity:

$$FV = (1 + 0.12) \times \$500,000 = \$560,000$$

Calculate the dollar interest amount as follows:

$$IA = \$560,000 - \$500,000 = \$60,000$$

or

$$IA = 0.12 \times \$500,000 = \$60,000$$

If you know the future value of the loan plus interest and you know the interest rate is 12%, calculate the present value as follows:

$$PV = \frac{\$560,000}{1 + 0.12} = \$500,000$$

How do I calculate present and future value over more than one period?

Future or Compound Value. If tomorrow's value were two years in the future rather than one, the relation between compound value and present value would be

$$FV = PV \times (1 + i)^2$$

Generally, this relationship for any number of periods is expressed as

$$FV = PV \times (1 + i)^n$$

where

n = number of periods of time

This is the formula for compound value. It can be somewhat impractical when the number of periods is more than two or three. Fortunately, standard tables are available that make the computations much easier. Table 4.1 (pages 134–136) shows computations for \$1 compounded at i over n periods. The interest amount owed on the loan is expressed as follows:

$$IA = FV - PV$$

or

$$IA = PV \times ([1 + i]^n - 1)$$

EXAMPLE 4.13

Assume Company C borrows \$500,000 for 20 years at 12% interest. Interest on the loan is to be compounded once a year for 20 years, and the company is not obligated to pay back the principal or any interest until the end of the 20-year period. How much would the company pay at the end of the 20-year period? The maturity value of the loan is shown as follows:

$$FV = PV \times (1 + i)^n$$
$$FV = (\$500,000) \times (1 + 0.12)^{20}$$

Using the table of compound values, you can determine the compound value of \$1 at 12% interest for 20 periods as 9.646293. Thus, the future value of \$500,000 is calculated as follows:

$$FV = (\$500,000) \times 9.646293 = \$4,823,146$$

The interest amount is \$4,323,156 (\$4,823,146 – \$500,000), which can alternatively be calculated as follows:

$$
\begin{aligned}
IA &= \$500,000 \times ([1 + 0.12]^{20} - 1) \\
&= \$500,000 \times (9.646293 - 1) \\
&= \$500,000 \times 8.646293 = \$4.323.146
\end{aligned}
$$

The calculation of future values of \$500,000 at the end of years one, two, three, and 20, as well as the interest amount as it accumulates on the loan for these years, is shown in Exhibit 4.1. NOTE: The compounding of interest takes place once a year at the end of each year.

EXHIBIT 4.1: CALCULATION OF THE FUTURE VALUE OF $500,000 AND CUMULATIVE INTEREST THEREON AT 12% PER YEAR FOR 20 YEARS

Present Value BOY1[a] (PV)	Future Value of 1 at 12%[b] (CV)	End of Period n	Future Value EOYn[c] (FV)	Cumulative Interest Amount (IA)
$500,000	1.120000	1	$560,000	$60,000
500,000	1.254400	2	627,200	127,200
500,000	1.404928	3	702,464	202,464
•	•	•	•	•
•	•	•	•	•
•	•	•	•	•
$500,000	9.646293	20	$4,823,146	$4,232,146

[a]BOY1: beginning of year 1.

[b]Compounded once a year as of the end of the year.

[c]EOYn: end of year n.

Present Value. Suppose you expect to receive $1 20 years from now. The present value of that dollar is not $1, but less. How much less depends on the interest rate used to reduce or discount tomorrow's value to its present value.

If you assume that future value is known along with the interest rate and number of periods, you can calculate present value as follows:

$$PV = \frac{FV}{(1 + i)^n}$$

As with compound values, this formula can be cumbersome to use. Standard tables are available that simplify the calculations, as least for certain typical values of interest rates and number of periods. Table 4.2 (pages 137-139) lists present values of $1 over n periods at i interest rate.

EXAMPLE 4.14

You expect to receive $1 in 20 years (periods) at a 12% discount rate. From Table 4.2, the present discounted value (PDV) is given as 0.103667. In other words, if $1 is discounted for 20 periods at a rate of 12%, then it is worth approximately 10.367 cents today.

A SHORTCUT: There is an inverse relationship between the compound value and the present discount value, as follows:

$$CV \times PDV = 1$$

You can get PDV by dividing the related CV into 1.

EXAMPLE 4.15

From Table 4.1, the future value of $1 compounded at 12% interest for 20 periods is 9.646293. To get the present discounted value of $1 at the same rate for the same number of periods, divide this number as follows:

$$PV = \frac{1}{9.646293} = 0.103667$$

Proof

$$CV \times PVD = 1$$
$$9.646293 \times 0.103667 = 1$$

EXAMPLE 4.16

In Example 4.13 we learned that the future value of $500,000 compounded at 12% for 20 years is $4,823,146. Reversing this, you can calculate the present value of this amount as follows:

$$PV = \frac{FV}{(1 + i)^n} = \frac{1}{(1 + i)^n} \times FV$$

$$PV = \frac{\$4,823,146}{(1 + 0.12)^{20}} = \frac{1}{(1 + 0.12)^{20}} \times \$4,823,146$$

$$PV = 0.103667 \times \$4,823,146 = \$500,001$$

Calculations of present values for several years are given in Exhibit 4.2.

EXHIBIT 4.2: ALTERNATIVE CALCULATION OF THE FUTURE VALUE OF $500,000 AT 12% PER YEAR FOR 20 YEARS

BOYn	Present Value BOYn[a] (PV)	Single Period Compounded at 12%	Future Value EOYn[b] (FV)
1	$ 500,000	1.12	$ 560,000
2	560,000	1.12	627,200
3	627,200	1.12	702,464
•	•	•	•
•	•	•	•
•	•	•	•
20	$4,306,380	1.12	$4,823,146

[a]BOYn: beginning of year n.
[b]EOYn: end of year n.

How do I determine present and future value of an ordinary annuity?

Present Value. An annuity is a series of payments over time. When the payments are made at the end of each period, it is known as an ordinary annuity. Annuities with payments made at the beginning of the period are called annuities due or annuity in advance.

One approach to determining the present or future value of an annuity is to separate each payment, calculate the values, and aggregate them over the length of its life. If the annuity consists of equal payments made at equal time intervals, then the calculations can be simplified considerably.

The amount an investor would be willing to invest in an annuity (or lease) is shown as follows:

$$PV = \frac{R}{(1+i)} + \frac{R}{(1+i)^2} + \cdots + \frac{R}{(1+i)^n}$$

$$PV = \frac{R}{i} - \frac{1}{(1+i)^n} \times \frac{R}{i}$$

where

PV = present value of the annuity (or lease)

R = equal annuity payments (or rentals)

i = interest rate (or rate of return desired by investor)

Notice that this formula really has two parts, each a present value calculation. The first part

$$PV = \frac{R}{i}$$

defines the formula for a perpetual annuity, that is, one whose payments continue indefinitely.

When an annuity is for a defined period of time, you need to subtract the present value of the annual payments for the years after the periods have expired. This is done with the following formula:

$$PV = \frac{1}{(1+i)^n} \times \frac{R}{i}$$

From this you can see that the first formula equals the difference of the second and third formulas. In other words, if you subtract the present value at the end of the periods from its present value today, you will arrive at the present value of the annuity.

The calculations can be simplified by using a standard table, such as Table 4.3 (pages 140–142). This shows the present values of an ordinary annuity of $1 per period for a given number of periods at a given interest rate.

EXAMPLE 4.17

Company C leases a property that it owns. The lease provides an annual rental income of $25,000 per year for 20 years. The lessee covers all costs associated with the leased property under the terms of the lease, so that the $25,000 per year is pure income to the lessor. Simple multiplication tells you that the rent payment to be paid over 20 years is $500,000. Assume this amount is to be paid in a series of equal payments. How much would be paid to produce a cash flow of $25,000 per year over 20 years? In other words, what is the present value of the 20 payments of $25,000 each?

Using the preceding formula, the calculations are as follows:

$$PV = \frac{\$25,000}{0.12} - \frac{1}{(1 + 0.12)^{20}} \times \frac{\$25,000}{0.12}$$
$$PV = \$208,333 - (0.103667)(\$208,333)$$
$$PV = \$208,333 - \$21,597$$
$$PV = \$186,736$$

In the case of the lease, payments of $25,000 per year continue forever; that is, perpetually. The present value of the leased property to the owner at the time it is leased for 20 years at $25,000 per year with payments made at the end of each year and at a desired rate of return of 12% would be calculated as follows:*

$$PV = \frac{\$25,000}{\$0.12} = \$208,333$$

Over a defined 20-year period, however, the present value of the lease is calculated as follows:

$$PV = \frac{1}{(1 + 0.12)^{20}} \times \frac{\$25,000}{0.12}$$
$$PV = 0.103667 \times \$208,333 = \$21,597$$

*This assumes the property will not deteriorate but will provide the same quality of services indefinitely.

From Table 4.3, the present value of $1 lease for 20 periods at 12% interest is 7.469444. Therefore, the present value of this lease is $25,000 × 7.469444, or $186,736.

Present Value of an Annuity Due. With an annuity due, periodic payments take place at the beginning of the period. The formula for calculating the present value of an annuity due is

$$PV_{ad} = R + \frac{R}{(1 + i)} + \frac{R}{(1 + i)^2} + \dots + \frac{R}{(1 + i)^{n-1}}$$
$$PV_{ad} = \frac{R(1 + i)}{i} - \frac{1}{(1 + i)^n} \times \frac{R(1 + i)}{i}$$

You can also use Table 4.3 to calculate the present value of an annuity due. To do so, find the present value of $1 for one period less than the life of the annuity. Then add 1 to this number.

EXAMPLE 4.18

Consider the preceding example to be an annuity due. Calculations for the present value are shown as follows:

$$PV = \frac{(\$25,000)(1 + 0.12)}{0.12} - \frac{1}{(1 + 0.12)^{20}}$$
$$\times \frac{(\$25,000)(1 + 0.12)}{0.12}$$

$$PV = \frac{\$28,000}{0.12} - 0.103667$$
$$\times \frac{\$28,000}{0.12}$$

$$PV = \$233,333 - 0.103667 \times \$233,333$$
$$PV = \$233,333 - \$24,189$$
$$PV = \$209,144$$

Table 4.3 gives the present value of $1 for 19 years as 7.365777. Thus,

$$PV = 8.365777 \times \$25,000 = \$209,144$$

The relationship between the present value of an annuity due to an ordinary annuity is shown as follows:

$$PV_{ad} = (1 + i) \times PV_{oa}$$

where

PV_{ad} = present value of an annuity due
PV_{oa} = present value of an ordinary annuity

Using the preceding examples, this formula can be applied as follows:

$$PV_{ad} = (1 + 0.12) \times \$186,736 = \$209,144$$

Future Value of an Ordinary Annuity. The formula for calculating the future value of an ordinary annuity is

$$FV_{oa} = R(1 + i)^{n-1} + R(1 + i)^{n-2} + \ldots$$
$$+ R(1 + i)^2 + R(1 + i) + R$$
$$FV_{oa} = (1 + i)^n$$
$$\times \frac{R}{i} - \frac{R}{i}$$

Table 4.4 (pages 143-145) is a standard table for calculation of future values.

EXAMPLE 4.19

Assume Company D plans to pay into a municipal bond fund $25,000 per year, at the end of each year, for the next 20 years. The fund earns an interest of 12% compounded once a year. What accumulated amount would be expected at the end of 20 years, or what is the future value of this ordinary annuity?

Calculations are

$$FV_{oa} = (1 + 0.12)^{20} \times \frac{\$205{,}000}{0.12} - \frac{\$205{,}000}{0.12}$$
$$FV_{oa} = (9.646293) \times (\$208{,}333) - \$208{,}333$$
$$FV_{oa} = \$2{,}009{,}641 - \$208{,}333 = \$1{,}801{,}308$$

By using Table 4.4 to calculate the accumulated value of the municipal bond fund at the end of 10 years, you can check your work:

$$FV_{oa} = 72.052442 \times \$25{,}000 = \$1{,}801{,}308$$

Actually, the future value of an ordinary annuity uses two future values. Consider the first part of the formula, which takes the present value of an ordinary perpetual annuity and calculates its future value. In terms of the municipal bond fund example, the present value is calculated at $208,333. This is then multiplied by the future value of $1 for 20 periods at 12 percent interest per period, yielding $2,009,641, or the future value of an ordinary perpetual annuity after 20 years. However, if the fund is not perpetual, but terminates after 20 years, the present value must be calculated for 20 periods. By subtracting $208,333 from $2,009,641, you arrive at the future value of the 20-year municipal bond fund at the end of its 20-year life. NOTE: You can speak of the present value of a perpetual annuity, but future value of a perpetual annuity must be tied into a specific future year.

Future Value of an Annuity Due. The formula for calculating the future value of an annuity due is given as follows:

$$FV_{ad} = R(1 + i)^n + R(1 + i)^{n-1} + \ldots$$
$$+ R(1 + i)^2 + R(1 + i)$$
$$FV_{ad} = (1 + i) \times \left([1 + i]^n + \frac{R}{i} - \frac{R}{i} \right)$$

You can also use Table 4.4 to calculate future value of an annuity.

EXAMPLE 4.20

Use the previous example of a 20-year municipal bond fund at 12% interest compounded once a year. This time, however, assume the annual payment is made at the beginning of the year. Of course, no payment will be made into the fund at the end of the twentieth year. The accumulated value of the fund is calculated as follows:

$$FV_{ad} = (1 + 0.12) \times \left([1 + 0.12]^{20} \right.$$
$$\left. \times \left[\frac{\$25000}{(0.12} - \frac{\$25000}{0.12} \right] \right)$$
$$FV_{ad} = 1.12 \times \$1{,}801{,}308 = \$2{,}017{,}465$$

Using Table 4.4, find the future value of $1 for 21 years (81.698736). Then subtract 1 from this to obtain 80.698736. This number is then used to calculate future value of the annuity due as follows:

$$FV_{ad} = 80.698736 \times \$25,000 = \$2,017,468$$

What are the uses of present and compound values?

Amortizing a Loan. The methods previously described can be used to calculate the payments required to amortize a loan when the loan possesses the appropriate characteristics. Use this formula to calculate the amount of equal payments required:

$$R = \frac{PV_{oa}}{IF_{poa}}$$

where
R = amount of the equal payment
PV_{oa} = present value of the ordinary annuity
IF_{poa} = interest factor of an ordinary annuity, obtained from Table 4.3

EXAMPLE 4.21

Company A borrows $500,000 for 20 years at an interest rate of 12% per year compounded once a year. The loan agreement requires the company to repay the loan, both interest and principal, in a series of 20 equal payments to be made at the end of each year. Such terms are in reality an ordinary annuity.

Calculations follow:

$$R = \frac{\$500,000}{7.469444} = \$66,939.99$$

The interest factor of 7.469444 is obtained from Table 4.4. The 20 equal installments of $66,939.39 will pay the $500,000 loan, both interest and principal, over the 20-year period. This is further demonstrated in Exhibit 4.3.

NOTE THIS: At the end of year one, the first installment of $66,939.39 is divided between interest and principal. Interest is calculated simply at 12% of $500,000, or $60,000. The balance of the payment, $6,939.39, is used to reduce the principal. As the balance of the loan is reduced, the amount of interest falls and the amount applied to the principal rises.

Market Value of a Bond. A long-term bond can be amortized in the same way as a loan. Present-value methods are appropriate here, too.

EXHIBIT 4.3: AMORTIZING A LOAN

End of Year	Balance of Loan	ANNUAL INSTALLMENTS		
		Interest	Principal	Total
0	$500,000.00			
1	493,060.61	$ 60,000.00	$ 6,939.39	$ 66,939.39
2	485,288.49	59,167.27	7,772.12	66,939.39
3	476,583.72	58,234.62	8,704.77	66,939.39
•	•	•	•	•
•	•	•	•	•
•	•	•	•	•
18	113,131.00	19,293.26	47,646.13	66,939.39
19	59,767.33	13,575.72	53,363.67	66,939.39
20	0.02	7,172.08	59,767.31	66,939.39
		$838,787.82	$499,999.98	$1,338,787.80

The formula for calculating the present value of a bond is

$$PV_b = \frac{1 - \frac{1}{(1 + i_m)^n}}{i_m} \times (i_c F) + \frac{1}{(1 + i_m)^n} \times M$$

where

PV_b = present value of the bond
i_m = market rate of interest
i_c = coupon rate of interest
F = face value of the bond used as the basis for calculating interest amount to be paid (IA)
M = maturity value or redemption value of the bond
n = number of years

This formula assumes annual compounding, since n has been defined by years. For semiannual compounding, use this slightly modified formula:

$$PV_b = \frac{1 - \frac{1}{\left(1 + \frac{i_m}{2}\right)^{2n}}}{\frac{i_m}{2}} \times \left(\frac{i_c}{2}\right)(F) + \frac{1}{\left(1 + \frac{i_m}{2}\right)^{2n}} \times M$$

NOTE: When the market rate of interest (annual or semiannual) is higher than the coupon rate, then the present value or market value of the bonds is lower than the face value of the bonds. You can use standard tables, such as Table 4.5 (pages 146-147) for calculating future present value of bonds. Here, the present values at different market rates of interest are given for a $100 bond that pays a 10-percent coupon rate of interest per year, compounded semiannually. The table also shows different present values for a given rate of interest for various maturities. For example, looking at the table, you will find that a 20-year bond at 10-percent coupon and market interest rate will have a face value equal to its market value of $100. However, if the 10-percent bond is issued to yield 12 percent, then the present value of the $100 bond falls to $84.95.

EXAMPLE 4.22

Company F issues $500,000 of 20-year bonds, which pay an annual interest rate of 10% compounded twice a year. The bonds are issued at a market rate of interest to yield the investor 12% per year, compounded twice a year. The interest is payable semiannually, on January 1 and July 1. Principal is to be repaid at the end of 20 years. The present or market value of the bonds on the date of issue is determined as follows: The present value consists of two parts: (1) present value of the principal and (2) present value of 40 semiannual interest payments over 20 years. Since the interest is compounded semiannually, present-value calculations would use 40 periods of six months each with a coupon rate of 5% and a market rate of 6% for each six-month period. Using the formula, calculations are

$$PV_b = \frac{1 - \frac{1}{\left(1 + \frac{0.12}{2}\right)^{(2)(20)}}}{\frac{0.12}{2}} \times \left(\frac{0.10}{2}\right)\left(\$500,000\right)$$

$$+ \frac{1}{\left(1 + \frac{0.12}{2}\right)^{(2)(20)}}\left(\$500,000\right)$$

$$PV_b = \frac{1 - \frac{1}{(1 + 0.06)^{40}}}{0.06}$$

$$\times (0.05)(\$500,000) + \frac{1}{(1 + 0.06)^{40}}(\$500,000)$$

$$PV_b = 15.046297 \times \$25,000$$
$$+ 0.097222 \times \$500,000$$

$$PV_b = \$376,157 + \$48,611 = \$424,768$$

Using Table 4.5, we find that the $500,000 bond issue is equivalent to 5,000 bonds of $100 face value each. The present or market value of $500,000 bonds issued at 12% interest is 5,000 × $84.95 = $424,750.

OBSERVATIONS: The present or market value of the bonds compounded semiannually is $424,768, whereas the face value is $500,000. Why? Because market interest rate is higher than the coupon rate. The reverse holds too: When market rate is below coupon rate, then market or present value is higher than face value.

Sinking Fund. A company would establish a sinking fund in order to accumulate financial resources for the purpose of paying off the maturity value of debt when due. You can use present or future value methods to calculate the company's annual contribution to the sinking fund. Use this formula:

$$R = \frac{M}{IF_{foa}}$$

where

R = annual payment to the sinking fund
M = maturity value of the bonds
IF_{foa} = interest factor that represents the future value of an ordinary annuity of $1

EXAMPLE 4.23

From the preceding example, Company F needs to set up and maintain a sinking fund for the retirement of the bond principal at the end of 20 years. The company is required to make annual payments into the fund at the end of each year. The future value of the sinking fund at the end of 20 years will be equal to the maturity value of the bonds. Management expects to earn 8% interest compounded annually on the sinking fund investment. Using the formula and Table 4.4, you can calculate the annual contribution to the sinking fund as follows:

$$R = \frac{\$500,000}{45.76194} = \$10,926.10$$

The sinking fund will grow as a result of both the annual contribution and the interest earnings. From the calculations you can see the growth of the sinking fund at 8% interest earnings. By year 20, the company will have enough funds to repay its principal as indicated in Exhibit 4.4.

Sales Growth and Compound Growth. Compound growth calculations can be used to simplify the calculation of anticipated sales when such sales are expected to grow in some uniform manner. WHAT TO DO: In applying future or compound growth techniques to sales growth, treat "no-growth" sales as if they were an annuity. Then calculate the anticipated growth rate using the following formula:

$$\text{Anticipated growth rate} = \frac{\text{Anticipated sales of year } n - \text{Anticipated sales of year } n-1}{\text{Anticipated sales of year } n-1}$$

Use Example 4.24 on this page as a guide.

EXAMPLE 4.24

Assume Company D anticipates sales growth of about 12% per year over the next four years, and expects this growth to be relatively uniform over the period. How would such a growth pattern look?

Assume anticipated sales will grow approximately 1% per month. The anticipated sales growth pattern is shown in Exhibit 4.5 on pages 130-131. Note that growth factors that are applied to the "no-growth" sales column in the Exhibit are simply compound interest factors taken from Table 4.1. Then note the cumulative growth factors applied to the no-growth sales. These are taken from Table 4.4, and are simply the future values of an ordinary annuity of $1 growing at 1% per period.

The calculations also show annual anticipated sales and their growth. If the monthly growth rate is 1%, the compound annual growth rate is 12.68% per year. Let us now look at the expected sales growth in Exhibit 4.5.

Proof

Using the preceding formula, anticipated growth rate is computed as follows:

$$\text{Anticipated growth rate} = \frac{\$1,286,250 - \$1,125,508}{\$1,125,508}$$
$$= 12.68\%$$

This assumes actual sales for the prior year also grew at 1% per month. In fact, you can easily reconstruct this using Exhibit 4.6.

WHAT TO DO NEXT: From Table 4.2, apply discount factors to no-growth sales at a rate of 1% per period. The cumulative discount factors are present values of an ordinary annuity of $1 (Table 4.3) that have been discounted at the rate of 1% per period.

What are the limitations of present and compound-value techniques?

What are some assumptions that underlie the present- and compound-value techniques? First, all the ingredients (or variables) used in the calculation of present or compound value (amounts being discounted or subject to growth, the interest rates used, and the discount or growth periods) are known with certainty. Second, the interest rate used for discounting or growth is constant over the given time period. Third, all amounts in a series are equal to each other. The second and third assumptions can be dropped, but doing so

EXHIBIT 4.4: SCHEDULE OF SINKING FUND PAYMENTS AND ACCUMULATION

Year	Beginning Balance	Annual Payment	Interest Earned	Annual Accumulation	Ending Balance
1	$ 0	$ 10,926.10	$ 0	$ 10,926.10	$ 10,926.10
2	10,926.10	10,926.10	874.09	11,800.19	22,726.29
3	22,726.29	10,926.10	11,818.10	12,744.20	35,470.49
•	•	•	•	•	•
•	•	•	•	•	•
•	•	•	•	•	•
18	368,758.35	10,926.10	29,500.67	40,426.77	409,185.12
19	409,185.12	10,926.10	32,734.81	43,660.91	452,846.03
20	452,846.03	10,926.10	36,227.68	47,153.78	499,999.81
		$218,522.00	$281,477.81	$499,999.81	

EXHIBIT 4.5: ANTICIPATED SALES GROWTH USING A COMPOUND GROWTH APPROXIMATION

End of Month	Monthly Sales— No Growth	Growth Factor (1%)	Monthly Sales at 1% Growth Rate	CUMULATIVE		ANNUAL	
				Growth Factor	Sales	Sales	Growth Rate
1	$ 100,000	1.000000	$100,000	1.000000	$ 100,000		
2	100,000	1.010000	101,000	2.010000	201,000		
3	100,000	1.020100	102,010	3.030100	303,010		
•	•	•	•	•	•		
•	•	•	•	•	•		
•	•	•	•	•	•		
10	100,000	1.093685	109,369	10.462213	1,046,221		
11	100,000	1.104622	110,462	11.566835	1,156,683		
12	100,000	1.115668	111,567	12.682503	1,268,250	$1,268,250	12.68%
•	•	•	•	•	•		
•	•	•	•	•	•		

22	100,000	1.232392	123,239	24.471586	2,447,159	
23	100,000	1.244716	124,472	25.716302	2,571,630	
24	100,000	1.257163	125,716	26.973465	2,697,346	1,429,096 12.68%
•	•	•	•	•	•	
•	•	•	•	•	•	
•	•	•	•	•	•	
34	100,000	1.388690	138,869	40.257699	4,025,770	
35	100,000	1.402577	140,258	41.660276	4,166,028	
36	100,000	1.416603	141,660	43.076878	4,307 688	1,610,342 12.68%
•	•	•	•	•	•	
•	•	•	•	•	•	
•	•	•	•	•	•	
46	100,000	1.564811	156,481	58.045885	5,804,588	
47	100,000	1.580459	158,046	59.626344	5,962,634	
48	100,000	1.596263	159,626	61.222608	6,122,261	1,814,573 12.68%
Totals	$4,800,000					$6,122,261

leads to an entirely new realm replete with difficulties. If the first assumption is dropped, then various statistical estimation techniques will be necessary, and present and compound values become subject to statistical estimation rather than arithmetic calculation.

In the real world, you are always confronted with uncertainty. This means that appropriate statistical techniques should be used to determine best estimates for each variable.

EXHIBIT 4.6: THE MOST RECENT YEAR'S ACTUAL SALES RECONSTRUCTED USING PRESENT VALUE

End of Month	Monthly Sales— No Growth	Discount Factor (1%)	Monthly Sales at 1% Discount Rate	CUMULATIVE Discount Factor	CUMULATIVE Sales
1	$100,000	0.990099	99,010	0.990099	99,010
2	100,000	0.980296	98,030	1.970395	197,040
3	100,000	0.970590	97,059	2.940985	294,099
•	•	•	•	•	•
•	•	•	•	•	•
•	•	•	•	•	•
10	100,000	0.905287	90,529	9.471305	947,130
11	100,000	0.896324	89,632	10.367628	1,036,763
12	100,000	0.887449	88,745	11.255077	1,125,508

TABLE 4.1

$$IF_f = \text{future or compound value of } \$1 = (1 + i)^n$$

ni	1%	2.5%	6%	8%	9%	10%	12%
1	0.010000	1.025000	1.060000	1.080000	1.090000	1.100000	1.120000
2	1.020100	1.050625	1.123600	1.166400	1.188100	1.210000	1.254400
3	1.030301	1.076891	1.191016	1.259712	1.295029	1.331000	1.404928
4	1.040604	1.103813	1.262477	1.360489	1.411582	1.464100	1.573519
5	1.051010	1.131408	1.338226	1.469328	1.538624	1.610510	1.762342
6	1.061520	1.159693	1.418519	1.586874	1.677100	1.771561	1.973823
7	1.072135	1.188686	1.503630	1.713824	1.828039	1.948717	2.210681
8	1.082857	1.218403	1.593848	1.850930	1.992563	2.143589	2.475963
9	1.093685	1.248863	1.689479	1.999005	2.171893	2.357948	2.773079
10	1.104622	1.280085	1.790848	2.158925	2.367364	2.593742	3.105848
11	1.115668	1.312087	1.898299	2.331639	2.580426	2.853117	3.478550
12	1.126825	1.344889	2.012196	2.518170	2.812665	3.138428	3.895976
13	1.138093	1.378511	2.132928	2.719624	3.065805	3.452271	4.363493
14	1.149474	1.412974	2.260904	2.937194	3.341727	3.797498	4.887112
15	1.160969	1.448298	2.396558	3.172169	3.642482	4.177248	5.473566
16	1.172579	1.484506	2.540352	3.425943	3.970306	4.594973	6.130394

17	1.184304	1.521618	2.692773	3.700018	4.327633	5.054470	6.866041
18	1.196147	1.559659	2.854339	3.996019	4.717120	5.559917	7.689966
19	1.208109	1.598650	3.025600	4.315701	5.141661	6.115909	8.612762
20	1.220190	1.638616	3.207135	4.660957	5.604411	6.727500	9.646293
21	1.232392	1.679582	3.399564	5.033834	6.108808	7.400250	10.803848
22	1.244716	1.721571	3.603537	5.436540	6.658600	8.140275	12.100310
23	1.257163	1.764611	3.819750	5.871464	7.257874	8.954302	13.552347
24	1.269735	1.808726	4.048935	6.341181	7.911083	9.849733	15.178629
25	1.282432	1.853944	4.291871	6.848475	8.623081	10.834706	17.000064
26	1.295256	1.900293	4.549383	7.396353	9.399158	11.918177	19.040072
27	1.308209	1.947800	4.822346	7.988061	10.245082	13.109994	21.324881
28	1.321291	1.996495	5.111687	8.627106	11.167140	14.420994	23.883866
29	1.334504	2.046407	5.418388	9.317275	12.172182	15.863093	26.749930
30	1.347849	2.097568	5.743491	10.062657	13.267678	17.449402	29.959922
31	1.361327	2.150007	6.088101	10.867669	14.461770	19.194342	33.555113
32	1.374941	2.203757	6.453387	11.737083	15.763329	21.113777	37.581726
33	1.388690	2.258851	6.840590	12.676050	17.182028	23.225154	42.091533
34	1.402577	2.315322	7.251025	13.690134	18.728411	25.547670	47.142517
35	1.416603	2.373205	7.686087	14.785344	20.413968	28.102437	52.799620
36	1.430769	2.432535	8.147252	15.968172	22.251225	30.912681	59.135574
37	1.445076	2.493349	8.636087	17.245626	24.253835	34.003949	66.231843

TABLE 4.1 (cont.)

n^i	1%	2.5%	6%	8%	9%	10%	12%
38	1.459527	2.555682	9.154252	18.625276	26.436680	37.404343	74.179664
39	1.474123	2.619574	9.703507	20.115298	28.815982	41.144778	83.081224
40	1.488864	2.685064	10.285718	21.724521	31.409420	45.259256	93.050970
41	1.503752	2.752190	10.902861	23.462483	34.236268	49.785181	104.217087
42	1.518790	2.820995	11.557033	25.339482	37.317532	54.763699	116.723137
43	1.533978	2.891520	12.250455	27.366640	40.676110	60.240069	130.729914
44	1.549318	2.963808	12.985482	29.555972	44.336960	66.264076	146.417503
45	1.564811	3.037903	13.764611	31.920449	48.327286	72.890484	163.987604
46	1.580459	3.113851	14.590487	34.474085	52.676742	80.179532	183.666116
47	1.596263	3.191697	15.465917	37.232012	57.417649	88.197485	205.706050
48	1.612226	3.271490	16.393872	40.210573	62.585237	97.017234	230.390776
49	1.628348	3.353277	17.377504	43.427419	68.217908	106.718957	258.037669
50	1.644632	3.437109	18.420154	46.901613	74.357520	117.390853	289.002190

TABLE 4.2

$$IF_p = \text{present value of \$1} = \frac{1}{(1+i)^n}$$

n^i	1%	2.5%	6%	8%	9%	10%	12%
1	0.990099	0.975610	0.943396	0.925926	0.917431	0.909091	0.892857
2	0.980296	0.951814	0.889996	0.857339	0.841680	0.826446	0.797194
3	0.970590	0.928599	0.839619	0.793832	0.772183	0.751315	0.711780
4	0.960980	0.905951	0.792094	0.735030	0.708425	0.683013	0.635518
5	0.951466	0.883854	0.747258	0.680583	0.649931	0.620921	0.567427
6	0.942045	0.862297	0.704961	0.630170	0.596267	0.564474	0.506631
7	0.932718	0.841265	0.665057	0.583490	0.547034	0.513158	0.452349
8	0.923483	0.820747	0.627412	0.540269	0.501866	0.466507	0.403883
9	0.914340	0.800728	0.591898	0.500249	0.460428	0.424098	0.360610
10	0.905287	0.781196	0.558395	0.463193	0.422411	0.385543	0.321973
11	0.896324	0.762145	0.526788	0.428883	0.387533	0.350494	0.287476
12	0.887449	0.743556	0.496969	0.397114	0.355535	0.318631	0.256675
13	0.878663	0.725420	0.468839	0.367698	0.326179	0.289664	0.229174
14	0.869963	0.707727	0.442301	0.340461	0.299246	0.263331	0.204620
15	0.861349	0.690466	0.417265	0.315242	0.274538	0.239392	0.182696

TABLE 4.2 *(cont.)*

n^i	1%	2.5%	6%	8%	9%	10%	12%
16	0.852821	0.673625	0.393646	0.291890	0.251870	0.217629	0.163122
17	0.844377	0.657195	0.371364	0.270269	0.231073	0.197845	0.145644
18	0.836017	0.641166	0.350344	0.250249	0.211994	0.179859	0.130040
19	0.827740	0.625528	0.330513	0.231712	0.194490	0.163508	0.116107
20	0.819544	0.610271	0.311805	0.214548	0.178431	0.148644	0.103667
21	0.811430	0.595386	0.294155	0.198656	0.163698	0.135131	0.092560
22	0.803396	0.580865	0.277505	0.183941	0.150182	0.122846	0.082643
23	0.795442	0.566697	0.261797	0.170315	0.137781	0.111678	0.073788
24	0.787566	0.552875	0.246979	0.157699	0.126405	0.101526	0.065882
25	0.779768	0.539391	0.732999	0.146018	0.115968	0.092296	0.058823
26	0.772048	0.526235	0.219810	0.135202	0.106393	0.083905	0.052521
27	0.764404	0.513400	0.207368	0.125187	0.097608	0.076278	0.046894
28	0.756836	0.500878	0.195630	0.115914	0.089548	0.069343	0.041869
29	0.749342	0.488661	0.184557	0.107328	0.082155	0.063039	0.037383
30	0.741923	0.476743	0.174110	0.099377	0.075371	0.057309	0.033378
31	0.734577	0.465115	0.164255	0.092016	0.069148	0.052099	0.029802
32	0.727304	0.453771	0.154957	0.085200	0.063438	0.047362	0.026609

33	0.720103	0.442703	0.146186	0.078889	0.058200	0.043057	0.023758
34	0.712973	0.431905	0.137912	0.073045	0.053395	0.039143	0.021212
35	0.705914	0.421371	0.130105	0.067635	0.048986	0.035584	0.018940
36	0.698925	0.411094	0.122741	0.062625	0.044941	0.032349	0.016910
37	0.692005	0.401067	0.115793	0.057986	0.041231	0.029408	0.015098
38	0.685153	0.391285	0.109239	0.053690	0.037826	0.026735	0.013481
39	0.678370	0.381741	0.103056	0.049713	0.034703	0.024304	0.012036
40	0.671653	0.372431	0.097222	0.046031	0.031838	0.022095	0.010747
41	0.665003	0.363347	0.091719	0.042621	0.029209	0.020086	0.009595
42	0.658419	0.354485	0.086527	0.039464	0.026797	0.018260	0.008567
43	0.651900	0.345839	0.081630	0.036541	0.024584	0.016600	0.007649
44	0.645445	0.337404	0.077009	0.033834	0.022555	0.015091	0.006830
45	0.639055	0.329174	0.072650	0.031328	0.020692	0.013719	0.006098
46	0.632728	0.321146	0.068538	0.029007	0.018984	0.012472	0.005445
47	0.626463	0.313313	0.064658	0.026859	0.017416	0.011338	0.004861
48	0.620260	0.305671	0.060998	0.024869	0.015978	0.010307	0.004340
49	0.614119	0.298216	0.057546	0.023027	0.014659	0.009370	0.003875
50	0.608039	0.290942	0.054288	0.021321	0.013449	0.008519	0.003460

TABLE 4.3

IF_{poa} = present value of an ordinary annuity of \$1

$$IF_{poa} = \frac{1 - \dfrac{1}{(1+i)^n}}{i}$$

n^i	1%	2.5%	6%	8%	9%	10%	12%
1	0.990099	0.975610	0.943396	0.925926	0.917431	0.909091	0.892857
2	1.970395	1.927424	1.833393	1.783265	1.759111	1.735537	1.690051
3	2.940985	2.856024	2.673012	2.577097	2.531295	2.486852	2.401831
4	3.901966	3.761974	3.465106	3.312127	3.239720	3.169865	3.037349
5	4.853431	4.645829	4.212364	3.992710	3.889651	3.790787	3.604776
6	5.795476	5.508125	4.917324	4.622880	4.485919	4.355261	4.111407
7	6.728195	6.349391	5.582381	5.206370	5.032953	4.868419	4.563757
8	7.651678	7.170137	6.209794	5.746639	5.534819	5.334926	4.967640
9	8.566018	7.970866	6.801692	6.246888	5.995247	5.759024	5.328250
10	9.471305	8.752064	7.360087	6.710081	6.417658	6.144567	5.650223
11	10.367628	9.514209	7.886875	7.138964	6.805191	6.495061	5.937699

12	11.255077	10.257765	8.383844	7.536078	7.160725	6.813692	6.194374
13	12.133740	10.983185	8.852683	7.903776	7.486904	7.103356	6.423548
14	13.003703	11.690912	9.294984	8.244237	7.786150	7.366687	6.628168
15	13.865053	12.381378	9.712249	8.559479	8.060688	7.606080	6.810864
16	14.717874	13.055003	10.105895	8.851369	8.312558	7.823709	6.973986
17	15.562251	13.712198	10.477260	9.121638	8.543631	8.021553	7.119630
18	16.398269	14.353364	10.827603	9.371887	8.755625	8.201412	7.249670
19	17.226009	14.978891	11.158116	9.603599	8.950115	8.364920	7.365777
20	18.045553	15.589162	11.469921	9.818147	9.128546	8.513564	7.469444
21	18.856983	16.184549	11.764077	10.016803	9.292244	8.648694	7.562003
22	19.660379	16.765413	12.041582	10.200744	9.442425	8.771540	7.644646
23	20.455821	17.332110	12.303379	10.371059	9.580207	8.883218	7.718434
24	21.243387	17.884986	12.550358	10.528758	9.706612	8.984744	7.784316
25	22.023156	18.424376	12.783356	10.674776	9.822580	9.077040	7.843139
26	22.795204	18.950611	13.003166	10.809978	9.928972	9.160945	7.895660
27	23.559608	19.464011	13.210534	10.935165	10.026580	9.237223	7.942554
28	24.316443	19.964889	13.406164	11.051078	10.116128	9.306567	7.984423
29	25.065785	20.453550	13.590721	11.158406	10.198283	9.369606	8.021806
30	25.807708	20.930293	13.764831	11.257783	10.273654	9.426914	8.055184
31	26.542285	21.395407	13.929086	11.349799	10.342802	9.479013	8.084986
32	27.269589	21.849178	14.084043	11.434999	10.406240	9.526376	8.111594

TABLE 4.3 *(cont.)*

n^i	1%	2.5%	6%	8%	9%	10%	12%
33	27.989693	22.291881	14.230230	11.513888	10.464441	9.569432	8.135352
34	28.702666	22.723786	14.368141	11.586934	10.517835	9.608575	8.156564
35	29.408580	23.145157	14.498246	11.654568	10.566821	9.644159	8.175504
36	30.107505	23.556251	14.620987	11.717193	10.611763	9.676508	8.192414
37	30.799510	23.957318	14.736780	11.775179	10.652993	9.705917	8.207513
38	31.484663	24.348603	14.846019	11.828869	10.690820	9.732651	8.220993
39	32.163033	24.730344	14.949075	11.878582	10.725523	9.756956	8.233030
40	32.834686	25.102775	15.046297	11.924613	10.757360	9.779051	8.243777
41	33.499689	25.466122	15.138016	11.967235	10.786569	9.799137	8.253372
42	34.158108	25.820607	15.224543	12.006699	10.813366	9.817397	8.261939
43	34.810008	26.166446	15.306173	12.043240	10.837950	9.833998	8.269589
44	35.455454	26.503849	15.383182	12.077074	10.860505	9.849089	8.276418
45	36.094508	26.833024	15.455832	12.108402	10.881197	9.862808	8.282516
46	36.727236	27.154170	15.524370	12.137409	10.900181	9.875280	8.287961
47	37.353699	27.467483	15.589028	12.164267	10.917597	9.886618	8.292822
48	37.973959	27.773154	15.650027	12.189136	10.933575	9.896926	8.297163
49	38.588079	28.071369	15.707572	12.212163	10.948234	9.906296	8.301038
50	39.196118	28.362312	15.761861	12.233485	10.961683	9.914814	8.304498

TABLE 4.4

$$IF_{foa} = \text{future value of an ordinary annuity of } \$1$$

$$IF_{foa} = \frac{(1+i)^n - 1}{i}$$

n^i	1%	2.5%	6%	8%	9%	10%	12%
1	1.000000	1.000000	1.000000	1.000000	1.000000	1.000000	1.000000
2	2.010000	2.025000	2.060000	2.080000	2.090000	2.100000	2.120000
3	3.030100	3.075625	3.183600	3.246400	3.278100	3.310000	3.374400
4	4.060401	4.152516	4.374616	4.506112	4.573129	4.641000	4.779328
5	5.101005	5.256329	5.637093	5.866601	5.984711	6.105100	6.352847
6	6.152015	6.387737	6.975319	7.335929	7.523335	7.715610	8.115189
7	7.213535	7.547430	8.393838	8.922803	9.200435	9.487171	10.089012
8	8.285671	8.736116	9.897468	10.636628	11.028474	11.435888	12.299693
9	9.368527	9.954519	11.491316	12.487558	13.021036	13.579477	14.775656
10	10.462213	11.203382	13.180795	14.486562	15.192930	15.937425	17.548735
11	11.566835	12.483466	14.971643	16.645487	17.560293	18.531167	20.654583
12	12.682503	13.795553	16.869941	18.977126	20.140720	21.384284	24.133133
13	13.809328	15.140442	18.882138	21.495297	22.953385	24.522712	28.029109

TABLE 4.4 *(cont.)*

n^i	1%	2.5%	6%	8%	9%	10%	12%
14	14.947421	16.518953	21.015066	24.214920	26.019189	27.974983	32.392602
15	16.096896	17.931927	23.275970	27.152114	29.360916	31.772482	37.279715
16	17.257864	19.380225	25.672528	30.324283	33.003399	35.949730	42.753280
17	18.430443	20.864730	28.212880	33.750226	36.973705	40.544703	48.883674
18	19.614748	22.386349	30.905653	37.450244	41.301338	45.599173	55.749715
19	20.810895	23.946007	33.759992	41.446263	46.018458	51.159090	63.439681
20	22.019004	25.544658	36.785591	45.761964	51.160120	57.274999	72.052442
21	23.239194	27.183274	39.992727	50.422921	56.764530	64.002499	81.698736
22	24.471586	28.862856	43.392290	55.456755	62.873338	71.402749	92.502584
23	25.716302	30.584427	46.995828	60.893296	69.531939	79.543024	104.602894
24	26.973465	32.349038	50.815577	66.764759	76.789813	88.497327	118.155241
25	28.243200	34.157764	54.864512	73.105940	84.700896	98.347059	133.333870
26	29.525632	36.011708	59.156383	79.954415	93.323977	109.181765	150.333934
27	30.820888	37.912001	63.705766	87.350768	102.723135	121.099942	169.374007
28	32.129097	39.859801	68.528112	95.338830	112.968217	134.209936	190.698887
29	33.450388	41.856296	73.629798	103.965936	124.135356	148.630930	214.582754
30	34.784892	43.902703	79.058186	113.283211	136.307539	164.494023	241.332684

31	36.132740	46.000271	84.801677	123.345868	149.575217	181.943425	271.292606
32	37.494068	48.150278	90.889778	134.213537	164.036987	201.137767	304.847719
33	38.869009	50.354034	97.343165	145.950620	179.800315	222.251544	342.429446
34	40.257699	52.612885	104.183755	158.626670	196.982344	245.476699	384.520979
35	41.660276	54.928207	111.434780	172.316804	215.710755	271.024368	431.663496
36	43.076878	57.301413	119.120867	187.102148	236.124723	299.126805	484.463116
37	44.507647	59.733948	127.268119	203.070320	258.375948	330.039486	543.598690
38	45.952724	62.227297	135.904206	220.315945	282.629783	364.043434	609.830533
39	47.412251	64.782979	145.058458	238.941221	309.066463	401.447778	684.010197
40	48.886373	67.402554	154.761966	259.056519	337.882445	442.592556	767.091420
41	50.375237	70.087617	165.047684	280.781040	369.291865	487.851811	860.142391
42	51.878989	72.839808	175.950545	304.243523	403.528133	537.636992	964.359478
43	53.397779	75.660803	187.507577	329.583005	440.845665	592.400692	1081.082615
44	54.931757	78.552323	199.758032	356.949646	481.521775	652.640761	1211.812529
45	56.481075	81.516131	212.743514	386.505617	525.858734	718.904837	1358.230032
46	58.045885	84.554034	226.508125	418.426067	574.186021	791.795321	1522.217636
47	59.626344	87.667885	241.098612	452.900152	626.862762	871.974853	1705.883752
48	61.222608	90.859582	256.564529	490.132164	684.280411	960.172338	1911.589803
49	62.834834	94.131072	272.958401	530.342737	746.865648	1057.189572	2141.980579
50	64.463182	97.484349	290.335905	573.770156	815.083556	1163.908529	2400.018249

TABLE 4.5 PRESENT BOND VALUES[a]

Annual Yield (1%)	Years to Maturity					
	1	5	10	15	20	30
7.0 . . .	102.85	112.47	121.32	127.59	132.03	137.42
7.5 . . .	102.37	110.27	117.37	122.29	125.69	129.67
8.0 . . .	101.89	108.11	113.59	117.29	119.79	122.62
8.5 . . .	101.41	106.01	109.97	112.58	114.31	116.19
9.0 . . .	100.94	103.96	106.50	108.14	109.20	110.32
9.5 . . .	100.47	101.95	103.18	103.96	104.44	104.94
10.0 . . .	100.00	100.00	100.00	100.00	100.00	100.00
10.5 . . .	99.54	98.09	96.95	96.26	95.85	95.46
11.0 . . .	99.08	96.23	94.02	92.73	91.98	91.28
11.5 . . .	98.62	94.41	91.22	89.39	88.35	87.41
12.0 . . .	98.17	92.64	88.53	86.24	84.95	83.84
12.5 . . .	97.72	90.91	85.95	83.24	81.77	80.53
13.0 . . .	97.27	89.22	83.47	80.41	78.78	77.45
13.5 . . .	96.82	87.57	81.09	77.73	75.98	74.59
14.0 . . .	96.38	85.95	78.81	75.18	73.34	71.92
14.5 . . .	95.95	84.38	76.62	72.77	70.85	69.43

15.0	95.51	82.84	74.51	70.47	68.51	67.10
15.5	95.08	81.34	72.49	68.30	66.31	64.92
16.0	94.65	79.87	70.55	66.23	64.23	62.87
16.5	94.22	78.44	68.68	64.26	62.26	60.94
17.0	93.80	77.04	66.88	62.39	60.40	59.13
17.5	93.38	75.67	65.15	60.80	58.64	57.42
18.0	92.96	74.33	63.49	58.91	56.97	55.81
18.5	92.55	73.02	61.89	57.29	55.39	54.28
19.0	92.14	71.75	60.34	55.74	53.89	52.84
19.5	91.73	70.50	58.86	54.27	52.46	51.47
20.0	91.32	69.28	57.43	52.87	51.10	50.16

[a]Bonds have a coupon rate of 10%, semiannual compounding, and semiannual interest payments.

5 _____

Capital Budgeting Techniques and Risk-Return Trade-Off

Capital budgeting involves planning for the best selections and financing of long-term investments. In this chapter, the following four techniques are described to help you select the best long-term investment proposals:

- Net present value
- Internal rate of return
- Payback
- Profitability index

Your selection will necessarily involve judgments about future events about which you have no direct knowledge. Your task will be to minimize your chances of being wrong. The risk-return trade-off method shown in this chapter is one way to help you come to grips with uncertainty.

5.1 CAPITAL BUDGETING: FOUR TECHNIQUES FOR EVALUATING AN INVESTMENT PROPOSAL

What is capital budgeting?

Capital budgeting is a selection technique used to evaluate long-term investment proposals. It can be done in a number of ways, four of which are described in this chapter. Understanding these techniques is important for managerial accountants and management executives in both for-profit and nonprofit industries. Mid-level managers should also be familiar with capital budgeting, because they are also concerned with investment and management of resources to a degree.

What are the uses of capital budgeting?

Whenever you are faced with a decision of how to invest major chunks of resources, you have a capital budgeting problem. Ask yourself these questions:

- Should I replace certain equipment?
- Should I expand facilities by renting additional space, buying an existing building, or constructing a new building?
- Do I have an opportunity to refinance an outstanding debt issue? Should I do it?
- I've been contemplating a merger. Should I go ahead with it?
- I've been thinking about adding a new product to our line. Should I?
- I'm considering a new major advertising campaign. Should I hold off?

How do I use the present value method?

The present value method compares present value of future cash flows expected from an investment project to the initial cash outflow attributable directly to the investment. Net cash inflows are defined as the difference between expected cash inflow received as a result of the investment and expected cash outflow of the investment. Net present value (NPV) is defined as follows:

$$NPV = PV + CI$$

where

CI = cash outflow resulting from the cost of the investment

$$PV = \frac{R_1}{(1 + i)} + \frac{R_2}{(1 + i)^2} + \cdots + \frac{R_n}{(1 + i)^n}$$
  = present value

where

R_n = expected cash flow of the nth period.

RULE OF THUMB: If the net present value is positive (NPV > 0), then the proposal would be a good candidate for investment by your company.

EXAMPLE 5.1

Company A is replacing some of its machinery in order to reduce costs and gain certain other savings. The cost savings will result in expected cash inflows over the six-year life of the replacement machinery as follows:

Year	Net Cash Inflows	Year	Net Cash Inflows
1	$10,000	4	$30,000
2	20,000	5	40,000
3	30,000	6	50,000

Initial cash outflow as a result of the investment consisted of the following elements:

Purchase price paid for new machinery	$86,000
Installation costs paid	3,000
Cash realized (net of taxes) from disposal of old machinery	1,000
Total initial cash outflow	**$90,000**

In addition, it is expected that, at the end of its useful life, the new machinery will result in a cash inflow (net of taxes) of $1,000. The incremental cost of capital to the company (also called its required rate of return) is assumed to be 12%.

Using the formula, calculations of present value and net present value are

$$PV = \frac{\$10,000}{(1 + 0.12)} + \frac{\$20,000}{(1 + 0.12)^2} + \cdots$$
$$+ \frac{\$50,000}{(1 + 0.12)^6}$$
$$NPV = \frac{\$10,000}{(1 + 0.12)} + \frac{\$20,000}{(1 + 0.12)^2} + \cdots$$
$$+ \frac{\$50,000}{(1 + 0.12)^6} - \$90\,000$$

In tabular format, calculations are presented in Exhibit 5.1. (See page 151.) (NOTE: The interest factors are present values of $1 at 12% taken from Table 4.2.)

CONCLUSIONS: The investment in the replacement machinery is expected to result in a net present value of $23,828. If the company has no other investment opportunities, then this positive value indicates the investment should be made.

What if I have two investment opportunities?

If you have two opportunities that cannot be undertaken simultaneously, then select the project with the highest positive present value. This assumes no other projects are more attractive. If both projects can be undertaken together, and

EXHIBIT 5.1: NET PRESENT VALUE OF EXPECTED NET CASH INFLOWS FROM REPLACEMENT OF MACHINERY

End of Year	Cash Outflow	Net Cash Inflows	IF at ICCa	PRESENT VALUES Inflows	PRESENT VALUES Outflows	Net Present Value	Cash Inflows Impact on NPV
0	-$90,000		1.000000		-$90,000	-$90,000	-$90,000
1		$10,000	0.892857	$ 8,929		8,929	- 81,071
2		20,000	0.797194	15,944		15,944	- 65,127
3		30,000	0.711780	21,353		21,353	- 43,774
4		30,000	0.635518	19,066		19,066	- 24,708
5		40,000	0.567427	22,697		22,697	- 2,011
6		50,000	0.506631	25,332		25,332	23,321
6		1,000	0.506631	507		507	23,828
				$113,828	-$90,000	$23,828	

aICC: incremental cost of capital.

your company has the financial capacity to do it, then select both projects. Also, you must know whether the projects can actually be handled at the same time. Example 5.2 is a case in point.

EXAMPLE 5.2

Company A has two choices for replacement machinery. The first, Project A, has been described in Example 5.1. The second, Project B, is expected to generate the following cost savings, also over a six-year period:

Year	Net Cash Inflows	Year	Net Cash Inflows
1	$50,000	4	$30,000
2	40,000	5	20,000
3	30,000	6	10,000

At the end of its life, the replacement machinery of Project B is expected to have a salvage value that will generate a cash inflow (net of taxes) of $1,000. Assume costs generate an initial cash outflow of $120,000. Calculations of NPV for Project B are presented in Exhibit 5.2 on page 154.

DISCUSSION: Project B also shows a positive NPV. If the projects can be undertaken at the same time, then both investments would be selected. However, since both projects replace the same machinery, then the more profitable one (Project A) would be the right choice.

What is the internal rate-of-return method?

The internal rate of return (IRR) refers to the yield or interest rate that equates present value of expected cash flows from an investment project to the cost of the investment project. IRR is determined by setting NPV equal to zero, as shown in this formula:

$$NPV = 0$$
$$\left(\frac{R_1}{(1 + IRR)} + \frac{R_2}{(1 + IRR)^2} + \cdots + \frac{R_n}{(1 + IRR)^n} \right) - CI = 0$$

In calculating NPV, the number of periods involved (n), cash flows for each period (R), timing of cash flows, discount interest rate (i), and cost of the investment (CI) are presumed known. In calculating IRR, NPV is no longer treated as unknown, but is set equal to zero. On the other hand, interest rate is now unknown. Generally speaking, calculation of IRR is a trial-and-error process.

With this method, IRR must be greater than or equal to the incremental cost of capital (ICC) in order for the project to be a good candidate for investment. Thus,

IRR ≥ ICC

EXAMPLE 5.3

Consider Project A from Example 5.1. Exhibit 5.3 (page 156) shows a simple trial-and-error process used to calculate the discount interest rate that approximates IRR. When the discount interest rate is set equal to 19%, NPV is just $9, which is sufficiently close to zero. Exhibit 5.4 (page 157) analyzes the result of setting this rate approximately equal to IRR.

DISCUSSION: The IRR of Project A is approximately 19%. In the initial calculations, the incremental cost of capital (ICC) was assumed to be 12%. At 19%, IRR is greater than ICC; therefore, Project A is a good candidate for use of capital funds.

EXAMPLE 5.4

Now consider Project B from Example 5.2. As shown in Exhibit 5.5, IRR would be approximately 17%.

DISCUSSION: Once again, IRR (17%) is greater than ICC (12%). Project A has a greater NPV and IRR than Project B. Thus, under either NPV or IRR methods, Project A should be selected over Project B if both cannot be undertaken at the same time.

How do I use the payback method?

The payback method focuses on the payback period (PB), which is defined as the amount of time a company expects to take before it recovers its initial investment. When the annual cash flows are constant and of equal amounts, then PB can be calculated by this simple formula:

$$PB = \frac{CI}{R}$$

NOTE: When periodic cash flows are not equal, then calculation of PB is more complex.

EXAMPLE 5.5

For Projects A and B, as discussed in the previous examples, calculation of the payback periods is shown in Exhibit 5.6. PB for Project A is four years, but only three years for Project B. Under this method, if the company cannot undertake both projects, then Project B with the

EXHIBIT 5.2: NET PRESENT VALUE OF EXPECTED NET CASH INFLOWS FROM REPLACEMENT OF MACHINERY

End of Year	Cash Outflow	Net Cash Inflows	IF_p at ICC	PRESENT VALUES Inflows	PRESENT VALUES Outflows	Net Present Value	Cash Inflows Impact on NPV
0	−$120,000		1.000000		−$120,000	−$120,000	−$120,000
1		$50,000	0.892857	44,643		44,643	− 75,357
2		40,000	0.797194	31,888		31,888	− 43,469
3		30,000	0.711780	21,353		21,353	− 22,116
4		30,000	0.635518	19,066		19,066	− 3,050
5		20,000	0.567427	11,349		11,349	8,299
6		10,000	0.506631	5,066		5,066	13,365
6		1,000	0.506631	507		507	13,872
				$133,872	−$120,000	$ 13,872	

shorter payback period would be chosen over Project A. CAUTION: This method works with undiscounted amounts, so it ignores entirely the time value of money. NOTICE THIS: Whereas NPV and IRR methods show a preference for Project A, this method concludes just the opposite!

How does the profitability index work?

The profitability index uses the same variables as NPV but combines them differently. Profitability index (PI) is defined as follows:

$$PI = \frac{PV}{CI}$$

If PI is greater than 1, then the project is a good candidate for investment.

Normally, when comparing more than one project, the one with the higher PI is the more profitable. CAUTION: A higher PI does not always coincide with the project with the highest NPV.

EXAMPLE 5.6

The calculations of PI for Projects A and B as defined in the previous examples are shown as follows:

$$PIA = \frac{\$113,828}{\$90\,000} = 1.26$$
$$PIB = \frac{\$113,872}{\$120,000} = 1.12$$

CONCLUSIONS: Project A is preferred over Project B. This agrees with the results of NPV and IRR methods.

EXAMPLE 5.7

Assume two projects X and Y. Project X has a PV of $1,000,000 and a CI of $500,000. Project Y has a PV of $225,000 and a CI of $100,000. According to NPV, both projects are candidates for investment. If only one can be undertaken, then Project X is preferable, because its NPV is greater. Now calculate PI for both projects as follows:

$$PIX = \frac{\$1,000,000}{\$500,000} = 2$$
$$PIY = \frac{\$225,000}{\$100,000} = 2.25$$

DISCUSSION: Since PI is greater than 1 for both projects, either is a potential candidate for investment. If only one can be undertaken, then Project Y would be preferred. However, it is clear that Project X has a signifi-

EXHIBIT 5.3: CALCULATION OF THE IRR

End of Year	Cash Flows	IF_p at 16%	NPV	IF_p at 22%	NPV	IF_p at 19%	NPV
0	-$90,000	1.000000	-$90,000	1.000000	-$90,000	1.000000	-$90,000
1	10,000	0.862069	8,621	0.819672	8,197	0.840336	8,403
2	20,000	0.743163	14,863	0.671862	13,437	0.706165	14,123
3	30,000	0.640658	19,220	0.550707	16,521	0.593416	17,802
4	30,000	0.552291	16,569	0.451399	13,542	0.498669	14,960
5	40,000	0.476113	19,045	0.369999	14,800	0.419049	16,762
6	50,000	0.410442	20,522	0.303278	15,164	0.352142	17,607
6	1,000	0.410442	410	0.303278	303	0.352142	352
			9,250		-5,036		9

EXHIBIT 5.4: SETTING THE YIELD OR DISCOUNT RATE OF INTEREST APPROXIMATELY EQUAL TO THE IRR—INVESTMENT PROJECT A

End of Year	Cash Outflow	Net Cash Inflows	IF_p appx[a] at IRR[b] = 19%	PV AT IRR Inflows	PV AT IRR Outflows	NPV at IRR	Cash Inflows Impact on NPV at IRR
0	−$90,000		1.000000		−$90,000	−$90,000	−$90,000
1		$10,000	0.840336	$8,403		8,403	− 81,597
2		20,000	0.706165	14,123		14,123	− 67,474
3		30,000	0.593416	17,802		17,802	− 49,672
4		30,000	0.498669	14,960		14,960	− 34,712
5		40,000	0.419049	16,762		16762	− 17,950
6		50,000	0.352142	17,607		17,607	− 343
6		1,000	0.352142	352		352	9
				$90,009	−$90,000	9	

aappx.: approximately.

bIRR: discount rate of interest approximately equal to IRR.

EXHIBIT 5.5: SETTING THE YIELD OR DISCOUNT RATE OF INTEREST APPROXIMATELY EQUAL TO THE IRR—INVESTMENT PROJECT B

End of Year	Cash Outflow	Net Cash Inflows	IF$_p$ appx. at IRR = 17%	PV AT IRR Inflows	PV AT IRR Outflows	NPV at IRR	Cash Inflows Impact on NPV at IRR
0	–$120,000		1.000000		–$120,000	–$120,000	–$120,000
1		$50,000	0.854701	$42,735		42,735	– 77,265
2		40,000	0.730514	29,221		29,221	– 48,044
3		30,000	0.624371	18,731		18,731	– 29,313
4		30,000	0.533650	16,010		16,010	– 13,303
5		20,000	0.456111	9,122		9,122	– 4,181
6		10,000	0.389839	3,898		3,898	– 283
6		1,000	0.389839	390		390	107
				$120,107	–$120,000	$ 107	107

cantly greater NPV and is, in fact, more economically attractive. CAUTION: This shows that the PI method does not really provide an unambiguous guide for ranking most profitable investment projects.

5.2 COMPARING AND SELECTING THE BEST PROPOSAL

How do the projects relate to each other?

Investment projects are either independent or mutually exclusive. They are *independent* if both can be undertaken simultaneously. When this occurs, there's no need to rank one project over another. Projects are *mutually exclusive* when only one project can be carried out. Then it is necessary to rank the projects to determine which is most attractive.

What methods are best for ranking projects?

NPV, IRR, and PI methods are considered equally effective in selecting economically viable independent investment projects. The payback method, however, is considered inadequate because it does not take the time value of money into account. For mutually exclusive projects, NPV, IRR, and PI methods are not always able to rank projects in the same order. That is, it is quite possible to end up with different rankings under each method. The payback method is also unsatisfactory for the same reason.

WHAT TO DO: You need to compare the techniques in greater depth. Then your decisions will be better informed.

How do I compare NPV with IRR?

This question is best answered with the following example.

EXAMPLE 5.8

Company A is considering three investment projects. Projects A and B were described in Section 5.1. Project C has identical cash flows to Project B, but its CI = $102,700. The calculation of NPV for Project C and the result of applying the IRR are shown in Exhibit 5.7. You can see that Project C has the highest NPV and IRR of the three projects. However, in order to compare the two methods, let's calculate NPV for the three projects with differing discount interest rates. This is shown in Exhibit 5.8.

OBSERVATIONS: The NPVs of the three projects vary,

EXHIBIT 5.6: CALCULATION OF PAYBACK PERIODS

| End of Year | INVESTMENT PROJECT A | | INVESTMENT PROJECT B | |
	Cash Flows	Undiscounted Investment Balance to Be Recovered	Cash Flows	Undiscounted Investment Balance to Be Recovered
0	$90,000	–$90,000	$120,00	–$120,000
1	10,000	– 80,000	50,000	70,000
2	20,000	60,000	40,000	30,000
3	30000	– 30,000	30,000	0
4	30,000	0		

as do the discount interest rates. In previous examples, the incremental cost of capital (ICC) was assumed to be 12%. However, ICC can change over time. Note the following observations:

- As ICC rises, NPV falls. This is an inverse relation.
- NPV for Project A is consistently higher than for Project B at each discount interest rate. The same is true for Project C compared with Project B. However, comparing Projects A and C, a consistent relationship cannot be observed. Below 6% interest, NPV is higher for Project A, but the relation is reversed when the rate rises above 6%.
- IRR of Project C is higher than for Project A, but NPVs are not always higher at every level of discount interest rate. This means you would choose Project A for certain interest rates and Project C for others. Yet, Project C has the higher IRR.

Figure 5.1 shows the NPV for each project at differing rates of interest (ICC). From it, you can see that the NPV for Project A is higher than Project B for interest rates below 6%, while the reverse is true for rates above 6%.

Which is the preferable project if NPV and IRR do not give consistent signals?

In order to resolve this conflict, you need to know the interest rate or rates at which the company will be able to reinvest net cash inflows from the projects as these funds are generated. In other words, you need to forecast future or compound values of the net cash inflows as of the end of the expected life of the projects.

EXHIBIT 5.7: NPV AND IRR FOR INVESTMENT PROJECT C

End of Year	Cash Flows	IF_p at ICC = 12%	Net Present Value	Cash Inflows Impact on NPV	IF_p appx. at IRR = 25%	NPV at IRR	Cash Inflows Impact on NPV at IRR
0	−$102,700	1.000000	−$102,700	−$102,700	1.000000	−$102,700	−$102,700
1	50,000	0.892857	44,643	− 58,057	0.800000	40,000	− 62,700
2	40,000	0.797194	31,888	− 26,169	0.640000	25,600	− 37,100
3	30,000	0.711780	21,353	− 4,816	0.512000	15,360	− 21,740
4	30,000	0.635518	19,066	14,250	0.409600	12,288	− 9,452
5	20,000	0.567427	11,349	25,597	0.327680	6,554	− 2,898
6	10,000	0.506631	5,066	30,665	0.26214	42,621	− 277
6	1,000	0.506631	507	31,172	0.262144	262	− 15
			$ 31,172			−$ 15	

EXHIBIT 5.8: BEHAVIOR OF NPV FOR INVESTMENT PROJECTS A, B, AND C

End of Year	Cash Flows—Investment Projects A	B	NET PRESENT VALUES AT ALTERNATIVE DISCOUNT INTEREST RATES 0%	6%	10%	12%	17%	19%	25%
0	-$90,000		-$90,000	-$90,000	-$90,000	-$90,000	-$90,000	-$90,000	-$90,000
1	10,000		10,000	9,434	9,091	8,929	8,547	8,403	8,000
2	20,000		20,000	17,800	16,529	15,944	14,610	14,123	12,800
3	30,000		30,000	25,189	22,539	21,353	18,731	17,802	15,360
4	30,000		30,000	23,763	20,490	19,066	16 010	14,960	12,288
5	40,000		40,000	29,890	24,837	22,697	18 244	16,762	13,107
6	50,000		50,000	35,248	28,224	25,332	19,492	17,607	13,107
6	1,000		1,000	705	564	507	390	352	262
NPVs—investment project A			$91,000	$52,029	$32,274	$23,828	$ 6,024	$ 9	–$15,076

163

EXHIBIT 5.8: (cont.)

End of Year	A	B	0%	6%	10%	12%	17%	19%	25%
0		–$120,000	–$120,000	–$120,000	–$120,000	–$120,000	–$120,000	–$120,000	–$120,000
1		50,000	50,000	47,170	45,455	44,643	42,735	42,017	40,000
2		40,000	40,000	35,600	33,058	31,888	29,221	28,247	25,600
3		30,000	30,000	25,189	22,539	21,353	18731	17,802	15,360
4		30,000	30,000	23,763	20,490	19,066	16,010	14,960	12,288
5		20,000	20,000	14,945	12,418	11,349	9,122	8,381	6,554
6		10,000	10,000	7,050	5,645	5,066	3,898	3,521	2,621
6		1,000	1,000	705	564	507	390	352	262
NPVs—investment project B			$61,000	$34,422	$20,169	$13,872	$107	–$4,720	–$17,315

Adjust cost of investment project B to that of investment project C:

			0%	6%	10%	12%	17%	19%	25%
Cost of project B	$120,000								
Cost of project C	102,700		17,300	17,300	17,300	17,300	17,300	17,300	17,300
NPVs—investment project C			$78,300	$51,722	$37,469	$31,172	$17,407	$12,580	–$15

164

FIGURE 5.1: NPV IN RELATION TO DIFFERING DISCOUNT RATES OF INTEREST

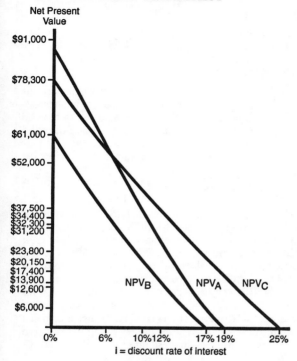

How to I calculate the future values of investment projects?

The calculation of the future values of investment projects is similar to that of an ordinary annuity where annual installments are equal to each other. However, while your investment projects generate an "annuity" of net cash inflows, the "installments" are not equal to each other. Recall this formula for future or compound value of an ordinary annuity

$$FV_{oa} = R_1(1 + i)^{n-1} + R_2(1 + i)^{n-2} + ... + R_{n-1}(1 + i) + R$$

Future values of investment projects can be calculated as follows:

$$FV_I = FV_R - FV_C$$
where
FV_I = future value of an investment project
FV_R = future value of net cash inflows as of the end of periods 1, 2, ... *n*

FV_C = future value of the net cash outflow due to the original cost of the project

Note that $FV_C = CI(1 + i)^n$. Thus

$$FV_I = R1(1 + i)^{n-1} + R_2(1 + i)^{n-2} + \ldots \\ + R_{n-1}(1 + i) + R_n - CI(1 + i)^n$$

EXAMPLE 5.9

For this example, use Projects A and C from the previous examples. Assume two companies, X and Y, are interested in both projects. Company X is assumed to have an ICC of 4%. Company Y has an ICC of 12%. Both companies can reinvest cash inflows generated from the projects at reinvestment rates (RR) equal to their respective ICCs.

Calculations for the two projects are shown in Exhibit 5.9.

DISCUSSION: You can see that the future value of Project A is greater than that of Project C for Company X (RR = 4%). On the other hand, the reverse is true for Company Y (RR = 12%). At RR less than 6%, both present and future values of Project A exceed those of Project C. At RR above 6%, the reverse holds.

The IRR can be interpreted as the potential RR for each project. For both Projects A and C, IRR is above 6%, and NPV of Project C is continually higher than that of Project A. Thus, NPV for Project A will become zero at a lower discount interest rate than will Project C. CONCLUSION: Only when RR is above 6% will IRR and NPV give consistent signals.

What do these calculations prove?

From these calculations of future values, you can see that the NPV method generally gives more reliable signals. By following this method and using your best estimates of reinvestment rates, you will select the projects expected to be most advantageous.

What is capital rationing?

Capital rationing occurs whenever a company cannot or will not undertake all investment projects with NPV greater than or equal to zero. Usually the company has set an upper limit to its capital budget, thereby preventing it from undertaking all projects.

EXAMPLE 5.10

Use Projects A, B, and C as described earlier. Assume there are three companies, X, Y, and Z, with capital bud-

EXHIBIT 5.9: FUTURE OR COMPOUND VALUES OF INVESTMENT PROJECTS A AND C AT ALTERNATIVE REINVESTMENT RATES

End of Year	*Cash Flows—Investment Projects*		IF_p at ICC = 4%	IF_p at ICC = 12%	*Future or Compound Values of Investment Projects at Reinvestment Rates (RR)*				*Differential Compound Values—Investment Project A less Investment Project C*	
					Company X		*Company Y*			
	A	C			A RR = 4%	C RR = 4%	A RR = 12%	C RR = 12%	RR = 4%	RR = 12%
0	–$90,000	–$102,700	1.265319	1.973823	–$113,879	–$129,948	–$177,644	–$202,712	$16,069	$25,068
1	10,000	50,000	1.216653	1.762342	12,167	60,833	17,623	88,117	– 48,666	– 70.494
2	20,000	40,000	1.169859	1.573519	23,397	46,794	31,470	62,941	– 23,397	– 31,471
3	30,000	30,000	1.124864	1.404928	33,746	33,746	42,148	42,148	0	0
4	30,000	30,000	1.081600	1.254400	32,448	32,448	37,632	37,632	0	0
5	40,000	20,000	1.040000	1.120000	41,600	20,800	44,800	22,400	20,800	22,400
6	50,000	10,000	1.000000	1.000000	50,000	10,000	50,000	10,000	40,000	40,000
6	1,000	1,000	1.000000	1.000000	1,000	1,000	1,000	1,000	0	0
					$ 80,479	$ 75,673	$ 47,029	$ 61,526	4,806	–$14,497

gets for the current year of $100,000, $150,000, and $200,000, respectively. Each company has ICC at 12%. Using the NPV method, the projects are ranked as follows:

Investment project	CI	NPV	Rank
A	$ 90.000	$23,828	2
B	120,000	13,872	3
C	102.700	31,173	1
	$312.700		

The investment projects to be financed by the capital budgets of Companies X, Y, and Z are summarized below.

CAPITAL BUDGETS AND SELECTION OF CAPITAL PROJECTS

		Companies		
Projects	Rank	X	Y	Z
C	1	—	$102,700	$102,700
A	2	$90,000	—	90,000
B	3	—	—	—
Projects financed		$90,000	$102,700	$192,700
Unutilized capital budget		10,000	47,300	7,300
Total capital budget		**$100,000**	**$150,000**	**$200,000**

NOTE: With capital rationing, the project with the highest ranking index and not the highest NPV will be selected for investment. Company X does not choose Project C but Project A instead. Company Y selects Project C only. Company Z selects Projects C and A but not Project B.

5.3 EVALUATING THE RISK-RETURN TRADE-OFF

5.3.1 One-Year Life Projects

As a manager, you are continually confronted with the risk of making wrong decisions. At the heart of the risk lies your uncertainty about future events that will bear upon the success of the project. The risk-return trade-off analysis is one way of trying to estimate the amount of risk associated with a particular project or set of projects. In this first part, let's consider the simplest case, an investment project with a one-year life.

What is the expected value of future cash flows?

Since you have no direct knowledge about future cash flows, you must rely on forecasts. These estimates take the form of probabilities that specific cash flows will be realized for the coming year. This is expressed in the following formula:

$$E(R) = \sum_{m=1}^{M} R_m P_m$$

where

$E(R)$ = expected value of R during a particular fiscal period (in this case, assumed to be the end of the fiscal period)

R_m = the mth value of R (cash flow) associated with P_m

P_m = probability of occurrence of R_m

m = number of occurrences of R and associated number of probabilities P, where $m = a, 2, \ldots M$

Σ = summation sign

EXAMPLE 5.11

Investment Project D is estimated to have cash flows for the coming fiscal year as follows:

Cash flows	Probability of occurrence
$ 8,000	.1
9,000	.2
10,000	.4
11,000	.2
$12,000	.1

The cash flows take place at the end of the year. Applying the above formula, calculations for the expected value of cash flows for the coming year are as follows:

$$E(R) = (.1)(\$8,000) + (.2)(\$9,000) + (.4)(\$10,000) + (.2)(\$11,000) + (.1)(\$12,000)$$
$$= \$800 + \$1,800 + \$4,000 + \$2,200 + \$1,200$$
$$= \$10,000$$

The expected value of cash flows is simply a weighted average of the cash flows, where the weights equal the probabilities of occurrence. Another notation for expected value would be

$$E(R) = \bar{R}$$
where

$\bar{R}$ = average of the expected cash flows (also called R bar)

If certain circumstances prevail, then the expected value of cash flows for the coming year would be the most probable value that you can expect to occur. MOST CRITICAL: Correct estimation of the probabilities and their associated cash flows will ensure your success. However, anyone with experience in forecasting knows how perilous any attempts to make useful guesses about the future can be.

How can I estimate risk associated with cash flow estimates?

Standard deviation measures the average dispersion of the individual cash flows, R_m, around the expected value of the cash flows, $E(R)$. First, the dispersion of cash flows, known as variance, is defined as follows:

$$\text{var}(R) = \sum_{m=1}^{M} (R_m - \bar{R})^2 P_m$$

or

$$\text{var(R)} = \delta^2{}_R$$

The standard deviation of the cash flows is given as follows:

$$\delta_R = \sqrt{\delta^2{}_R}$$

or

$$\delta_R = \sqrt{\sum_{m=1}^{M} (R_m - \bar{R})^2 P_m}$$

EXAMPLE 5.12

Consider Project D from the previous example. The calculation of expected value, variance, and standard deviation are given in Exhibit 5.10.

NOTE: Standard deviation is considered a measure of absolute risk. The higher the standard deviation, the greater the risk.

How do these measures affect net present value?

When comparing investments, you do not really compare their cash flows but their net present values or yields. You need to understand how variability of future cash flows affect these figures. The expected value of NPV is given by the following formula:

$$E(\text{NPV}) = \sum_{m=1}^{M} \text{NPV}_m P_m$$

The standard deviation of NPV is given in Exhibit 5.10.

EXAMPLE 5.13

Begin again with Project D, but note some additional information. The cost of the project is $8,000, and the company estimates an incremental cost of capital of 12%. Assume the investment cost is incurred at the beginning of next year and cash flows occur at the end of next year.

The calculations of NPV for expected cash flows, as well as their variance and standard deviation, are shown in Exhibits 5.11 and 5.12.

EXHIBIT 5.11: CALCULATION OF NPV

m	R_m	IF_p at $ICC = 12\%$	$PV(R_m)$	CI	NPV_m
1	$ 8,000	0.892857	$ 7,143	$8,000	–$857
2	9,000	0.892857	8,036	8,000	36
3	10,000	0.892857	8,929	8,000	929
4	11,000	0.892857	9,821	8,000	1,821
5	12,000	0.892857	10,714	8,000	2,714

Recall that NPV depends on R, as shown in Section 5.1. Since this example considers just one future year, the following expected net present value, $E(\text{NPV})$, can be computed as follows:

EXHIBIT 5.10: CALCULATION OF EXPECTED VALUE, VARIANCE, AND STANDARD DEVIATION OF EXPECTED CASH FLOWS

m	R_m	P_m	$R_m P_m$	$(R_m - \bar{R})$	$(R_m - \bar{R})^2$	$(R_m - \bar{R})^2 P_m$
1	$8,000	.1	$800	$8,000 − $10,000	$4,000,000	$400,000
2	9,000	.2	1,800	9,000 − 10,000	1,000,000	200,000
3	10,000	.4	4,000	10,000 − 10,000	0	0
4	11,000	.2	2,200	11,000 − 10,000	1,000,000	200,000
5	12,000	.1	1,200	12,000 − 10,000	4,000,000	400,000
		1.0	$10,000		$10,000,000	$1,200,000

$E(R) = \bar{R} = \$10,000$

$\text{var}(R) = \$1,200,000$

$\sigma_R = \$1,095$

$$E(\text{NPV}) = \frac{E(R)}{(1 + i)} - CI$$

$$E(\text{NPV}) = \frac{\$10,000}{(1 + 0.12)} - \$8,000$$

$$E(\text{NPV}) = \$8,929 - \$8,000 = \$929$$

NOTE: In the previous example, both CI and i are assumed to be known with certainty. If they are not, then these variables must also be treated in terms of expected values. WHAT TO DO: Treat all variables in terms of expected values. For illustrative purposes in this chapter, however, only future cash flows are considered in terms of net present value.

What is the relation between standard deviation of future cash flows and standard deviation of net present value?

The relation between standard deviation of NPV and standard deviation of R is given by the following formula:

$$\delta_{\text{NPV}} = \sqrt{\sum_{m=1}^{M}(\text{NPV}_m - \overline{\text{NPV}})^2 P_m}$$

With the previous example, this formula yields a standard deviation of NPV and R as follows:

$$\delta_{\text{NPV}} = \frac{\$1,095}{(1 + 0.12)} = \$978$$

5.3.2 Two-Year Life Projects

This section continues where the last left off. Here, expected value and standard deviation of future cash flows will be considered for a two-year investment project.

How do I compute expected value and standard deviation of the second year's cash flows?

The formulas for the calculation of expected value, variance, and standard deviation of the expected cash flows of the second year of a project parallel those of the first year.

$$E(R_2) = \sum_{m=1}^{M} R_{2m}P_{2m}$$

$$\text{var}(R_2) = \sum_{m=1}^{M}(R_{2m} - \bar{R}_{2m})^2 P_{2m}$$

$$\delta_{R2} = \sqrt{\sum_{m=1}^{M}(R_{2m} - \bar{R}_{2m})P_{2m}}$$

EXHIBIT 5.12: CALCULATION OF $E(NPV)$, var (NPV), AND σ_{NPV}

m	NPV_m	P_m	$E(NPV)$	$NPV_m - \overline{NPV}$	$(NPV_m - \overline{NPV})^2$	var(NPV)
1	−$ 857	.1	−$ 85.7	− 1,786	$3,189,796	$318,980
2	36	.2	7.2	− 893	797,449	159,490
3	929	.4	371.6	0	0	0
4	1,821	.2	364.2	892	795,664	159,133
5	2,714	.1	271.4	1,785	3,186,225	318,623
			$928.7			$956,226

$E(NPV) = \overline{NPV} = \$ \quad 929$

var $(NPV) = \$956,226$

$\sigma_{NPV} = \$ \quad 978$

EXAMPLE 5.14

Investment Project E is estimated to have cash flows and probabilities of occurrence as follows:

	YEAR 1		YEAR 2
Cash Flows	Probability of Occurrence	Probability of Cash Flows	Occurrence
$ 8,000	.1	$16,000	.1
9,000	.2	18,000	.2
10,000	.4	20,000	.4
11,000	.2	22,000	.2
$12,000	.1	$24,000	.1

All cash flows are assumed to take place at the end of each of the two future years. Calculations for the expected value, variance, and standard deviation of the expected cash flows for the first year are given in Example 5.12. For the second year, calculations are given in Exhibit 5.13.

How do I compute expected value of net present value?

Formulas for the calculation of the expected value and standard deviation for net present value are as follows:

$$E(\text{NPV}) = \frac{E(R_1)}{(1 + i)} + \frac{E(R_2)}{(1 + i)^2} - \text{CI}$$

$$E(\text{NPV}) = \frac{\sum_{m=1}^{M} R_{1m}P_{1m}}{1 + i} + \frac{\sum_{m=1}^{M} R_{2m}P_{2m}}{(1 + i)^2} - \text{CI}$$

Note the similarity between these formulas and those for a one-year project. Once again, these assume that CI and i are known with certainty.

For present purposes, let's assume the probabilities that certain cash flows would materialize at the end of each year are the same. That is,

$$Pn,m = Pn+1, m \text{ for } n = 1, 2, \ldots, n$$

where

Pn,m = the probability of year n that the mth cash flow will be realized

EXHIBIT 5.13: CALCULATION OF EXPECTED VALUE, VARIANCE, AND STANDARD DEVIATION OF EXPECTED CASH FLOWS FOR THE SECOND YEAR OF INVESTMENT PROJECT E

m	R_{2m}	P_{2m}	$R_{2m}P_{2m}$	$R_{2m} - \bar{R}_2$	$(R_{2m} - \bar{R}_2)^2$	$(R_{2m} - \bar{R}_2)^2 P_{2m}$
1	$16,000	.1	$ 1,600	$16,000 − $20,000	$16,000,000	$1,600,000
2	18,000	.2	3,600	18,000 − 20,000	4,000,000	800,000
3	20,000	.4	8,000	20,000 − 20,000	0	0
4	22,000	.2	4,400	22,000 − 20,000	4,000,000	800,000
5	24,000	.1	2,400	24,000 − 20,000	16,000,000	1,600,000
		1.0	$20,000		$40,000,000	$4,800,000

R_{2m} = the mth value of R_2 (the second year's cash flow) associated with P_{2m}

P_{2m} = the second year's probability of occurrence of R_{2m}

$\bar{R}_2 = E(R_2)$ = expected value of R during the second year, assumed in the present case to take place at the end of the second year

$\bar{R}_2$ = $20,000

var(R_2) = $4,800,000

σR_2 = $2,191

EXAMPLE 5.15

Use Project E as described previously. Assume the cost of investment (CI) equals $20,800 and the incremental cost of capital (i) is 12%.

The calculation of the expected values of the future cash flows of the first and second future years, $E(R_1)$ and $E(R_2)$, are shown in Exhibit 5.14.

EXHIBIT 5.14: CALCULATION OF THE EXPECTED VALUES OF THE FUTURE CASH FLOWS OF INVESTMENT PROJECT E

m	R_{1m}	P_{1m}	$R_{1m}P_{1m}$	R_{2m}	P_{2m}	$R_{2m}P_{2m}$
1	$ 8,000	.1	$ 800	$16,000	.1	$ 1,600
2	9,000	.2	1,800	18,000	.2	3,600
3	10,000	.4	4,000	20,000	.4	8,000
4	11,000	.2	2,200	22,000	.2	4,400
5	12,000	.1	1,200	24,000	.1	2,400
			$10,000			**$20,000**

$E(R_1) = \$10,000$

$E(R_2) = \$20,000$

From the formula for E(NPV) given in Section 5.3, you can calculate E(NPV) for Project E as follows:

$$E(\text{NPV}) = \frac{\$10,000}{(1 + 0.12)} + \frac{\$20,000}{(1 + 0.12)^2} - \$20,800$$
$$E(\text{NPV}) = (0.892857)(\$10,000) + (0.797194)(\$20,000) - \$20,800$$
$$E(\text{NPV}) = \$8,929 + \$15,944 - \$20,800$$
$$E(\text{NPV}) = \$4,073$$

How do I compute standard deviation of net present value?

The variance of net present value, var(NPV), is equal to the variance of the present value, var(PV), or

var(NPV) = var(PV)

where

var (CI) = 0

This assumes that the cost of the project, CI, is known with certainty and is a given constant.

Assume also that variations in the expected cash flows of

the first future year are independent of those of the second year. This leads to the following formula:

$$\text{var(PV)} = \sum_{m=1}^{M} (PV_{1m} - E[PV_1])^2 P_{1m}$$
$$+ \sum_{m=1}^{M} (PV_{2m} - E[PV_2])^2 P_{2m}$$

$$\text{var(PV)} = \text{var(PV}_1) + \text{var(PV}_2)$$

where
$$\text{cov(PV}_1, PV_2) = 0$$

The covariance, cov(PV1, PV2), is a measure of whether the variations in the expected cash flows of future year one are associated with those of future year two. Since these variations are assumed to be independent of each other, cov(PV_1, PV_2) = 0.

EXAMPLE 5.16

The present values of the probable cash flows for the first and second years for Project E are given in Exhibit 5.15. With these calculations completed, the variances of the present values of future cash flows can be shown as in Exhibit 5.16.

EXHIBIT 5.15: CALCULATION OF THE PRESENT VALUES AND EXPECTED VALUES OF PROBABLE FUTURE CASH FLOWS OF INVESTMENT PROJECT E

m	R_{1m}	One-Year Discount $ICC = 12\%$	$PV(R_{1m})$	P_{1m}	$PV(R_{1m})$ $\times P_{1m}$
1	$ 8,000	.892857	$ 7,142.86	.1	$ 714.29
2	9,000	.892857	8,035.71	.2	1,607.14
3	10,000	.892857	8,928.57	.4	3,571.43
4	11,000	.892857	9,821.43	.2	1,964.29
5	12,000	.892857	10,714.28	.1	1,071.43
					$ 8,928.58

m	R_{1m}	Two-Year Discount $ICC = 12\%$	$PV(R_{1m})$	P_{1m}	$PV(R_{1m})$ $\times P_{1m}$
1	$16,000	.797194	$12,755.10	.1	$ 1,275.51
2	18,000	.797194	14,349.49	.2	2,869.90
3	20,000	.797194	15,943.88	.4	6,377.55
4	22,000	.797194	17,538.27	.2	3,507.65
5	24,000	.797194	19,132.66	.1	1,913.27
					$15,943.88

$E(PV_1)$ = $8,928.57
$E(PV_2)$ = $15,943.88

The overall variance of Project E would then be

$$var(PV) = \$956,632 + \$3,050,496 = \$4,007,128$$

Remember, cash flows of future years one and two are independent of each other.

Having calculated var(PV), then the standard deviation of the present value would be given by this formula:

$$\delta_{PV} = \sqrt{var(PV)}$$

For Project E, then,

$$\delta_{PV} = \sqrt{\$4,007,128} = \$2,002$$

NOTE: The standard deviation of the present value, δ_{PV}, is also the standard deviation of the net present value

$$\delta_{NPV} = \delta_{PV} = \$2,002.$$

What is the relation between standard deviation of net present value and standard deviation of future cash flows?

In order to derive a relation between the standard deviation of the present value and net present value to those of future cash flows, use the following formulas:

$$var(PV_1) = \frac{var(R_1)}{(1 + i)^2}$$

and

$$var(PV_2) = \frac{var(R_2)}{(1 + i)^4}$$

By substitution, you can obtain the following relation:

$$var(NPV) = \frac{var(R_1)}{(1 + i)^2} + \frac{var(R_2)}{(1 + i)^4}$$

where

$$cov(R_1, R_2) = 0$$

Thus, the relationship for the standard variations would be expressed as follows:

$$\delta_{NPV} = \sqrt{\frac{var(R_1)}{(1 + i)^2} + \frac{var(R_2)}{(1 + i)^4}}$$

where

$$cov(R_1, R_2) = 0$$

EXHIBIT 5.16: CALCULATION OF THE VARIANCES OF THE PRESENT VALUES OF INVESTMENT PROJECT E

m	$PV_{1m} - E(PV_1)$			$(PV_{1m} - E[PV_1])^2$	P_{1m}	$PV_{1m} - E[PV_{1m}])^2 P_{1m}$
1	$7,142.86	–	$8,928.57	$-1,785.71	$3,188,760	.1	$318,876
2	8,035.71	–	8,928.57	– 892.86	797,199	.2	159,440
3	8,928.57	–	8,928.57	0	0	.4	0
4	9,821.43	–	8,928.57	+892.86	797,199	.2	159,440
5	10,714.28	–	8,928.57	+1,785.71	3,188,760	.1	318,876
							$956,632

1	$12,755.10 – $15,943.88	$–3,188.78	$10,168,318	.1	$1,016,832
2	14,349.49 – 15,943.88	–1,594.39	2,542,079	.2	508,416
3	15,943.88 – 15,943.88	0	0	.4	0
4	17,538.27 – 15 943.88	+1,594.39	2,542,079	.2	508,416
5	19,132.66 – 15 943.88	+3,188.78	10 168318	.1	1,016,832
					$3,050,496

var(PV$_1$) = $956,632

var(PV$_2$) = $3,050,496

5.3.3 Multiyear Life Projects

How do I compute expected value of future cash flows and net present value?

In Section 5.3, determination of net present value (NPV) was based on the assumption that future cash flows are known with certainty. When you consider the notion of probable future cash flows, then you must calculate the expected value of NPV, E(NPV), according to the following formula:

$$E(\text{NPV}) = \frac{E(R_1)}{1+i} + \frac{E(R_2)}{(1+i)^2} + \ldots + \frac{E(R_N)}{(1+i)^N} - \text{CI}$$

where

$$E(R_n) = \sum_{m=1}^{M} R_{nm}P_{nm} \text{ for } n = 1, 2, \ldots, N$$

The formula can also be written as follows:

$$E(\text{NPV}) = \left(\frac{\sum_{m=1}^{M}R_{1m}P_{1m}}{(1+i)} + \frac{\sum_{m=1}^{M}R_{2m}P_{2m}}{(1+i)^2} + \ldots \frac{\sum_{m=1}^{M}R_{Nm}P_{Nm}}{(1+i)n} \right) - \text{CI}$$

EXAMPLE 5.17

The cost of investment project F is $68,928. The incremental cost of capital is 12%. Project F is assumed to have a five-year horizon as well as five probable levels of future cash flows, given as follows:

PROBABLE FUTURE CASH FLOWS FOR PROJECT F

n (year)	\multicolumn{5}{c}{m (probable future cash flow)}
	1	2	3	4	5
1	$ 8,000	$ 9,000	$10,000	$11,000	$12,000
2	16,000	18,000	20,000	22,000	24,000
3	24,000	27,000	30,000	33,000	36,000
4	32,000	36,000	40,000	44,000	48,000
5	40,000	45,000	50,000	55,000	60,000

Also, assume the probabilities of occurrence do not change. As a result, the probability of occurrence for the *m*th cash flows is .1 for $m = 1$, .2 for $m = 2$, .4 for $m = 3$, and .1 for $m = 5$.

WHAT TO DO: First, calculate the expected values of the future cash flows for each five years. For years 1 and 2, these values are shown in Example 5.16 above. Calculations for years 3, 4, and 5 are shown in Exhibit 5.17 on page 184.

The calculation of the expected value of PV and NPV are given in Exhibit 5.18.

How do I measure variance and standard deviation of future cash flows?

You would measure variance and standard deviation of the probable cash flows of subsequent years as you would for years 1 and 2.

EXAMPLE 5.18

For Project F, variance and standard deviation of future cash flows for years 1 and 2 are shown.

EXHIBIT 5.18: CALCULATION OF THE EXPECTED VALUE OF THE PRESENT VALUE AND NET PRESENT VALUE OF THE FUTURE CASH FLOWS OF INVESTMENT PROJECT F

End of Year n	$E(R_n)$	IF_p at ICC = 12%	EV of Present Value
1	$10,000	0.892857	$ 8,929
2	20,000	0.797194	15,944
3	30,000	0.711780	21,353
4	40,000	0.635518	25,421
5	50,000	0.567427	28,371
			$100,018

$E(\text{NPV}) = E(\text{PV}) - \text{CI}$

$E(\text{NPV}) = \$100,018 - \$68,928$

$E(\text{NPV}) = \$31,090$

EXHIBIT 5.17: CALCULATION OF THE EXPECTED VALUES OF THE FUTURE CASH FLOWS OF INVESTMENT PROJECT F FOR YEARS 3, 4, AND 5

m	R_{3m}	P_{3m}	$R_{3m}P_{3m}$	R_{4m}	P_{4m}	$R_{4m}P_{4m}$	R_{5m}	P_{5m}	$R_{5m}P_{5m}$
1	$24,000	.1	$ 2,400	$32,000	.1	$ 3,200	$40,000	.1	$ 4,000
2	27,000	.2	5,400	36,000	.2	7,200	45,000	.2	9,000
3	30,000	.4	12,000	40,000	.4	16,000	50,000	.4	20,000
4	33,000	.2	6,600	44,000	.2	8,800	55,000	.2	11,000
5	36,000	.1	3,600	48,000	.1	4,800	60,000	.1	6,000
			$30,000			$40,000			$50,000

$E(R_3) = \$30,000$

$E(R_4) = \$40,000$

$E(R_5) = \$50,000$

**EXHIBIT 5.19: CALCULATION OF THE
VARIANCES AND STANDARD DEVIATIONS OF
THE FUTURE CASH FLOWS OF INVESTMENT
PROJECT F FOR YEARS 3, 4, AND 5**

m	$R_{3m} - \bar{R}_3$	$(R_{3m} - \bar{R}_3)^2$	P_{3m}	$(R_{3m} - \bar{R}_3)^2 P_{3m}$
1	$24,000 - $30,000	$ 36,000,000	.1	$3,600,000
2	27,000 - 30,000	9,000,000	.2	1,800,000
3	30,000 - 30,000	0	.4	0
4	33,000 - 30,000	9,000,000	.2	1,800,000
5	36,000 - 30,000	36,000,000	.1	3,600,000
				$10,800,000

m	$R_{4m} - \bar{R}_4$	$(R_{4m} - \bar{R}_4)^2$	P_{4m}	$(R_{4m} - \bar{R}_4)^2 P_{4m}$
1	$32,000 - $40,000	$ 64,000,000	.1	$ 6,400,000
2	36,000 - 40,000	16,000,000	.2	3,200,000
3	40.000 - 40,000	0	.4	0
4	44,000 - 40,000	16,000,000	.2	3,200,000
5	48,000 - 40,000	64,000,000	.1	6,400,000
				$ 19,200,000

m	$R_{5m} - \bar{R}_5$	$(R_{5m} - \bar{R}_5)^2$	P_{5m}	$(R_{5m} - \bar{R}_5)^2 P_{5m}$
1	$40,000 - $50,000	$100,000,000	.1	$10,000,000
2	45,000 - 50,000	25,000,000	.2	5,000,000
3	50,000 - 50,000	0	.4	0
4	55,000 - 50,000	25,000,000	.2	5,000,000
5	60,000 - 50,000	100,000,000	.1	10,000,000
				$30,000,000

$\text{var}(R_3) = \$10,800,000; \sigma R_3 = \$3,286$
$\text{var}(R_4) = \$19,200,000; \sigma R_4 = \$4,382$
$\text{var}(R_5) = \$30,000,000; \sigma R_5 = \$5,477$

For years 3, 4, and 5, these values are computed as
shown in Exhibit 5.19.

How to I compute variance and standard deviation of net present value?

The formula for the calculation of the variance of the net
present value, var(NPV) of an investment project with independent probable cash flows for any number of future years,
would be as follows:

$$\text{var(NPV)} = \left(\frac{\text{var}[R_1]}{[1+i]^2} + \frac{\text{var}[R_2]}{[1+i]^4} + \ldots \right.$$
$$\left. + \frac{\text{var}[R_n]}{[1+i]2n} \right) - \text{CI}$$

$$\text{var(NPV)} = \sum_{n=1}^{N} \frac{\text{var}(R_n)}{(1+i)2n}$$

where

$$\text{var}(R_n, R_n + 1) = 0 \text{ for } n = 1, 2, \ldots, N$$

The formula for the calculation of the standard deviation of the net present value would be as follows:

$$\delta_{\text{NPV}} = \sqrt{\sum_{n=1}^{N} \frac{\text{var}(R_n)}{(1+i)^{2n}}}$$

where the $\text{cov}(R_n, R_{n+1}) = 0$ for $n = 1, 2, \ldots, N$

EXAMPLE 5.19

Use the data from Project F for this example. The calculation of the var(NPV) and the δ(NPV) is shown in Exhibit 5.20.

EXHIBIT 5.20: CALCULATION OF THE VAR(NPV) AND σ_{NPV} OF INVESTMENT PROJECT F

n	$\text{var}(R_n)$	$\dfrac{1}{(1+i)^{2n}}$	$\text{var}(R_n) \cdot \left[\dfrac{1}{(1+i)^{2n}} \right]$
1	\$ 1,200,000	.797194	\$ 956,633
2	4,800,000	.635518	3,050,486
3	10,800,000	.506631	5,471,615
4	19,200,000	.403883	7,754,554
5	30,000,000	.321973	9,659,190
			\$26,892,478

var(NPV) = \$26,892,478
σ_{NPV} = \$5,186

What is relative risk and how is it measured?

Relative risk, also called the coefficient of variation (CV), is defined as the ratio of the standard variation of the net present value to the net present value of the investment. The formula is stated as follows:

$$\text{CV}_{\text{NPV}} = \frac{\delta_{\text{NPV}}}{E(\text{NPV})}$$

EXAMPLE 5.20

For Projects D, E, and F from the previous examples, see the calculations of CV as follows:

Investment Project	σ_{NPV}	$E(NPV)$	CV_{NPV}
D	978	$ 929	1.05
E	2,002	4,073	0.49
F	5,186	31,090	0.17

CONCLUSIONS: Project F has the lowest level of risk compared with the others. Notice that as the level of absolute risk (as measured by δ_{NPV}) rises, the level of return (as measured by $E([NPV])$) rises even more. THE RESULT: Relative risk falls.

What is the trade-off between risk and return?

Typically you want to minimize the risk to which your investments are exposed. In order to consider bearing a greater risk, you would require a higher return. The desired trade-off between risk and return is shown in Figure 5.2. This graph, called an indifference curve, assumes the return will have to be increased at an increasing rate as the level of risk rises. Because the curve shows only the level of return required to compensate for the burden of additional risk, the investor is indifferent among the investments found on the curve. The curve also shows the minimal level of return desired by an investor even when risk is absent (zero level of risk).

What are the limitations of capital budgeting techniques?

Now that you have reviewed the techniques of capital budgeting, you should be aware of their limitations. First, such techniques require that certain types of data be forecast, and this holds special perils that must not be neglected.

The net present value method basically assumes you can forecast future cash flows with some degree of usefulness. It also assumes the incremental cost of capital will be constant over the future forecast periods. In order to use this method, you must know or be able to reasonably forecast the cost of the investment project. When uncertain, and this is the usual state of affairs, you must be able to forecast not only the amount and timing of future cash flows but also the probabilities of their occurrence.

Capital budgeting techniques also require evaluation of

not only the returns expected to be generated by the investment projects but also an evaluation of the risk perceived to be associated with the returns. The calculation of standard deviation of the NPV is itself dependent on the calculation of the NPV.

FIGURE 5.2: THE DESIRED TRADE-OFF BETWEEN RISK AND RETURN

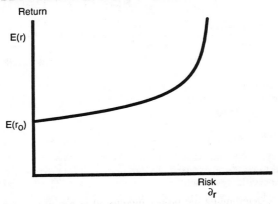

$E(r)$ = the expected value of return (normally measured in percent)

σr = the standard deviation of return

$E(r_0)$ = the expected value of return on an investment that an investor desires in the absence of risk

6

Assets Management and Financing Techniques

In this chapter you will learn how to manage your company's assets and liabilities in order to generate the highest return at the lowest possible risk. Whether you are a financial manager, managerial accountant, or investment analyst, you should be concerned with

- Determining the proper mixture of assets in the total asset structure
- Receiving cash promptly while delaying its payment
- Selling to the right customers
- Formulating a sound investment strategy

This chapter also helps you develop techniques for obtaining financing. If you're a financial manager, you'll learn how to go about raising funds on a short-, intermediate-, and long-term basis. Or, if you're a management executive, the following factors will be very much your concern:

- The cost of capital for examining financing alternatives
- The appropriateness of your company's dividend policy
- The effects of inflation
- The effects of the business cycle

ECONOMISTS AND FINANCIAL MANAGERS: You'll learn how to use economic indicators of performance for purposes of evaluating your own company's financial health. All these techniques will help you cope with situations as they arise every day.

6.1 MANAGING WORKING CAPITAL

What is working capital?

Working capital equals current assets less current liabilities. It is a measure of liquidity. CAUTION TO FINANCIAL MANAGERS: A higher balance in total current assets means greater ability to meet your debt. But it also means less return earned on total assets. Remember: Fixed assets generate a higher rate of return than current assets.

What is the risk-return trade-off in current versus fixed assets?

Fixed assets comprise the basic structure of a business, representing plant and manufacturing equipment. Assuming a viable business, you would expect a higher return on machinery than marketable securities which, in fact, usually come to less than the overall cost of capital. You can see a risk-return trade-off here, since current assets represent less risk but lower return. Similarly, financing with current liabilities rather than long-term debt typically involves lower cost but greater liquidity risk. The greater the debt maturity, the more uncertainty and hence generally the greater the cost.

What approach should I use for financing assets?

FOR MANAGEMENT EXECUTIVES: It's probably best to use a hedging approach whereby assets are financed by liabilities of similar maturity. This will ensure that adequate funds are available to meet the debt when due.

6.2 MAXIMIZING YOUR RETURN ON CASH

What is necessary for good cash management?

If you're a financial manager or management executive, cash management is important to you. If you are holding on to cash unnecessarily, you are losing a return that could be earned by investing. The cash balance held should depend on forecasted cash flows, probability of running out of cash, maturity of debt, and ability to borrow. You'll need forecasting information to determine (1) the best time to incur and pay back debt and (2) the amount to transfer daily between accounts. Use such techniques as accounting budgets, zero base budgeting (see Section 3.6) and quantitative models like time series and probabilities (see Section 7.3).

MANAGEMENT EXECUTIVES USE THIS RULE: Required cash balance equals transaction balances (required for normal business activity) plus precautionary balances (needed for emergencies) plus compensating balances (needed for financing commitments).

How can I accelerate cash receipts?

Use the following techniques.

CHECKLIST OF WAYS
TO ACCELERATE CASH RECEIPTS

- Lockbox. This is a location where customer payments are mailed, usually a strategic post office box. Payments are then picked up several times during the day by the bank.
- Concentration banking. Funds are collected in local banks and transferred to a main concentration account.
- Immediate transfer of funds between banks. Transfers would be accomplished through depository transfer checks or via wire.
- Cash discounts for early payment.
- Accelerated billing practices.
- Personal collection efforts.
- Cash-on-delivery.
- Postdated customer checks.
- Depositing checks promptly.
- Obtaining cash tied up unnecessarily in other accounts (for example, loans to company of ficers).

WHAT TO DO: Compare the return earned from the newly acquired cash to the cost of implementing an accelerated cash management system. Lockbox services are primarily good for collecting large dollar, low-volume receipts. Because of its high per-item cost, a lockbox does not always provide net savings.

EXAMPLE 6.1

Akel Corporation is considering a lockbox arrangement costing $350,000 per year. Daily collections average $1,000,000. Mailing and processing time will be reduced by four days with the arrangement. The rate of return is 10%. The cost-benefit analysis is shown as follows:

Annual return on freed cash	
10% × 4 × $1,000,000	$400,000
Annual cost	350,000
Savings	**$ 50,000**

CONCLUSION: The lockbox arrangement is profitable.

EXAMPLE 6.2

Loft Corporation presently has a lockbox with Colt Bank. The bank handles $1.5 million per day for $300,000 compensating balance. Loft is considering canceling this arrangement and instead dividing its western region through arrangements with two other banks. Most Bank will handle $1 million a day, with a compensating balance of $225,000, and Davis Bank will handle $500,000 a day, with a compensating balance of $200,000. In both instances, collections will improve by one half-day. The rate of return is 11%. A cost-benefit analysis shows the following:

Accelerated cash receipts of $1.5 million per day × 1/2 day	$750,000
Increased compensating balance	125,000
Increased cash flow	$625,000
Return rate	× 11%
Net annual savings	**$ 68,750**

CONCLUSION: The new arrangement is financially feasible.

How can I delay cash payments?

Try these techniques:

CHECKLIST OF WAYS
TO DELAY CASH PAYMENTS

- Centralize the payable operation. This enables you to meet obligations at the most profitable time. It also enhances your ability to predict disbursement float in the system.
- Use drafts. A draft is given to the bank for collection, which in turn goes to the issuer for acceptance. After that, the funds are deposited to pay the draft.
- Use a computer terminal to transfer funds between various bank accounts at opportune times.
- Draw checks on remote banks, for example, a New York company could use a California bank.
- Mail checks from post offices with limited services or where mail must go through several handling points.
- Use probability analysis to determine the expected time for checks to clear. For example, funds deposited on payday may not equal the entire payroll since not all checks will be cashed on that day.
- Make partial payments.

SUGGESTION FOR MANAGEMENT EXECUTIVES: Consider "payment float," that is, the difference between the checkbook balance and the bank balance. When float is used effectively, a company can hold a higher bank balance even though a lower cash balance appears on the books.

EXAMPLE 6.3

Company X writes checks averaging $50,000 per day; each check takes three days to clear. The company will have a checkbook balance $150,000 less than the bank's records.

How much cash do I need on hand?

You can predict the optimum amount of transaction cash needed under conditions of certainty. First, compute the sum of the fixed cost applicable to transactions and the opportunity cost of holding cash balances as follows:

$$\frac{F(T)}{C} + \frac{i(C)}{2}$$

where

C = given cash balance
F = fixed cost of transaction
T = total cash required for time period
i = interest rate on marketable securities

The following formula was developed by W. Baumol to compute the optimal cash level (K):

$$K = \sqrt{\frac{2FT}{i}}$$

Average cash balance equals

$$\frac{K}{2}$$

and the number of required transactions equals

$$\frac{\text{transaction cash}}{K}$$

EXAMPLE 6.4

Company B expects a cash need of $4,000,000 over a one-month period, to be paid out at a constant rate. The opportunity interest rate is 0.5% for one month. The cost for each transaction is $100. The optimal transaction size is computed as follows:

$$K = \sqrt{\frac{2FT}{i}} = \sqrt{\frac{2\,(100)(4,000,000)}{0.005}} = \$400,000$$

The average cash balance equals:

$$\frac{K}{2} = \frac{\$400,000}{2} = \$200,000$$

The number of transactions required equals:

$$\frac{\$400,000}{400,000} = 10$$

SUGGESTION FOR FINANCIAL MANAGERS: You can use a stochastic model for cash management when major uncertainty regarding cash payments exists. The Miller-Orr model places an upper ceiling (referred to as d dollars) and lower limit ("zero" dollars) for cash balances. When the upper limit is reached, a transfer takes place from securities to cash. The transaction will not occur as long as the cash balance falls within the limits of the model.

You should take the following factors into account when using the Miller-Orr model:

- Fixed costs of a securities transaction (F)
- The daily interest rate on marketable securities (i)
- The deviation in daily net cash flows (σ^2)

Your objective is to meet cash requirements at the lowest possible cost. When the cash balance reaches d, this amount less the cost of securities bought (z) reduces the balance to z dollars. When the cash balance equals zero, z dollars are sold and the new balance again reaches z. NOTE TO MANAGEMENT EXECUTIVES: The minimum cash balance is established at an amount greater than zero to act as a safety buffer as, for example, delays in transfer.

Use these formulas for optimal and average cash balance:

Optimal cash balance $(z) = \sqrt[3]{\dfrac{3F\sigma^2}{4i}}$

Optimal upper limit $(d) = 3z$

Average cash balance $= \dfrac{(z + d)}{3}$

EXAMPLE 6.5

Company J wishes to use the Miller-Orr model. The following data are given:

Fixed cost of a securities transaction	$10
Deviation in daily net cash flows	$50
Daily interest rate on securities (10%/360)	0.0003

The optimal cash balance, the upper limit of cash needed, and the average cash balance are computed as follows:

$$z = \sqrt[3]{\frac{3(10)(50)}{4(0.0003)}} = \sqrt[3]{\frac{3(10)(50)}{0.0012}} = \sqrt[3]{\frac{1500}{0.0012}}$$

$$= \sqrt[3]{1,250,000} = \$102$$

The optimal cash balance (z) = \$102

The upper limit (d) = $3 \times \$102 = \$306$

The average cash balance = $\dfrac{\$102 + \$106}{3} = \$136$

DISCUSSION: When the upper limit (\$306) is reached, \$204 of securities (\$306 – \$102) will be purchased, thereby obtaining the optimal cash balance of \$102. When the lower limit of \$0 dollars is reached, \$102 of securities will be sold, again bringing the optimal cash balance to \$102.

6.3 MANAGING ACCOUNTS RECEIVABLE

What can I do to manage receivables properly?

Whether you're a financial manager, managerial accountant, or management executive, you'll want to manage receivables in order to maximize return and minimize risk. Here are some of the many things you can do:

CHECKLIST OF APPROACHES TO THE MANAGEMENT OF ACCOUNTS RECEIVABLE

- Age accounts receivable for overdue balances and compare them to industry and competitive norms as well as your own prior years.
- Periodically revise credit limits based on your customers' changing financial health.
- When there might be a problem with collection, obtain collateral at least equal in amount to the account balance.
- Use collection agencies when warranted.
- Factor (sell) accounts receivable when net savings occur.
- Bill large sales immediately.
- Employ cycle billing for uniformity in the billing process.
- Mail customer statements within one day of the period end.
- Offer delayed payment terms to stimulate demand.
- Carefully evaluate customers' financial health before giving credit.

- Obtain credit insurance to guard against abnormal losses from bad debt.
- Avoid typically high-risk receivables, for example, customers in a financially troubled industry or country.

Should I consider cash discounts?

MANAGEMENT EXECUTIVES: You must decide whether cash discounts should be given for early payment. WHAT TO DO: Implement discount policy provided the return on funds obtained from early collection is greater than the cost of the discount.

EXAMPLE 6.6

Blake Company provides the following data:

Current annual credit sales	$8,000,000
Collection period	2 months
Terms	net/30
Minimum rate of return	15%

The financial manager is considering whether to offer a 2/10, net/30 discount. He anticipates that 25% of the customers will take advantage of it. The collection period should decline to 1.5 months.

The advantage of the policy is shown as follows:

Return

Average accounts receivable balance prior to change in policy:

$$\frac{\text{credit sales}}{\text{accounts receivable turnover}} = \frac{\$8,000,000}{6}$$

$1,333,333

Average accounts receivable balance subsequent to change in policy:

$$\frac{\$8,000,000}{8}$$

1,000,000

Decrease in average accounts receivable	$ 333,333
Rate of return	× 15%
Return	$ 50,000

Discount

Cost of discount 0.02 × 0.25 × $8,000,000	$ 40,000
Net advantage of discount policy	$ 10,000

When should I give credit to marginal customers?

MANAGEMENT EXECUTIVES: You are often faced with a decision of whether to give credit to somewhat marginal customers. WHAT TO DO: Give credit when the profitability of the additional sales is greater than the additional cost associated with the discount. When idle capacity exists, this additional profitability equals the contribution margin (sales minus variable cost). But, remember to add these costs, too: higher bad debts, opportunity cost of putting funds in receivables for a longer period of time, and increased clerical costs for servicing an additional customer base.

EXAMPLE 6.7

Long Corporation provides the following data:

Selling price per unit	$5
Variable cost per unit	$2
Fixed cost per unit	$2
Annual credit sales	600,000 units
Collection period	1 month
Minimum return	24%

The financial manager is considering a proposal to liberalize credit. He expects sales to increase by 20%. The collection period on total accounts will be two months. Bad debts will increase by $90,000.

The following calculations show that the policy should be implemented:

Additional profit on increased sales

Additional units (600,000 × 20%)		120,000
Contribution margin per unit		
Selling price	$5	
Less variable cost	$2	× $3
Additional profitability		$360,000

Bad debts

Higher bad debts	$90,000

Opportunity cost of increased balance in accounts receivable

Current average investment in accounts receivable:

Average accounts receivable

$$\frac{\text{credit sales}}{\text{accounts receivable turnover}} \times \frac{\text{cost}}{\text{selling price}}$$

$$\times \frac{\text{cost}}{\text{selling price}}$$

$$\frac{\$3,000,000^a}{12} \times \frac{\$4}{\$5} \qquad \underline{\$200,000}$$

Average investment in accounts receivable after change in credit policy:

$$\frac{\$3,600,000^b}{6} \times \frac{\$3.67^c}{\$5} \qquad \$440,000$$

Increased average investment in accounts receivable	$240,400
Minimum rate	× 0.24
Opportunity cost	$ 57,696

Net advantage to policy

Additional profitability		$360,000
Additional cost		
Bad debts	$90,000	
Opportunity cost	57,696	(147,696)
Savings		**$212,304**

Calculations

a) $5 × 600,000 units = $3,000,000
b) $3,000,000 + 0.20 ($3,000,000) = $3,600,000
c) New average unit cost:

	Units	×	*Unit Cost*	=	*Total Cost*
Current volume	600,000		$4		$2,400,000
Additional volume	120,000		2		240,000
After proposal	720,000				$2,640,000

New average unit cost = $2,640,000/720,000 units = $3.67

The new average unit cost went down from $4 to $3.67 because the fixed cost is spread over more units.

How much credit should I give?

MANAGEMENT EXECUTIVES: Sometimes you must decide whether to give full credit to presently limited- or no-credit customers. REMEMBER THIS: Use full credit only when it will lead to a net profit.

EXAMPLE 6.8

Company D classifies its customers by risk ratings:

Category	Uncollectible Account (%)	Collection Period	Credit Policy	Increase in Annual Sales if Credit Restrictions Are Relaxed
A	1	20 days	Unlimited	$ 50,000
B	4	40	Restricted	500,000
C	18	70	No credit	700,000

Gross profit averages 20% of sales. The minimum rate of return is 14%. Of course, Category A receives unlimited credit. However, full credit should be extended only to Category B, and not Category C, as indicated in the following table.

	Category B	Category C
Gross profit		
$500,000 \times 0.2$	$100,000	
$700,000 \times 0.2$		$140,000
Less bad debts addition		
$500,000 \times 0.04$	(20,000)	
$700,000 \times 0.18$		(126,000)
Incremental average investment in accounts receivable		
$\frac{40}{360} \times (80\% \times 500,000)$	$44,444	
$\frac{70}{360} \times (80\% \times 700,000)$		$108,889
Opportunity cost	$\times .14$ (6,222)	$\times 0.14$ (15,244)
Net earnings	**$73,778**	**($1,244)**

6.4 FORMULATING THE BEST INVESTMENT STRATEGY

What factors should I consider when selecting an investment portfolio?

When you are selecting an investment portfolio, look at these factors:

- Financial
- Risk versus return
- Tax implications

A company's present financial picture governs the magnitude and type of risk you can undertake. For example, if liquidity is strong, you might choose long-term securities. Or, if you want to maintain needed liquidity, short-term bills (e.g., market certificates, treasury bills) might be better. REMEMBER THIS: With greater liquidity there is less return, because short-term securities yield less.

What are the various types of investments?

CHECKLIST OF INVESTMENT TYPES

- Direct *equity* claims
    - Common stock
    - Options
    - Warrants
- Indirect *equity* claims
    - Mutual funds
- *Creditor* claims
    - Savings accounts
    - Money market certificates
    - Money market funds
    - Treasury securities
    - Commercial paper
    - Bonds
- Preferred stock

How should I manage the investment portfolio?

FINANCIAL MANAGERS: Stagger the maturity dates of the securities. For example, if all the securities mature on a single date, your reinvestment may be subject to low returns if interest rates are low at that time. MANAGEMENT EXECUTIVES: Examine the risk. Look at the degree of diversification and stability of the portfolio. INVESTMENT ANALYSTS: Consider securities with negative correlations to each other. BE ON GUARD: Declines in portfolio market values may not be entirely reflected in the accounts. Use the ratio of revenue (dividend income, interest income, etc.) to the carrying value as a clue. Also, examine the footnotes for subsequent event disclosure regarding any unrealized losses that have taken place in the portfolio. FINANCIAL MANAGERS: You may want to adjust downward the extent to which an investment account can be realized in the case of such declines. You should also appraise the riskiness of the portfolio by computing the standard deviation of its rate of return.

EXAMPLE 6.9

Winston Company reports the following data for year-ends 19X1 and 19X2:

	19X1	*19X2*
Investments	$30,000	$33,000
Income from investments (dividends and interest)	4,000	3,200

The 19X2 annual report has a footnote titled "Subsequent Events," which indicates a $5,000 decline in the portfolio as of March 2, 19X3. The ratio of investment income to total investments went from 0.133 in 19X1 to 0.097 in 19X2, indicating a higher realization risk in the portfolio. Additionally, the post balance sheet disclosure of a $5,000 decline in value should prompt you to adjust downward the amount to which the year-end portfolio can be realized.

What kinds of risks are involved in investing?

CHECKLIST OF INVESTING RISKS

- *Business risk.* This relates to factors such as financial condition and product demand.
- *Liquidity risk.* This applies to the possibility that an investment may not be sold on short notice for its market value. A security sold at a high discount may have high liquidity risk.
- *Default risk.* This refers to the borrower's inability to make interest payments or principal repayments on debt. A bond issued by a company with significant financial problems might be a default risk.
- *Market risk.* This relates to changes in the stock price caused by changes in the market itself.
- *Purchasing power risk.* This applies to the likelihood of decreased purchasing power. Bonds are a good example of this because the issuer pays back in cheaper dollars.

- *Interest rate risk.* This refers to the variability in the value of an investment as interest rates, money market, or capital market conditions change. This factor applies to fixed-income securities such as bonds. As interest rates increase, bond prices decrease.
- *Concentration risk.* This reflects a lack of diversification in the portfolio.

What should I know about taxes?

FINANCIAL MANAGERS: When formulating an optimal investment strategy, tax aspects must be considered. For example, interest income on bonds is fully taxable, whereas dividend income has an 85 percent tax exclusion (only 15 percent of dividends are subject to tax). When securities held for more than six months are sold at a gain only 40 percent of the profit is taxable. Thus, you have an advantage in holding appreciated securities for longer than six months. REMEMBER THIS: Income from U.S. government securities are taxable for federal purposes but are exempt from local taxes. Income from municipals are exempt from both federal and local taxes.

What is a technical analysis?

A technical analysis looks at the direction and magnitude of the market in determining when or what to buy or sell. Technical analysts believe stock prices of individual companies tend to move with the market as they react to various supply and demand forces. Charts and graphs of internal market data, including prices and volume, are also helpful.

What are the key indicators of stock market performance?

A discussion of six major indicators of market performance follows.

Trading volume. This points to the health and trend of the market. Market volume of stocks depends on supply and demand relationships, which in turn point to market strength or weakness. For instance, you can expect higher prices when demand increases. An *upside-downside index* illustrates the difference between stock volume advancing and decreasing, typically based on a ten-day or thirty-day moving average. The index assists in identifying expected market turning points.

Market breadth. This relates to the dispersion of general price fluctuation and may be useful as an advance indicator of major price declines or advances. The *breadth index* involves computing daily the net advancing or declining issues of a broad range of securities from the New York

Stock Exchange. The index is determined by dividing net advances (number of securities with price increases less declines) by the number of securities traded. This index differs from a limited stock market average (like the Dow Jones Industrial Average of 30 Stocks) by virtue of the greater spread between the number advances and declines.

EXAMPLE 6.10

Assume net declines equal 40, securities traded equals 1,100, and the breadth index equals –3.6.

This figure can be related to a base year or combined in a 150-day moving average. The figures obtained are then related to the Dow Jones Industrial Average. When *both* indexes are increasing, this indicates market strength.

You can also determine the market breadth for individual securities by computing net volume (up-ticks less down-ticks).

EXAMPLE 6.11

Bette Corporation trades 90,000 shares for the day with 60,000 on the upside, 20,000 on the downside, and 10,000 at no change. The net volume difference at day's end is 40,000 traded on up-ticks.

FINANCIAL MANAGERS: Look for any sign of divergence between the price trend and net volume. If one occurs, you can anticipate a reversal in the price trend.

The Barron's Confidence index. This is useful when evaluating the trading patterns of bond investors and helps determine when to buy and sell. The index assumes bond traders are more knowledgeable than stock traders and that they identify trends more quickly. The index equals

$$\frac{\text{Yield on Barron's 10 top-grade corporate bonds}}{\text{Yield on Dow Jones 40 bond average}}$$

The numerator reflects a lower yield than the denominator because it uses higher-quality bonds. For example, if the Dow Jones yield is 14 percent and the Barron's yield is 11.5 percent, the confidence index is 0.821. RULE OF THUMB: When bond investors are bullish, yield differences between high-grade and low-grade bonds will be small.

Odd-lot trading. This refers to transactions of 100 shares or less and is used as a reflection of popular opinion. THE RULE OF CONTRARY OPINION: The investment analyst determines what small traders are doing and then does the opposite. An *odd-lot index* consists of the ratio of odd-lot purchases to odd-lot sales.

Charts. These are used to appraise market conditions and price behavior of individual securities. By looking at past trends, you can possibly predict the future.

Relative strength analysis. This relates to predicting individual stock prices and consists of computing a ratio of monthly average stock prices to a monthly average "market index" or "industry group index." Or, you can compute the ratios of specific industry group indexes to the total market index. OBSERVATION: If a stock or industry group outperforms the market, you may view this as a positive sign.

6.5 HOW TO BEST FINANCE YOUR BUSINESS

What financing alternatives are available?

As a financial manager or executive, you should be familiar with three alternative sources of financing: short-term (less than one year), intermediate-term (one to five years), and long-term (longer than five years). To plan the best financing strategy, evaluate the risks and costs applicable to each alternative. Consider these factors:

- Your company's financial position (cash flow, debt position, etc.)
- Cost of alternative funding sources
- Availability of future financing
- Risk
- Inflation rate
- Expected money market trends
- Tax rate
- Stability of operations
- Overall management objectives

What type of financing should I select?

Here are some sources of short- and intermediate-term financing:

Trade credit. Trade credit is easy to get, has no or minimal cost, and requires no collateral. Creditors tend to be more lenient when payment problems occur, too.

Bank. To obtain a bank loan, you must have a good financial position with sufficient stockholders' equity. Loans may be secured (collateralized) or unsecured. In a secured loan, you have to pledge an asset to back the security. Or you can obtain a line of credit that promises loans up to a maximum amount.

Finance company. If a bank loan is unavailable, a

finance company may be necessary. There will be a higher interest rate and required collateral.

Commercial paper. This is a short-term, unsecured note issued by the highest-quality companies. Their interest rate is less than the prime rate charged by banks.

Receivable financing. Accounts receivable may be sold outright (factored) or assigned to a bank or finance company in return for immediate cash. There's a high financing cost involved here.

Inventory financing. This typically occurs when receivable financing has been used up. Inventory must be marketable.

Leasing. By leasing property, only a minor cash outlay may be required. Usually, a purchase option accompanies the agreement.

Here are some sources of long-term financing:

Mortgages. These are notes payable to banks that are secured by real property. Mortgages have favorable interest rates, fewer financing restrictions, long payment schedules, and ready availability.

Bonds. These are long-term debt issued to the public. Bonds offer some advantages over stocks. For instance, interest from bonds are tax deductible, whereas stock dividends are not; the payback is in cheaper dollars because of inflation; and equity interests (i.e., voting rights) remain intact. Also, call provisions enable you to buy back the bonds before maturity. On the other hand, you must accept certain risks, including the inability to meet debt payments as well as indenture restrictions. Indenture refers to the agreement between the bond issuer and the bond investor.

Equity securities (preferred and common stock). Common stock refers to residual equity ownership in the business. Common stockholders have voting power but come after preferred stockholders in receiving dividends and in liquidation. Equity securities do not involve fixed charges, maturity dates, or sinking fund requirements. You need not pay dividends during periods of financial distress. However, dividend payments are not tax deductible and therefore will incur higher costs to the company. And since they also hold greatest risk to common stockholders, the cost of funds will be greater. Common stocks dilute ownership and voting rights as well.

What is the cost of raising funds?

VITAL FOR FINANCIAL MANAGERS: The cost of capital is calculated from a weighted average of debt and equity security costs. Compare these averages under various alternative financing strategies. Your input will bear heavily when deciding the best source of financing in a given situation. REMEMBER THIS: The alternative with the least overall cost of capital is best.

What is the cost of short-term debt?

The cost of short-term debt applies to the interest rate on bank or finance company loans. Remember this: Interest is a tax-deductible expense.

$$\text{Cost of short-term debt} = \frac{\text{Interest}}{\text{Proceeds received}}$$

If a bank discounts a loan, interest is deducted from the face of the loan to get the proceeds. When a compensating balance is required (that is, a percent of the face loan is held by the bank as collateral), proceeds are also reduced. In either case, the effective or real interest rate on the loan is higher than the face interest rate owing to the proceeds received from the loan being less than the amount (face) of the loan.

EXAMPLE 6.12

Company A takes a $150,000, one-year, 13% loan. The loan is discounted, and a 10% compensating balance is required. The effective interest rate is computed as follows:

$$\frac{13\% \times \$150,000}{\$115,500^a} = \frac{\$19,500}{\$115,500} = 16.89\%$$

ᵃProceeds received =

Face of loan	$150,000
Less interest	(19,500)
Compensating balance (10% × $150,000)	(15,000)
Proceeds	**$115,500**

Notice how the effective cost of the loan is significantly greater than the stated interest rate.

What is the cost of long-term debt?

The real cost of bonds is obtained by computing two types of yield: simple (face) yield and yield to maturity (effective interest rate). The first involves an easy approximation, but the second is much more accurate.

WHAT YOU SHOULD KNOW: The nominal interest rate equals the interest paid on the face (maturity value) of the bond and is always stated on a per-annum basis. Bonds are always issued in $1,000 denominations and may be sold above face value (at a premium) or below (at a discount). A bond is sold at a discount when the interest rate is below the going market rate. In this case, the yield will be higher than the nominal interest rate. The opposite holds for bonds issued at a premium.

$$\text{Simple yield} = \frac{\text{nominal interest}}{\text{present value of bond}}$$

$$\text{Yield to maturity} = \frac{\text{nominal interest} + \frac{\text{discount}}{\text{years}}\left(\frac{\text{or-premium}}{\text{years}}\right)}{\frac{\text{present value} + \text{maturity value}}{2}}$$

EXAMPLE 6.13

Prentice Corporation issues a \$400,000, 12%, 10-year bond for 97% of face value. Yield computations follow:

$$\text{Nominal annual payment} = 12\% \times \$400{,}000 = \$48{,}000$$

$$\text{Bond proceeds} = 97\% \times \$400{,}000 = \$388{,}000$$

$$\text{Bond discount} = 3\% \times \$400{,}000 = \$12{,}000 \text{ or } \$400{,}000 - \$388{,}000 = \$12{,}000$$

Simple yield =

$$\frac{12\%. \times \$400{,}000}{97\% \times \$400{,}000} = \frac{\$48{,}000}{\$388{,}000} = 12.4\%$$

$$\text{Yield to maturity} = \frac{\$48{,}000 + \frac{\$12{,}000}{10}}{\frac{\$388{,}000 + \$400{,}000}{2}} = \frac{\$48{,}000 + \$1{,}200}{\$369{,}000} = \frac{449{,}200}{\$394{,}000} = 12.5\%$$

NOTE: Because the bonds were sold at a discount, the yield exceeds the nominal interest rate (12%).

What is the cost of equity securities?

The cost of equity securities comes in the form of dividends, which are not tax deductible.

The cost of common stock

$$= \frac{\text{dividends per share for current year}}{\text{net proceeds per share}} + \text{growth rate in dividends}$$

where
    net proceeds per share = market price per share − flotation costs (that is, cost of issuing securities, such as brokerage fees and, printing costs). The cost of preferred stock is stated in the dividend rate. If this is not given, the cost of preferred stock would be computed as for common stock.

EXAMPLE 6.14

ABC Company's dividend per share is $10, net proceeds per share are $70, and the dividend growth rate is 5%.

$$\text{The cost of the stock} = \frac{\$10}{\$70} + 0.05 = 19.3\%$$

How do I compute the weighted average cost of capital?

When computing the weighted average cost of capital, consider the percent of the total and after-tax cost of each financing alternative.

EXAMPLE 6.15

Bloated Company provides the following from its financial statements:

Bonds payable (16%)	$ 4 million
Preferred stock (dividend rate = 13%)	1 million
Common stock	5 million
Total	**$10 million**

Dividends per share on common stock are $11; net proceeds per share are $80; growth rate on dividends is 4%; and tax rate is 40%.

The weighted average cost of capital is computed as follows:

	Percent	After-Tax Cost	Weighted Average Cost
Bonds payable	0.40	0.096[a]	0.038
Preferred stock	0.10	0.130	0.013
Common stock	0.50	0.178[b]	0.089
	1.00		0.140

[a]Cost of bonds payable: 16% × 60% = 0.096

$$^{[b]}\text{Cost of bonds payable} = \frac{\text{dividends per share}}{\text{net proceeds per share}} + \text{growth rate in dividends}$$

$$\frac{\$11}{\$80} + 004 = 0.178$$

What is the cost of not taking a discount on accounts payable?

If you do not take a discount on accounts payable by pay-ing earlier, you have lost an opportunity cost or the return foregone from an alternative use of funds or time. TAKE NOTICE: Financial managers who do not take the discount typically show a lack of financial astuteness. Why? The cost of paying is usually higher than the cost of borrowing money.

You can compute the opportunity cost with this formula:

$$\frac{\text{discount foregone}}{\text{use of proceeds}} \times \frac{360}{\text{days use of money}}$$

EXAMPLE 6.16

XYZ Company purchases $500,000 of merchandise on credit terms of 2/10, net/30. The company does not pay within 10 days and thus loses the discount.

$$\begin{aligned}
\text{Opportunity cost} &= \frac{0.02 \times \$500,000}{0.98 \times \$500,000} \times \frac{360}{20} \\
&= \frac{\$10,000}{\$490,000} \times 180 = 36.7\%
\end{aligned}$$

Surely management would have been better off to take advantage of the discount by borrowing $490,000 at the prime interest rate.

How do I evaluate a dividend policy?

FOR FINANCIAL MANAGERS: A dividend policy must be attractive to the investing public by satisfying cur-rent stockholders and prompting new investment. Psychologically, investors like to receive stable dividends. If you cut dividends, stockholders may become worried and sell. The result: Your stock price declines.

On the other hand, from a purely financial perspective, earnings should be retained by the business rather than dis-tributed to stockholders. Why? First, the company typically earns a greater return than the individual stockholder does, and this will result in appreciation in the market price of the stock. Second, there is a tax advantage to the investor. When stock held for more than six months is sold, only 40 percent of the gain is taxable. On the other hand, dividends will only provide a $100 exclusion to the investor.

MANAGEMENT EXECUTIVES: If financial problems exist within your company, the distribution will seriously impair the company's health. By distributing earnings, you'll have to refinance, and cost of capital will be very high. YOUR DILEMMA: It's generally best to retain funds rather than distribute them in the form of dividends to the company or individual investor. But, since stockholders are basically unsophisticated in financial analysis, they will demand dividends.

WHAT TO DO: To satisfy stockholders while retaining as much as possible, you have two options. You can establish a *minimum* dividend base and give a bonus dividend during very good times, or you can create the impression of a growth company that typically retains earnings for expansion purposes.

FINANCIAL MANAGERS: Look at the trends in these dividend-related ratios:

$$\text{Dividend payout} = \frac{\text{dividends per share}}{\text{earnings per share}}$$

$$\text{Dividend yield} = \frac{\text{dividends per share}}{\text{market price per share}}$$

Investors generally favor increasing trends.

How does the business cycle affect a company?

One company or industry cannot control fundamental economic conditions. To the extent that you can insulate yourself from the effects of a broader economy, your corporate stability will be greater. HINT: Look for stability in operations because it enhances predictability and planning.

Companies having product lines with inelastic demand (such as food and medicine) are affected less by the business cycle. Companies with product lines or services correlated positively to changes in real gross national product (such as the airlines) have greater earnings instability.

PART III

QUANTITATIVE METHODS AND COMPUTER APPLICATIONS

7

Decision Making
with Statistics
and Forecasting

As a decision maker, you'll find yourself in many situations in which large volumes of data need to be analyzed. These data could be sales figures, income, or a multitude of other possibilities. And they could be used for a variety of purposes, including risk analysis, figuring return on investments, or other financial decisions. Effective use of statistics and forecasting techniques will prove necessary as your company grows.

7.1 HOW TO USE BASIC STATISTICS

The most commonly used statistics that describe characteristics of data are the mean and the standard deviation.

What is a mean and how is it used?

The mean gives an average (or central) value of your data. Three such means are common. They are

- Arithmetic mean
- Weighted mean
- Geometric mean

What is an arithmetic mean?

The arithmetic mean is a simple average. To find it, sum the values of your data and divide by the number of data entries or observations:

$$\bar{x} = \frac{\sum x}{n}$$

where
$\bar{x}$ = the arithmetic mean (called x-bar)
x = the data values
n = number of observations

EXAMPLE 7.1

John Jay Lamp Company has a revolving credit agreement with a local bank. Last year, the loan showed the following month-end balances:

January	$18,500
February	21,000
March	17,600
April	23,200
May	18,600
June	24,500
July	60,000
August	40,000
September	25,850
October	33,100
November	41,000
December	28,400

The mean monthly balance is computed as follows;

$$\bar{x} = \frac{\begin{array}{l} \$18,500 + \$21,000 + \$17,600 + \$23,200 \\ + \$18,600 + \$24,500 + \$60,000 + \$40,000 \\ + \$25,850 + \$33,100 + \$41,000 + \$28,400 \end{array}}{12}$$

$$= \frac{\$351,750}{12} = \$29,312.50$$

What is a weighted mean?

When your observations have different degrees of importance or frequency, a weighted mean enables you to account for this. The formula for a weighted mean is

Weighted mean = $\Sigma(w)(x)$

where
w = weight assigned to each observation, expressed as a percentage or relative frequency

EXAMPLE 7.2

Company J uses three grades of labor to produce a finished product as follows:

Grade of Labor	Labor Hours per Unit of Labor	Hourly Wages (x)
Skilled	6	$10.00
Semiskilled	3	8.00
Unskilled	1	6.00

The arithmetic mean (average cost) of labor per hour for this product can be computed as follows:

$$\text{Arithmetic mean} = \frac{\$10.00 + \$8.00 + \$6.00}{3}$$
$$= \$8.00 \text{ per hour}$$

However, this implies that each grade of labor was used in equal amounts, and this is not the case. To calculate the average cost of labor per hour correctly, the weighted average should be computed as follows:

$$\text{Weighted mean} = \$10.00(6/10) + \$8.00(3/10)$$
$$+ \$6.00(1/10) = \$9.00 \text{ per hour}$$

NOTE: The weights equal the proportion of the total labor required to produce the product.

What is a geometric mean?

Sometimes quantities change over a period of time; for example, the rate of return on investment or rate of growth in earnings over a period of years In such cases, you need to know the geometric mean, which uses the average rate or percentage of change. Use this formula:

Geometric mean
$$= \sqrt[n]{(1 + x_1)(1 + x_2) + \ldots + (1 + x_n)} - 1$$

where
x = the rate of change (in percent)
n = number of periods

EXAMPLE 7.3

A stock doubles during one period and then depreciates back to the original price, as shown in the following table:

	Time Periods		
	$t = 0$	$t = 1$	$t = 2$
Price (end of period)	$80	$160	$80
Rate of return	—	100%	–50%

The rate of return for periods 1 and 2 are computed as follows:

Period 1 ($t = 1$) $= \dfrac{\$160 - \$80}{\$80} = \dfrac{\$80}{\$80} = \$100\%$

Period 2 ($t = 2$) $= \dfrac{\$80 - \$160}{\$160} = \dfrac{-\$80}{\$160} = -50\%$

The arithmetic mean return over the two periods equals the average of 100% and -50%, or 25%, as shown:

$$\bar{x} = \frac{100\% + (-50\%)}{2} = 25\%$$

Clearly, you can see that the stock purchased for $80 and sold for the same price two periods later does not return 25%, but zero. Here's proof:

$$\text{Geometric mean return} = \sqrt[2]{(1+1)(1+0.5)} - 1$$

$$= \sqrt[2]{(2)(0.5)} - 1$$

$$= \sqrt[2]{1} - 1 = 0\%$$

where
$n = 2$
$x_1 = 100\%$ or 1
$x_2 = -50\%$ or -0.5

What is standard deviation?

The standard deviation measures the extent to which data spread out or disperse. MANAGERS: You can make important inferences from past data with this statistic, for example, when measuring the risk of purchasing a financial asset. Standard deviation, denoted σ, is defined as follows:

$$\sigma = \sqrt{\frac{\sum(x - \bar{x})^2}{n - 1}}$$

where

$\bar{x}$ = the arithmetic mean

WHAT TO DO: Calculate the standard deviation using these five steps:

- Subtract the mean from each observation value
- Square each difference obtained in Step 1
- Sum all the squared differences
- Divide the sum of all the squared differences by the number of observations minus one
- Take the square root of the quotient

EXAMPLE 7.4

United Motors stock lists six consecutive quarterly returns as follows:

Time Period	x	$(x-\bar{x})$	$(x-\bar{x})^2$
1	10%	0	0
2	15	5	25
3	20	10	100
4	5	-5	25
5	-10	-20	400
6	<u>20</u>	10	<u>100</u>
	60		**700**

The mean return and standard deviation over this period are computed as follows:

$$\bar{x} = 60/6 = 10\%$$

$$6 = \sqrt{\frac{\Sigma(x+\bar{x})^2}{n-1}} = \sqrt{\frac{700}{6-1}} = \sqrt{140} = 11.83\%$$

CONCLUSION: United Motors stock has returned on average 10% over the last six periods, and the variability about its mean return is 11.83%. This high standard deviation relative to the average return indicates this stock is very risky.

2 USING FORECASTING TECHNIQUES

7.2.1 Moving Averages

How do I use moving averages?

With a moving average, simply take the most recent observations (*n*) to calculate an average. Then, use this as the forecast for the next period. Moving averages are updated continually as new data are received. NOTE: You can choose the number of periods to use on the basis of the relative importance you attach to old versus current data.

EXAMPLE 7.5

The marketing manager has the following sales data:

Date	Actual Sales (y_t) (in Thousands of Dollars)
Jan. 1	46
2	54
3	53
4	46
5	58
6	49
7	54

In order for the marketing manager to predict sales for the seventh and eighth days of January, he must pick the number of observations to be averaged. He used two possibilities, a six-day and a three-day period:

1. $y_7 = \dfrac{46 + 54 + 53 + 46 + 58 + 49}{6} = 51$

   $y_8 = \dfrac{54 + 53 + 46 + 58 + 49 + 54}{6} = 52.3$

2. $y_7 = \dfrac{46 + 58 + 49}{3} = 51$

   $y_8 = \dfrac{58 + 49 + 54}{3} = 53.6$

Date	Actual Sales (y_t)	PREDICTED SALES ($\hat{y}_t$) Case 1	Case 2
Jan. 1	46		
2	54		
3	53		
4	46		
5	58		
6	49		
7	54	51	51
8		52.3	53.6

In terms of the relative importance of new versus old data, in Case 1, the old data received a weight of $5/6$ and current data $1/6$. In Case 2, the old data received a weight of $2/3$, whereas current observation received $1/3$ weight.

7.2.2 Exponential Smoothing

What is the basis of exponential smoothing?

Exponential smoothing is a popular technique for short-run forecasting. It uses a weighted average of past data as the basis of the forecast. The procedure assumes the future is most dependent upon the recent past and thus gives heaviest weight to more recent data and smaller weights to those of the more distant past. WHEN TO USE IT: The method is most effective when there are random demand and no seasonal fluctuations. CAUTION: The method does not include industrial or economic factors such as market conditions, prices, or competitive actions.

What is the model?

Here is the formula for exponential smoothing:

$$\hat{y}_{t+1} = \alpha y_t + (1 - \alpha)\hat{y}_t$$

or

$$\hat{y}_{new} = \alpha y_{old} + (1 - \alpha)\hat{y}_{old}$$

where

$y_{new} = $ Exponentially smoothed average to be used as the forecast

$y_{old} = $ Most recent smoothed forecast

$\alpha = $ Smoothing constant

REMEMBER THIS: The higher the α, the greater the weight given to most recent data.

EXAMPLE 7.6

Company Y provides the following sales data:

Time Period (t)	Actual Sales (y_t) (in Thousands of Dollars)
1	$60.0
2	64.0
3	58.0
4	66.0
5	70.0
6	60.0
7	70.0

Time Period (t)	Actual Sales (y_t) (in Thousands of Dollars)
8	74.0
9	62.0
10	74.0
11	68.0
12	66.0
13	60.0
14	66.0
15	62.0

The manager decides to use a six-period average as the initial forecast $(\hat{y}_7)$ with a smoothing constant = 0.40.

$$\hat{y}_7 = \frac{60 + 64 + 58 + 66 + 70 + 60}{6} = 63$$

Note that $y_7 = 70$. Then $\hat{y}_8$ is computed as follows:

$$
\begin{aligned}
\hat{y}_8 &= \alpha y_7 + (1 - \alpha)\hat{y}_7 \\
&= (0.40)(70) + (0.60)(63) \\
&= 28.00 + 37.80 = 65.80
\end{aligned}
$$

Similarly,

$$
\begin{aligned}
\hat{y}_9 &= \alpha y_8 + (1 + \alpha)\,\hat{y}_8 \\
&= (0.40)(74) + (0.60)(65.80) \\
&= 29.60 + 39.48 = 69.08
\end{aligned}
$$

and

$$
\begin{aligned}
\hat{y}_{10} &= \alpha y_9 + (1 + \alpha)\,\hat{y}_9 \\
&= (0.40)(62) + (0.60)(69.08) \\
&= 24.80 + 41.45 = 66.25
\end{aligned}
$$

By using the same procedures, the values of $\hat{y}_{11}$ through $\hat{y}_{15}$ can be calculated. The following shows a comparison between actual and predicted sales by the exponential smoothing method:

Time Period (t)	Actual Sales (y_t)	Predicted Sales $(\hat{y}_t)$	Difference $(y_t - \hat{y}_t)$	Difference Squared $(y_t - \hat{y}_t)^2$
1	60.0			
2	64.0			
3	58.0			
4	66.0			

Time Period (t)	Actual Sales (y_t)	Predicted Sales ($\hat{y}_t$)	Difference ($y_t - \hat{y}_t$)	Difference Squared ($y_t - \hat{y}_t)^2$
5	70.0			
6	60.0			
7	70.0	63.00	7.00	49.00
8	74.0	65.80	8.20	67.24
9	62.0	69.08	−7.08	50.13
10	74.0	66.25	7.75	60.06
11	68.0	69.35	−1.35	1.82
12	66.0	68.81	−2.81	7.90
13	60.0	67.69	−7.69	59.14
14	66.0	64.61	1.39	1.93
15	62.0	65.17	−3.17	10.05
				307.27

How do I determine the best smoothing constant?

You can use a higher or lower smoothing constant in order to adjust your prediction to large fluctuations in the data series. For example, if the forecast is slow in reacting to increased sales (if the difference is negative), then you might want to try a higher α value. For practical purposes, the optimal α may be picked by minimizing the mean square error (MSE), which is the average sum of the variations between the historical data and forecast values for the corresponding periods. MSE is computed as follows:

$$MSE = \frac{\sum_{t-1}^{n}(y_t - \hat{y}_t)^2}{n - i}$$

where

   i = the number of observations used to determine the initial forecast

In the previous example, $i = 6$ and

$$MSE = \frac{307.27}{15 - 6} = \frac{307.25}{9} = 34.14$$

WHAT TO DO: Try to select the α that minimizes MSE.

Can a computer help?

As a manager, you will be confronted with complex problems requiring large sample data. You will also need to try different values of α for exponential smoothing. A computer can assist you here. To demonstrate, consider the following sales data.

Time Period	Actual Sales (in Thousands of Dollars)
1	117
2	120
3	132
4	141
5	140
6	156
7	169
8	171
9	174
10	182

Figure 7.1 is a printout of an exponential smoothing program. The input data entry is straightforward.

The best α for this particular example is 0.9, because it gives the least mean square error (MSE).

FIGURE 7.1 EXPONENTIAL SMOOTHING PROGRAM

PLEASE ENTER THE NUMBER OF OBSERVATIONS.
?10
ENTER YOUR DATA NOW.
THE DATA SHOULD BE SEPARATED BY COMMAS.
?117,120,132,141,140,156,169,171,174,182
ENTER THE NUMBER OF PERIODS OVER WHICH YOU COMPUTE THE AVERAGE TO BE USED AS THE FIRST FORECAST VALUE.
?1

**********EXPONENTIAL SMOOTHING PROGRAM-SINGLE SMOOTHING**********

JAE K. SHIM

PERIOD	ACTUAL VALUE	ESTIMATED VALUE	ERROR
1	117.00	.00	
2	120.00	117.00	

THE VALUE OF THE EXPONENTIAL SMOOTHER IS .1

3	132.00	117.30	14.70
4	141.00	118.77	22.23

FIGURE 7.1 (*cont.*)

5	140.00	120.99	19.01
6	156.00	122.89	33.11
7	169.00	126.20	42.80
8	171.00	130.48	40.52
9	174.00	134.54	39.46
10	182.00	138.48	43.52

THE TOTAL ABSOLUTE ERROR IN ESTIMATE IS 255.34

THE MEAN SQUARED ERROR IS 1136.48

THE VALUE OF THE EXPONENTIAL SMOOTHER IS .2

3	132.00	117.60	14.40
4	141.00	120.48	20.52
5	140.00	124.58	15.42
6	156.00	127.67	28.33
7	169.00	133.33	35.67
8	171.00	140.47	30.53
9	174.00	146.57	27.43
10	182.00	152.06	29.94

THE TOTAL ABSOLUTE ERROR IN ESTIMATE IS 202.24

THE MEAN SQUARED ERROR IS 690.23

THE VALUE OF THE EXPONENTIAL SMOOTHER IS .3

3	132.00	117.90	14.10
4	141.00	122.13	18.87
5	140.00	127.79	12.21
6	156.00	131.45	24.55
7	169.00	138.82	30.18
8	171.00	147.87	23.13
9	174.00	154.81	19.19
10	182.00	160.57	21.43

THE TOTAL ABSOLUTE ERROR IN ESTIMATE IS 163.66

THE MEAN SQUARED ERROR IS 447.49

THE VALUE OF THE EXPONENTIAL SMOOTHER IS .4

3	132.00	118.20	13.80
4	141.00	123.72	17.28

FIGURE 7.1 (cont.)

5	140.00	130.63	9.37
6	156.00	134.38	21.62
7	169.00	143.03	25.97
8	171.00	153.42	17.58
9	174.00	160.45	13.55
10	182.00	165.87	16.13

THE TOTAL ABSOLUTE ERROR IN ESTIMATE IS 114.16

THE MEAN SQUARED ERROR IS 308.97

THE VALUE OF THE EXPONENTIAL SMOOTHER IS .5

3	132.00	118.50	13.50
4	141.00	125.25	15.75
5	140.00	133.12	6.88
6	156.00	136.56	19.44
7	169.00	146.28	22.72
8	171.00	157.64	13.36
9	174.00	164.32	9.68
10	182.00	169.16	12.84

THE TOTAL ABSOLUTE ERROR IN ESTIMATE IS 114.16

THE MEAN SQUARED ERROR IS 226.07

THE VALUE OF THE EXPONENTIAL SMOOTHER IS .6

3	132.00	118.80	13.20
4	141.00	126.72	14.28
5	140.00	135.29	4.71
6	156.00	138.12	17.88
7	169.00	148.85	20.15
8	171.00	160.94	10.06
9	174.00	166.98	7.02
10	182.00	171.19	10.81

THE TOTAL ABSOLUTE ERROR IN ESTIMATE IS 98.13

THE MEAN SQUARED ERROR IS 174.23

THE VALUE OF THE EXPONENTIAL SMOOTHER IS .7

3	132.00	119.10	12.90
4	141.00	128.13	12.87

FIGURE 7.1 (cont.)

5	140.00	137.14	2.86
6	156.00	139.14	16.86
7	169.00	150.94	18.06
8	171.00	163.58	7.42
9	174.00	168.77	5.23
10	182.00	172.43	9.57

THE TOTAL ABSOLUTE ERROR IN ESTIMATE IS 85.76

THE MEAN SQUARED ERROR IS 140.55

THE VALUE OF THE EXPONENTIAL SMOOTHER IS .8

3	132.00	119.40	12.60
4	141.00	129.48	11.52
5	140.00	138.70	1.30
6	156.00	139.74	16.26
7	169.00	152.75	16.25
8	171.00	165.75	5.25
9	174.00	169.95	4.05
10	182.00	173.19	8.81

THE TOTAL ABSOLUTE ERROR IN ESTIMATE IS 76.05

THE MEAN SQUARED ERROR IS 117.91

THE VALUE OF THE EXPONENTIAL SMOOTHER IS .9

3	132.00	119.70	12.30
4	141.00	130.77	10.23
5	140.00	139.98	.02
6	156.00	142.25	3.75
7	169.00	154.40	14.60
8	171.00	167.54	3.46
9	174.00	170.65	3.35
10	182.00	173.67	8.33

THE TOTAL ABSOLUTE ERROR IN ESTIMATE IS 68.30

THE MEAN SQUARED ERROR IS 102.23

FIGURE 7.1 (cont.)
SUMMARY RESULTS

THE EXPONENTIAL SMOOTHER	.1	WITH A MEAN SQUARED ERROR OF	1136.48
THE EXPONENTIAL SMOOTHER	.2	WITH A MEAN SQUARED ERROR OF	690.23
THE EXPONENTIAL SMOOTHER	.3	WITH A MEAN SQUARED ERROR OF	447.49
THE EXPONENTIAL SMOOTHER	.4	WITH A MEAN SQUARED ERROR OF	308.97
THE EXPONENTIAL SMOOTHER	.5	WITH A MEAN SQUARED ERROR OF	226.07
THE EXPONENTIAL SMOOTHER	.6	WITH A MEAN SQUARED ERROR OF	174.23
THE EXPONENTIAL SMOOTHER	.7	WITH A MEAN SQUARED ERROR OF	140.55
THE EXPONENTIAL SMOOTHER	.8	WITH A MEAN SQUARED ERROR OF	117.91
THE EXPONENTIAL SMOOTHER	.9	WITH A MEAN SQUARED ERROR OF	102.23

7.3 REGRESSION ANALYSIS FOR SALES AND EARNINGS PROJECTIONS

What is regression analysis?

Regression analysis is a statistical procedure for estimating mathematically the average relationship between a dependent variable and an independent variable or variables. Simple regression involves one independent variable, and multiple regression involves two or more. First, we will discuss simple linear regression, defined by the following formula·

$$y = a + bx$$

where

y = dependent variable
x = independent variable
a = a constant or y intercept of regression line
b = the slope of the regression line

How do I use the method of least squares?

The method of least squares attempts to find a line of best fit for the graph of a regression equation. To better explain this, let's define error, or u, as the difference between the observed and estimated values of sales or earnings. Symbolically,

$$u = y - \hat{y}$$

where

y = observed value
$\hat{y}$ = estimated value based on $\hat{y} = a + bx$

The least-squares method requires that the sum of the squares of the errors be the smallest possible value, that is,

$$\text{Min}\sum u^2 = \sum(y - \hat{y})^2 \ (= \text{sum of the errors squared})$$

The typical line of best fit from the observed data points is shown in Figure 7.2.

How do I compute the coefficients?

From differential calculus, the formula for b is as follows:

$$b = \frac{\text{cov}(x,y)}{\sigma_x^2}$$

where

$\text{cov}(x,y)$ = covariance of x and y

FIGURE 7.2 ACTUAL VERSUS ESTIMATED

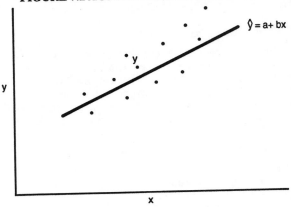

Use these simplified formulas for a and b:

$$b = \frac{n\sum xy - (\sum x)(\sum y)}{n\sum x^2 - (\sum x^2)}$$
$$a = \bar{y} - b\bar{x}$$

where

$$\bar{y} = \sum y/n$$
$$\bar{x} = \sum x/n$$

EXAMPLE 7.7

Company M provides the following data of sales and advertising expenses:

Advertising (in Hundreds of Dollars)	Sales (in Thousands of Dollars)	xy	x²	y²
$ 9	$15	135	81	225
19	20	380	361	400
11	14	154	121	196
14	16	224	196	256
23	25	575	529	625
12	20	240	144	400
12	20	240	144	400
22	23	506	484	529
7	14	98	49	196
13	22	286	169	484
15	18	270	225	324
17	18	306	289	324
$174	$225	$3,414	$2,792	$4,359

From this table:

$$\Sigma x = 174$$
$$\Sigma y = 225$$
$$\Sigma xy = 3,414$$
$$\Sigma x^2 = 2,792$$
$$\bar{x} = \Sigma x/n = 174/12 = 14.5$$
$$\bar{y} = \Sigma y/n = 225/12 = 18.75$$

You can calculate the values of a and b as follows:

$$b = \frac{(12)(3,414) - (174)(225)}{(12)(2,792) - (174)2} = \frac{1,818}{3,228} = 0.5632$$
$$a = 18.75 - (0.5632)(14.5) = 18.75 - 8.1664$$
$$= 10.5836$$

Assume \$10 in advertising will be expensed for the next year. Sales projections would be computed as follows:

$$\hat{y} = \$10.5836 + \$0.5632x$$
$$= \$10.5836 + \$0.5632(\$10)$$
$$= \$10.5836 + \$5.632$$
$$= \$16.2156$$

The final regression equation is

$$\hat{y} = \$10.5836 + \$0.5632x$$

where

$\hat{y}$ = estimated sales
x = advertising expense

How can I use trend analyses?

Trend analysis is a special type of regression analysis often used by financial executives for forecasting sales or earnings. This method involves a regression whereby a trend line is fitted to a time series of data according to the following equation:

$$y = a + bx$$

A time series refers to the relationship of variables over a period of time.

The formulas for the coefficients a and b are essentially the same as those used for simple regression. Each time period is assigned a number so that $\Sigma x = 0$. With an odd number of periods, the middle period is assigned zero value. If there are an even number of periods, then -1 and $+1$ are assigned to the two middle periods. Thus, in both cases, $\Sigma x = 0$.

EXAMPLE 7.8

Case 1	19X1	19X2	19X3	19X4	19X5	19X6
x =	−2	−1	0	+1	+2	

Case 2						
x =	−3	−2	−1	+1	+2	+3

In each case, $\sum x = 0$

The formulas for b and a thus reduce to the following:

$$b = \frac{n \sum xy}{n \sum x^2}$$
$$a = \sum y/n$$

EXAMPLE 7.9

TK Company reports its historical earnings per share (EPS) as follows:

Year	EPS
19X1	$1.00
19X2	1.20
19X3	1.30
19X4	1.60
19X5	1.70

Since there is an odd number of years, the middle year is assigned zero value. Thus:

Year	x	EPS(y)	xy	x²	y²
19X1	−2	$1.00	−2.00	4	1.00
19X2	−1	1.20	−1.20	1	1.44
19X3	0	1.30	0	0	1.69
19X4	+1	1.60	1.60	1	2.56
19X5	+2	1.70	3.40	4	2.89
	0	**$6.80**	**1.80**	**10**	**9.58**

$$b = \frac{(5)(\$1.80)}{(5)(10)} = \frac{\$9}{50} = \$.18$$
$$a = \frac{\$6.80}{5} = \$1.36$$

The estimated trend equation is

$$\hat{y} = \$1.36 + \$0.18x$$

where

$\hat{y}$ = estimated EPS
x = year index value

To project sales for 19X6, assign +3 to the value of x. Thus

$$\hat{y} = \$1.36 + \$0.18(+3)$$
$$= \$1.36 + \$0.54 = \$1.90$$

A summary of the five forecasting methods described in this chapter is provided in Figure 7.3. Use it as a guide for determining which method is best for your specific circumstance.

7.4 WHAT STATISTICS TO LOOK FOR IN REGRESSION ANALYSIS

7.4.1 Simple Regression

A variety of statistics can be used to tell you about the accuracy and reliability of the regression result. We described three in this section:

- Correlation coefficient (r) and coefficient of determination (r^2)
- Standard error of the estimate (s_e)
- Standard error of the regression coefficient (S_b) and t statistic.

How can I measure the appropriateness of the regression equation?

The correlation coefficient (r) measures the degree of correlation between y and x. It takes a range of values between −1 and +1. The coefficient of determination (r^2) is more widely used, however. Simply put, r^2 tells how well the estimated equation fits the data, or, the "goodness of fit" in the regression. RULE OF THUMB: The higher the r^2, the more confidence you can have in your equation.

The coefficient of determination represents the proportion of the total variation in y that is explained by the regression equation. Its value ranges between 0 and 1. For example, the statement "Sales is a function of advertising with $r^2 = 0.70$" can be interpreted as, 70 percent of the total variation of sales is explained by the regression equation (or the change in advertising), and 30 percent is explained by some

FIGURE 7.3 SUMMARY OF MORE COMMONLY USED FORECASTING METHODS

Technique	Moving Average	Exponential Smoothing	Trend Analysis	Regression Analysis
Description	Each point of a moving average of a time series is the arithmetic or weighted average of a number of consecutive points of the series, where the number of data points is chosen so that the effects of seasonals or irregularity or both are eliminated.	Similar to moving average, except that more recent data points are given more weight. Descriptively, the new forecast is equal to the old one plus some proportion of the past forecasting error. Effective when there are random demand and no seasonal fluctuations in the data series.	Fits a trend line to a mathematical equation and then projects it into the future by means of this equation. There are several variations: the slope-characteristic method, polynomials, logarithms, and so on.	Functionally relates sales to other economic, competitive, or internal variables an and estimates an equation using the least-squares technique. Relationships are primarily analyzed statistically, although any relationship could be selected for testing on a rational ground.
Accuracy:				
Short-term (0-3 months)	Poor to good	Fair to very good	Very good	Good to very good
Medium-term (3 months-2 years)	Poor	Poor to good	Good	Good to very good

Long-term (2 year and over)	Very poor	Very poor	Good	Poor
Identification of turning point	Poor	Poor	Poor	Very good
Typical application	Inventory control for low-volume items.	Production and inventory control, forecast of sales, and financial data.	New product forecasts (particularly intermediate and long-term).	Forecasts of sales by product classes, forecasts of income and other financial data.
Data required	A minimum of two years of sales history if seasonals are present. Otherwise, fewer data. (Of course, the more history the better.) The moving average must be specified.	The same as for a moving average.	Varies with the technique used. However, a good rule of thumb is to use a minimum of five years' annual data to start. Thereafter, the complete history.	Several years' quarterly history to obtain good, meaningful relationships. Mathematically necessary to have two more observations than there are independent variables.

FIGURE 7.3 (cont.)

Technique	Moving Average	Exponential Smoothing	Trend Analysis	Regression Analysis
Cost of forecasting with a computer	Very minimal	Minimal	Varies with application	Varies with application
Is calculation possible without a computer?	Yes	Yes	Yes	Yes
Time required to develop an application and make forecasts	1 day→	1 day→	1 day→	Depends on ability to identify relationships

Source: Reprinted by permission of the *Harvard Business Review.* An exhibit from "How to Choose the Right Forecasting Technique" by John C. Chambers, Satinder K. Mullick and Donald D. Smith (July/August 1971). Copyright © 1971 by the President and Fellows of Harvard College; all rights reserved.

other factor (perhaps price or income).

The coefficient of determination is computed from the following formula:

$$r^2 = 1 - \frac{\sum(y - \hat{y})^2}{\sum(y - \hat{y})^2}$$

In simple regression, you can use this shortcut formula:

$$r^2 = \frac{(n\sum xy - [\sum x][\sum y])^2}{(n \sum x^2 - [\sum x]^2)(n\sum y^2 - [\sum y]^2)}$$

EXAMPLE 7.10

Refer to the table in Example 7.7. With $y^2 = 4,359$, you can compute r^2 using the shortcut formula as follows:

$$r^2 = \frac{(1,818)^2}{(3,228)([12][4,359] - [225]^2)}$$

$$= \frac{1,305,124}{(3,228)(52,308 - 50,625)}$$

$$= \frac{3,305,124}{(3,228)(52,308 - 50,625)}$$

$$= \frac{3,305,124}{(3,228)(1,683)} = \frac{3,305,124}{5,432,724}$$

$$= 0.6084$$

INTERPRETATION: About 60.84% of the variation in total sales is explained by advertising, and the remaining 39.16% is still unexplained. This relatively low r^2 indicates that lots of room for improvement still exists in the estimated sales forecast equation $y = \$10.5836 + \$0.5632x$.

EXAMPLE 7.11

Now examine the data presented in Example 7.9. The r^2 is computed as follows:

$$r^2 = \frac{9^2}{(50) [(5)(9.58) (6.80)]^2}$$

$$= \frac{81}{50(47.9 - 46.24)}$$

$$= \frac{81}{(50)(1.66)} = \frac{81}{83} = 0.9759$$

CONCLUSION: A very high r^2 (0.9759) indicates that the trend line is an excellent fit, and there is a growing trend in EPS over time.

How can I measure the accuracy of management predictions?

You can use the standard error of the estimate, designated s_e, and defined as the standard deviation of the regression.

The formula for s_e is

$$s_e = \sqrt{\frac{\sum(y-\hat{y})^2}{n-2}} = \sqrt{\frac{\sum y^2 - a\sum y - b\sum xy}{n-2}}$$

Confidence interval relates to the probability that the sampled result accurately portrays the population. If you want the prediction to be 95-percent confident, compute a confidence interval.

Confidence interval = $y + t(s_e)$

where

t =   table t-value from Table 7.1 determined according to the manager's desired confidence level and the degrees of freedom $(n-2)$.

For example, $t = 2.228$ for a 95% confidence level and 10 degrees of freedom $(12 - 2 = 10)$.

EXAMPLE 7.12

Refer again to Example 7.7. The standard error of the estimate is computed as follows:

$$s_e = \sqrt{\frac{(4,359) - (10.5836)(225) - (0.5632)(3,414)}{12-2}}$$

$$= \sqrt{\frac{54.9252}{10}} = \sqrt{5.49252} = 2.3436$$

If you want your prediction to be 95% confident, the confidence interval would equal the estimated sales ± 2.228(2.3436). The computations are \$16.2156 ± 2.228 (2.3436) = \$16.2156 ± 5.2215, or

\$10.9941 ~ \$21.4371

How can I test the appropriateness of the coefficients?

The standard error of the coefficient, designated s_b, gives an estimate of the range within which the true coefficient may actually be. The standard error of the coefficient is calculated as follows:

$$s_b = \sqrt{\frac{s_e}{\sum(x-\bar{x})^2}}$$

or, in shortcut form,

$$s_b = \sqrt{\frac{s_e}{\sum x^2 - \bar{x}\sum x}}$$

The t statistic shows the statistical significance of x in explaining y. It is determined by dividing the estimated coefficient b by its standard error s_b:

$$t \text{ statistic} = \frac{b}{s_b}$$

The t statistic really measures how many standard errors the coefficient is away from zero. RULE OF THUMB: Any value of t greater than $+2$ or -2 is acceptable. The higher the t value, the more significant is b and therefore the greater your confidence in the coefficient as a predictor.

NOTE: You can also find the t value from Table 7.1.

EXAMPLE 7.13

Once again, refer to Example 7.7. Note the following:

$$s_e = 2.3436$$
$$\Sigma x2 = 2{,}792$$
$$\bar{x} = 14.5$$
$$\Sigma x = 174$$

The standard error of the regression coefficient (0.5632) is computed as follows:

$$s_b = \sqrt{\frac{2.3436}{2{,}792 - (14.5)(174)}} \qquad 2.3426$$

$$= \sqrt{\frac{2.3436}{2{,}792 - 2{,}523}}$$

$$= \sqrt{\frac{2.3436}{269}} = \frac{2.3436}{16.40} = 0.143$$

The t statistic = b/s_b = $0.5632/0.143 = 3.94$

CONCLUSION: Since $t = 3.94 > 2$, the coefficient b is statistically significant.

NOTE: Many computer spreadsheet software such as Microsoft Excel, Lotus 1-2-3, or Quattro Pro have regression routines. See the Lotus 1-2-3 regression command and output in Figure 7.4.

FIGURE 7.4 USING LOTUS 1-2-3 REGRESSION COMMAND

Step 1 Enter the data on X and Y as shown below

(X) Adv. (000)	(Y) Sales (000)
9	15
19	20
11	14
14	16
23	25
12	20
12	20
22	23
7	14
13	22
15	18
17	18

Step 2 Press "/Data Regression"
Step 3 Define X and Y range
Step 4 Define output range
Step 5 Hit Go

This will produce the following regression output:

$$a = 10.58364$$
$$s_e = 2.343622$$
$$r^2 = 0.608373$$
$$n = 12$$
$$n - 2 = 10$$
$$b = 0.563197$$
$$s_b = 0.142893$$

The result shows:

$$\hat{y} = 10.58364 + 0.563197x$$

7.4.2 Multiple Regression

Multiple regression involves more than one independent or explanatory variable. You need to take note of the following statistics when doing multiple regression:

- t statistic
- r-bar squared ($\bar{r}^2$) and F statistic
- Multicollinearity
- Autocorrelation (or serial correlation)

TABLE 7.1 VALUES OF t_P FOR SPECIFIED PROBABILITIES P AND DEGREES OF FREEDOM ν

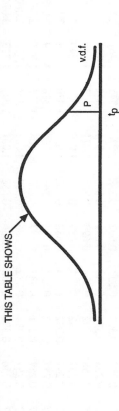

THIS TABLE SHOWS

Level of Significance P for One-Sided Statements

Degrees of Freedom ν	0.45	0.40	0.35	0.30	0.25	0.20	0.15	0.10	0.05	0.025	0.01	0.005	0.0005
1	0.158	0.325	0.510	0.727	1.000	1.376	1.963	3.078	6.314	12.706	31.821	63.657	636.692
2	0.142	0.289	0.445	0.617	0.816	1.061	1.386	1.886	2.920	4.303	6.965	9.925	31.598
3	0.137	0.277	0.424	0.584	0.765	0.978	1.250	1.638	2.353	3.182	4.541	5.841	12.924
4	0.134	0.271	0.414	0.569	0.741	0.941	1.190	1.533	2.132	2.776	3.747	4.604	8.610
5	0.132	0.267	0.408	0.559	0.727	0.920	1.156	1.476	2.015	2.571	3.365	4.032	6.869
6	0.131	0.265	0.404	0.553	0.718	0.906	1.134	1.440	1.943	2.447	3.143	3.707	5.959
7	0.130	0.263	0.402	0.549	0.711	0.896	1.119	1.415	1.895	2.365	2.998	3.499	5.408

TABLE 7.1 (cont.)

	Level of Significance P for One-Sided Statements												
Degrees of Freedom ν	0.45	0.40	0.35	0.30	0.25	0.20	0.15	0.10	0.05	0.025	0.01	0.005	0.0005
8	0.130	0.262	0.399	0.546	0.706	0.889	1.108	1.397	1.860	2.306	2.896	3.355	5.041
9	0.129	0.261	0.398	0.543	0.703	0.883	1.100	1.383	1.833	2.262	2.821	3.250	4.781
10	0.129	0.260	0.397	0.542	0.700	0.879	1.093	1.372	1.812	**2.228**	2.764	3.106	4.587
11	0.129	0.260	0.396	0.540	0.697	0.876	1.088	1.363	1.796	2.201	2.718	3.106	4.437
12	0.128	0.259	0.395	0.539	0.695	0.873	1.083	1.356	1.782	2.179	2.681	3.055	4.318
13	0.128	0259	0.394	0.538	0.694	0.870	1.079	1.350	1.771	2.160	2.650	3.012	4.221
14	0.128	0.258	0.393	0.537	0.692	0.868	1.076	1.345	1.761	2.145	2.624	2.977	4.140
15	0.128	0.258	0.393	0.536	0.691	0.866	1.074	1.341	1.753	2.131	2.602	2.947	4.073
16	0.128	0.258	0.392	0.535	0.690	0.865	1.071	1.337	1.746	2.120	2.583	2.921	4.015
17	0.128	0.257	0.392	0.534	0.689	0.863	1.069	1.333	1.740	2.110	2.567	2.898	3.965
18	0.128	0.257	0.392	0.534	0.688	0.862	1.067	1.330	1.734	2.101	2.552	2.878	3.922
19	0.127	0.257	0.392	0.534	0.688	0.861	1.066	1.328	1.729	2.093	2.539	2.861	3.883
20	0.127	0.257	0.391	0.533	0.687	0.860	1.064	1.325	1.725	2.086	2.528	2.854	3.850
21	0.127	0.257	0.391	0.532	0.686	0.859	1.063	1.323	1.721	2.080	2.518	2.831	3.819
22	0.127	0.256	0.390	0.532	0.686	0.858	1.061	1.321	1.717	2.074	2.508	2.819	3.792

23	0.127	0.256	0.390	0.532	0.685	0.858	1.060	1.319	1.714	2.069	2.500	2.807	3.767
24	0.127	0.256	0.390	0.531	0.685	0.857	1.059	1.318	1.711	2.064	2.492	2.797	3.745
25	0.127	0.256	0.390	0.531	0.684	0.856	1.058	1.316	1.708	2.060	2.485	2.787	3.725
26	0.127	0.256	0.390	0.531	0.684	0.856	1.058	1.315	1.706	2.056	2.479	2.779	3.707
27	0.127	0.256	0.389	0.531	0.684	0.855	1.057	1.314	1.703	2.052	2.473	2.771	3.690
28	0.127	0.256	0.389	0.530	0.683	0.855	1.056	1.313	1.701	2.048	2.467	2.763	3.674
29	0.127	0.256	0.389	0.530	0.683	0.854	1.055	1.311	1.699	2.045	2.462	2.756	3.659
30	0.127	0.256	0.389	0.530	0.683	0.854	1.055	1.310	1.697	2.042	2.457	2.750	3.646
40	0.126	0.255	0.388	0.529	0.681	0.851	1.050	1.303	1.684	2.021	2.423	2.704	3.551
60	0.126	0.254	0.387	0.527	0.679	0.848	1.046	1.296	1.671	2.000	2.390	2.660	3.460
120	0.126	0.254	0.386	0.526	0.677	0.845	1.041	1.289	1.658	1.980	2.358	2.617	3.373
∞	0.126	0.253	0.385	0.524	0.674	0.842	1.036	1.282	1.645	1.960	2.326	2.576	3.291

t_P is the value of the student's t random variable such that the probability of obtaining a sample t value at least as large as t_P is P. The value of P must be doubled if two-sided statements are made using the same t_P value.

Source: This table is taken from Table III of Fisher and Yates, *Statistical Tables for Biological, Agricultural and Medical Research,* published by Oliver and Boyd, Edinburgh, and by permission of the authors and publishers.

What does the t statistic show?

Even though the t statistic was discussed in the previous section, we take it up again because it is even more valid in multiple regression. The t statistic shows the significance of each independent variable in predicting the dependent variable. In multiple regression, the t statistic is defined as follows:

$$t \text{ statistic} = \frac{b_i}{S_{b_i}}$$

where

$i = i$th independent variable

RULE OF THUMB: It's best to have a large t statistic (either positive or negative) for each independent variable. Generally, a value greater than $+2$ or less than -2 is acceptable. You can usually eliminate variables with a low t value without substantially decreasing r^2 or increasing the standard error. Table 7.2 provides t-value for a specified level of significance and degrees of freedom.

How do I measure goodness of fit?

For multiple regressions, goodness of fit is best represented by r-bar squared (r^2), shown as follows:

$$\bar{r}^2 = 1 - (1 - r^2)\ \frac{n-1}{n-k}$$

where

n = number of observations
k = number of coefficients to be estimated

An alternative to the r-bar squared would be the F test. The F statistic is defined as follows:

$$F = \frac{\sum(\hat{y} - \bar{y})^2/k}{\sum(y - \hat{y})^2/n - k - 1}$$

$$= \frac{\text{Explained variation} / k}{\text{Unexplained variation} / n - k - 1}$$

Values for F for specified probabilities and degrees of freedom are given in Table 7.3. If the F statistic is greater than the table value, you can conclude that the regression equation is statistically significant in overall terms.

NOTE: Virtually all computer programs for regression analysis show $\bar{r}^2$ and an F statistic.

TABLE 7.2 STUDENT'S t DISTRIBUTION

Degree of freedom $= n - k - 1$	Probability												
	0.9	0.8	0.7	0.6	0.5	0.4	0.3	0.2	0.1	0.05	0.02	0.01	0.001
1	0.158	0.325	0.510	0.727	1.000	1.376	1.963	3.078	6.314	12.706	31.821	63.657	636.619
2	0.142	0.289	0.445	0.617	0.816	1.061	1.386	1.886	2.920	4.303	6.965	9.925	31.598
3	0.137	0.277	0.424	0.584	0.765	0.978	1.250	1.638	2.353	3.182	4.541	5.841	12.924
4	0.134	0.271	0.414	0.569	0.741	0.941	1.190	1.533	2.132	2.776	3.747	4.604	8.610
5	0.132	0.267	0.408	0.559	0.727	0.920	1.156	1.476	2.015	2.571	3.365	4.032	6.869
6	0.131	0.265	0.404	0.553	0.718	0.906	.134	1.440	1.943	2.447	3.143	3.707	5.959
7	0.130	0.263	0.402	0.549	0.711	0.896	1.119	1.415	1.895	2.365	2.998	3.499	5.408
8	0.130	0.262	0.399	0.546	0.706	0.889	1.108	1.397	1.860	2.306	2.896	3.355	5.041
9	0.129	0.261	0.398	0.543	0.703	0.883	1.100	1.383	1.833	2.262	2.821	3.250	4.781
10	0.129	0.260	0.397	0.542	0.700	0.879	1.093	1.372	1.812	2.228	2.764	3.169	4.587
11	0.129	0.260	0.396	0.540	0.697	0.876	1.088	1.363	1.796	2.201	2.718	3.106	4.437
12	0.128	0.259	0.395	0.539	0.695	0.873	1.083	1.356	1.782	2.179	2.681	3.055	4.318
13	0.128	0.259	0.394	0.538	0.694	0.870	1.079	1.350	1.771	2.160	2.650	3.012	4.221
14	0.128	0.258	0.393	0.537	0.692	0.868	1.076	1.345	1.761	2.145	2.624	2.977	4.140
15	0.128	0.258	0.393	0.536	0.691	0.866	1.074	1.341	1.753	2.131	2.602	2.947	4.073

TABLE 7.2 (cont.)

Degree of freedom = $n - k - 1$	Probability												
	0.9	0.8	0.7	0.6	0.5	0.4	0.3	0.2	0.1	0.05	0.02	0.01	0.001
16	0.128	0.258	0.392	0.535	0.690	0.865	1.071	1.337	1.746	2.120	2.583	2.921	4.015
17	0.128	0.257	0.392	0.534	0.689	0.863	1.069	1.333	1.740	2.110	2.567	2.898	3.965
18	0.127	0.257	0.392	0.534	0.688	0.862	1.067	1.330	1.734	2.101	2.552	2.878	3.922
19	0.127	0.257	0.391	0.533	0.688	0.861	1.066	1.328	1.729	2.093	2.539	2.861	3.883
20	0.127	0.257	0.391	0.533	0.687	0.860	1.064	1.325	1.725	2.086	2.528	2.845	3.850
21	0.127	0.257	0.391	0.532	0.686	0.859	1.063	1.323	1.721	2.080	2.518	2.831	3.819
22	0.127	0.256	0.390	0.532	0.686	0.858	1.061	1.321	1.717	2.074	2.508	2.819	3.792
23	0.127	0.256	0.390	0.532	0.685	0.858	1.060	1.319	1.714	2.069	2.500	2.807	3.767
24	0.127	0.256	0.390	0.531	0.685	0.857	1.059	1.316	1.711	2.064	2.492	2.797	3.745
25	0.127	0.256	0.390	0.531	0.684	0.856	1.058	1.315	1.708	2.060	2.485	2.787	3.725
26	0.127	0.256	0.390	0.531	0.684	0.856	1.058	1.315	1.706	2.056	2.479	2.779	3.707
27	0.127	0.256	0.389	0.531	0.684	0.855	1.057	1.314	1.703	2.052	2.473	2.771	3.690
28	0.127	0.256	0.389	0.530	0.683	0.855	1.056	1.313	1.701	2.048	2.467	2.763	3.674
29	0.127	0.256	0.389	0.530	0.683	0.854	1.055	1.311	1.699	2.045	2.462	2.756	3.659
30	0.127	0.256	0.389	0.530	0.683	0.854	1.055	1.310	1.697	2.042	2.457	2.750	3.646

40	0.126	0.255	0.388	0.529	0.681	0.851	1.050	1.303	1.684	2.021	2.423	2.704	3.551
60	0.126	0.254	0.387	0.527	0.679	0.848	1.046	1.296	1.671	2.000	2.390	2.660	3.460
120	0.126	0.254	0.386	0.526	0.677	0.845	1.041	1.289	1.658	1.980	2.358	2.617	3.373
∞	0.126	0.253	0.385	0.524	0.674	0.842	1.036	1.282	1.645	1.960	2.326	2.576	3.291

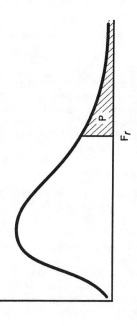

Values of F_r for Probabilities P

In Table 7.2 the level of significance P is 0.05 for the first entry of n^1 and 0.01 for the second entry of n^2. For example, an $n^1 = 5$ and $n^2 = 16$ results in an F value of 2.85 for a 0.05 significance level.

How can I be sure the independent variables are unrelated?

When you use more than one independent variable in a regression equation, the variables themselves may be correlated. *Multicollinearity* occurs when these variables interfere with each other. When this is the case, you may produce spurious (accidental) or inaccurate forecasts.

Here's how to recognize multicollinearity:

- The t statistics of two seemingly important independent variables are suspiciously low
- The estimated coefficients on independent variables have signs opposite from what you would logically expect

You can solve the problem of multicollinearity two ways:

- Drop one of the highly correlated variables from the regression
- Change the structure of the equation by (1) dividing all variables by some factor that will leave the basic economic logic but will remove multicollinearity; (2) estimating the equation on a "first-difference" basis; or (3) combining the collinear variables into a new variable that equals their weighted sum

What is autocorrelation?

Autocorrelation indicates a correlation between successive errors. In other words, it usually shows that an important part of the variation of the dependent variable has not been explained. WHAT TO DO: When autocorrelation exists, search for other independent variables to include in the regression equation.

The Durbin-Watson statistic provides the standard test for autocorrelation. Table 7.4 provides values of the Durbin-Watson statistic for specified sample sizes and independent variables. Generally, you can interpret the statistic as follows:

Durbin-Watson Statistic	*Autocorrelation*
Between 1.5 and 2.5	No autocorrelation
Below 1.5	Positive autocorrelation
Above 2.5	Negative autocorrelation

An example showing applications of all the tests discussed in this section can be found in Section 7.6.

TABLE 7.3 F DISTRIBUTION

	n_1 = degrees of freedom for numerator = k											
	1	2	3	4	5	6	7	8	9	10	11	12
1	161	200	216	225	230	234	237	239	241	242	243	244
	4,052	**4,999**	**5,408**	**5,625**	**5,764**	**5,559**	**5,928**	**5,981**	**6,023**	**6,054**	**6,082**	**6,106**
2	18.51	19.00	19.16	19.25	19.30	19.33	19.36	19.37	19.38	19.39	19.40	19.41
	98.49	**99.01**	**99.17**	**99.25**	**99.30**	**99.33**	**99.34**	**99.36**	**99.38**	**99.40**	**99.41**	**99.42**
3	10.13	9.55	9.28	9.12	9.01	8.94	8.88	8.84	8.81	8.78	8.76	8.74
	34.12	**30.81**	**29.46**	**28.71**	**28.24**	**27.91**	**27.67**	**27.49**	**27.34**	**27.23**	**27.13**	**27.06**
4	7.71	6.94	6.59	6.39	6.26	6.16	6.09	6.04	6.00	5.96	5.93	5.91
	21.20	**18.00**	**16.69**	**15.98**	**15.52**	**15.21**	**14.98**	**14.80**	**14.66**	**14.54**	**14.45**	**14.37**
5	6.61	5.79	5.41	5.19	5.05	4.95	4.88	4.82	4.78	4.74	4.70	4.68
	16.26	**13.27**	**12.06**	**11.39**	**10.37**	**10.67**	**10.45**	**10.27**	**10.15**	**10.05**	**9.96**	**9.89**
6	5.99	5.14	4.76	4.53	4.39	4.28	4.21	4.15	4.10	4.06	4.03	4.00
	13.74	**10.92**	**9.78**	**9.15**	**8.76**	**8.47**	**8.26**	**8.10**	**7.98**	**7.87**	**7.79**	**7.72**
7	5.59	4.74	4.35	4.12	3.97	3.87	3.79	3.73	3.68	3.63	3.60	3.57
	12.25	**9.55**	**8.45**	**7.85**	**7.44**	**7.19**	**7.00**	**6.84**	**6.71**	**6.62**	**6.54**	**6.47**
8	5.32	4.48	4.07	3.84	3.69	3.58	3.50	3.44	3.39	3.34	3.31	3.28
	11.26	**8.64**	**7.69**	**7.01**	**6.63**	**6.37**	**6.19**	**6.03**	**5.91**	**5.82**	**5.74**	**5.67**

TABLE 7.3 (cont.)

			n_1 = degrees of freedom for numerator = k								
	1	*2*	*3*	*4*	*5*	*6*	*7*	*8*	*9*	*10*	*11*	*12*
9	5.12	4.26	3.86	3.63	3.48	3.37	3.29	3.23	3.18	3.13	3.10	3.07
	10.66	**8.02**	**6.99**	**6.42**	**6.06**	**5.30**	**5.62**	**5.47**	**5.35**	**5.26**	**5.18**	**5.11**
10	4.96	4.10	3.71	3.48	3.33	3.22	3.14	3.07	3.02	2.97	2.94	2.91
	10.04	**7.54**	**6.55**	**5.99**	**5.64**	**5.39**	**5.21**	**5.06**	**4.95**	**4.85**	**4.78**	**4.71**
11	4.84	3.98	3.59	3.36	3.20	3.09	3.01	2.95	2.90	2.86	2.82	2.79
	9.65	**7.20**	**6.22**	**5.67**	**5.32**	**5.07**	**4.88**	**4.74**	**4.63**	**4.54**	**4.46**	**4.40**
12	4.75	3.88	3.49	3.26	3.11	3.00	2.92	2.85	2.80	2.76	2.72	2.69
	9.33	**6.93**	**5.95**	**5.41**	**5.04**	**4.82**	**4.65**	**4.50**	**4.39**	**4.30**	**4.22**	**4.16**
13	4.67	3.80	3.41	3.18	3.02	2.92	2.84	2.77	2.72	2.67	2.63	2.60
	9.07	**6.70**	**5.74**	**5.20**	**4.86**	**4.62**	**4.44**	**4.30**	**4.19**	**4.10**	**4.02**	**3.96**
14	4.60	3.74	3.34	3.11	2.96	2.85	2.77	2.70	2.65	2.60	2.56	2.53
	8.86	**6.51**	**5.56**	**5.03**	**4.69**	**4.46**	**4.28**	**4.14**	**4.03**	**3.94**	**3.86**	**3.80**
15	4.54	3.68	3.29	3.06	2.90	2.79	2.70	2.64	2.59	2.55	2.51	2.48
	8.62	**6.36**	**5.42**	**4.89**	**4.56**	**4.32**	**4.14**	**4.00**	**3.89**	**3.80**	**3.73**	**3.67**
16	4.49	3.63	3.24	3.01	2.85	2.74	2.66	2.59	2.54	2.49	2.45	2.42
	8.53	**6.23**	**5.29**	**4.77**	**4.44**	**4.20**	**4.03**	**3.89**	**3.78**	**3.69**	**3.61**	**3.55**

n_2												
17	4.45	3.59	3.20	2.96	2.81	2.70	2.62	2.55	2.50	2.45	2.41	2.38
	8.40	**6.11**	**5.18**	**4.67**	**4.34**	**4.10**	**3.93**	**3.79**	**3.68**	**3.59**	**3.52**	**3.45**
18	4.41	3.55	3.16	2.93	2.77	2.66	2.58	2.51	2.46	2.41	2.37	2.34
	8.26	**6.01**	**5.09**	**4.58**	**4.25**	**4.01**	**3.86**	**3.71**	**3.60**	**3.51**	**3.44**	**3.37**
19	4.38	3.52	3.13	2.90	2.74	2.63	2.55	2.48	2.43	2.38	2.34	2.31
	8.18	**5.98**	**5.01**	**4.50**	**4.17**	**3.94**	**3.77**	**3.63**	**3.52**	**3.43**	**3.36**	**3.30**
20	4.35	3.49	3.10	2.87	2.71	2.60	2.52	2.45	2.40	2.35	2.31	2.28
	8.10	**5.86**	**4.94**	**4.43**	**4.10**	**3.87**	**3.71**	**3.56**	**3.45**	**3.37**	**3.30**	**3.23**
21	4.33	3.47	3.07	2.84	2.68	2.57	2.49	2.42	2.37	2.32	2.28	2.25
	8.10	**5.78**	**4.87**	**4.37**	**4.04**	**3.81**	**3.65**	**3.51**	**3.40**	**3.31**	**3.24**	**3.17**
22	4.30	3.44	3.05	2.82	2.66	2.55	2.47	2.40	2.35	2.30	2.26	2.23
	7.94	**5.72**	**4.82**	**4.31**	**3.99**	**3.76**	**3.69**	**3.45**	**3.35**	**3.26**	**3.18**	**3.12**
23	4.28	3.42	3.03	2.80	2.64	2.53	2.45	2.38	2.32	2.28	2.24	2.20
	7.88	**5.64**	**4.76**	**4.28**	**3.94**	**3.71**	**3.45**	**3.41**	**3.30**	**3.21**	**3.14**	**3.07**
24	4.26	3.40	3.01	2.78	2.62	2.51	2.43	2.36	2.30	2.26	2.22	2.18
	7.82	**5.61**	**4.72**	**4.22**	**3.90**	**3.67**	**3.50**	**3.36**	**3.25**	**3.17**	**3.09**	**3.03**
25	4.24	3.38	2.99	2.76	2.60	2.49	2.41	2.34	2.28	2.24	2.20	2.16
	7.77	**5.57**	**4.68**	**4.13**	**3.86**	**3.63**	**3.46**	**3.32**	**3.21**	**3.13**	**3.05**	**2.99**
26	4.22	3.37	2.98	2.74	2.59	2.47	2.39	2.32	2.27	2.22	2.18	2.15
	7.72	**5.83**	**4.64**	**4.14**	**3.82**	**3.59**	**3.42**	**3.29**	**3.17**	**3.09**	**3.02**	**2.96**

n_2 = degrees of freedom for denominator = $n - k - 1$

TABLE 7.3 (cont.)

				n_1 = degrees of freedom for numerator = k								
	14	16	20	24	30	40	50	75	100	200	500	∞
1	245	246	248	249	250	251	252	253	253	254	254	254
	6,142	**6,169**	**6,208**	**6,334**	**6,258**	**6,286**	**6,302**	**6,323**	**6,334**	**6,352**	**6,361**	**6,364**
2	19.42	19.43	19.44	19.45	19.46	19.47	19.47	19.48	19.49	19.49	19.50	19.50
	99.43	**99.44**	**99.45**	**99.46**	**99.47**	**99.48**	**99.48**	**99.49**	**99.49**	**99.49**	**99.50**	**99.50**
3	8.71	8.69	8.66	8.64	8.62	8.60	8.58	8.57	8.56	8.54	8.54	8.53
	26.92	**26.83**	**26.69**	**26.60**	**26.50**	**26.41**	**26.35**	**26.27**	**26.23**	**26.18**	**26.14**	**26.12**
4	5.87	5.84	5.80	5.77	5.74	5.71	5.70	5.68	5.66	5.65	5.64	5.63
	14.24	**14.15**	**14.02**	**13.93**	**13.83**	**13.74**	**13.69**	**13.61**	**13.57**	**13.52**	**13.48**	**13.46**
5	4.64	4.60	4.56	4.53	4.50	4.46	4.44	4.42	4.40	4.38	4.37	4.36
	9.77	**9.68**	**9.55**	**9.47**	**9.38**	**9.29**	**9.24**	**9.17**	**9.13**	**9.07**	**9.04**	**9 02**
6	3.96	3.92	3.87	3.84	3.81	3.77	3.75	3.72	3.71	3.69	3.68	3.67
	7.60	**7.52**	**7.39**	**7.31**	**7.23**	**7.14**	**7.09**	**7.02**	**6.99**	**6.94**	**6.90**	**6.88**
7	3.52	3.49	3.44	3.41	3.38	3.34	3.32	3.29	3.28	3.25	3.24	3.23
	6.35	**6.27**	**6.15**	**6.07**	**5.98**	**5.90**	**5.85**	**5.78**	**5.75**	**5.70**	**5.67**	**5.65**
8	3.23	3.20	3.15	3.12	3.08	3.05	3.03	3.00	2.98	2.96	2.94	2.93
	5.56	**5.48**	**5.36**	**5.28**	**5.20**	**5.11**	**5.06**	**5.00**	**4.96**	**4.91**	**4.88**	**4.86**

9	3.02	2.98	2.93	2.90	2.86	2.82	2.80	2.77	2.76	2.73	2.72	2.71
	5.00	4.92	4.80	4.73	4.64	4.56	4.51	4.45	4.41	4.36	4.33	4.31
10	2.86	2.82	2.77	2.74	2.70	2.67	2.64	2.61	2.59	2.56	2.55	
	4.60	4.52	4.41	4.33	4.25	4.17	4.12	4.05	4.01	3.96	3.93	3.91
11	2.74	2.70	2.65	2.61	2.57	2.53	2.50	2.47	2.45	2.42	2.41	2.40
	4.29	4.21	4.10	4.02	3.94	3.86	3.80	3.74	3.70	3.66	3.62	3.60
12	2.64	2.60	2.54	2.50	2.46	2.42	2.40	2.36	2.35	2.32	2.31	2.30
	4.50	3.98	3.86	3.78	3.70	3.61	3.56	3.49	3.46	3.41	3.38	3.36
13	2.55	2.51	2.46	2.42	2.38	2.34	2.32	2.28	2.26	2.24	2.22	2.21
	3.85	3.78	3.67	3.59	3.51	3.42	3.37	3.30	3.27	3.21	3.18	3.16
14	2.48	2.44	2.39	2.35	2.31	2.27	2.24	2.21	2.19	2.16	2.14	2.13
	3.70	3.62	3.51	3.43	3.34	3.26	3.21	3.14	3.11	3.06	3.02	3.00
15	2.43	2.39	2.33	2.29	2.25	2.21	2.18	2.15	2.12	2.10	2.08	2.07
	3.56	3.48	3.36	3.29	3.20	3.12	3.07	3.00	2.97	2.92	2.89	2.87
16	2.37	2.33	2.28	2.24	2.20	2.16	2.13	2.09	2.07	2.04	2.02	2.01
	3.45	3.37	3.25	3.18	3.10	3.01	2.96	2.89	2.86	2.80	2.77	2.75
17	2.33	2.29	2.23	2.19	2.15	2.11	2.08	2.04	2.02	1.99	1.97	1.96
	3.35	3.27	3.16	3.08	3.00	2.92	2.86	2.79	2.76	2.70	2.67	2.65
18	2.29	2.25	2.19	2.15	2.11	2.07	2.04	2.00	1.98	1.95	1.93	1.92
	3.27	3.19	3.07	3.00	2.91	2.83	2.78	2.71	2.68	2.62	2.59	2.57

TABLE 7.3 (cont.)

n_1 = degrees of freedom for numerator = k

	14	16	20	24	30	40	50	75	100	200	500	∞
19	2.26 **3.19**	2.21 **3.12**	2.15 **3.00**	2.11 **2.92**	2.07 **2.84**	2.02 **2.76**	2.00 **2.70**	1.96 **2.63**	1.94 **2.60**	1.91 **2.54**	1.90 **2.51**	1.88 **2.49**
20	2.23 **3.13**	2.18 **3.05**	2.12 **2.94**	2.08 **2.86**	2.04 **2.77**	1.99 **2.69**	1.96 **2.63**	1.92 **2.56**	1.90 **2.53**	1.87 **2.47**	1.85 **2.44**	1.84 **2.42**
21	2.20 **3.07**	2.15 **2.99**	2.09 **2.88**	2.05 **2.80**	2.00 **2.72**	1.96 **2.63**	1.93 **2.58**	1.89 **2.51**	1.87 **2.47**	1.84 **2.42**	1.82 **2.38**	1.81 **2.36**
22	2.18 **3.02**	2.13 **2.94**	2.07 **2.83**	2.03 **2.75**	1.98 **2.67**	1.93 **2.58**	1.91 **2.53**	1.87 **2.46**	1.84 **2.42**	1.81 **2.37**	1.80 **2.33**	1.78 **2.31**
23	2.14 **2.97**	2.10 **2.89**	2.04 **2.78**	2.00 **2.70**	1.96 **2.62**	1.91 **2.53**	1.88 **2.48**	1.84 **2.41**	1.82 **2.37**	1.79 **2.32**	1.77 **2.28**	1.76 **2.26**
24	2.13 **2.93**	2.09 **2.85**	2.02 **2.74**	1.98 **2.66**	1.94 **2.58**	1.89 **2.49**	1.86 **2.44**	1.82 **2.36**	1.80 **2.33**	1.76 **2.27**	1.74 **2.23**	1.73 **2.21**
25	2.11 **2.89**	2.06 **2.81**	2.00 **2.70**	1.96 **2.62**	1.92 **2.54**	1.87 **2.45**	1.84 **2.40**	1.80 **2.32**	1.77 **2.29**	1.74 **2.23**	1.72 **2.19**	1.71 **2.17**
26	2.10 **2.86**	2.05 **2.77**	1.99 **2.66**	1.95 **2.58**	1.90 **2.50**	1.85 **2.41**	1.82 **2.36**	1.78 **2.28**	1.76 **2.25**	1.72 **2.19**	1.70 **2.15**	1.69 **2.13**

TABLE 7.4 DURBIN-WATSON VALUES

LEVEL OF SIGNIFICANCE: 0.01

Number of residuals T	K = 1		K = 2		K = 3		K = 4		K = 5	
	d_L	d_U	d_L	d_U	d_L	d_U	d_L	d_U	d_L	d_U
15	1.08	1.36	0.95	1.54	0.82	1.75	0.69	1.97	0.56	2.21
16	1.10	1.37	0.98	1.54	0.86	1.73	0.74	1.93	0.62	2.15
17	1.13	1.38	1.02	1.54	0.90	1.71	0.78	1.90	0.67	2.10
18	1.16	1.39	1.05	1.53	0.93	1.69	0.82	1.87	0.71	2.06
19	1.18	1.40	1.08	1.53	0.97	1.68	0.86	1.85	0.75	2.02
20	1.20	1.41	1.10	1.54	1.00	1.68	0.90	1.83	0.79	1.99
21	1.22	1.42	1.13	1.54	1.03	1.67	0.93	1.81	0.83	1.96
22	1.24	1.43	1.15	1.54	1.05	1.66	0.96	1.80	0.86	1.94
23	1.26	1.44	1.17	1.54	1.08	1.66	0.99	1.79	0.90	1.92
24	1.27	1.45	1.19	1.55	1.10	1.66	1.01	1.78	0.93	1.90
25	1.29	1.45	1.21	1.55	1.12	1.66	1.04	1.77	0.95	1.89
26	1.30	1.46	1.22	1.55	1.14	1.65	1.06	1.76	0.98	1.88
27	1.32	1.47	1.24	1.56	1.16	1.65	1.08	1.76	1.01	1.86
28	1.33	1.48	1.26	1.56	1.18	1.65	1.10	1.75	1.03	1.85
29	1.34	1.48	1.27	1.56	1.20	1.65	1.12	1.74	1.05	1.84

TABLE 7.4 (cont.)

LEVEL OF SIGNIFICANCE: 0.01

Number of residuals T	K = 1 d_L	K = 1 d_U	K = 2 d_L	K = 2 d_U	K = 3 d_L	K = 3 d_U	K = 4 d_L	K = 4 d_U	K = 5 d_L	K = 5 d_U
30	1.35	1.49	1.28	1.57	1.21	1.65	1.14	1.74	1.07	1.83
31	1.36	1.50	1.30	1.57	1.23	1.65	1.16	1.74	1.09	1.83
32	1.37	1.50	1.31	1.57	1.24	1.65	1.18	1.73	1.11	1.82
33	1.38	1.51	1.32	1.58	1.26	1.65	1.19	1.73	1.13	1.81
34	1.39	1.51	1.33	1.58	1.27	1.65	1.21	1.73	1.15	1.81
35	1.40	1.52	1.34	1.58	1.28	1.65	1.22	1.73	1.16	1.80
36	1.41	1.52	1.35	1.59	1.29	1.65	1.24	1.73	1.18	1.80
37	1.42	1.53	1.36	1.59	1.31	1.66	1.25	1.72	1.19	1.80
38	1.43	1.54	1.37	1.59	1.32	1.66	1.26	1.72	1.21	1.79
39	1.43	1.54	1.38	1.60	1.33	1.66	1.27	1.72	1.22	1.79
40	1.44	1.54	1.39	1.60	1.34	1.66	1.29	1.72	1.23	1.79
45	1.48	1.57	1.43	1.62	1.38	1.67	1.34	1.72	1.29	1.78
50	1.50	1.59	1.46	1.63	1.42	1.67	1.38	1.72	1.34	1.77

Note: This table displays the values of the Durbin-Watson d for sample sizes T and explanatory variables $K1$ where $K1 = K - 1$.

254

LEVEL OF SIGNIFICANCE: 0.05

Number of residuals T	K = 1		K = 2		K = 3		K = 4		K = 5	
	d_L	d_U	d_L	d_U	d_L	d_U	d_L	d_U	d_L	d_U
15	0.81	1.07	0.70	1.25	0.59	1.46	0.49	1.70	0.39	1.96
16	0.84	1.09	0.74	1.25	0.63	1.44	0.53	1.66	0.44	1.90
17	0.87	1.10	0.77	1.25	0.67	1.43	0.57	1.63	0.48	1.85
18	0.90	1.12	0.80	1.26	0.71	1.42	0.61	1.60	0.52	1.80
19	0.93	1.13	0.83	1.26	0.74	1.41	0.65	1.58	0.56	1.77
20	0.95	1.15	0.86	1.27	0.77	1.41	0.68	1.57	0.60	1.74
21	0.97	1.16	0.89	1.27	0.80	1.41	0.72	1.55	0.63	1.71
22	1.00	1.17	0.91	1.28	0.83	1.40	0.75	1.54	0.66	1.69
23	1.02	1.19	0.94	1.29	0.86	1.40	0.77	1.53	0.70	1.67
24	1.04	1.20	0.96	1.30	0.88	1.41	0.80	1.53	0.72	1.66
25	1.05	1.21	0.98	1.30	0.90	1.41	0.83	1.52	0.75	1.65
26	1.07	1.22	1.00	1.31	0.93	1.41	0.85	1.52	0.78	1.64
27	1.09	1.23	1.02	1.32	0.95	1.41	0.88	1.51	0.81	1.63
28	1.10	1.24	1.04	1.32	0.97	1.41	0.90	1.51	0.83	1.62
29	1.12	1.25	1.05	1.33	0.99	1.42	0.92	1.51	0.85	1.61

TABLE 7.4 *(cont.)*

LEVEL OF SIGNIFICANCE: 0.05

Number of residuals T	$K = 1$		$K = 2$		$K = 3$		$K = 4$		$K = 5$	
	d_L	d_U	d_L	d_U	d_L	d_U	d_L	d_U	d_L	d_U
30	1.13	1.26	1.07	1.34	1.01	1.42	0.94	1.51	0.88	1.61
31	1.15	1.27	1.08	1.34	1.02	1.42	0.96	1.51	0.90	1.60
32	1.16	1.28	1.10	1.35	1.04	1.43	0.98	1.51	0.92	1.60
33	1.17	1.29	1.11	1.36	1.05	1.43	1.00	1.51	0.94	1.59
34	1.18	1.30	1.13	1.36	1.07	1.43	1.01	1.51	0.95	1.59
35	1.19	1.31	1.14	1.37	1.08	1.44	1.03	1.51	0.97	1.59
36	1.21	1.32	1.15	1.38	1.10	1.44	1.04	1.51	0.99	1.59
37	1.22	1.32	1.16	1.38	1.11	1.45	1.06	1.51	1.00	1.59
38	1.23	1.33	1.18	1.39	1.12	1.45	1.07	1.52	1.02	1.58
39	1.24	1.34	1.19	1.39	1.14	1.45	1.09	1.52	1.03	1.58
40	1.25	1.34	1.20	1.40	1.15	1.46	1.10	1.52	1.05	1.58
45	1.29	1.38	1.24	1.42	1.20	1.48	1.16	1.53	1.11	1.58
50	1.32	1.40	1.28	1.45	1.24	1.49	1.20	1.54	1.16	1.59

7.5 MEASURING THE ACCURACY OF YOUR FORECASTS

One of the most important aspects of any forecast is the amount of error associated with it. DEFINITION:

Error = Actual − Forecast

What measures are commonly used for summarizing errors?

Two measures are commonly used to summarize errors: mean absolute deviation (MAD) and mean squared error (MSE). MAD is defined as the average error, or

$$\text{MAD} = \frac{\sum |\text{ actual} - \text{forecast }|}{n}$$

Note: Vertical lines indicate absolute values (or positive values).

MSE is the average of squared errors, expressed as follows:

$$\text{MAD} = \frac{\sum (\text{actual} - \text{forecast})^2}{n - 1}$$

EXAMPLE 7.14

Company Z reports the following sales data:

Time Period	Actual	Forecast	Error	|Error|	(Error)^2
1	$217	$215	2	2	4
2	213	216	− 3	3	9
3	216	215	1	1	1
4	210	214	− 4	4	16
5	213	211	2	2	4
6	219	214	5	5	25
7	216	217	− 1	1	1
8	212	216	− 4	4	16
				22	76

Computations for MAD and MSE are

$$\text{MAD} = \frac{\sum |\text{ error }|}{n} = \frac{22}{8} = 2.75$$

$$\text{MSE} = \frac{\sum (\text{error})^2}{n - 1} = \frac{76}{8 - 1} = 10.86$$

How do I choose the best forecasting equation?

Choosing among alternative forecasting equations basically involves two steps:

- Eliminate the obvious losers
- Select a winner from among the remaining contenders

You can eliminate the losers by asking these questions:

- Does the equation make sense either intuitively or theoretically? If not, then eliminate.
- Does the equation have independent variables with low t statistics? If so, they should be reestimated or dropped in favor of equations in which all independent variables are significant. This test will probably eliminate equations facing problems with multicollinearity.
- How about a low $\bar{r}^2$? This statistic can be used to rank the remaining equations and to select the best candidates. REMEMBER THIS: A low $\bar{r}^2$ could mean (1) a wrong functional form was fitted (linear, quadratic, etc.); (2) an important independent variable or variables is or are missing; or (3) other combinations of independent variables might be more desirable.

Here's how to select the best equation:

- Given equations that survive all previous tests, the equation with the Durbin-Watson statistic closest to 2.0 can provide a basis for selection.
- The equation whose prediction accuracy is best as measured by MAD or MSE generally provides the best basis for forecasting.

7.6 HOW TO USE THE COMPUTER FOR MULTIPLE REGRESSION

Are computers helpful for statistical analyses?

Software packages can greatly assist decision makers and forecasters with a variety of statistical analyses.

How does the computer handle multiple regression?

Here's an example of how a computer handles multiple regression. REMEMBER THIS: Each software package is different. For this example, we use SPSS, one of the easiest programs to use. In Figure 7.5, you'll find a computer listing containing the input data and output results using three independent variables. To help you, illustrative comments have been added where applicable.

EXAMPLE 7.15

Cypress Consumer Products Corporation wishes to develop a forecasting model for its dryer sales by using multiple regression analysis. The marketing department prepared the following sample data that appears in the following table using three independent variables: sales of washers, disposable income, and savings.

Month	Sales of Washers (x_1)	Disposable Income (x_2)	Savings (x_3)	Sales of Dryers (y)
	(000)	(000)	(000)	(000)
January	$45	$16	$71	$29
February	42	14	70	24
March	44	15	72	27
April	45	13	71	25
May	43	13	75	26
June	46	14	74	28
July	44	16	76	30
August	45	16	69	28
September	44	15	74	28
October	43	15	73	27

The Forecasting Equation. From the SPSS output, you can see that

$$\hat{y} = -45.796 + 0.597x_1 + 1.177x_2 + 0.405x_3$$

Suppose expectations for November are as follows:

x_1 = sales of washers = $43,000
x_2 = disposable income = $15,000
x_3 = savings = $75,000

FIGURE 7.5 SPSS Program Output

SPSS for MS Windows Release 6.1

Multiple Regression

Equation Number 1
Dependent Variable. .   SALESDRY

Block Number 1.
Method: Enter   SALESWAS
                        INCOME SAVINGS

FIGURE 7.5 *(cont.)*

Variable(s) Entered on Step Number

1. SAVINGS
2. SALESWAS sales
3. INCOME

NOTE:
Multiple R = .99167
r^2 = .98340
$\bar{r}^2$ = .97511
s_e = .28613

Analysis of Variance

	DF	Sum of Squares	Mean Square
Regression	3	29.10878	9.70293
Residual	6	.49122	.08187

F = 118.51727   Signif F = .0000

Variables in the Equation

Variable	B	SE B	Beta	T	Sig T
SALESWAS	.596972	.081124	.394097	7.359	.0003
INCOME	1.176838	.084074	.752425	13.998	.0000
SAVINGS	.405109	.042234	.507753	9.592	.0001
(Constant)	−45.796348	4.877651		−9.389	.0001

Residuals Statistics:

	Min	Max	Mean	Std Dev	N
*PRED	24.1098	30.0881	27.2000	1.7984	10
*RESID	−.2908	.4445	.0000	.2336	10
*ZPRED	−1.7183	1.6059	.0000	1.0000	10
*ZRESID	−1.0163	1.5536	.0000	.8165	10

Total Cases = 10
Durbin-Watson Test = 2.09377

The forecasted sales for this month would be

$$\hat{y} = -45.796 + 0.597(43) + 1.177(15) + 0.405(75)$$
$$= -45.796 + 25.671 + 17.655 + 30.375$$
$$= 27.905 \text{ or } \$27,905$$

The Coefficient of Determination.

$$r^2 = 0.983$$

For multiple regression, $\bar{r}^2$ is more appropriate.

$$\bar{r}^2 = 0.975$$

CONCLUSION: 97.5 percent of total variation in sales of dryers is explained by the three independent variables. The remaining 2.5 percent remains unexplained by this equation.

The Standard Error of the Estimate (s_e). From the output, s_e is shown to equal 0.28613, which measures the dispersion of actual sales around the estimated equation.

Computed t. From the output, t statistics are for the three variables as follows:

x_1 : 7.359
x_2 : 13.998
x_3 : 9.592

Remember the rule of thumb that a t value greater than 2.0 is acceptable. Here, all values are greater than 2.0. Strictly speaking, with $n - k - 1 = 10 - 3 - 1 = 6$ degrees of freedom, and a level of significance of, say, 0.01, the t value from Table 7.2 = 3.707. CONCLUSION: All three independent variables are statistically significant.

Durbin-Watson Test. The output shows 2.094 which is between 1.5 and 2.5. No autocorrelation exists.

F Test. From the output, $F = 118.517$. At a 0.01 level of significance, this F value is far above 9.78. CONCLUSION: The regression as a whole is highly significant.

Conclusions. Based on these statistical considerations, you can conclude that

• The estimated equation is a good fit
• All three independent variables are highly significant
• No autocorrelation exists
• The regression as a whole is highly significant
• The model can be used as a forecasting equation with a high degree of confidence

8

Making Use of Quantitative Decision Making

Quantitative methods (or models) are used in operations research or management science. They refer to sophisticated mathematical and statistical techniques for solving problems pertaining to managerial planning and decision making. Numerous such techniques are available, eight of which are discussed in this chapter. They are

- Decision making under certainty and conflict
- Decision making under uncertain conditions
- Decision theory
- Zero sum games
- Linear programming
- Learning curve
- Inventory planning and control
- Queuing models

8.1 DECISION MAKING UNDER CERTAINTY AND CONFLICT

Decision making involves managing three major elements:

- *Decision strategy.* A decision maker implements a decision strategy which utilizes known existing organizational resources.
- *States of nature.* Elements of the environment over which the manager has little or no control. States of nature include the weather, political environment, the economy, technological developments, etc. They can dramatically affect the outcome of any decision strategy.

• *Outcome.* The result of the interaction of the implementation of a decision strategy with the states of nature. Because of the variable nature of the states of nature, outcomes can be extremely difficult to forecast. Thus, outcomes of a decision strategy, O, the dependent variable, is a function of the interaction of the two independent variables, D, decision strategies and, S, the states of nature. Figure 8.1 shows a decision matrix. The rows are strategic choice a manager can make while the columns represent decision outcomes. An outcome O_{ij} is a function of a decision strategy D_i and a state of nature S_i.

FIGURE 8.1 DECISION MATRIX

	States of Nature					
Strategies	S_1	S_2	S_x	S_x	S_x	S_j
D_1	O_{11}	O_{12}	*	*	*	O_{1j}
D_2	O_{21}	O_{22}	*	*	*	O_{2j}
D_x	*	*				*
D_x	*	*				*
D_i	O_{i1}	O_{i2}	*	*	*	O_{ij}

Mathematically this relationship can be expressed as:

$O_{ij} = f(D_i\ S_j)$

What is decision making under certainty?

This is the simplest type of decision making since it has a known state of nature. Therefore, the outcomes are the direct result of the chosen decision strategy, and can be predicted with certainty. In reality, this situation rarely occurs.

The manager simply evaluates all the available decision strategies and then chooses the one best meeting the outcome criteria. Various optimization techniques can be utilized to maximize a decision strategy.

Decision making under certainty occurs with problems that can be analyzed using basic inventory models, break-even analysis, linear programming, incremental analysis, and other methods where an outcome having one state of nature can be determined.

What is decision making under conflict?

In this situation, the decision maker is opposed by another party who is designing states of nature strategies to offset the decision maker's strategy to gain a competitive advantage. The decision maker must develop decision strategies to defeat an opponent's state of nature control strategy.

This is the ideal setting for developing game strategies. Games are dependent on rules governing a competitive situation where the number of players, the strategies, the states of nature between the players, and the degree of conflict control the outcomes.

What are the types of games?

Games are classified according to the degree of conflict of interest between the opponents. A zero sum game has a perfect inverse relationship between the gains and losses of the opponents. One opponent's gain is the other's loss. The total sum remains the same.

In nonzero-sum games the gains of one participant do not necessarily represent a comparable loss for the other party to the game. In the business environment, most competitive situations are nonzero-sum games.

How does a zero sum game work?

In a zero sum game the gains and losses are always equal. No player can gain more than the other player loses. Therefore, the game is always in equilibrium.

The simplest type of zero sum game is the two-person zero sum game. Each player has a choice of game strategies. Since each player's gain will equal the other's loss, the outcome for each game strategy is known to each player.

In the two-person zero sum game, the outcomes can be expressed numerically. A two-person zero sum game outcome matrix is shown in Example 8.1. A positive number indicates a payoff to the player for rows A, and a negative number indicates a payoff to the player for columns B. In Example 8.1 the maximum any player can win/lose is 11.

EXAMPLE 8.1

Two-player zero sum game outcome matrix

Player A	Player B	
	Strategy F r_1	Strategy H r_2
Strategy D p_1	A wins 5	A wins 8
Strategy E p_2	A wins 6	B wins 2 (or A loses 2)

What is a pure strategy?

A pure strategy exists when there is one strategy for player A and one for player B that will be played every time. An equilibrium point is reached when it is at an optimum point for each respective player. This is termed a saddle point. A saddle point occurs where it is both the smallest numerical value in its row and the largest numerical value in its column.

EXAMPLE 8.2

Example 8.2 shows a sample saddle point in a two-person zero sum game. Since 13 is the row minimum and the column maximum, this is the saddle point strategy. The value of this game is 13. As the first choice Player A gains 13 while Player B loses 13.

Saddle Point for two-person Zero Sum Game

Player B

20	13	18
8	4	7

Player A

What is a mixed strategy?

When no player has one strategy that will be used each time, then there is no pure strategy used in the zero sum game. In this case the optimum point, or saddle point, is found using a mixed strategy. In this case, each player's strategy is chosen using a random number process. Nonetheless, one player's gain is another player's loss.

EXAMPLE 8.3

Using the Two-Player Zero Sum Game Outcome Matrix in Example 8.1, it is possible to establish a mixed strategy. Assuming p_1 and p_2 are the probabilities for A's strategies, and n_1 and n_2 are the probabilities for B's strategies, their values can be determined using the following process in Section 8.2.

2 DECISION MAKING UNDER UNCERTAIN CONDITIONS

Under what conditions are decisions made?

Decisions are made under conditions of certainty or

uncertainty (risk). Under certainty implies that for each decision there is only one event and therefore only one outcome for each action. Under uncertainty, which is more common realistically, several events are involved for each action and with each a different probability of occurrence. WHAT TO DO: Under uncertainty, it's often helpful to compute the following:

- Expected value
- Standard deviation
- Coefficient of variation

What does expected value tell me?

For decisions involving uncertainty, the concept of expected value ($\overline{A}$) provides a rational means for selecting the best course of action. Expected value is defined as a weighted mean using the probabilities as weights. It is found by multiplying the probability of each outcome by its payoff:

$$\overline{A} = \overline{\sum} A_x P_x$$

where:

A_x = outcome for the xth possible event
P_x = the probability of occurrence for that outcome

What is the significance of the standard deviation?

The standard deviation (s) measures the dispersion of a probability distribution (see also Section 7.1). It can be defined as the square root of the mean of the squared deviations from the expected value; thus

$$\sigma = \sqrt{\sum_{x=1}^{n} (Ax - \overline{A})^2 P_x}$$

Standard deviation is commonly used as an absolute measure of risk. RULE OF THUMB: The higher the standard deviation, the higher the risk.

What does the coefficient of variation mean?

The coefficient of variation (cv) is a measure of relative dispersion, or relative risk. You can compute it by dividing the standard deviation by the expected value:

$$\sigma v = \frac{\sigma}{\overline{A}}$$

EXAMPLE 8.4

Investment Projects A and B have the following probability distribution of cash inflows in each of the next four years:

Cash Inflows

Probability	(.2)	(.3)	(.4)	(.1)
Project A	$ 50	200	300	400
Project B	$100	150	250	850

The expected value of the cash inflow is computed as follows:

Project A

$\bar{A}$ = $500(.2) + $200(.3) + $300(.4) + $400(.1) = $230

Project B

$\bar{A}$ = $100(.2) + $140(.3) + $240(.4) + $850(.1) = $250

The standard deviations are computed as follows:

Project A

$$\sigma = \sqrt{\begin{array}{l}([\$50 - \$230]^2\,[0.2] + [200 - 230]^2\,[0.3] \\ + [300 - 230]^2\,[0.4] + [400 - 230]^2\,[0.1])\end{array}}$$

σ = $107.70

Project B

$$\sigma = \sqrt{\begin{array}{l}([\$100 - 250]^2\,[0.2] + [150 - 250]^2\,[0.3] \\ + [250 - 250]^2\,[0.4] + [850 - 250]^2\,[0.1])\end{array}}$$

σ = $208.57

The coefficients of variation are computed as follows:

Project A

$$cv = \frac{\$107.70}{\$230} = 0.47$$

Project B

$$cv = \frac{\$208.57}{\$250} = 0.83$$

CONCLUSIONS: Project B is riskier than Project A because its standard deviation is greater. And, because its coefficient of variation is also greater, the degree of risk is also greater for Project B.

8.3 DECISION THEORY

What is decision theory?

Decision theory refers to a systematic approach to making decisions, particularly under conditions of uncertainty. While the statistics mentioned in Section 7.1 are essential for making your best choice, the decision problem can best be approached by using a payoff table or decision matrix. This consists of three basic components:

- *The row.* Each row represents a set of available alternative courses of action.
- *The column.* Each column represents the "states of nature," or conditions that are likely to occur and over which you have no control.
- *The entries.* These appear in the body of the table and represent the outcome of the decision, known as payoffs. These may be in the form of costs, revenues, profits, or cash flows.

What is the role of expected value in decision theory?

By computing the expected value of each action, you will be able to pick the best one.

Suppose you can obtain a perfect prediction of which event will occur. The expected value with such perfect information would be the total expected value of selected actions. Thus, expected value of perfect information (EVPI) can be computed as follows:

> EVPI = expected value with perfect information minus expected value with existing information

EXAMPLE 8.5

The daily demand for strawberries is expressed by the following probability distribution:

daily demand	0	1	2	3
probability	.2	.3	.3	.2

Assume

> unit cost = \$3
> selling price = \$5 (i.e., profit on sold unit = \$2)
>
> salvage value
> on unsold units = \$2
> (i.e., loss on unsold unit = \$1)

The company can stock 0, 1, 2, or 3 units. Problem: How many units should be stocked daily? Assume that units from one day cannot be sold on the next. The payoff table can be constructed as follows:

		STATE OF NATURE				
		Demand (Probability)				Expected
	Stock	0 (.2)	1 (.3)	2 (.3)	3 (.2)	Value (A)
	0	$0	$0	$0	$0	$0
Actions	1	−1	2	2	2	1.40
	2	−2	1a	4	4	1.90b
	3	−3	0	3	6	1.50

aProfit for (stock 2, demand 1) = (no. units sold) (profit per unit) − (no. units unsold) (loss per unit)
= (1)($5 − 3) − (1)($3 − 2)
= $2 − 1 = $1

bExpected value for (stock 2) = − 2(.2) + 1(.3) + 4(.3) + 4(.2)
= $1.90

With perfect information, you can make the following analysis:

		STATE OF NATURE				
		Demand (Probability)				Expected
	Stock	0 (.2)	1 (.3)	2 (.3)	3 (.2)	Value (Ā)
	0	$0				0
Actions	1		2			.6
	2			4		1.2
	3				6	1.2
						$3.0

CONCLUSIONS: The optimal stock action is stock 2, with the highest expected value of $1.90. Thus, with existing information, the best you can do is to select stock 2 units to obtain $1.90. With perfect information, you could make as much as $3. Therefore, the expected value of perfect information (EVPI) = $3.00 + $1.90, or $1.10. This is the maximum price you should be willing to pay for additional information.

8.4 LINEAR PROGRAMMING AND SHADOW PRIC

8.4.1 Linear Programming

What is linear programming?

Linear programming (LP) is concerned with optimal allocation of limited resources among competing activities. Specifically, it's a technique used to maximize revenue, contribution margin, or profit, or it is used to minimize a cost function subject to constraints.

What does linear programming consist of?

Linear programming consists of two important components:

- Objective function
- Constraints that typically are inequalities

Here's an example: A company wishes to find an optimal product mix in order to maximize its total contribution without violating restrictions imposed by the availability of resources. Or, it may want to determine a least-cost combination of input materials while satisfying production requirements, maintaining required inventory levels, staying within production capacities, and using available employees. The objective function is to minimize production costs. The constraints are production requirements, inventory levels, production capacity, and available employees.

What are applications of linear programming?

In addition to the preceding example, some applications for which you can use LP follow.

CHECKLIST OF APPLICATIONS FOR LINEAR PROGRAMMING

- Selecting an investment mix
- Blending chemical products
- Scheduling flight crews
- Assigning jobs to machines
- Determining transportation routes
- Determining distribution or allocation patterns

What is involved in the formulation of linear programming?

To formulate the LP problem, first define the "decision variables" that you are trying to solve. Next, express th objective function and constraints in terms of these decision variables. NOTE: All expressions must be in linear form.

EXAMPLE 8.6

Company J produces two products, A and B. Both require time in two processing departments, the Assembly Department and the Finishing Department. Data for the two products are given as follows:

	PRODUCTS		Available Hours
Processing	A	B	
Assembly	2	4	100
Finishing	3	2	90
Contribution margin per unit	$25	$40	

The company wants to find the most profitable mix of these two products. First define the decision variables as follows:

A = the number of units of Product A to be produced

B = the number of units of Product B to be produced

The objective function is to maximize the total contribution margin (CM), expressed as follows:

Total CM = $25A + $40B

Then, formulate the constraints as inequalities, as follows:

- Assembly constraint: $2A + 4B \leq 100$
- Finishing constraint: $3A + 2B \leq 90$
- Nonnegativity constraints: $A, B \geq 0$

The LP model would be constructed as follows:

- Maximize total CM = 25A + 40B
- Subject to $2A + 4B \leq 100$
  $3A + 2B \leq 90$
  $A, B \geq 0$

How do I solve LP problems?

There are several methods available for solving LP problems. Here are two common ones:

- *The simplex method.* This is the most commonly used method of solving LP problems. It uses an algorithm, which can be defined as an iterative method of computation, to move from one solution to another until it reaches the best one.

- *The graphical method.* This solution is easier to use but is limited to problems involving two or at most three decision variables.

To use the graphical method, follow these five steps:

- Change inequalities to equalities
- Graph the equalities
- Identify the correct side for the original inequalities
- After all this, identify the feasible region or area of feasible solutions wherein values of the decision variables satisfy all the restrictions simultaneously
- Determine the contribution margin at all corners in the feasible region

EXAMPLE 8.7

Using Example 8.6, obtain the feasible region by going through steps one through four. This is shown as the shaded area in Figure 8.2. Then evaluate all the corner points within the feasible region in terms of their CM. Computations follow.

	Corner Points		Contribution Margin	
	A	*B*	*$25A + $40B*	
(*a*)	30	0	$25(30) + $40(0) =	$ 750
(*b*)	20	15	25(20) + 40(15) =	1,100
(*c*)	0	25	25(0) + 40(25) =	1,000
(*d*)	0	0	25(0) + 40(0) =	0

CONCLUSION: Corner *b* (20*A*, 15*B*) produces the most profitable solution.

FIGURE 8.2 GRAPHICAL SOLUTION

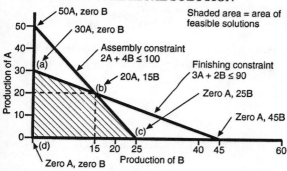

8.4.2 Shadow Prices

What are shadow prices?

If you have solved an LP problem, you might still wish to know whether it pays to add capacity in hours in a particular department. For example, you would be interested to know the monetary value to the company by adding, say, an hour per week of assembly time. This value is the additional contribution margin that could be earned, or the shadow price of a given resource. Shadow prices constitute a form of *opportunity cost* if you consider it as the contribution margin that would be lost by not adding capacity.

To justify a decision in favor of a short-term capacity expansion, you must be sure the shadow price exceeds the actual price of the expansion. Here's how to compute shadow prices (or opportunity costs):

- Add one hour (or preferably more) to the constraint under consideration
- Resolve the problem and find the maximum CM
- Compute the difference between CM of the original LP problem and the CM determined in the previous step; this is the shadow price

NOTE: Other methods, such as using the dual problem, are available to compute shadow prices.

EXAMPLE 8.8

Use the data from the previous example to compute the shadow price of the assembly capacity. To facilitate graphing, add eight hours of capacity to this department. The new assembly constraint is shown in Figure 8.3.

	Corner Points A	B	Contribution Margin $25A + $40B
(a)	30	0	$25(30) + $40(0) = $ 750
(b)	18	18	25(18) + 40(18) = 1,170
(c)	0	27	25(0) + 40(27) = 1,080
(d)	0	0	25(0) + 40(0) = 0

The new optimal solution, Corner b (18A, 18B) has a total CM of $1,170 per week. The shadow price of the assembly capacity = $1,170 − $1,100 = $70. YOUR CONCLUSION: The company should be willing to pay up to $70 to obtain an additional eight hours per week, or $8.75 per hour per week.

FIGURE 8.3 GRAPHICAL SOLUTION

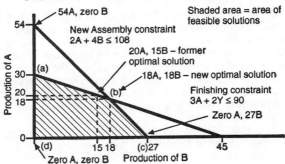

8.4.3 How to Use the Computer for Linear Programming

How does the computer handle linear programming?

Here's an example of how a computer can help solve a linear programming problem. For this example, we use LINDO computer software.

EXAMPLE 8.9

CSULB Company makes two products: snowmobiles and outboard motors. The selling price and variable manufacturing and selling expense data are given as follows:

	Snowmobiles	Outboard Motors
Selling price	$1,400	$1,000
Variable cost	1,200	700
Contribution margin	**$ 200**	**$ 300**

Production is carried out in a single plant. Parts for each product are first produced in the machining department and then moved to the assembly line.

	Snowmobiles	Outboard Motors
Standard machining time	10 hours	30 hours
Standard assembly time	20	20
Total capacity of machining department	150	200

Each unit of snowmobile requires 300 units of material no. 444, and each unit of outboard motor requires 500 units. Currently, 4,800 units are available.

The company wants to determine (1) the most profitable mix of these products and (2) the shadow price for each scarce resource, that is, machining time, assembly time, and material.

The Optimal Solution. From LINDO output:

x_1 = the number of units of snowmobiles to be produced = 7.5

x_2 = the number of units of outboard motors to be produced = 2.5

NOTE: If you must have an integer solution, you should use the integer programming method.

The Shadow Prices. Shadow prices are as follows:

For machining time	$5.00
For assembly time	7.50
For material	0.00

LINDO Output for Example 8.9

```
:   max 200x1+300x2
?   st
?   10x1+30x2<150
?   20x1+20x2<200
?   300x1+500x2<4800
?   end
    look all
```

MAX   200 X1 + 300 X2

SUBJECT TO
  2)   10 X1 + 30 X2 < = 150
  3)   20 X1 + 20 X2 < = 200
  4)   300 X1 + 500 X2 < = 4800

END
: 90

LP OPTIMUM FOUND AT STEP   2

     OBJECTIVE FUNCTION VALUE

  1)   2250.00000

VARIABLE	VALUE	REDUCED COST	
X1	7.500000	.000000	$X_1 = 7.5$
X2	2.500000	.000000	$X_2 = 2.5$

ROW	SLACK OR SURPLUS	DUAL PRICES SHADOW PRICES
2)	.000000	5.000000
3)	.000000	7.500000
4)	1300.000000	1300.000000

NO. ITERATIONS =   2

INTERPRETATION: The company would be willing to pay $5 and $7.50 to buy one additional hour of machining time and assembly time, respectively. By not buying, the company would lose $5 and $7.50 in potential contribution. On the other hand, the company is unwilling to pay anything for material. Why? Adding one extra unit of material no. 444 will not bring any additional contribution to the company.

NOTE: You may use Microsoft Excel to solve a linear programming problem.

8.5 LEARNING CURVE

How does the learning curve work to estimate labor hours?

The learning curve is based on the proposition that labor hours decrease in a definite pattern as labor operations are repeated. Statistical findings show that as the cumulative output doubles, the cumulative average input will be reduced by some constant percentage, ranging from 10 to 40 percent. Thus, the learning curve is an expression of this phenomenon as it applies to labor hours needed per unit produced.

How do I properly express the learning curve relationship?

The curve is usually designated by its complement. That is, if the rate of reduction is 20 percent, then you would refer to the curve as an 80-percent learning curve.

The following illustrates the 80-percent learning curve relationship:

QUANTITY (IN UNITS)		TIME (IN HOURS)	
Per lot	Cumulative	Total Cumulative	Average time per unit
15	15	600	40.0
15	30	960	32.0 (40.0 × 0.8)
30	60	1,536	25.6 (32.0 × 0.8)
60	120	2,460	20.5 (25.6 × 0.8)
120	240	3,936	16.4 (20.5 × 0.8)

TAKE NOTE: As production quantities double, the average time needed per unit reduces by 20 percent from its immediately previous time.

EXAMPLE 8.10

Stanley Electronics Products, Inc., finds that new-product production is affected by an 80% learning curve. The company has just produced 50 units at 100 hours per unit. Costs were as follows:

Materials @ $20	$1,000
Labor and labor-related costs	
Direct labor (100 hr @ $8)	800
Variable overhead (100 hr @ $2)	200
	$2,000

The company has just received a contract for another 50 units. Management wants to add a 50% markup to the cost of materials, labor, and labor-related costs. You can compute the price for this job as follows:

The learning curve table shows the following:

Quantity	Total Time (in hours)	Average Time (per unit)
50 units	100	2 hours
100	160	1.6 (80% × 2 hr)

The new 50-unit job requires 60 total hours of production time.

Contract Price Computations

Materials @ $20	$1,000
Labor and labor-related costs	
Direct labor (60 hr @ $8)	480
Variable overhead (60 hr @ $2)	120
	$1,600
Markup (50%)	800
Contract price	**$2,400**

In what other ways can I use the learning curve?

CHECKLIST OF APPLICATIONS
FOR THE LEARNING CURVE

- Scheduling labor requirements
- Making capital budgeting decisions
- Setting incentive wage rates

8.6 INVENTORY PLANNING AND CONTROL

Why are inventory planning and control important?

The purpose of inventory planning and control is to develop policies that will achieve an optimal inventory investment. You can do this by determining the optimal inventory level necessary to minimize related costs.

What kinds of costs are associated with inventory?

Inventory costs fall into three categories. They are

- *Order costs.* These include all costs associated with preparing a purchase order.
- *Carrying costs.* These include storage costs for inventory items plus opportunity cost (that is, the cost incurred by investing in inventory).
- *Shortage (stockout) costs.* These are costs incurred when an item is out of stock. They include the lost contribution margin on sales plus lost customer goodwill.

When and how much should I order?

Several inventory planning and control models are available that try to answer these questions. Three such models are

- Economic order quantity (EOQ)
- Reorder point (ROP)
- Determination of safety stock

How does the Economic Order Quantity (EOQ) model work?

The EOQ model determines the order size that minimizes the sum of carrying and ordering costs.

ASSUMPTIONS: Demand is assumed to be known with certainty and to remain constant throughout the year. Order cost is also assumed to be fixed. Also, unit carrying costs are assumed to be constant. Since demand and lead time (time interval between placing an order and receiving delivery) are assumed to be determinable, no shortage costs exist.

EOQ is computed as follows:

$$EOQ = \sqrt{\frac{2 \ (\text{annual demand}) \ (\text{ordering cost})}{\text{carrying cost per unit}}}$$

Total inventory costs

$$= \text{carrying cost per unit} \times \frac{EOQ}{2}$$

$$+ \text{order cost} \times \frac{\text{annual demand}}{EOQ}$$

$$\text{Total number of orders per year} = \frac{\text{annual demand}}{EOQ}$$

EXAMPLE 8.11

Oakman, Inc. buys sets of steel at $40 per set from an outside vendor. Oakman will need 6,400 sets evenly throughout the year. Management desires a 16% return on its inventory investment (cost of capital). In addition, rent, insurance, taxes, etc., for each set in inventory comes to $1.60. The order cost is $100.

The carrying cost per set = $1.60 + 16%(40) = $8.00.
Thus,

$$EOQ = \sqrt{\frac{2 \ (6,400) \ (100)}{\$8.00}}$$

$$= \sqrt{160,000} = 400 \text{ sets}$$

$$\begin{aligned}
\text{Total inventory costs} &= \$8.00 \\
&\quad (400/2) + \$100 \ (6400/400) \\
&= \$1,600 + \$1,600 = \$3,200
\end{aligned}$$

Total number
of annual orders = 6,400/400
= 16 orders

How do I determine the reorder point?

Reorder point tells you when to place an order. However, this method requires that you know the lead time from placing to receiving an order.

Reorder point is computed as follows:

ROP = lead time × average usage per unit of time.

This tells you the level of inventory at which a new order should be placed. NOTE: If you need a safety stock, then add this amount to the ROP model.

EXAMPLE 8.12

Using the preceding example, assume lead time is constant at one week. There are 50 working weeks in the year. Reorder point is computed as follows:

$$\text{Reorder point} = 1 \text{ week} \times \frac{6,400}{50 \text{ weeks}}$$
$$= 1 \times 128 = 128 \text{ sets}$$

CONCLUSION: When the inventory level drops to 128 sets, a new order should be placed.

Figure 8.4 shows this inventory system when the order quantity equals 400 sets.

FIGURE 8.4 BASIC INVENTORY SYSTEM

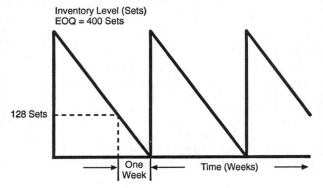

When are these models realistic to use?

The EOQ model described here is appropriate for a pure inventory system; that is, for single-item, single-stage inventory decisions for which joint costs and constraints can be ignored. EOQ and ROP assume that both lead time and demand rates are constant and known with certainty. CAUTION: This may be unrealistic. Still, these models have been proved useful in inventory planning for many companies. There are, for instance, many businesses for which these assumptions hold to some extent. They include:

- Subcontractors who must supply parts on a regular basis to a primary contractor
- Automobile dealerships, in which demand varies from week to week but tends to even out over a season

CAUTION: When demand is not known precisely and/or other complications arise, you should not use these models. You should instead refer to probabilistic models.

What about quantity discounts?

EOQ does not take quantity discounts into account, which is often unrealistic in actual practice. Usually the more you order, the lower the unit price you pay. A typical price discount schedule follows:

Order Size	Unit Cost
$0 < E < 500$	$ 40.00
$500 < E < 1000$	39.90
$1000 < E$	39.80

where E = order size

WHAT TO DO: With the price discounts shown here, you must include unit costs in your cost model as follows:

Total costs = total inventory costs + cost of product
= carrying cost per unit
$\times \dfrac{E}{2}$ + unit price
$\times \dfrac{\text{annual demand}}{E}$
+ unit price × annual demand

Use these three steps to find the economic order size with price discounts:

- Compute the EOQ when price discounts are ignored and the corresponding costs using the new cost after discount.
- Compute the costs for those quantities greater than EOQ at which price reductions occur.
- Select the value of E that results in the lowest annual cost.

EXAMPLE 8.13

Using the information from the previous two examples and the discount schedule shown previously, try to determine the economic order size. Recall that EOQ = 400. The further you move from point 400, the greater will be the sum of the ordering and carrying points. Thus, 400 is the only candidate for the minimum total cost value within the first price range. The only candidate within the $39.90 price range is $E = 500$, and $E = 1,000$ is the only candidate within the $39.80 range. The evaluation of these three points follows, and they are illustrated in Figure 8.5.

FIGURE 8.5 COSTS FOR PRICE DISCOUNT PROBLEM

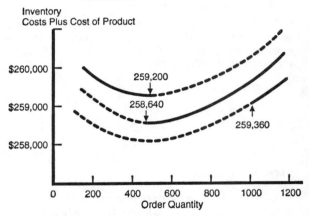

CONCLUSION: The economic order quantity with price discounts is 500. The manufacturer is justified in going to the first price break, but the extra carrying cost of the second price break more than outweighs the savings in ordering and in the cost of the product itself

ANNUAL COSTS WITH VARYING ORDER SIZES

Order Size	400	500	1,000
Ordering cost $\dfrac{(\$100 \times 6,400)}{\text{order size}}$	$ 1,600	$ 1,280	$ 640
Carrying cost $\dfrac{(\$8 \times \text{order size})}{2}$	1,600	2,000	4,000
Product cost (unit price × 6,400)	256,000	255,360	254,720
Total cost	$259,200	$258,640	$259,360

What can I do when lead time and demand are uncertain?

When lead time and demand are uncertain, you must carry extra units of inventory, called safety stock, as protection against possible stockouts.

Service level can be defined as the probability that demand will not exceed supply during lead time. Thus, a service level of 90 percent implies a probability of 90 percent that demand will not exceed supply during lead time. To determine the optimal level of safety stock size, you might want to measure costs of not having enough inventory, or stockout costs. Here are three cases for computing the safety stock. The first two do not recognize stockout costs; the third case does.

Case 1: Variable usage rate, constant lead time

ROP = Expected usage during lead time
+ safety stock

$$= \bar{u} \, LT + z \sqrt{LT} \, (\sigma_u)$$

where

$\bar{u}$ = average usage rate
LT = lead time
σ_u = standard deviation of usage rate
z = standard normal variate as defined in Table 8.1

For a normal distribution, a given service level amounts to the shaded area under the curve to the left of ROP in Figure 8.6.

FIGURE 8.6 SERVICE LEVEL

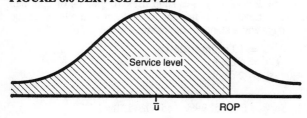

EXAMPLE 8.14

Ken's Pizza uses large cases of tomatoes at an average rate of 50 cans per day. Usage can be approximated by a normal distribution with a standard deviation of five cans per day. Lead time is four days. Thus:

$\bar{u}$ = 50 cans per day
σ_u = 5 cans
LT = 4 days

How much safety stock is necessary for a service level of 99%? And what is the ROP?

For a service level of 99%, $z = 2.33$ (from Table 8.1). Thus:

Safety stock $= 2.33\sqrt{4}\,(5) = 23.3$ cans

$$ROP = 50(4) + 23.3 = 223.3 \text{ cans}$$

FIGURE 8.7 SERVICE LEVEL = 99%

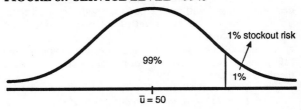

Case 2: Constant usage rate, variable lead time

For constant usage with variable lead time, the reorder point is computed as follows:

ROP = expected usage during lead time + safety stock
$$= \overline{u}\,\overline{LT} + zu\,\sigma_{LT}$$

where

u = constant usage rate
$\overline{LT}$ = average lead time
σ_{LT} = standard deviation of lead time

EXAMPLE 8.15

The local hamburger shop uses 10 gallons of cola per day. Lead time is normal distribution with a mean of six days and a standard deviation of 2 days. Thus,

u = 10 gallons per day
$\overline{LT}$ = 6 days
σ_{LT} = 2 days

How much safety stock should be carried to achieve a service level of 99%, and what is the ROP?

Safety stock $= 2.33(10)(2) = 46.6$ gallons
$$ROP = 10(6) + 46.6 = 106.6 \text{ gallons}$$

(Note: 2.33 = z at 99% service level.)

TABLE 8.1   **VALUES OF z_P FOR SPECIFIED PROBABILITIES P**

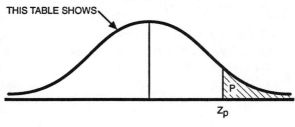

THIS TABLE SHOWS

P	z_P	P	z_P	P	z_P
0.0005	3.29053	0.005	2.57583	0.11	1.22653
0.0010	3.09023	0.010	2.32635	0.12	1.17499
0.0015	2.96774	0.015	2.17009	0.13	1.12639
0.0020	2.87816	0.020	2.05375	0.14	1.08032
0.0025	2.80703	0.025	1.95996	0.15	1.03643
0.0030	2.74778	0.030	1.88079	0.16	0.99446
0.0035	2.69684	0.035	1.81191	0.17	0.95417
0.0040	2.65207	0.040	1.75069	0.18	0.91537
0.0045	2.61205	0.045	1.69540	0.19	0.87790
0.0050	2.57583	0.050	1.64485	0.20	0.84162
0.006	2.51214	0.06	1.55477	0.25	0.67449
0.007	2.45726	0.07	1.47579	0.30	0.52440
0.008	2.40892	0.08	1.40507	0.35	0.38532
0.009	2.36562	0.09	1.34076	0.40	0.25335
0.010	2.32635	0.10	1.28155	0.45	0.12566

z_p is the value of the standardized normal (mean = 0, standard deviation = 1) random variable z such that the probability of obtaining a sample z value at least as large as z_p is P. The value of P must be doubled if two-sided statements are made using the same z_p value.

Source: Croxton/Cowden/Bolch, *Practical Business Statistics,* 4th Ed., © 1969, p. 393. Reprinted by permission of Prentice-Hall, Inc., Englewood Cliffs, N.J.

Case 3: Incorporation of stockout costs

This case specifically recognizes the cost of stockouts or shortages, which can be quite expensive. Lost sales, disgruntled customers, idle machines, and disrupted production scheduling are examples of internal and external costs caused by stockouts.

WHAT TO DO: You can use the probability approach to determine the optimum stock size in the presence of stock-out costs. Here's an example:

EXAMPLE 8.16

Refer to Example 8.12. The total usage over a one-week period is estimated as follows:

Total Use	Probability
78	.2
128	.4
178	.2
228	.1
278	.1
	1.0

A stockout cost is estimated at $12 per set. Recall that the carrying cost is $8 per set. Computation of safety stock is shown on page 287.

CONCLUSIONS: The table shows that total costs are minimized at $1,200 when a safety stock of 150 sets is maintained. Thus, ROP = 128 sets + 150 sets = 278 sets.

8.7 QUEUING (WAITING LINE) MODELS

What is the purpose of queuing theory?

Queuing, or waiting line, theory investigates the everyday hassle of waiting in line. If you are an operating, marketing or production manager, you could apply this tool should waiting time involve you.

Like EOQ, queuing theory involves minimization of overall costs; that is, the sum of waiting costs borne by customers or businesses and the cost of providing extra service facilities and/or attendants.

What are the applications of queuing theory?

The applications of queuing theory are numerous. For example, you may want to determine the number of doctors that should be on call at a clinic.

What are some queuing models?

Before investigating queuing models, you need to know three things. They are

Safety Stock Levels in Units	Stockout and Probability	Average Stockout in Units	Average Stockout Costs	Total Annual No. of Orders	Stockout Costs	Carrying Costs	Total
0	50 with .2 100 with .1 150 with .1	35[a]	$420[b]	16	$6,720[c]	0	$6,720
50	50 with .1 100 with .1	15	180	16	2,880	400[d]	3,280
100	50 with .1	5	60	16	960	800	1,760
150	0	0	0	16	0	1,200	1,200

[a]50(.2) + 100(.1) + 150(.1) = 10 + 10 + 15 = 35 units

[b]35 units × $12.00 = $420

[c]$420 × 16 times = $6,720

[d]50 units × $8.00 = $400

287

- Your company's experience with the daily ebb and flow of customers
- The probability assumptions as the nature of this process unfolds; for example, what are the chances of experiencing an unusually large bunching of arrivals
- Determination of costs associated with waiting and improving the rate of service

There are many queuing models from which you can choose. One, called the Single Channel Exponential Service Time Model, assumes a Poisson arrival rate and infinite source. For this model, use the following symbols:

A = mean arrival rate
S = mean service rate

Management scientists have developed the following equations for this single-channel model:

- System utilization = probability that the servers are busy = $\dfrac{A}{S}$
- Average number in the system = number of units in the queue plus number being served = $\dfrac{A}{(S-A)}$
- Average number waiting for service to begin = number of units in the queue = $\dfrac{A^2}{S(S-A)}$
- Average time spent waiting in the system = queue time plus service time = $\dfrac{1}{S-A}$
- Average time spent waiting before service begins = time in queue = $\dfrac{A}{S(S-A)}$
- Percent of idle time = $1 - \dfrac{A}{S}$

EXAMPLE 8.17

Los Alamitos Car Wash is an automatic operation with a single bay. On a typical Saturday morning, cars arrive at a mean rate of nine per hour, with arrivals tending to follow a Poisson distribution. Service time, including manual drying time, is assumed to be exponentially distributed. Past experience suggests that the mean service time should average five minutes. Thus

A = 9 cars per hour
S = 1 per 5 minutes or 12 per hour

You can determine the following:

- System utilization $= \dfrac{9}{12} = 75\%$. This means the system is busy 75% of the time.

- Average number of cars in line and service $=$
  $\dfrac{9}{12-9} = 3$ cars

- Average number of cars in line $= \dfrac{9_2}{12(\,12-9)} =$
  $\dfrac{81}{36} = 2.25$ cars

- Average time cars spend waiting in line and for service $= \dfrac{1}{121-9} = 1/3$ hour or 20 minutes

- Average time cars spend waiting for service $=$
  $\dfrac{9}{12(12-9)} = 9/36 = 1/4$ or 15 minutes

- Percent of idle time $= 1 - 0.75 = 0.25$ or 25%

The following is Microsoft Excel's queuing output for this example.

M/M/s queuing computations

Arrival rate	9
Service rate	12
Number of servers	1 (max of 40)

Assumes Poisson process for arrivals and services.

Utilization	75.000%	System utilization
P(0), probability that the system is empty	0.2500	Percent of idle time
Lq, expected queue length	2.2500	Average # of cars in line
L, expected number in system	3.0000	Average # of cars in line and service
Wq, expected time in queue	0.2500	Average time cars spending waiting for service
W, expected total time in system	0.3333	Average time cars spending waiting in line and for service
Probability that a customer waits	0.7500	

PART IV

MANAGEMENT, MARKETING, AND LEGAL STRATEGIES

Chapters 9, 10, and 11 were written by Stephen W. Hartman; Chapter 12 was written by Joyce O. Moy.

9

Management

Management is a process that utilizes various functions and activities to help an organization accomplish its goals. Managers are charged with the responsibility of achieving the organization's goals by getting things done. Above all else, the management process is dependent on coordinating and motivating people in the organization to achieve high quality outcomes. The study of management involves theories, principles and concepts used in this process.

9.1 JUST-IN-TIME (JIT) INVENTORY

Inventory is maintained to prevent production problems caused by the lack of supply of needed materials. JIT is an inventory system that maintains the smallest amount of inventory necessary to continue the organizational production process and to minimize costs.

What is the cost of inventory?

Inventory entails many hidden and obvious costs. Among these are the costs of carrying, ordering, and storing supplies as well as the risks of obsolescence, spoilage, shrinkage, inadequate insurance, and undetected defects. Inventory costs can involve an enormous amount of money.

How does the Just-in-Time (JIT) Inventory Management System work?

The Just-in-Time Inventory Management System seeks to have the exact amount of production materials available when needed, without having shortages or excess inventory.

In order to maintain this exacting performance specification, the methodology is designed to minimize system variances both inside and outside of the production process.

What are system variances and what causes them?

Basically, production system variances occur because of ineffective management practices and insufficient utilization and/or processing of production materials, i.e., waste. One bottleneck can be an ineffective procurement system which includes purchasing, source, supply, and materials management.

Waste occurs because:

- Production results have unacceptable quality, quantity, or timeliness due to poor employee training, low quality production resources, or poor quality materials.

- Design specifications are faulty.

- Customer specifications are incomplete or unrealistic.

How does JIT minimize production variances?

JIT minimizes production variances in the following ways:

- Small lot sizes are used. Small lot sizes require smaller material inventory needs, and delivery times can be more reliably estimated and managed.

- The stages of the manufacturing process are carefully synchronized. This prevents unanticipated material demands.

- Inventory is used only when required instead of accumulating waiting for need. This is called an inventory "pull" strategy, as opposed to a "push" strategy.

- Smaller lot size produces a steadier inventory demand since maximum and minimum inventory levels are reduced. This can be demonstrated by calculating a mean inventory level:

$$\text{Mean Inventory Level} = \frac{\text{Maximum Inventory} + \text{Minimum Inventory Level}}{2}$$

EXAMPLE 9.1

A manager wants to understand the Mean Inventory Levels in two different production departments. The first has large lot production of 5,000 units while the second only produces in small lot sizes of 200 units. The manager must calculate the mean inventory levels:

Lot Size	Minimum Inventory	Maximum Inventory	Mean Inventory Level = Max. Inventory + Min. Inventory / 2
5,000	500	9,000	4,750
200	150	250	200
Difference			4,550

The large lot size has a mean inventory level of 4,750 while the small lot size has a mean inventory level of 200. The difference between the large and small lot sizes in Mean Inventory Levels is 4,550.

9.2 MATERIAL REQUIREMENTS PLANNING (MRP)

A Material Requirements Planning system provides a methodology for analyzing and forecasting material needs for the purpose of developing a schedule of the material necessary to complete production goals. MRP requires the existence of a production schedule, a bill of material, inventory and purchase records, and lead times for each production item. The MRP graphically demonstrates when inventory materials need to be ordered or when production on an item must begin so a particular item will meet the production schedule.

Normally, an MRP is computerized. It is a widely used inventory management system in companies involved in mass assembly.

EXAMPLE 9.2

A company produces a consumer item which consists of several components it also manufactures. Using these items, an MRP is constructed:

Gross Material Requirements plan for 75 units of A									
Component Deadline and Start Dates		*Weeks*							*Lead Time*
	1	2	3	4	5	6	7	8	
A. Deadline Date								75	1 week
Start Date							75		
B. Deadline Date							150		3 weeks
Start Date				150					
C. Deadline Date							200		2 weeks
Start Date					200				
D. Deadline Date					350				1 week
Start Date				350					
E. Deadline Date					400				1 week
Start Date				400					
F. Deadline Date				550					1 week
Start Date			550						
G. Deadline Date			400						2 weeks
Start Date	400								
H. Deadline Date			500						2 weeks
Start Date	500								

In this gross material requirements example, in order to produce 75 units of A in week eight, their manufacture must begin in week seven. However, that requires that 150 components of B and 200 of C be available at that time. In turn, that means manufacture of components B and C must start at weeks 4 and 5, respectively. The MRP shows the start and deadline dates of the other required components in the manufacturing chain. Transforming these dates into an actual calendar allows managers to quickly view their progress in the manufacturing process.

How is an MRP adjusted when there is inventory on hand?

When there is inventory on hand, the MRP manufacturing schedule is adjusted to the actual net requirements to meet the production deadlines.

9.3 PLANNING

What is planning?

Planning is a fundamental management process that influences an organization's mission, goals and objectives, and determines a future course of action. Planning is dynamic and continually responds to changes in the business environment. Rather than reacting to changes, planning allows the proactive control of future environmental variables. The planning process normally results in a management plan that can be widely distributed throughout the organization.

Why is planning essential?

Planning requires an organization to consider its future actions. The reality is that the organizational environment is becoming far more competitive and complex because of increasing international competition and technological progress. While research and development expenditures are increasing, product life cycles are getting steadily shorter.

Planning is absolutely essential in order to develop an understanding of where an organization should be devoting its resources and energy. Without planning, proactive strategies and programs cannot be developed to secure the organization's future success. Planning allows the organization to develop a rational method for controlling and developing the future.

Who has the responsibility for planning?

The real question in planning authority is whether it is centralized or decentralized. Traditionally, the planning function was centralized as a staff management responsibility. The role of the centralized planner was to help shape the organization's mission, goals and objectives, and to develop management strategies for future actions. This was predicated on the advantage management traditionally had in accessing strategic information. It was only natural for planning to be positioned in a centralized management environment.

As the organizational environment has become more dynamic, with management information systems becoming more sophisticated and ubiquitous, information management capabilities have proliferated throughout all levels of an organization. Thus, the planning function has become integrated into the operational levels of organizations. This provides for a dynamic environment where the organization's mission, goals, and objectives are continuously being tested and shaped by those having the responsibility for operationalizing them.

What are the advantages of planning?

Planning makes it possible for an organization to:

- Achieve a coordinated system where all levels of the organization have input into operationalizing its mission, goals, and objectives.

- Control and manage the future consistent with the organization's capabilities and resources.
- Develop a sophisticated management information system so the organization can increase its information processing capability.
- Define organizational and performance objectives to achieve higher quality and productivity.
- Coordinate an overall management development effort throughout the organization.

What are the types of planning?

There are several ways of categorizing plans. Two methods are specificity and timeliness.

1. *Functionally specific plans.* These plans apply to individual organizational functions including human resource management, operations, financial, and marketing management.
2. *Time range of the plan.* The time range of a plan can correspond with the time parameters of objectives from short- and medium- to long-range.

Organizational plans are normally classified into several general categories which encompass a wide range of activities and functions:

- *Strategic Planning.* Strategic planning encompasses the broadest and most comprehensive type of planning. It includes the main purpose of the organization, its mission, as well as the organization's short-, intermediate- and long-range objectives, including the specific details of how the objectives and goals will be achieved. Strategic planning contains within it operational and tactical planning as well as standing and single-use plans.
- *Tactical Planning.* This type of planning is concerned with specific methods of implementing an overall strategic plan. If an organization, for example, would like to enter into a new market, tactical planning would be concerned with the types of products or services that might be necessary to do that.
- *Operational Planning.* Operational planning is very specific and is concerned with actual methods of operationalizing tactical plans which are designed to implement the overall strategic plan. For example, an operational plan might be concerned with managing a manufacturing process to produce a specific product that a tactical plan developed.
- *Single-use Plans.* Single-use plans have very specific

time limits and purposes. Single-use plans are used to implement a program, product, project, or service. A single-use plan might, for example, be used for designing and implementing a specific manufacturing process for the production of a particular product within a clearly defined time frame.

- *Standing Plans.* Standing plans are ongoing management plans for particular organizational policies.

What are the steps in the planning process?

Basically there are six steps in the planning process:

1. *Survey the current organizational environment.* Before a strategic plan can be established, management must conduct a thorough review of the organization's overall environment. This must include the firm's strengths and weaknesses, the competitive and regulatory environment, and current economic and market developments. This review will help the organization form a strategic plan; however, this must be coordinated with the organization's operational plan based on current cash flow, market performance, and overall capabilities.

2. *Develop goals and objectives.* The survey of the organization's current environment assists the organization in determining short-term objectives and future goals. Organizational objectives have different time spans depending on the nature of the objectives and the type of organization. Long-range plans can be for as long as 25 years. Short-term plans can last up to one year while intermediate-term plans can last from one to five years. All objectives must be met prior to achieving the organization's long-term goals. Complex organizations often have multiple objectives which create additional planning and budgeting challenges.

There are several types of organizational objectives:

- Quality and productivity objectives. Quality and productivity go hand-in-hand. Productivity is a ratio of the input of organizational resources to its output. An example is labor to units produced. However, without some standard of quality, there can be no productivity, while high quality increases productivity by decreasing imperfections and waste.

- Marketing objectives. Marketing objectives are the degree of success the organization is experiencing in achieving market, product, and service growth. Management also seeks to evaluate an organization's overall market mix in order to determine where resources should be allocated.

  – Profitability objectives. Profitability objectives include the total increase in profits relative to sales, and net assets. Numerous financial ratios are used to measure profitability. Profitability objectives are important to management for monitoring an organization's financial progress.

3. *Create an organizational action plan.* The net result of the planning process is the establishment of an organizational action plan designed to achieve short-term objectives and longer-term goals. An organizational action plan is derived from the careful definition and understanding of the organization's short-term objectives which are consistent and instrumental in achieving intermediate to longer-term objectives. After establishing a consensus with those having responsibility for carrying it out, the plan is transformed into a clearly written document. While the plan must encompass all of the short-, intermediate- and long-term objectives in order to achieve the organization's longer-term goals, it must also be flexible to permit adaptation to future changes in the organizational and external environment.

4. *Earmark resources.* In order to implement an action plan, a careful assessment of the quantity and nature of the necessary resources is required. A budget is developed for the purpose of allocating the required resources. The budget is based upon a priority analysis of each objective. It must be consistent with the organization action plan's short-, intermediate- and longer-term objectives. Budget allocations require constant monitoring to measure their success in achieving objectives.

5. *Execute the plan.* An organizational action plan will have no effect unless it is carried out. Organizational action plans are executed through the cooperation and teamwork of those within the organization. Management efforts must be coordinated while employees are oriented and trained in the plan's implementation.

6. *Manage the plan.* The management process involves constant feedback of information regarding the success of the plan in achieving its stated objectives. The use of a management information system would be extremely instrumental in managing the plan's implementation.

EXAMPLE 9.3

A beer brewery is planning to establish an organizational action plan. The company has several short-term objectives designed to achieve its long-term goal of increasing its overall market share.

- *Offset server liability.* One of the objectives of the company is to offset the server's legal liability when selling alcoholic beverages. The company creates a series of posters intended to be posted in establishments serving alcoholic beverages. Some posters illustrate the effects of drunk driving, and others urge the necessity of choosing a designated driver. The company also develops beer having a lower alcohol content.

- *Offset the actions of the Mothers Against Drunk Driving (MADD) and other groups such as the Students Against Drunk Driving (SADD).* The company decides to initiate a social responsibility campaign which emphasizes not consuming more than an individual's limit, and the need for responsible automobile driving.

- *Change the image of its products.* In addition to introducing a low-alcohol beer, it also introduces a low-calorie "lite beer" including a non-alcohol product.

- *Develop a sales training program.* In order to achieve higher sales, the company develops a sales training program that emphasizes the importance of educating customers about the company's variety of beer products including low-alcohol and low-calorie beverages. It also seeks to demonstrate the company's commitment to social responsibility.

After creating a consensus regarding its organizational action plan, the brewery initiates a training program where its sales managers and representatives are trained in the significance of the newly developed plan. The company also develops a sophisticated management information system containing a large database where sales representatives can continuously update the database from remote locations using telecommunications.

Over time the company makes steady progress in increasing its market share while improving relations with MADD and SADD. The company has also achieved success in reducing the number of server liability cases as well as witnessing a reduction in driving-while-intoxicated convictions in its market area.

Finally, the company's market share, net profit, and stockholder equity show steady growth.

9.4 TOTAL QUALITY MANAGEMENT (TQM)

TQM is an extremely well-publicized organizational methodology. It is intended to involve all parts of the organization, beginning with total commitment from top management. It is a system-wide concept where all parts of the organization must function congruently in order for it to be functional. A major component of TQM is employee involvement, which management strongly encourages in every step of the decision-making process. This is accomplished by in-depth training and the delegation of extensive quality responsibility to operational employees.

What are the main components of TQM?

The following are some of the basic components of TQM:

- Organizations succeed through constant product and service development and innovation.
- Organizations must embrace a new management philosophy where traditional management views are rejected.
- Quality is achieved by design rather than by inspection.
- Purchasing must be made based on total cost. Short-term material savings could be disastrous if their quality is unacceptable.
- Production and service methods must be continuously improved. Single or occasional standard review and revision is unacceptable.
- Employees must receive training.
- Management needs to demonstrate leadership by teaching others what must be done on a continuous basis.
- A positive and personally rewarding organizational environment must be established for employees to be productive.
- Organizational communications must be open and free at all levels.
- Slogans and short-term employee objectives are not successful.
- Quotas are not successful motivators.
- Employees should be recognized and rewarded for the work they do.
- Continuous education and training programs should be made available to employees.
- A management program must be created to implement TQM or else it will never happen. Implementing TQM needs the active support of top management.

What is the role of quality in TQM?

Quality is a central focus in TQM. The concept of quality goes far beyond the acceptance of a standard minimum number of defects. It essentially means preventing defects from occurring in the first place. This concept has come to be known as "Zero Defects." However, TQM does not limit itself to zero defects in products. It also means providing superb service to develop loyal customers who are so impressed with the quality of the service and products delivered that they recommend the organization to others. TQM's operational definition of quality is nothing less than total customer satisfaction. This is achieved by meeting or exceeding the customer's expectations.

Quality itself is not a fixed objective. Rather it is a continuously evolving target. Organizations cannot be satisfied merely with achieving zero defects in a product or a high level of customer satisfaction. Continuous improvement is essential where previous quality levels are used as the basis for future improvements.

What is necessary to achieve continuous improvement?

Continuous improvement is dependent on continuously improving work methods where employees and customers have unlimited opportunities to express their points of view. This involves developing a dynamic, continually changing, flexible and broad, organizationally based quality planning process. This process would not only lead to new levels of quality performance, but also to new opportunities.

How does TQM compare with the traditional view of management?

TQM goes far beyond the traditional view of management where a defect standard was defined as acceptable. Table 9.1 compares the traditional management view with TQM.

TABLE 9.1 TRADITIONAL MANAGEMENT VIEW COMPARED WITH TQM

Traditional Management View	TQM
High quality is unaffordable. Low quality produces lower costs.	Low quality is unaffordable. High quality produces lower costs.
A percentage standard of defects is acceptable.	Only zero defects are acceptable.
Defects are a function of employees.	Defects are a function of the system designed by management.

TABLE 9.1 (*cont.*)

Annual quality standards are established.	Continuously improve quality standards to maintain competitive advantage.
Manage by using quotas and standards.	Eliminate quotas and standards.
Employees are a cost center.	Employees are a profit center.
Manage by fear.	Drive out fear.
Low costs create profits.	Loyal customers create profits.
Buy on the basis of price.	Buy on the basis of total cost.
Manage on the basis of profits.	Profits are historical and do not predict the future.

9.5 OTHER QUALITY CONTROL TECHNIQUES

What are the Baldrige National Quality Award Criteria?

In 1987 the Malcolm Baldrige National Quality Award (MBNQA) was created to recognize outstanding companies in quality management and control. The criteria specified in the MBNQA are leadership, information and analysis, strategic quality planning, human resource utilization, quality assurance, quality results, and customer satisfaction. Each company uses its own unique approach to winning the award. They define the management strategies and techniques required for each category.

The winning companies share certain characteristics:

- They dedicate themselves to changing former management practices in order to implement newer strategies often requiring radically different operational procedures.
- They display a singular resolve in committing the organization to the new strategy for the long term. They do not expect quick "fixes" will solve their problems.

Various innovative practices often emerge including outside partnering, human resource empowerment, and developing operational strategies to achieve new objectives and long-term goals.

What is the ISO 9000 standard?

ISO 9000 is the general name for the quality standard accepted throughout the European Economic Community. It was initially adopted in 1987. ISO is a series of documents on quality assurance published by the Geneva based International Standards Organization. The five documents outline standards for developing Total Quality Management and a Quality Improvement Process. ISO 9000 consists of guidelines for the selection and use of the quality systems contained in 9001-9003. ISO 9001 outlines a model for quality assurance in design, development, production, installation, and servicing. ISO 9002 outlines a model for quality assurance in production and installation. ISO 9003 outlines a model for quality assurance for finance inspection and testing. ISO 9004 is not a standard but contains guidelines for quality management and quality system elements.

Today, over fifty trading countries, including the United States, use the ISO 9000 standard. It is anticipated that certification in the ISO 9000 standard will be mandatory for firms involved in international trade. Companies doing business with many U.S. agencies are required to meet ISO 9000 standards.

What is Statistical Process Control (SPC)?

SPC is a widely used statistical variation measurement system which plots data graphs over time to illustrate upper and lower control limits for a particular process. The basic concept seeks to monitor excessive variations in a process.

What is special cause variation?

Special cause variations are those process variations caused by external influences. In order to use SPC effectively, management must undertake the demanding process of detecting and eliminating all special cause variations from a process. For example, a special cause variation may be electrical surges experienced from a power source causing manufacturing equipment failures. In order to eliminate this special cause, management installs a surge protector on the line.

What is common cause variation?

Common cause variations are random variations in a process. While management procedures can be developed to control for common cause variation, its complete elimination is unrealistic. However, common cause that exceeds upper or lower control limits around a predetermined mean value must be carefully investigated by management.

What is a stable system?

A stable system is a process operating within the toler-ances of common cause variation. This can also be described as operating in statistical control. This does not mean there is no variation in the process; rather it is operat-ing within the upper and lower control limits of common cause variation around a predetermined mean value.

How is SPC computed?

Standard deviation measures of a data sample mean are used to establish upper and lower process control limits. A process operating in statistical control should be within three standard deviation units from the mean. (See figure 9.1.)

FIGURE 9.1 PRODUCTION PROCESS VARIABILITY

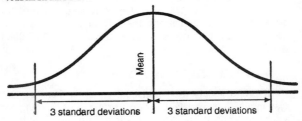

*99.7% confidence level

What are control charts?

Control charts are used to assist management in deter-mining when excessive variation is occurring in a process. This is determined by setting upper control limits (UCL) and lower control limits (LCL) for a given data sample.

A method for determining upper and lower control limits for the percent defective in a large sample, a *p*-chart, is as follows:

$$UCL = \bar{p} + z\sigma_p$$
$$LCL = \bar{p} - z\sigma_p$$

where

$\bar{p}$ = average defectives in a sample
z = number of standard deviates (3 = 99.7% confidence level)
σ_p = standard deviation of the sample population
n = sample size

σ_p is calculated by the following formula:

$$\sigma_p = \sqrt{\overline{p}\ \frac{(1-\overline{p})}{n}}$$

EXAMPLE 9.4

An automobile tire manufacturing company is seeking to develop a statistical process control chart of defective tires manufactured over a period of time. The manufacturer takes a weekly sample of 100 tires over a 20-week period.

Weekly Sample	Number of defects	Fraction defective	Weekly sample	Number of defects	Fraction defective
1	11	0.11	11	7	0.07
2	3	0.03	12	3	0.03
3	4	0.04	13	4	0.04
4	6	0.06	14	9	0.09
5	9	0.09	15	5	0.05
6	5	0.05	16	8	0.08
7	4	0.04	17	10	0.10
8	14	0.14	18	13	0.13
9	10	0.10	19	7	0.07
10	15	0.15	20	5	0.05
Total Defects				152	
Mean					0.076

$$\overline{p} = \frac{\text{Total number of defects}}{\text{Total number of tires examined}}$$
$$= \frac{152}{(100 \times 20)} = .076$$

$$\sigma_p = \sqrt{\frac{(.076)(1 - .076)}{(100)}} = 0.0265$$

$$\text{UCL}_p = \overline{p} + z\sigma_p = .076 + 3(.0265) = .1555$$

$$\text{LCL}_p = \overline{p} + z\sigma_p = .076 - 3(.0265) = .00*$$

* cannot have a negative LCL

When the process chart for the tire manufacturer is developed. it becomes apparent that no sample of defects exceeds the control limits, and it is therefore in statistical control. Only in week 10 does it approach the upper control limit with 15 defects. (See Figure 9.2.)

FIGURE 9.2 TIRE MANUFACTURER PROCESS (p) CHART

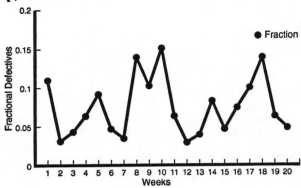

9.6 MANAGING QUALITY CONTROL

Quality control management is a crucial organizational responsibility. Now, as never before, organizations are vigorously competing on the basis of quality. ISO 9000 standards and global competition are pushing quality performance standards to ever higher levels. A major responsibility of quality control management is to develop procedures to locate quality bottlenecks and to ensure that products are made right the first time.

How should a quality control program be designed?

Management should develop and implement a quality control program using these four steps:

1. *Delineate product and service quality requirements.* The quality interrelationship between products and services and market requirements has to be carefully established. Performing market surveys in appropriate market segments may be helpful in understanding the level of quality available and required by the marketplace. Management, however, has greater understanding of products and services than customers do, and this knowledge can be used for developing their full quality potential and competitive advantage.

2. *Develop quality standards.* Products and services should be designed to the highest quality standards available. Manufacturers who use computer aided design (CAD) and computer automated manufacturing (CAM) are able to achieve the highest technical stan-

dards possible in achieving lasting quality. It is quantitatively cheaper to design quality prior to manufacturing or delivering a service than correcting flaws at the customer level where the costs escalate beyond control. Additionally, global competition demands the highest quality standards available.

3. *Develop a quality analysis program.* Management must develop a consistent and systematic program for insuring high quality. Not only does this mean selecting samples for a continual review process, but it also means constantly improving products and services to achieve ever improving quality standards.

4. *A total organizational commitment to quality must be established.* Management not only has the obligation of designing quality requirements and standards, but also has the responsibility to ensure a total organizational commitment to achieving them. This means developing an employee training program where all will gain the ability to perform to their highest potential.

What is benchmarking and how is it useful?

Benchmarking is a process of comparing an organization's products or services against those considered to be the best in a particular industry or market segment. There are several types of benchmarking. These include:

- Comparison of internal departments within one organization including its subsidiary elements
- Careful examination of the functional units of several different organizations
- An analysis of the competitive practices of several different industries within a particular market segment

The benchmarking procedures that should be followed include the following:

- Identify a particular product, service, procedure, or function that could be improved
- Create a benchmarking team
- Target a particular organization or group of organizations having characteristics that would be most suitable for analysis
- Evaluate practices, procedures, and functions within a given market that are the most productive and then adapt and implement those that would be most useful to the target organization

What are quality circles (QC) and how are they used?

The purpose of QC is to allow a forum within an organization where those who are charged with the operational responsibilities interact with colleagues to improve the quality and productivity of the workplace and organization. Most QC groups have ten or fewer members, and all are volunteers.

Normally, although their schedules are flexible, most quality circles meet weekly or monthly depending on the group's needs. The most successful QC groups consist of highly dedicated and disciplined members who strongly desire to improve the work methods and procedures followed in the organization. They seek to work together as a group to share their experience and abilities to solve common problems.

QC groups work best when they are integrated into an ongoing organizational quality control program having strong management support. QC programs are ongoing and seek to improve the overall organization through constant quality improvements.

The benefits of QC groups have been dramatic increases in organizational productivity and quality, increased job satisfaction, and lowered rates of absenteeism, job-related accidents, and turnover.

9.7 QUALITY CONTROL TOOLS

What is a flow chart and how is it used?

Flow charts are graphical depictions of a logical sequence of activities for a particular process. Management uses flow charts to understand the dynamics of an ongoing process. The objective analysis of the interrelationships of the parts of a process provided by a flow chart allow management to conceptualize alternative process configurations.

EXAMPLE 9.5

A furniture manufacturer wishes to draw a flow chart of the processes involved in the fabrication of its product from receiving the unfinished wood to final sales. (See Figure 9.3.)

FIGURE 9.3 FLOW CHART FOR A FURNITURE MANUFACTURER

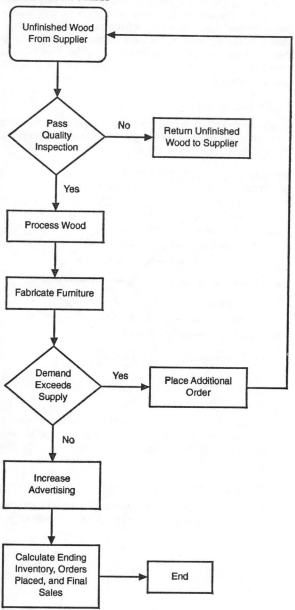

What are fishbone charts and how are they used?

Fishbone charts are graphical charts used to help identify sources of quality deficiencies. In appearance they resemble fishbones. The deficiency, defined as the effect, is at the "head" of the fishbone, while the procedures contributing to the effect are termed causes, and they are the "bones." The bones are viewed as the potential causes of the problem being examined.

EXAMPLE 9.6

An automobile manufacturer wants to prepare a fishbone chart to discover what is causing defects in the cars being produced. (See Figure 9.4.)

FIGURE 9.4 FISHBONE CHART FOR AN AUTOMOBILE MANUFACTURER

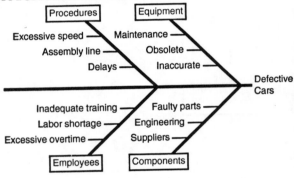

What is a Pareto chart?

A Pareto chart is a bar graph display of the number of component errors that occur in a specified period of time. Pareto charts allow management to focus on individual component errors in order to isolate problem areas.

EXAMPLE 9.7

A computer manufacturer wants to prepare a Pareto chart to do an analysis of weekly component defects (Figure 9.5).

FIGURE 9.5 WEEKLY COMPONENT DEFECTS

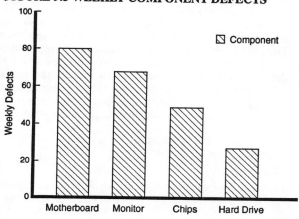

What is a histogram?

Histograms are bar graph displays of measurements of a particular component within a specified period of time. This allows management to observe the aspects of a particular component or process over time.

EXAMPLE 9.8

A firm wants to prepare a histogram in order to have a weekly breakdown of data errors at its various sites (Figure 9.6).

FIGURE 9.6 WEEKLY DATA ERRORS

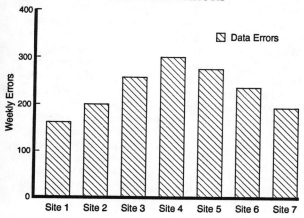

9.8 GROUP DECISION MAKING

Group decision making involves the activities of two or more people working together to resolve a particular issue. The relative merits of group decision making versus individual decision making is a controversial issue. There is general agreement that group decision making is superior when nonprogrammed decisions are required; that is, when an unusual or unique set of events needs to be conceptualized involving several related elements of information.

What are the advantages and disadvantages of group decision making?

Advantages

1. Groups have greater knowledge and insight for evaluating group goals and objectives.

2. A group of organizational members brings broader knowledge for developing situational alternatives.

3. Groups bring greater knowledge and a wider breadth of experience for evaluating alternatives.

4. Groups bring more resources to bear when doing research for particular subjects of interest.

5. Those who participate in the forming of a group decision are highly motivated to implement resulting decisions. Consensus is a strong motivator.

6. Group decisions can be much more creative than individual decisions since many points of view are considered.

Disadvantages

1. Group decisions may result in the risky shift phenomenon where groups will take greater risks than individuals will. However, individual managers have the responsibility for implementing group decisions.

2. Group scheduling difficulties can result in long delays between meeting times.

3. Group decisions are very costly since they take much longer to develop than individual decisions.

4. "Group think" can develop where conformity to the general consensus is more important than individual expression of ideas.

5. Groups can be used as scapegoats for managers seeking to avoid responsibility for implementing group decisions.

6. Dominant personalities or supervising managers can result in group members being reluctant to express their points of view and conforming to one individual's point of view.

What is brainstorming and how is it used?

Brainstorming is a group decision-making technique operating under the rules that no one's idea should be criticized no matter how outrageous it may appear. The basic purpose of the technique is to generate ideas and original thinking. Ideas generated through brainstorming can be discussed at a later period and may act as the genesis for new organizational policies.

What is the Delphi technique?

The Delphi technique is a process of soliciting ideas from a group of anonymous volunteers using a series of mailed questionnaires together with a summary of previous results. Using the summaries from earlier responses, the respondents are subsequently asked to further evaluate and focus their positions on the same range of issues. The basic concept is to reach a consensus among the respondents after at least two sets of questionnaires have been circulated. Normally, while many rounds of questionnaires can be circulated, after two responses a consensus begins to emerge.

What is the nominal group technique (NGT)?

In the nominal group technique a group of people initially discusses ideas in writing rather than having an open discussion. At a later point the group members individually express their ideas to a moderator who records them in full view, often using a flip chart.

After all of the ideas have been recorded, a vote is taken where they are prioritized. The rankings of the group members are then tallied to reach a final consensus on the relative priorities of the ideas discussed.

9.9 ORGANIZATIONAL STRUCTURE

Organizational structure consists of the methods used for disseminating power and authority throughout an organization. The rationale of an organization is that people work together more effectively than they do alone. This is the basis for synergy. However, an organization must be structured effectively to achieve synergy.

A traditional discussion in organizational theory is whether to centralize or decentralize an organizational structure.

What functions do centralization and decentralization perform?

The processes of centralization and decentralization determine who will have authority and power in an organization. In a centralized organization, authority and power are retained by just a few managers, whereas in a decentralized organization authority and power is disseminated to many managers through several levels.

Centralization allows high-level management to retain direct control over the organizational operations. Decentralization creates an environment where decisions are made by those having responsibility at the organization's operational level.

Centralization's advantage of direct control is offset by its distance from and possible misunderstanding of the organization's operations. This is particularly acute when the organization has geographically dispersed operations.

Decentralization's advantage of giving operational managers direct decision-making authority is offset by a lack of coordination at the organization's staff management levels. Some of these disadvantages can be offset through the implementation of a management information system which permits direct access to management staff levels.

In reality, organizations often are both centralized and decentralized in that certain functions, such as finance, are directed through a centralized management control system while other operational functions are decentralized. This permits an organization to have direct staff management control over certain designated functions, such as finance, while permitting flexible decentralized control where it is most functional.

What is the chain of command?

The chain of command is the line of authority that connects superior and subordinate positions in a hierarchical organization. Following the chain of command, subordinate positions must seek approval from the next immediately superior position prior to going to the next superior position for authorization. Similarly, superior positions must follow the chain of command going downward when passing instructions to lower levels of the organization (Figure 9.7). In flat organizations, the chain of command often has little relevance.

FIGURE 9.7 CHAIN OF COMMAND

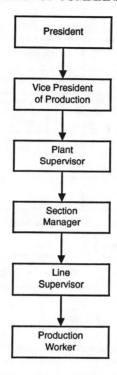

What is the line and staff division of authority?

Line and staff is a concept first developed by the military. Respectively, line and staff describe the direct functional roles and advisory relationships existing in an organization. In modern terms, line functions are those that have direct operational responsibilities such as production or customer service. Staff responsibilities are essentially management services provided to line functions. Staff responsibilities include human resource management, strategic planning, quality control, finance, and marketing (Figure 9.8).

FIGURE 9.8 LINE AND STAFF MANAGEMENT

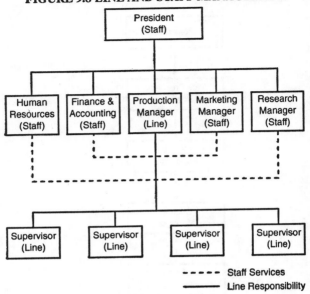

9.10 DEPARTMENTATION

Departmentation is a method of grouping organizational activities in order to achieve organizational objectives. A primary purpose of departmentation is to provide an organization similar specialized services or activities. For example, a marketing department normally consists of people primarily concerned with developing markets for particular products and services an organization may offer. It is not concerned with production, although it may interface from time-to-time with the production department in order to better understand products as well as the department's functional capabilities.

Departments are created to fulfill the following objectives:

- *Functional.* A functional department performs a specific role. Functional departments would include accounting and finance, human resources, marketing, production, research, and development.

- *Product.* A product department is created to build or complete a specific product. Job duties are highly functional in nature, and have the completion of a particular product as its end goal. General Motors, for example, has organized according to automobile product divisions.

- *Customer.* These are departments created to serve specific customer needs. For example, a department store may have the following customer departmentation: babies, boys and girls, teens, ladies and mens wear, maternity, etc. Customer departmentation allows an organization to group its activities to best serve specific customer requirements.

- *Geographic.* National or international organizations have specific geographic needs. It is unrealistic to have one central management center for an organization having large nationwide and/or international operations. The communication and logistical needs are simply too great. Geographic departmentation can be used to manage specific regional needs. For example, an organization may have southern, western, eastern, and northern divisions or Asian, European, and Latin American divisions.

9.11 PERFORMANCE EVALUATION

Performance evaluation is the appraisal of employee performance using a systematic method of analysis. The essential process of performance evaluation is predicated on observation and judgmental analysis. The judgmental nature of performance evaluation precludes the possibility of completely eliminating subjective evaluations. Therefore, rigorously following an objective methodology is essential to have creditable evaluations.

What is the graphic rating scales performance evaluation method?

Graphic rating scales show a number of employee performance rating factors on which a supervisor indicates an evaluation. Rating factors include quantity and quality of work, attendance, timeliness, behavior attitudes, willingness to learn new techniques, and other factors that management feels are important. These factors are then rated using an evaluation scale. In a five-point rating system, the highest rating is usually given a value of 5 while the lowest rating is given a rating of 1. All the points are added up to form a total for each employee.

EXAMPLE 9.9

A manager wants to create a graphic rating scale for the purpose of rating the employees in a production environment. To do this the manager creates a form having a series of performance categories with rating criteria which are to be used by the production supervisors for rating their employees.

GRAPHIC RATING SCALES

Employee Name: Dept:		Date:		
Rating Scale	Exceptional Good	Average	Acceptable	Poor
Units of Work normally produced				
Work Quality				
Timeliness				
Attendance				
Work Attitude				
Cooperativeness				
Dependability				

What are behaviorally anchored rating scales (BARS)?

Behaviorally anchored rating scales are developed by rating specific job-related behaviors. Several scales can be developed covering various job-related behaviors, and BARS points can be given for various aspects of the job behavior. Figure 9.9 shows one area to be evaluated for a teacher:

FIGURE 9.9 BEHAVIORALLY ANCHORED RATING SCALES

Teaching Ability

(the ability to successfully interface with students and teach subject materials)

Above Average Outstanding teacher who is well rated by students	— 4 — 3.75 — 3.5 X — 3.25 — 3	Teacher is considered an expert in the field, communicates well, and has strong student acceptance. Teacher receives numerous student recommendations.
Average Performance Enthusiastic teacher who is very familiar with the material	— 2.75 — 2.5 — 2.25 — 2 — 1.75	This teacher can be relied upon to do a professional job and be well prepared.
Poor Performance Teacher shows little professional interest	— 1.5 — 1.25 — 1	Teacher is not well prepared and has poor interaction with students. Frequent student complaints.

9.12 COMPENSATION

Compensation often is the largest organizational budgetary expense. It consists of the direct financial earnings an employee receives for work performed as well as associated employee benefits. Generally, direct financial earnings include one or more of the following: salary, commission, bonuses, and/or merit pay. Benefits, which can be an additional 40% of the total compensation package, may include health, life and other forms of insurance, subsidized pension plans, compensated time including vacations, personal and/or sick leave, stock options, and subsidized services including cafeterias and recreational facilities.

Is there a relationship between compensation and performance?

The relationship between compensation and performance is controversial. Some research indicates a direct and positive relationship between the compensation levels and the quantity and quality of production. Others argue that tying compensation to performance destroys intrinsic motivation. It does seem fair to say that some behaviors can be more effectively motivated by compensation than others.

What common compensation methods exist and how successful are they?

Generally management seeks to fairly compensate its employees. However, it also expects comparable output for its compensatory policies. In the final analysis, employee productivity is necessary to generate the profits essential to form the basis of a compensation plan.

A basic type of salary compensation is a straight-time compensation plan while others provide employee incentives:

- *Flat rates.* Wage rates are based on an established pay scale for a specified job in a straight-time compensation plan. Flat rate plans do not recognize seniority, performance, or other individual differences. For example, an assembler on a particular job gets paid a flat rate of $7.00 per hour irrespective of experience. Flat rates are often found in unionized environments where the union does not wish to distinguish between individual capabilities. Flat rates prevent management from creating employee performance incentives.

- *Incentive plans.* The piece rate system and commission plans are types of individual incentive plans. In a piece rate system the employee works from an established pay level with additional stated levels of compensation being paid for production exceeding a base quota. The base production level is established after production research is completed.

    The commission plan is usually associated with sales personnel. It is an established rate that is paid on the basis of sales. The greater the sales, the greater the commission. It is probably one of the oldest forms of incentive plans.

    A gainsharing plan is an incentive plan that shares compensation, normally in the form of cash bonuses, with a group's members based on their performance. It is probably one of the most successful forms of employee incentive plans.

9.13 MOTIVATING PERFORMANCE THROUGH JOB DESIGN

Job design is essential for the organizational process. Job design not only structures the way work is done in the organization, but is also a critical factor in determining how an employee is motivated to perform useful work. There are several forms of job design.

What is job specialization?

Job specialization is the process of dividing work into smaller processes for the purpose of simplification. Job specialization, originally alluded to by Adam Smith, was fully developed by Frederick W. Taylor in *Principles of Scientific Management* (New York: Harper Bros., 1911) for the purpose of increasing production efficiencies. Job specialization makes work so simple that workers become interchangeable. The disadvantage is that the lack of challenge in simplified work processes oftentimes lead to boredom and subsequent accidents.

What is job rotation?

Job rotation is a form of job design where employees are systematically moved, or rotated, from one job to another. An objective of job rotation is to diminish the boredom and accidents often associated with job specialization. One advantage of job rotation is that employees have an opportunity to experience a cross section of jobs in the work place and thus become familiar with them all.

Nonetheless, when each individual job is specialized, the objective of avoiding the boredom and accidents associated with job specialization is unrealistic.

What is job enlargement?

Job enlargement simply consists of expanding the number of job responsibilities an individual has without increasing his or her authority to decide how the work is to be accomplished or what priorities work should receive. The rationale for job enlargement is it increases worker motivation; however, the only change is that the employee has more to do than before the job was enlarged. If the work consists of specialized tasks, the rationale for work enlargement has little inherent justification.

What is job enrichment?

The concept of job enrichment was developed by Frederick Herzberg in the late 1960s. The essential component of job enrichment is increasing the extent of control an employee has over the work for which he or she is responsible. The assumption in job enrichment is that the work itself is the motivator. The employee controls the type of work, work methods, and the degree of freedom or autonomy he or she has in making decisions regarding these work issues.

What is flextime?

Flextime is a method of developing work schedules that reflect worker preferences and needs. Using a range established by management, employees can determine at what hours they will begin and end the workday. Flextime is particularly useful for employees who must balance family and work responsibilities. It has proven to be popular, useful, and productive for employees and organizations.

What is the quality of work life?

The quality of work life is the personal significance the work environment has for individual employees. A high quality work life is personally fulfilling and has a high degree of significance. A low quality work life will produce worker alienation.

A positive quality of work life is associated with lower absenteeism and tardiness as well as higher productivity.

9.14 EFFECTIVE LEADERSHIP

Leadership is an extremely important concept in organizational dynamics. Basically, leadership consists of the manipulation of power. Power is the leader's ability to get others to do what the leader wants. The way power is managed distinguishes one leader from another.

What are the sources of leader power?

There are several sources of leader power:

- *Legitimate power.* Legitimate power is conferred by the organization itself, not by the person who occupies a particular position. For example, the role of bank president confers an ability on the person occupying the role to manage the overall affairs of the bank as well as to have a certain level of conferred status.

- *Reward power.* Managers have the ability to grant financial, status, and promotional rewards to the organization's human resources. This is an important management source of power.

- *Coercive power.* Coercive power is the ability of the manager to force others to carry out functions they would not otherwise perform because of the manager's ability to impose sanctions.

- *Expert power.* Expert power is derived from particular knowledge and expertise an individual has. For example, a computer expert is one who has demonstrated accumulated insight into the functioning of computers and is able to make computers perform as desired.

- *Information power.* Information power is derived from access to sources of information that others do not have. Thus, those having information power have the ability to gain particular organizational and competitive advantages.

- *Referent power.* Referent power is power derived from the esteem in which one is regarded by others. It therefore enables those having referent power to more effectively lead an organization.

What skills do leaders need?

Effective leadership depends on the exercise of several skills:

- *Flexibility.* Flexibility is an essential skill for managers. Not only is the environment of business extremely dynamic, the workplace itself consists of great cultural diversity which requires constant modification of the organizational culture.

- *Communication.* The understanding, processing, and transferring of information is a central management function. The ability to interface with others in the organizational and business environment requires excellent communication skills.

- *Human resource management.* Organizations consist of people. A critical management role is managing the organization's human resources. This consists of developing and managing training programs, organizational development strategies, counseling, and other skills.

- *Conceptualization.* The ability to understand the implications of information and strategic developments is required for managers to succeed in a progressively evolving technological and internationally competitive environment.

10

Production and Operations Management (P/OM)

This chapter provides a discussion of production and operations management including:

- Mission statement
- Threats, Opportunities, Weaknesses, and Strengths (TOWS) analysis
- Management decision making
- Simulation
- Capacity management
- Location analysis
- Time-study procedures
- Aggregate planning schedules
- Inventory management
- Scheduling, including project scheduling

Production and operations management is a vital management activity in both manufacturing and service organizations. It is primarily concerned with the process of transforming organizational resource inputs into final organizational outputs. It is a comprehensive process that treats the organization as a system of interconnected functions. The major functions of P/OM incorporate design, planning, decision making, operations, and system controls.

10.1 THE ORGANIZATIONAL MISSION STATEMENT

What is the purpose of a mission statement?

A mission statement describes the basic operational intent of an organization. It takes a long-term perspective and states the reason for a firm's existence. Its function is to provide guidance for its shareholders, customers, and employees about the organization's overall direction and rationale.

How is a mission statement developed?

A mission statement should be consistent with the organization's history, including past achievements, organizational culture, attributes, and basic policies. A new organization will take into consideration the history of the industry they are joining as well as the purpose they wish to serve. Successful mission statements emphasize areas where an organization has its greatest strengths and resources.

What are the key elements of a mission statement?

A mission statement must be:

- Meaningful for the organization's client or customer base. Organizations must be constantly aware of who their clientele is, and their requisite needs.
- Realistic and attainable. Unrealistic mission statements will cause the organization to fail.
- Stimulating and inspiring. A motivating mission statement will enhance employee creativity and commitment.
- Definitive and explicit. Unclear mission statements result in dispersed and unsuccessful organizational strategies.

EXAMPLE 10.1

An independent power producer states that its mission consists of four central values:

1. *Integrity:* To act with integrity and honor its commitments.
2. *Fairness:* To treat fairly its employees, customers, suppliers, and the governments and communities in which it operates.
3. *Fun:* To create and maintain an atmosphere where employees can advance in their skills while enjoying their time at work.
4. *Social Responsibility:* To undertake projects that pro-

vide social benefits, such as lower costs to customers, a high degree of safety and reliability, increased employment, and a cleaner environment.

EXAMPLE 10.2

A rapidly growing petroleum company states that its mission is to create value by adding substantial oil and gas reserves while minimizing geological risk and leveraging staff expertise.

EXAMPLE 10.3

A company which introduced the first independent, electronic, product information database (EDI) that uses the industry standard Universal Product Code (UPC) numbering system states that its mission is to provide quality electronic merchandise management services and technologies to the retail industry.

10.2 STRATEGY DEVELOPMENT PROCESS

What is the purpose of an organizational strategy?

The purpose of an organizational strategy is to achieve the goals of the mission statement. This is done by developing a logical plan for utilizing the organization's strengths and resources. An organizational strategy provides direction for the organization's activities and its human resources within the context of its mission statement's objectives.

What strategy must an organization develop to achieve its mission?

An organizational strategy must be developed for each functional area within its mission statement. The resulting strategies contain:

1. A clear purpose
2. Measurable expected outcomes
3. Fall-back plans in the event the primary strategy cannot be implemented
4. Costs and benefits

Developing an organizational strategy using the Threats, Opportunities, Weaknesses, and Strengths (TOWS) analysis.

The purpose of the TOWS analysis is to develop a concept for producing competitive advantage by analyzing an organization's environmental threats and opportunities. Elements analyzed within the organization's environment consist of the following variables:

1. culture
2. demographics
3. economic technology
4. organizational publics:
   a. capital originators including shareholders, creditors, bankers, and underwriters
   b. raw material and component providers
   c. customers
   d. human resources
   e. competitive rivals
   f. governmental and legal environment including regulators
   g. special-interest lobbying groups

The TOWS analysis allows managers to develop a strategic plan by examining organizational strengths and weaknesses in terms of the opportunities and threats presented by its environmental elements. Subsequent strategies and tactical decisions can produce a competitive advantage.

10.3 MANAGERIAL DECISION MAKING

All managers have a shortage of knowledge, resources, and time. Working within these parameters, the management process culminates in decisions to implement various actions. Decision making is the focal point of all organizational dynamics, and management effectiveness is judged on the basis of the quality of these decisions.

What is managerial decision making?

Managerial decisions are deliberate choices made from a range of alternatives. Before making the decision, the manager must evaluate each choice according to its projected outcomes in terms of the organization's resources as well as the amount of information and time available. Thus, every managerial decision is a best-effort compromise made in an environment of uncertainty.

What are the types of management decisions?

From a management perspective there are three types of decisions:

1. Long-term strategic decisions concerning the external environment of the organization
2. Administrative decisions intended to order the functions of the organization in the most cost-effective way
3. Operational decisions designed to maximize a firm's profitability through productive procedures

What are the types of strategic decisions?

There are several types of strategic decisions in P/OM:

1. *Product or service strategies.* Management decisions regarding product line market strategies (including design. quality and cost) determine production cost parameters.

2. *Process strategy.* Management decisions regarding process methods are critical in determining technological and organizational production requirements. The process strategy decision is also crucial in determining capital and financial requirements.

3. *Research and Development (R&D) strategy.* R&D is critical for organizational survival in today's rapidly changing marketplace. The R&D strategy includes total resources being devoted to the effort, the type of research to be performed including pure vs. applied research, manufacturing vs. market research, and product development vs. process development.

4. *Location strategy.* Often the success or failure of a business, production, or service is determined by a location decision.

5. *Inventory management strategy.* It is essential to develop a strategy for coordinating production needs with raw material and component inventories. However, the inventory strategy is determined by whether the demand is dependent or independent of the demand for other components. If the demand for one product, such as air conditioners, is independent of another product, such as kitchen chairs, then an independent inventory management strategy is required. However, if the overall component demand is dependent on the demand for the product, then a Material Requirements Planning (MRP) strategy is needed. MRP is a component manufacturing planning method in which items required for a manufacturing process are indexed to overall product demand. With MRP it is not essential that all inventory items are available at all times, but only when they are required in the production process. Thus, under MRP, inventory needs are coordinated with production needs. (See Chapter 9 on inventory management for a more complete discussion.)

6. *Human resource planning and management strategy.*
As a rule of thumb more than 75% of a firm's operating expense is for human resources. Therefore, adequate hiring, training, and utilization of human resources is a critical operational strategy for achieving success.

EXAMPLE 10.4

The management of an organization makes a strategic decision to develop a five-year marketing plan to achieve a competitive advantage through the introduction of a new service.

EXAMPLE 10.5

An automobile manufacturer makes a process strategy decision to offer a standard group of options on its automobiles in order to reduce the variation in its production needs and lower unit costs.

EXAMPLE 10.6

A computer chip manufacturer makes a strategy decision to increase R&D expenditures on an advanced CPU chip design enabling compatibility with multiple computer operating systems.

EXAMPLE 10.7

A firm makes a location strategy decision to conduct a nationwide survey of state industrial development agencies to evaluate where the company could receive the greatest financial and environmental location benefits.

EXAMPLE 10.8

A lawn mower and snow blower manufacturer makes an inventory management decision to use an MRP system to coordinate their need for lawn mower and snow blower components with seasonal manufacturing schedules.

EXAMPLE 10.9

A manufacturer makes a human resource strategy decision to give more responsibility to its employees by creating work teams to assemble entire products rather than components in the belief that it will obtain greater productivity because of job enrichment.

What are the types of administrative decisions?

1. *Programmed decisions.* Decisions typically made

regarding highly routine situations where little discretion is required.

2. *Nonprogrammed decisions.* Decisions made in unstructured situations where problem conceptualization and original thinking is required.

EXAMPLE 10.10

Management makes a programmed administrative decision to establish a vehicle maintenance schedule.

EXAMPLE 10.11

Management makes a nonprogrammed administrative decision to implement an organizational downsizing plan to reduce duplication of services, decrease costs, and increase profitability.

What are the types of operational decisions?

1. *Quality.* Decision making regarding product and service quality is a vital operations responsibility necessitating comprehensive organizational support. Quality decisions are made in the design stage of the product or service plan and require the creation and maintenance of standards.

2. *Process.* Operational decisions are made regarding the design of the process used in the manufacturing or servicing of a final product. Process decisions normally are long range and cannot easily be reversed.

3. *Capacity.* Operational capacity decisions are concerned with the long-term capability of an organization to produce the required amount of output over time. Capacity planning determines not only the size of an organization's physical productive capability, but also its human resource needs.

4. *Inventory.* Inventory decisions are crucial in fulfilling management's inventory management strategy. The challenge for operations management is to create a balance in inventory between product demand, cost, and supply needs. (See Chapter 9 on inventory management for a more detailed discussion.)

5. *Human Resources.* Human resources are an extremely important operational management responsibility. Organizations pay a major portion of their revenues to employees. Therefore, selection, hiring, training, termination, and general management of human resources are critical for the future of the organization.

EXAMPLE 10.12

The franchise management of a fast-food retail chain makes a determination concerning quality standards in terms of the content and temperature of the food when it is served to the customer. It implements a program to ensure the individual franchises meet the quality standards.

EXAMPLE 10.13

The management of a car-washing company makes a process decision to utilize a brushless car-washing facility that requires fewer workers, results in less damage to the car finish, and is more productive.

EXAMPLE 10.14

A seasonal manufacturer of lawn equipment makes a capacity operational decision to hire and train a second shift of employees during peak demand periods rather than increase overall plant capacity. This will make more productive use of existing capacity without increasing long-term overhead costs including plant maintenance and capital financing costs.

EXAMPLE 10.15

The franchise manager of a chain of job printers makes an operational decision to allow the individual store managers to buy their own printing supply inventory as long as they use the franchise's equipment.

EXAMPLE 10.16

A franchise manager makes a human resource operational decision to allow individual franchisees to hire, train, and supervise their own employees. Thus, the individual franchisee has the entire human resource operational responsibility.

What are the steps in the decision-making process?

Making good decisions is essential to the management process. As discussed, decisions are rational choices among a group of alternatives. Good decisions are the result of a sequential series of analytical steps:

1. *Identify and delineate the problem.* No management action can occur unless there is a need to resolve an issue. Additionally, when identifying a problem, it is necessary to assess the seriousness of the issue. Highly critical issues require more immediate attention and a

greater demand on existing resources. Difficulties in identifying problems include:

Perceptual errors. Often problems are not identified because of personal biases which do not allow the individual to perceive that there is a problem needing attention. Preconceived notions of how something should be (as well as personal preferences) will interfere with the ability to identify a problem.

Insufficient information. Insufficient research about a specific problem can lead to misleading and unwarranted conclusions regarding the true nature of the problem and its possible solution.

– Mistaking a symptom as the cause of the problem. An apparent cause of a problem may just mask a systemic cause. Again, further research is essential to clearly identify the cause and nature of a problem.

2. *Establish decision priorities and goals.* Managers constantly deal with problems. However, all organizations have limited resources. They must assign priorities to problems in terms of their importance relative to the organization's goals. This process results in a matching of organizational resources with priorities and creates a management methodology for administering solutions to problems.

3. *Ascertain the cause of the problem.* In order to develop a solution to a problem, it is essential to understand its cause. This requires a systemic understanding of the dynamics of the situation that has caused the problem.

4. *Develop realistic alternatives.* It is important for the manager to develop a range of alternative realistic solutions. This means doing extensive research into the nature of the problem and discovering what alternatives would be a good fit.

5. *Weigh the best alternative.* This requires extensive evaluation and comparison using a cost benefit analysis. The alternative solutions are developed within the constraints of limited time and resources, and with a degree of uncertainty.

6. *Choose a solution.* After conducting extensive research, a decision will have to be made regarding an optimal solution. Managers operate within an environment of incomplete information, time deadlines, and limited resources. All solutions represent opportunity choices having limited outcome predictability. Therefore, managers must make decisions within a range of known alternatives having unknown outcomes.

7. *Implement the decision.* This requires developing human resources to carry out the decision. This mandates a high communication level between the manager and the human resource team.

8. *Follow up.* All decisions require constant monitoring. Changes will have to be made over time to ensure optimum results. This requires an effective organizational control and evaluation system for future organizational decisions.

EXAMPLE 10.17

A word processing software manufacturer that has been very successful in the text-based operating system market is facing a crucial decision when the industry standard operating system is changed to a graphical user interface system (GUI). The company's text-based word processor is extremely successful and has a large following. The commands used in the text-based word processor are difficult to learn, but once learned, it is a very versatile word processor.

If the word processor is converted to a graphical user interface, then a portion of the installed user base may be lost, and its competitive advantage based on powerful nonintuitive commands may also be compromised. However, failure to convert the word processor to a graphical user interface will mean losing its market share since the major competitors have already released GUI word processors.

After deciding to develop a GUI word processor, the company had to decide whether to do a fundamental rewrite of the program, which could take at least two years, or simply update it and make it GUI compatible.

The company decides to release a GUI update to its word processing program with a fundamental GUI rewrite scheduled for a future date.

What is decision making under certainty and conflict?

Decision making involves managing three major elements:

1. *Decision strategy.* A decision maker develops a plan affecting long-term organizational outcomes utilizing existing organizational resources.

2. *States of nature.* These are elements of the environment over which the manager has little or no control. States of nature include the weather, political environment, the economy, technological developments, etc. They can dramatically affect the outcomes of any decision strategy.

3. *Outcome.* This is the result of the interaction of the implementation of a decision strategy with the states of nature. Because of the many variables within the states of nature, outcomes can be extremely difficult to forecast.

Thus, outcomes of a decision strategy, O, the dependent variable, is a function of the interaction of the two independent variables, D, decision strategies and, S, the states of nature. Figure 10.1 shows a decision matrix. The rows are strategic choices a manager can make while the columns represent decision outcomes. An outcome O_{ij} is a function of a decision strategy D_i and a state of nature S_i.

FIGURE 10.1 DECISION MATRIX

		States of Nature			
Strategies	S_1	S_2	S_x	S_x	S_x	S_j
D_1	O_{11}	O_{12}	*	*	*	O_{1j}
D_2	O_{21}	O_{22}	*	*	*	O_{2j}
D_x	*	*				*
D_x	*	*				*
D_j	O_{i1}	O_{i2}	*	*	*	O_{ij}

Mathematically this relationship can be expressed as:

$O_{ij} = f(D_i \, S_j)$

What are decision trees and decision tables?

Developing a graphical display is an effective way of mapping the alternatives and probable events that can occur in a complex decision-making environment. Decision trees use symbols consisting of squares and circles. Branches of the decision tree that extend from a square depict an area where several choices can be made while a circle connotes a unique state of nature having certain outcomes.

A decision tree is analyzed in reverse order from right to left going back chronologically. Decision trees are normally accompanied by a payoff or decision table where all the alternatives are listed down the left side of the table with states of nature listed across the top of the table and payoffs stated in the main part of the table.

EXAMPLE 10.18

The Jackson Lawn Products Corporation is studying the possibility of manufacturing a new line of lawn mowers. Since the market for the new mowers is uncertain, the corporation must decide whether to construct a large or small plant, or do nothing. Figure 10.2 presents a decision tree depicting the Jackson Lawn Products decision choices.

FIGURE 10.2 JACKSON LAWN PRODUCTS CORPORATION DECISION TREE

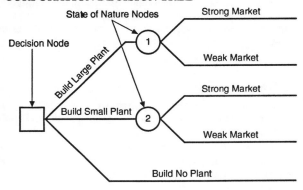

A payoff or decision table can be developed to assist Jackson Lawn Products in determining what type of a lawn mower plant they should build. There is an outcome for each decision and state of nature that can be described in units of monetary value. The units of monetary value are also described as conditional values.

Exhibit 10.1 describes all of Jackson's decision alternatives in the left column of the exhibit, the states of nature across the top, and the payoffs (conditional values) in the main part of the exhibit. In the case of building a large plant, a strong market will produce a $250,000 net profit, whereas a weak market will result in a $125,000 net loss. If a small plant is built, a strong market will produce a $125,000 net profit with a $60,000 net loss in a weak market.

EXHIBIT 10.1 DECISION TABLE WITH CONDITIONAL VALUES FOR JACKSON LAWN PRODUCTS CORP.

Decision Alternatives	*States of Nature*	
	Strong Market	*Weak Market*
Build Large Plant	$250,000	–$125,000
Build Small Plant	$125,000	–$60,000
Build No Plant	$0	$0

What is decision making in a Total Quality Environment?

Total Quality Management evolved from W. Edwards Deming's 14 points, which was termed Total Quality Control. Decision making in a total quality environment essentially involves the elements of a continuous process focusing on three essential components: continuous improvement, assessment management, and teamwork. Implementing decision making in a total quality environment requires:

- Making quality improvement a central organizational focus
- Extensive and continuous employee training
- Total involvement of the employees and management concerning the organization's mission, goals, and operational objectives
- Continual improvement of organizational processes rather than focusing on employees as the source of quality failures
- Team decision making
- A recognition that the customer defines quality, and that a total quality decision objective is to meet or exceed customer satisfaction standards

Decision making in a TQM environment is a shared experience for all employees throughout the organization. Information is an organizational resource essential for making quality decisions. Increased quality leads to increased productivity, lower unit costs, and higher customer satisfaction.

EXAMPLE 10.19

A transmission manufacturing company was machining highly exacting parts to be used in automatic transmissions. The parts consisted of gears, bearings, and assorted spacers and shafts. The parts were engineered to be within the industry standard of + or − .003" of specifications. However, other manufacturers were able to produce the same transmissions at two-thirds of the price and achieve higher productivity and quality.

Management decided to make a 300% improvement in the tolerances of the parts by reducing them to + or − .001" tolerance. The net result was there were fewer returns, lower unit costs, and higher overall customer satisfaction. Consequently, productivity and profits grew substantially.

10.4 SIMULATION MODELS

Management uses simulation techniques to replicate the characteristics and dynamics of a real system. Simulations enable management to test models of performance when it is too expensive, risky, or time consuming to do it with the real materials, workers, and/or equipment. Using simulation, a manager can test the effects of a decision in a wide variety of situations including time compression scenarios without disrupting an operational system. It allows the manager to evaluate alternative system designs when implementing a given operational strategy. Additionally, simulation permits the manager to evaluate the effects of interactions between individual system components and various when/if tactics.

The weaknesses of simulations are that they are syllogistic in that they can evaluate only the information built into the model. Therefore, variables not included or not capable of being included in the model cannot be evaluated. Another limitation for simulation is that it is typically designed for unique situations restricting transferability to other scenarios.

How is simulation implemented by management?

When implementing a simulation model, management is required to:

1. Delineate the problem.
2. Categorize the factors associated with the problem.
3. Develop an analytical model.
4. Construct strategic alternatives for testing.
5. Implement the simulation.
6. Analyze the outcomes of the simulation.
7. Apply the analysis to an operational system.

What is the Monte Carlo simulation?

When a scenario contains elements of chance, the Monte Carlo simulation can be used to estimate outcomes. The Monte Carlo simulation analyzes the probability distribution of variables in a problem and uses random sampling of the data. Using random sampling these probabilities are calculated to estimate a problem's solution.

The Monte Carlo simulation is developed through the following procedures:

1. Probability distributions for major elements of the problem are established. A critical feature of the Monte Carlo simulation is the generation of probability distributions. The probability distribution must correspond to the actual data as closely as possible in order for the

simulation to be valid and reliable. A commonly accepted method for doing this is historical frequency.

2. Cumulative probability distributions are developed for each variable. After establishing a probability distribution for each variable in the model, the probabilities are sequentially totalled.

3. Random samples are established using the cumulative probability distributions to obtain specific element values for each observation. A random number table is often used to generate numbers for the sampling distribution.

4. Perform several simulation trials. The actual number of trials needed is determined by statistical tests of significance.

Monte Carlo simulations have a wide number of applications including estimating inventory demand on a time interval basis, times between machine failures, project scheduling times, and servicing schedules. Exhibit 10.2 presents a Random Number Table.

EXAMPLE 10.20

A computer memory chip manufacturer's records show the following failure rates of a particular memory chip when tested individually:

Memory Chip Failures	
Failures	*Frequency of Failure in Hours*
2	10
5	20
6	30
8	40
2	50
1	60
Total Hours	210

The initial step in developing the Monte Carlo simulation is to develop a cumulative probability distribution for the memory chip failures. After the cumulative probability distribution is established, then random number intervals, otherwise known as Monte Carlo numbers, are allotted for each possible outcome. The Monte Carlo numbers are intervals of random numbers that correspond with the probability that a given interval of hours of operation will have a stated occurrence of memory chip failures.

Memory Chip Failures, Frequency of Failure, Failure Probability, Cumulative Probability, and Monte Carlo Numbers

Failures	Frequency of Failure in Hours	Probability (Frequency / Total Hours)	Cumulative Probability	Monte Carlo Numbers
2	10	0.05	0.05	01-05
5	20	0.10	0.15	06-15
6	30	0.14	0.29	16-29
8	40	0.19	0.48	30-48
3	50	0.24	0.72	49-72
1	60	0.29	1.01*	73-00
Total Hours	210	1		

* Rounding error.

Random numbers are then assigned, using a computer-generated table of random numbers.

EXHIBIT 10.2 RANDOM NUMBER TABLE

75	55	41	96	97	38	33	79	91	22	20	24
39	75	58	48	68	6	62	30	21	96	4	56
91	88	78	58	94	5	51	61	59	90	40	14
79	93	62	48	73	88	17	56	48	22	53	3
50	22	76	38	2	46	68	94	89	17	83	76
5	21	35	52	95	79	19	51	26	46	2	10
76	44	51	15	98	71	33	75	26	47	58	99
77	71	51	20	75	9	91	92	22	99	33	11
4	89	54	62	67	9	65	79	47	39	25	77
88	18	17	46	7	16	98	90	54	56	95	66
56	31	44	50	29	74	66	35	55	81	43	76
55	61	97	16	32	31	66	29	65	61	6	26
65	82	50	68	26	53	76	6	99	98	14	46
30	1	20	47	92	61	76	17	72	15	57	94

EXHIBIT 10.2 (cont.)

95	45	83	50	100	49	58	32	19	0	13	79
70	94	39	19	64	33	28	61	81	6	88	99
87	38	16	34	9	89	19	69	77	24	33	84
47	26	29	96	9	96	2	70	9	34	42	91
85	90	31	79	89	3	86	75	61	59	40	73
48	94	57	21	70	72	23	57	97	50	4	39

The next step is to simulate the memory chip failures. In this example, twenty simulations are run using random numbers from the first column of the random number table. The number of memory chip failures is derived from where the random number coincides with the Monte Carlo interval, as shown in Exhibit 10.3.

EXHIBIT 10.3 FAILURE RATES

Simulation	Random Number	Simulated Failures
1	75	1
2	39	8
3	91	1
4	79	1
5	50	3
6	5	2
7	76	1
8	77	1
9	4	2
10	88	1
11	56	3
12	55	3
13	65	3
14	30	8
15	95	1
16	70	3
17	87	1
18	47	8
19	85	1
20	48	8
Total Number of Failures		60
Average Failure Rate 60/20 =		3

A frequency distribution for the Hours and Failures of the simulation can now be tabulated, as shown in Exhibit 10.4.

EXHIBIT 10.4 SIMULATION FREQUENCY DISTRIBUTION

Hours	Failures	Probability of Failure
10	4	0.07
20	0	0
30	0	0
40	32	053
50	15	0.25
60	9	0.15
		1

In this simulation, the average failure rate for the memory chips is 3; however, the greatest number of failures occurs between 40 and 50 hours of operation. Assuming enough simulated iterations occurred, the simulated outcomes will represent real operations.

In this example, running more simulations could have changed the average failure rate for the memory chips. The expected failure rate for the memory chips can be calculated from the failure rates and their probabilities:

$$\text{Expected failure rate} = \sum_{i=1}^{5} \begin{array}{l} (\text{probability of } i \text{ units}) \times \\ (\text{failure rate of } i \text{ units}) \end{array}$$

$$= (.05)(2) + (.10)(5) + (.14)(6) \\ + (.19)(8) + (.24)(3) + \\ (.29)(1)$$

$$= .1 + .5 + .84 + 1.52 + .72 \\ + .29$$

$$= 3.97 \text{ failure rate}$$

The expected failure rate for the memory chips is higher than the average for the sample simulation. Assuming more simulations were run, the average failure rate would more closely approximate the expected failure rate.

0.5 CAPACITY MANAGEMENT

Capacity is the total productive capability of a system during a unit of time. For a manufacturing facility, capacity is simply the maximum output that can be attained with the existing capital equipment during a period of time. Thus, an automobile manufacturer may define its capacity as the number of cars that can be assembled in an hour, day, week, or month. Capacity is critically important for a productive organization because:

- It provides the output required to meet product demand.
- It directly impacts the cost and efficiency of productive capability.
- It is a major organizational investment.

What is design capacity?

Design capacity is the total achievable capacity under perfect conditions. Normally, perfect conditions are not achievable, and few organizations operate for any period of time at design capacity. Furthermore, operating at designed capacity can cause rapid wear and breakdowns. Operating at design capacity essentially means operating at the organization's productive limits.

What is effective capacity or utilization?

Effective capacity or utilization is a ratio between the expected capacity of a firm and its design capacity. It can be computed by the following formula:

$$\text{EFFECTIVE CAPACITY OR UTILIZATION} = \frac{\text{EXPECTED CAPACITY}}{\text{DESIGN CAPACITY}}$$

Effective capacity is affected by an organization's product mix, production scheduling, age of equipment, and maintenance standards.

EXAMPLE 10.21

A television manufacturing company has a design capacity of 50 televisions per hour, but due to intensive quality control standards, it normally produces only 40 televisions per hour. The effective capacity or utilization of the television manufacturing company is calculated in the following manner:

$$\text{EFFECTIVE CAPACITY OR UTILIZATION} = \frac{\text{EXPECTED CAPACITY}}{\text{DESIGN CAPACITY}}$$

$$\text{EFFECTIVE CAPACITY OR UTILIZATION} = \frac{40}{50} = 80\%$$

What is capacity efficiency?

Capacity efficiency is a ratio of production output to effective capacity. It is a measure of effective management in utilizing effective capacity. It is calculated using the following formula:

$$\text{EFFICIENCY} = \frac{\text{ACTUAL OUTPUT}}{\text{EFFECTIVE CAPACITY}}$$

EXAMPLE 10.22

The effective capacity of a candy manufacturing company is 1,000 units of candy per hour; however, it actually produces only 850 units per hour. The efficiency of the candy manufacturing company can be computed in the following manner:

$$\text{EFFICIENCY} = \frac{\text{ACTUAL OUTPUT}}{\text{EFFECTIVE CAPACITY}}$$

$$\text{EFFICIENCY} = \frac{850}{1000} = 85\%$$

What is rated capacity?

Rated capacity is a determination of the maximum usable capacity of manufacturing capability. Rated capacity can never exceed design capacity. It is a product of design capacity times effective capacity times efficiency. The formula used to calculate rated capacity is:

Rated capacity = Design capacity × Effective capacity
× Efficiency

EXAMPLE 10.23

A computer printer manufacturer has a manufacturing facility operating at an effective capacity of 80% with 85% efficiency. It has two assembly lines operating five days a week with two shifts a day. Each assembly line has a designed capacity of 40 printers per hour.

The rated capacity of the computer printer manufacturer is calculated by multiplying the design capacity times the effective capacity times the efficiency of the plant. To determine the design capacity, the two production lines have to be multiplied by the number of printers times the combined number of hours of production.

Design Capacity = 40 printers/hour × 2 assembly lines
× 80 hours = 6,400

Rated capacity = Design capacity × Effective capacity
× Efficiency

Rated capacity = 6,400 × .8 × .85 = 4,352 printers
per week

What factors affect capacity?

Many factors affect an organization's productive capacity. Some are within management's control while others are not. Factors within management's control include the acquisition and supervision of land, physical resources, and the utilization of labor.

Management challenges affecting organizational capacity include personnel issues, technological maximization, and issues that are not directly controllable such as the impacts of weather events, political issues, or war.

10.6 LOCATION ANALYSIS

Few decisions have more long-lasting and critical-cost implications than plant location. Costs affected by location decisions include:

- Transportation—the geographic location will determine how far products must be transported to markets.

- Energy—utility geographic service areas determine the respective energy costs for any particular location. These costs can vary widely.

- Taxation—local and state tax rates vary widely. Location decisions have major taxation cost implications.

- Wages—wage levels vary widely depending on geographic regions. However, a location decision made solely on the basis of wage levels without considering labor productivity is counterproductive.

- Raw materials—certain industries are extremely dependent on the ready availability of specified raw materials such as wood or iron ore. Location analysis therefore must include the availability of these raw materials.

What is locational break-even and profit analysis?

Locational break-even analysis is an economic comparison of locational options based on a cost-volume examination. Location decisions can be compared in graph form using alternative production/sales volumes.

In order to perform locational break-even analysis it is essential to:

1. Establish the fixed and variable costs for each location.
2. Graph the costs for each location where costs are on the Y axis and production/sales volume is on the X axis of the graph.

3. Determine which location has the lowest production/ sales volume.

EXAMPLE 10.24

A washing machine manufacturer is analyzing three possible locations—Buffalo, New York; Toledo, Ohio; and Orlando, Florida—to build an additional manufacturing facility. Research analyses indicate the annual fixed costs for the sites are respectively $45,000; $60,000; and $95,000. The variable unit costs respectively are $235; $205; and $185. The anticipated selling price for the washing machines is $350. The company is seeking the most economical location for an expected volume of 5,000 units annually.

The total cost for each city at the expected volume of 5,000 units is calculated using the following formula:

Total cost = Fixed cost + Variable cost × Total volume

Buffalo:

Total cost = $45,000 + $235 × 5,000 = $1,220,000

Toledo:

Total cost = $60,000 + $205 × 5,000 = $1,085,000

Orlando:

Total cost = $95,000 + $185 × 5,000 = $1,020,000

Expected annual profits for each location can be calculated using the following formula:

Total revenue = (Selling price × 5,000) − Total cost (Fixed cost + Variable cost × total volume)

Buffalo:

$1,750,000 − $1,220,000 = $530,000

Toledo:

$1,750,000 − $1,085,000 = $665,000

Orlando:

$1,750,000 − $1,020,000 = $730,000

Assuming a maximum production of 5,000 units, Orlando provides the lowest cost location at $1,020,000 and the highest annual profit of $730,000.

Figure 10.3 shows the locational break-even analysis. At 500 units Buffalo and Toledo are both cheaper than Orlando. At 1,500 units Toledo is the cheapest location, but at 2,000 units of production Orlando becomes the cheapest. Therefore, the crossover points in the break-even analysis are 500 and 1,500 units of production.

FIGURE 10.3 LOCATIONAL BREAK-EVEN ANALYSIS

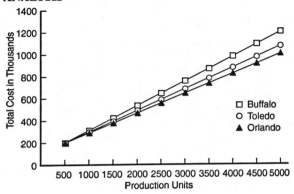

Figure 10.4 shows the location profit analysis. At 500 units both Buffalo and Toledo earn a profit of $12,500. At 1,000 units Toledo earns a profit of $85,000, while Buffalo and Orlando earn $70,000. At 1,500 units Buffalo shows a profit of $127,500, while Orlando shows a profit of $152,500 and Toledo's profit is $157,500. From 2,000 to 5,000 units Orlando is clearly more profitable than either Buffalo or Toledo. The crossover points are 500, 1,000, 1,500 and 2,000 units for location profitability.

FIGURE 10.4 LOCATIONAL PROFIT ANALYSIS

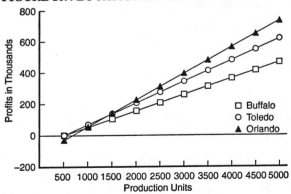

Therefore, from both a cost analysis and profit analysis, Orlando at 2,000 units and over is the best locational choice.

What is the center of gravity location method?

The center of gravity location method relies on mathematical analysis for determining where a warehouse should be located to service a number of retail stores in disparate locations. The method considers three factors:

- Market location
- The volume of goods handled in these markets
- Shipping expenses to each location

In order to develop the center of gravity location method, each retail outlet has to be given coordinates within a map grid system where the geographical distances are correctly established.

The center of gravity is determined by using the following formula:

$$C_x = \frac{\sum i \, d_{ix} \, V_i}{\sum i \, W_I}$$

$$C_Y = \frac{\sum i \, d_{iy} \, V_i}{\sum i \, V_I}$$

where

C_x = x coordinate of the center of gravity
C_y = y coordinate of the center of gravity
d_{ix} = x coordinate of the center of gravity
d_{iy} = y coordinate of the center of gravity
V_i = volume of goods moved to or from location i

In order to accurately reflect the true cost of distance on shipping, the center of gravity method evaluates the distance as well as the total volume actually being shipped to any respective location. The ideal location for a warehouse servicing several retail outlets is that which has the lowest weighted cost of distance and volume of units actually shipped.

EXAMPLE 10.25

Good Worth Hardware is a chain of six retail hardware stores being supplied by an outdated warehouse close to its first store. Stores are located in cities A, B, C, D, E, and F in Ohio, Pennsylvania, and New York.

The monthly volume of goods shipped to the respective stores is shown in Exhibit 10.5.

EXHIBIT 10.5 MONTHLY VOLUME OF GOODS SHIPPED TO STORES

Hardware Store Location	Volume of Monthly Shipments
City A	600
City B	800
City C	900
City D	1,200
City E	850
City F	1,100

The company needs to find a more centralized location in which to locate a modern warehouse to supply all the hardware stores.

The data from the coordinate locations is then used in the formulas for coordinates x and y.

$$C_x = \frac{\begin{array}{c}(40)(600) + (100)(800) + (150)(900) + \\ (165)(1,200) + (50)(850) + (110)(1,100)\end{array}}{600 + 800 + 900 + 1,200 + 850 + 1,100}$$

$$C_y = \frac{\begin{array}{c}(30)(600) + (90)(800) + (140)(900) + \\ (180)(1,200) + (60)(850) + (120)(1,100)\end{array}}{600 + 800 + 900 + 1,200 + 850 + 1,100}$$

The center of gravity coordinate is shown in the coordinate locations in Figure 10.5.

FIGURE 10.5 COORDINATE LOCATIONS FOR HARDWARE STORES

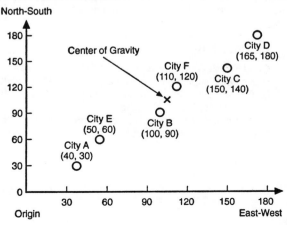

10.7 TIME STUDIES

The classical approach to time studies was developed by Frederick W. Taylor in 1911, and is the accepted procedure for production analysis. A time study, also termed a stopwatch time study, is an analysis of a worker's performance against a time standard. Time studies are normally performed on short repetitive production types of tasks.

How is a time study performed?

There are several basic steps which must be followed in any time study:

1. Define the job to be analyzed.
2. Break the job into discrete tasks.
3. Measure the actual time required for each task.
4. Develop a statistically significant sample size of the task work cycles to be measured. Work measurement depends on sampling the work process. However, in order to counter inherent variability in the work samples, a sufficient representation of the sample universe must be selected. Therefore, it is essential to determine an adequate work cycle sample size. In order to do this, a preliminary analysis must be performed usually consisting of anywhere from 5 to 20 repetitive work cycles in order to determine variability.

The work sample size is dependent on three factors:

a. Observed variance in the work cycles.
b. How closely the sample will conform to the average work cycle (accuracy).
c. The desired statistical level of confidence.

The work cycle element having the greatest variability will determine the sample size needed to obtain an acceptable statistical level of confidence.

The typical statistical level of confidence expected is 95% with a reliability of ± 5%. The following formula will determine required sample sizes:

$$N = \frac{nZ^2 \left[n\sum X^2 - (\sum X)^2 \right]}{(n-1)a^2 (\sum X)^2}$$

where

n = initial sample size
X = cycle time
a = accuracy
Z = confidence level ($Z = 1$ for 68.3% confidence level, $Z = 2$ for 95.5% confidence level, and $Z - 3$ for 99.7% confidence level)

5. Calculate the average time required for each job element using the following formula:

$$\frac{\text{AVERAGE JOB}}{\text{ELEMENT TIME}} = \frac{\text{SUM OF THE TIME NEEDED TO PERFORM EACH TASK}}{\text{NUMBER OF JOB CYCLES}}$$

6. Rate the performance of each worker (Performance Rating).

7. Calculate the normal time required for each job element using the following formula:

$$\text{Normal time} = \Sigma \left[(\text{average element time}) \frac{\text{Performance rating}}{100} \right]$$

Here the observed time, normal time, for a particular employee is rated against the average job element time.

8. Determine allowances that may be permitted for a particular job task. This may take into consideration personal factors as well as unavoidable constraints encountered in the work situation. Allowances include all unavoidable delays, but rule out avoidable delays. An allowance factor represents time lost due to personal factors, shift adjustments, improper equipment, fatigue, and related issues. The performance rating is adjusted for any allowances.

9. Calculate the standard time. When calculating the standard time, three different types of time are actually utilized. Actual time is the time a particular employee actually takes to perform a particular job operation. Normal time is the time needed to complete an operation by an employee working at 100% efficiency having no delays. Standard time is the time needed to complete an operation by an employee working at 100% efficiency with unavoidable delays:

$$\text{standard time} = \text{normal time} + \text{allowance time}$$
$$\text{standard time} = \frac{\text{normal time}}{1 - \text{allowance fraction}}$$

EXAMPLE 10.26

A work operation consisting of three procedures is observed using a stopwatch time procedure. The allowance for the work operation is 15%. It is necessary to determine the standard time for the operation and what the standard should be in hours per 1,500 units. The observed data are contained in Table 10.1:

TABLE 10.1 STOPWATCH TIME STUDY

Job Element	Performance rating (%)	Observations (seconds / element)										Mean Time (sec)	Normal Time (sec)
		1	2	3	4	5	6	7	8	9	10		
1	85	10	4	8	8	5	6	8	6	8	8	7	6
2	90	11	9	12	12	14	11	10	9	11	13	11	10
3	105	8	9	9	7	8	6	10	7	8	9	8	9
												Total	25

$$\text{standard time} = \frac{\text{normal time}}{1 - \text{allowance factor}}$$

$$\text{standard time} = \frac{24.6}{1 - .15} = 28.94 \text{ sec./unit}$$

$$1500 \text{ units} \times 28.94 \text{ sec/unit} = 43410 \times 1/60 \text{ sec/min} \times 1/60 \text{ min/hr}$$

$$= 12.06 \text{ hr.}$$

The standard time is 28.94 seconds/unit and the standard for 1500 units is12.06 hr.

EXAMPLE 10.27

A manager wants to determine the required sample size for three different work cycle elements after having performed 12 sample observations. The manager is seeking a 95.5% statistical confidence level with an accuracy of ± 5%. Refer to Exhibit 10.6.

EXHIBIT 10.6 REQUIRED SAMPLE SIZE AT .005 LEVEL OF CONFIDENCE

Sample Observation	Element 1		Element 2		Element 3	
	X	X2	X	X2	X	X2
1	8	64	12	144	7	49
2	7	49	13	169	6	36
3	10	100	14	196	9	81
4	9	81	16	256	8	64
5	6	36	18	324	9	81
6	8	64	1 5	225	7	49
7	9	81	16	256	9	81
8	10	100	17	289	8	64
9	9	81	14	196	7	49
10	9	81	15	225	8	64

EXHIBIT 10.6 (*cont.*)

11	7	49	16	256	7	49
12	8	64	14	196	9	81
Total	100	850	180	2,732	94	748

$Z = 95.5\%$ confidence level $= 2$

Element 1:

$$N = \frac{nZ^2\,[nX^2 - (X)^2]}{(n-1)a^2(X)^2} = \frac{12(4)[12(850) - 10,000]}{11(.0025)\,10,000} = 34.91$$

Element 2:

$$N = \frac{12(4)[12(2,732) - 32.400]}{11(.0025)\,32,400} = 20.69$$

Element 3:

$$N = \frac{12(4)[12(748) - 8,836]}{11(.0025)\,8,836} = 27.66$$

Element 1 has the largest required sample size of 35. Therefore, the manager needs to make another 23 sample observations to complete the total sample size of 35.

10.8 WORK SAMPLING

Work sampling is a work measurement methodology that estimates the proportion of time an employee utilizes in performing assigned job tasks. The methodology uses random observations of actual worker activity and is dependent on the laws of probability. Since it does not require a formalized time study procedure conducted by qualified stopwatch analysts, it is less costly. The methodology requires that the manager simply determines whether an employee is actually working or is idle during any particular observation.

After all the observations have been completed, the percentage of working observations is computed from the total observations. The greater the number of observations, the more accurate the technique is.

How is work sampling used?

Work sampling is used for the following:

1. *Ratio delay studies.* Worker allowances are determined by calculating the percentage of time an employee spends on unavoidable delays.
2. *Percent utilization of equipment.* The technique is used to determine the actual utilization of machinery and other equipment.

3. *Determining labor standards.* The technique is useful in determining work standards for various tasks by rating the employee's performance.

4. *Evaluating employee performance.* A performance standard can be calculated utilizing the work sampling procedure and resulting standards.

How is work sampling performed?

1. *Sample observations.* Several sample observations are performed to act as the basis for developing a correct sample size based on the problem's parameters.

2. *Compute the actual sample size.* The sample size is dependent on the desired level of statistical confidence and accuracy. Normally, the acceptable level of confidence is 95% with an accuracy level of ± 5%. The following formula determines the actual sample size necessary for a work sampling procedure:

$$N = \frac{Z^2(1-p)}{a^2 p}$$

where

p = estimate of time utilized in an activity

$1 - p$ = estimate of time not utilized in an activity

a = accuracy level fraction

Z = confidence level ($Z = 1$ for 68.3% confidence level, $Z = 2$ for 95.5% confidence level, and $Z = 3$ for 99.7% confidence level)

A higher confidence level and a reduced accuracy level fraction will increase the required sample size. The 95% confidence level and ± 5% accuracy level establish that in 95 cases out of 100 the sampling activity will be accurate within ± 5% of the proportion of time utilized in an activity (p).

3. Prepare a random schedule of employee observations.

4. Observe and rate the employee's work performance.

5. Total the number of units produced and calculate the normal time per unit.

6. Compute the standard time per unit.

EXAMPLE 10.28

The supervisor of a large production organization wants to determine what the idle time is with a confidence level of 95.5% and an accuracy level of 5%. After performing a random sample of 75 observations, it is determined there is 20% idleness. What is necessary to analyze the percentage of operational idleness?

The required sample size is determined by using the following formula:

Z = 95.5% confidence level = 2

$$N = \frac{Z^2(1-p)}{a^2 p} = \frac{4(1-.20)}{0.0025(0.2)} = 6400$$

Additional observations needed for sample
= 6,400 − 75 = 6,325

For establishing labor standards, work samples are used in a similar manner to time studies. However, work samples are more appropriate for operations having long production cycles, group service or production operations, and work using indirect labor. A determination is made as to whether the employee is busy or idle during the observation, a rating is given to the employee, and the units produced are totaled in order to produce an average. Using this data, the normal time and standard time can be determined:

$$\text{Normal time} = \frac{\text{(total study time)} \times \text{(working time percent)} \times \text{(performance rating)}}{\text{number of units produced}}$$

The standard time is the normal time plus allowance time:

$$\text{standard time} = \text{normal time} + \text{allowance time}$$

$$= \frac{\text{normal time}}{1 - \text{allowance time}}$$

EXAMPLE 10.29

A work sample study of a production operator was conducted over 60 hours (3,600 minutes) and disclosed the following data:

Number of pieces produced	580
Total number of observations	800
Total number of observations working	650
Average performance rating	95%

The total allowance given by the company for this operation is 15%. What is the standard time for each operation?

$$\text{Normal time} = \frac{\text{(total study time)} \times \text{(working time percent)} \times \text{(performance rating)}}{\text{number of units produced}}$$

$$= \frac{(3600 \text{ min.})(0.8125)(.95)}{580} = 4.8 \text{ minutes/unit of production}$$

$$\text{Standard time} = \frac{\text{normal time}}{1 - \text{allowance time}}$$

$$= \frac{4.8}{1 - .15} = 5.65 \text{ minutes/unit of production}$$

10.9 AGGREGATE PLANNING STRATEGIES

Planning is a primary management responsibility. Aggregate planning is concerned with organizing the quantity and timing of production over a medium period of time up to eighteen months with undetermined demand. Specifically, aggregate planning means combining all of an organization's resources into one aggregate production schedule for a predetermined intermediate time period. The objective of aggregate planning is to maximize resources while minimizing costs over the planning period.

The aggregate production plan is midway between short-range planning and long-range planning. Aggregate planning includes the following factors:

1. Work force size and composition
2. Demand forecasts and orders
3. Raw material planning
4. Plant capacity management
5. Utilizing outside subcontractors
6. Inventory management

Aggregate planning is the link between short-term scheduling and long-term capacity planning.

What are aggregate planning strategies?

There are three types of aggregate planning strategies:

Pure Strategy. In this strategy, only one production or supply factor is changed.

Mixed Strategy. This strategy simultaneously alters two or more production or supply factors or some combination.

Level Scheduling. This strategy has been adopted by the Japanese and it embodies maintaining constant monthly production schedules.

What aggregate planning strategies influence demand?

Aggregate planning can influence demand in the following ways:

1. *Pricing strategies.* Pricing can be used to increase or reduce demand. All things being equal, increasing prices reduces demand while lowering prices will increase demand.
2. *Advertising and promotion strategies.* Advertising and promotion are pure demand management strategies in

that they can increase demand by making a product or service better known as well as positioning it for a particular market segment.

3. *Delayed deliveries or reserving orders.* Managing future delivery schedules is a strategy for managing orders when demand exceeds capacity. The net effect of delayed deliveries, or back ordering, and reservations is to shift demand to a later period of time, often to a more slack period, which provides a smoothing effect for overall demand. However, the negative is that a percentage of orders will be lost as consumers are unwilling or unable to wait the additional amount of time.

4. *Diversifying the product mix.* Product mix diversification is a method used to offset demand seasonality. For example, a lawn mower manufacturing company may diversify into snow removal equipment to offset the seasonality of the lawn mower industry.

What aggregate planning strategies influence supply?

Aggregate planning is also used to manage supply considerations by using the following strategies:

1. *Subcontracting.* Subcontracting is a method of increasing capacity without incurring large capital investment charges. It can turn the competitive advantage of other corporations to the contracting organization's advantage. However, subcontracting can be costly, and also reveals part of the business to potential competitors.

2. *Overtime and idle time.* A direct short-term strategy for managing production capacity is to either increase or decrease the number of the work force. This strategy has the advantage of utilizing the currently existing work force. However, overtime is expensive and can produce job burnout if relied upon too extensively. On the other hand, enforcing idle time on the work force can result in resistance as well as a drop in morale.

3. *Hiring and laying off employees.* Hiring and laying off employees is a medium- to long-term strategy for increasing or decreasing capacity. Hiring employees usually involves the cost of training while laying off employees can incur severance charges. Laying off employees can also cause labor difficulties with unions and reduce morale.

4. *Stockpiling inventory.* Accumulating inventory is a strategy for smoothing variances which may occur between demand and supply.

5. *Part-time employees.* Certain industries have seasonal

requirements for lower skilled employees. Aggregate planning can be used to manage these seasonal requirements.

What is the charting method of aggregate planning?

Charting is a highly utilized trial-and-error aggregate planning method. It is relatively simple to use and is easily understood. Essentially, the charting approach uses a few variables in forecasting demand, applying current production capacity. While the charting method does not assure an accurate prediction, it is simple to implement requiring only minimal calculations.

The charting method requires five steps to implement:

1. Calculate each period's demand.
2. Calculate each period's production capacity for regular time, overtime, and subcontracting.
3. Determine all labor costs including costs for hiring and layoffs as well as the cost of holding inventory.
4. Evaluate organizational employee and stock policies.
5. Create optional policies and evaluate their costs.

EXAMPLE 10.30

A Florida men's suit manufacturer has created expected demand forecasts for the period June–January, as shown in Table 10.2.

TABLE 10.2 EXPECTED DEMAND FOR MEN'S SUITS, PRODUCTION DAYS, AND DAILY DEMAND

Month	Expected Demand	Production Days	Daily Demand
July	5,500	20	275
August	5,200	22	236
September	5,300	21	252
October	4,800	21	229
November	4,300	19	226
December	4, 100	20	205
Average			237

The daily demand is calculated by dividing the total expected demand by the number of monthly working days:

$$\text{AVERAGE DEMAND} = \frac{\text{TOTAL EXPECTED DEMAND}}{\text{NUMBER OF PRODUCTION DAYS}}$$

FIGURE 10.6 MONTHLY AND AVERAGE MEN'S SUIT DEMAND

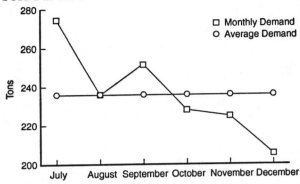

The graph in Figure 10.6 illustrates that there is a substantial variance between the monthly and average men's suit demand.

What are the costs of aggregate planning?

Aggregate planning is a systems methodology having major organizational impacts. Every strategy has associated costs and benefits. Increasing hiring means increasing training costs and incurring associated employment benefit costs. Increasing inventory increases carrying costs consisting of capital and storage costs, deterioration, and obsolescence. Using part-time employees involves the costs and risks of using improperly trained and inexperienced personnel as well as creating possible union conflicts. Using subcontractors has the cost of exposing an organization to potential competitors.

EXAMPLE 10.31

Using the data in Example 10.30, it is possible to develop cost estimates for the men's suit manufacturer. Basically, the manufacturer has three choices:

1. The manufacturer can meet expected monthly production fluctuations by varying the work force size, hiring and laying off employees as needed. In this scenario, an assumption is made that the men's suit manufacturer has a constant staff of 55 employees. (See page 362.)
2. Another alternative is to maintain a constant work force of 51 employees and subcontract for additional expected demand. (See page 363.)

3. A third alternative is to maintain a work force of 69 employees and store suits during slack demand months. (See page 364.)

Organizational Costs

Inventory Holding Cost Per Unit Per Month	$3
Subcontracting Cost Per Unit	$25
Labor Hours Per Men's Suit	2
Layoff Cost Per Employee	$500
Hiring and Training Cost Per Employee	$650

THREE PLAN SUMMARY COSTS

Item	Plan 1 Hiring and Laying Off	Plan 2 Subcon- tract	Plan 3 Store Inventory
Hiring Cost	19,278		
Layoff Cost	2,000		
Inventory Holding Cost			14,244
Subcontractor Cost		102,700	
Total	21,278	102,700	14,244

In this example, the best production plan is plan 3 which maintains a work force of 69 employees and stores men's suit inventory during low demand months.

10.10 TRANSPORTATION METHOD

The objective of the transportation method is to limit shipment costs from several points of origin to several points of destination. Organizations having an origin and destination network must maximize effectiveness in order to limit costs while expediting the shipments.

How is the transportation method implemented?

The transportation method is implemented initially by determining point of origin predictive capacities, destination requirements, and shipment costs to the various destinations from the points of origin. The analysis is structured utilizing a matrix containing these factors.

PLAN 1

Month	Required Number of Suits	Required Production Hours (Suits Required × 2)	Hours Available Per Employee per Month (no. of days × 8)	Workers Required (Required Production Hours / Hours Available)	Workers Hired	Workers Laid Off	Hiring Cost (Workers Hired × $650)	Layoff Cost (Workers Laid Off × $500)
July	5,500	11,000	160	69	14	0	8,938	
August	5,200	10,400	176	59	4	0	2,659	
September	5,300	10,600	168	63	8	0	5,262	
October	4,800	9,600	168	57	2	0	1,393	
November	4,300	8,600	152	57	2	0	1,026	
December	4,100	8,200	160	51		4		2,000
Total							19,278	2,000

PLAN 2

Month	Required Number of Suits	Available Production Hours (no. of days × 8 × 51)	Suits Produced (Available Hours /2)	Suits Subcontracted	Subcontractor Cost (Tons Subcontracted × $25)
July	5,500	8,160	4,080	1,420	35,500
August	5,200	8,976	4,488	712	17,800
September	5,300	8,568	4,284	1,016	25,400
October	4,800	8,568	4,284	516	12,900
November	4,300	7,752	3,876	424	10,600
December	4,100	8,160	4,080	20	500
Total					102,700

PLAN 3

Month	Required Number of Suits	Available Production Hours (no. of days × 8 × 69)	Number of Suits Produced (Available Hours /2)	Ending Inventory of Suits	Inventory Holding Cost (Ending Inventory × $3)
July	5,500	11,040	5,520	20	60
August	5,200	12,144	6,072	872	2,616
September	5,300	11,592	5,796	496	1,488
October	4,800	11,592	5,796	996	2,988
November	4,300	10,488	5,244	944	2,832
December	4,100	11,040	5,520	1,420	4,260
Total					14,244

EXAMPLE 10.32

A company manufactures furnaces in three different cities, A, B, and C located in various regions of the country. They are shipped to three different warehouses, D, E, and F also located in various regions of the country. Each manufacturing site has different capacities, and each warehouse has different requirements. A transportation matrix is developed to illustrate the data in Figure 10.7.

FIGURE 10.7 A TRANSPORTATION MATRIX

To \ From	Warehouses			Production Capacity
	D	E	F	
A	$12	$10	$8	200
B	$15	$11	$9	300
C	$16	$13	$8	400
Warehouse Requirement	400	200	300	900

B to D Destination

Shipping Cost From Point B to Point E

Warehouse F Demand

Total Demand and Supply

What is the Northwest corner rule?

In the Northwest corner rule the maximum amount of a shipment is shipped from the upper left-hand corner (Northwest corner) of the matrix and distributed through the other cells going to the right and down throughout the matrix until all demands are met.

EXAMPLE 10.33

Develop an initial feasible transportation solution from the previous example as shown in Figure 10.8. The following shipments are assumed to have occurred:

1. 200 furnaces are shipped from A to D (this consumes A's production capacity)
2. 200 furnaces are shipped from B to D (this fulfills D's warehouse requirement)
3. 100 furnaces are shipped from B to E (this consumes B's production capacity)
4. 100 furnaces are shipped from C to E (this fulfills E's warehouse requirement)

5. 300 furnaces are shipped from C to F (this fulfills F's warehouse requirement and C's production capacity)

FIGURE 10.8 WAREHOUSES, DEMAND, AND SHIPPING COST

To / From		Warehouses D	E	F	Production Capacity
	A	$12 / 200	$10	$8	200
Factories	B	$15 / 200	$11 / 100	$9	300
	C	$16	$13 / 100	$8 / 300	400
Warehouse Requirement		400	200	300	900

Using this information, furnace shipping costs are calculated for each respective destination, as shown in Table 10.3.

TABLE 10.3 RESPECTIVE FURNACE SHIPPING COSTS FOR EACH DESTINATION

Route	Furnaces Shipped	Unit Cost	Total Cost
From A to D	200	$12	$1,200
From B to D	200	$15	$3,000
From B to E	100	$11	$1,100
From C to E	100	$13	$1,300
From C to F	300	$8	$2,400
Total Cost			$9,000

This is an initial solution where all demands and capacities were utilized. However, this may not be the least expensive transportation solution for this set of variables since no consideration was given to limiting costs.

What is the stepping-stone method and how does it reach an optimum transportation solution?

The stepping-stone method is a technique for optimizing an initial transportation solution. The methodology calculates cost by testing each unused square in a transportation table. The following methodology is followed to calculate an optimal transportation solution:

1. Choose any unused square in a transportation table such as Figure 10.8.
2. Develop a closed horizontal and vertical path back to the original square through the squares that are being used. Unused squares are skipped in the process.
3. The first unused square is marked with a + sign and subsequent corner squares in the developed closed path are alternately marked with – and + signs.
4. An evaluation index is created by adding the unit cost figures in each square containing a plus sign and then subtracting the unit costs in each square containing a minus sign.
5. The methodology repeats all of these steps until an evaluation index is calculated for all the unused squares. An optimal solution is achieved when all the results are equal to or greater than zero. If a square evaluation is negative, cost reductions can be accomplished by transferring as many units as possible to that square.

EXAMPLE 10.34

Using the transportation matrix for the furnace company, the stepping-stone method can be used to evaluate an optimal shipping route. Every empty cell must be tested using a closing pathway of engaged cells.

In the stepping-stone method, the number of engaged squares has to equal the number of rows in the table plus the number of columns minus 1 ($R + C - 1 =$ number of engaged cells). In the furnace example we have:

$R + C - 1 =$ number of engaged cells

$3 + 3 - 1 = 5$

If there are fewer engaged cells than the stepping-stone rule calls for, there is a degeneracy, meaning it is not possible to trace a closed path for one or more unoccupied squares.

Shipping route A to E: starting in empty cell AE, a route is traced using only engaged squares. Thus, a route is traced from AE to AD to AB to BE and alternate + and – signs are placed in each square. This is shown in Figure 10.9.

FIGURE 10.9 SHIPPING ROUTE AE

From \ To	Warehouses D	Warehouses E	F	Production Capacity
A	$12 − 200 ◄ − − −	$10 +	$8	200
B (Factories)	$15 + 200 − − −	$11 ► 100 −	$9	300
C	$16	$13 100	$8 300	400
Warehouse Requirement	400	200	300	900

A shipping cost index for route AE is calculated using the shipment costs in the upper right-hand corner of each square:

$$\$10 - \$12 + \$15 - \$11 = +\$2$$

Thus, for route AE an additional cost of \$2 would be incurred for each furnace shipped. Figure 10.10 shows shipping route AF.

FIGURE 10.10 SHIPPING ROUTE AF

From \ To	Warehouses D	Warehouses E	F	Production Capacity
A	$12 − 200 ◄ − − − − − −	$10	$8 +	200
B (Factories)	$15 + 200 − − −	$11 − ► 100	$9	300
C	$16	$13 + 100 − − −	$8 − ► 300	400
Warehouse Requirement	400	200	300	900

The shipping cost index for shipping route AF is:

$$\$8 - \$12 + \$15 - \$11 + \$13 - \$8 = +\$5$$

Using route AF will increase furnace shipping costs by \$5 per unit.

Shipping route BF (not shown) would start in square BF going to square BE to square CE and back to square BF.

The shipping cost index for shipping route BF is:

$9 - $11 + $13 - $8 = + 3

Using route BF will increase furnace shipping costs by $3 per unit. Figure 10.11 presents route CD.

FIGURE 10.11 SHIPPING ROUTE CD

From \ To	Warehouses D	Warehouses E	F	Production Capacity
A	$12 200	$10	$8	200
B (Factories)	$15 − 200◄ − − ─▲100	+ $11	$9	300
C	$16 + ◄ − − − ─►│	− $13 100	$8 300	400
Warehouse Requirement	400	200	300	900

The shipping cost index for route CD is:

$16 - $13 + $11 - $15 = - 1

Of the three routes, shipping route CD is the optimum since it would reduce the furnace shipping costs by $1 per unit.

The total amount that may be shipped on the optimum route is the smallest number in the squares having minus signs. Thus, in shipping route CD 100 furnaces, found in square CE, is the greatest amount that can be shipped. Using shipping route CD reduces furnace shipping costs by $100 (100 units × $1 = $100).

10.11 SCHEDULING

Scheduling is the management of organizational resources to achieve an orderly and uninterrupted workflow process. The basic objective of scheduling is to maintain high organizational productivity, low inventory levels, and high levels of customer satisfaction. Scheduling involves the use of time and the setting of priorities into operational rules.

Scheduling is generally categorized into forward and backward scheduling.

What is forward scheduling?

Forward scheduling begins as soon as demand is known. This type of scheduling is generally used by custom fabricators and manufacturers who rely on individual customer orders. Normally, forward scheduling assumes a very short delivery date. It is essential that fabrication and manufacturing times be accurately estimated in order to develop reliable deadlines. This mandates the development of reliable estimates of fabrication and manufacturing capacities.

What is backward scheduling?

In backward scheduling, start and due dates as well as the required capacity for individual jobs are developed by calculating processing times and required capacities sequentially from the last job back to the first.

What is shop loading?

Shop loading is the apportioning of jobs to production centers. While the method determines which manufacturing centers receive specific jobs, it does not specify processing priorities. When job orders can be performed equally well by several manufacturing centers, a prioritizing of the manufacturing centers becomes necessary.

What are the two shop loading methods?

The two types of shop loading method are infinite loading and finite loading. Infinite loading does not consider capacity limitations when apportioning jobs to work centers, while finite loading apportions work to manufacturing centers consistent with their production capacities. Infinite loading monitors and measures production underloads and overloads and projects the timing sequence of their occurrence. The net result of infinite loading's monitoring and measuring of the production process results in a determination of capacity requirements. An overload occurs when a manufacturing center cannot finish scheduled jobs because of capacity constraints, whereas an underload occurs when a manufacturing center experiences periods of idleness because of insufficient job scheduling.

Since finite loading does not permit capacity overloads, it mandates job rescheduling based upon existing manufacturing capacities.

What are the advantages of finite and infinite loading?

All jobs must be prioritized before implementing finite loading. Since finite loading cannot exceed capacity, it should generate more realistic completion times. Those jobs not having the highest priority are rescheduled for a later period of time.

Infinite loading's advantage is that it does not consider capacity. Therefore, it gives a more realistic assessment of what production capacity is really required to complete designated jobs. Using the capacity requirements that infinite loading provides allows management to more accurately schedule work among the available manufacturing centers.

How are Gantt charts useful in loading and scheduling?

The Gantt load chart depicts the apportioning of jobs to a production center. While many variations exist, normally the load chart is a table depicting the production center, assigned jobs, hours required for the assigned jobs, and remaining capacity in hours arranged along horizontal and vertical lines.

A Gantt schedule chart is a graph used to analyze the progress of currently scheduled jobs. It is a visual method for surveying the actual progress of jobs in production.

What are the advantages and disadvantages of the Gantt loading and scheduling charts?

Gantt charts are a very popular management tool for assessing job loading for production centers as well as for analyzing actual job progress in the production centers. They are easy to develop and understand.

However, criticisms are that they are unsophisticated in the sense that no allowance is provided for uncontrollable production delays resulting from human error, unavoidable technical failures, or material shortages. They also require continual adjustment as conditions change. Also, when there is more than one production center equally capable of processing job orders, the Gantt methodology does not provide the required sophistication to help management make decisions as to which should process particular jobs. Essentially, Gantt charts tend to be more useful in simply maintaining records regarding current operations.

EXAMPLE 10.35

It is necessary to chart the loading of ten jobs and calculate the remaining production hours available in three different production centers. A Gantt load chart, shown in Figure 10.12, is prepared to demonstrate the loading of the jobs.

FIGURE 10.12 GANTT LOAD CHART

	Production Center					
Job	*#1*		*#2*		*#3*	
Number	*Required*	*Available*	*Required*	*Available*	*Required*	*Available*
1	7	70	2	50	3	60
2	3	63	4	48	6	57
3	6	60	5	44	4	51
4	4	54	3	39	7	47
5	9	50	7	36	8	40
6	2	41	6	29	4	32
7	4	39	4	23	8	28
8	7	35	8	19	5	20
9	3	28	4	11	7	15
10	4	25	5	7	2	8
Remaining Hours		21		2		6

EXAMPLE 10.36

Management needs to visualize the scheduling and production status of four different job orders, 1, 2, 3, and 4. A Gantt scheduling chart shown in Figure 10.13 displays the scheduling and production status of the four products.

FIGURE 10.13 GANTT SCHEDULING CHART

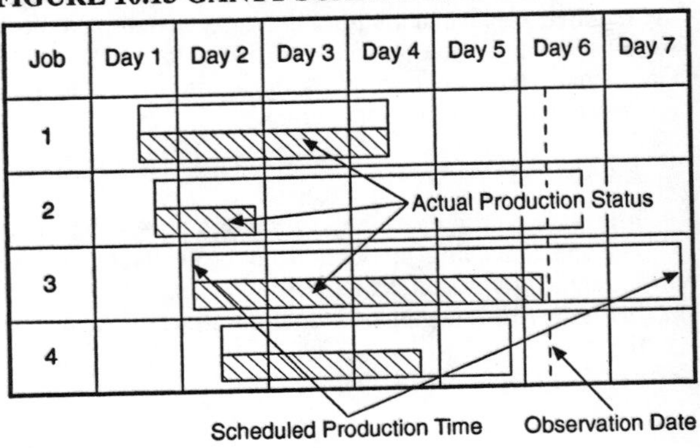

10.12 SEQUENCING

While the Gantt charts are useful for tracking job loading, they do not have the sophistication to help management determine what job order priorities should be. Sequencing is a process that determines the priorities job orders should have in the manufacturing process. Sequencing results in priority rules for job orders.

What are priority rules?

The basic function of priority rules is to provide direction for developing the sequence in which jobs should be performed. This assists management in ranking job loading decisions for manufacturing centers.

There are several priority rules which can be applied to job loading. The most widely used priority rules are:

DD—Due Date of a job. The job having the earliest due date has the highest priority.

FCFS—First Come, First Served. The first job reaching the production center is processed first.

LPT—Longest Processing Time. Jobs having the longest processing time have the highest priority.

PCO—Preferred Customer Order. A job from a preferred customer receives the highest priority.

SPT—Shortest Processing Time. The job having the shortest processing time has the highest priority.

EXAMPLE 10.37

Using the data contained in the table Job Processing Data, it is necessary to schedule orders according to the priority rules of Due Date (DD), First Come, First Served (FCFS), Longest Processing Time (LPT), Preferred Customer Order (PCO), and Shortest Processing Time (SPT).

Job Processing Data

Job	Preferred Customer Status (1 = Highest)	Processing Time (days)	Due Date (days)
A	3	7	9
B	4	4	6
C	2	2	4
D	5	8	10
E	1	3	5

PRIORITY RULES AND JOB SEQUENCING OUTCOMES

Priority Rules

Due Date	First Come, First Served	Longest Processing Time	Preferred Customer Order	Shortest Processing Time
C	A	D	E	C
E	B	A	B	E
B	C	B	A	B
A	D	E	C	A
D	E	C	D	D

What is the critical ratio method?

The critical ratio method assigns a priority that is a continually updated ratio between the time remaining until due date and the required job processing time. When used in conjunction with other jobs waiting to be processed, it is a relative measure of critical job order priority.

The critical ratio gives the highest priority to jobs that must be done to maintain a predetermined shipping schedule. Jobs that are falling behind a shipping schedule receive a ratio of less than 1, while a job receiving a critical ratio greater than 1 is ahead of schedule and is less critical. A job receiving a critical ratio score of 1.0 is precisely on schedule.

The critical ratio is calculated by dividing the remaining time until the date due by the remaining process time using the following formula:

$$\text{critical ratio} = \frac{\text{remaining time}}{\text{remaining process time}}$$
$$= \frac{\text{Due Date} - \text{Today's date}}{\text{days of remaining process time}}$$

EXAMPLE 10.38

On day 16, four jobs, A, B, C, and D, are on order for Ferguson's Kitchen Installation Service:

Jobs on Order

Job	Due Date	Days of Remaining Process Time
A	27	8
B	34	16
C	29	15
D	30	14

Using this data, the critical ratios and priority order are computed.

Critical Ratios and Priority

Job	Critical Ratio	Priority
A	$(27 - 16) / 8 = 1.38$	4
B	$(34 - 16) / 16 = 1.13$	3
C	$(29 - 16) / 15 = .87$	1
D	$(30 - 16) / 14 = 1$	2

Job C has a critical ratio less than one indicating it has fallen behind schedule. Therefore, it gets the highest priority. Job D is exactly on schedule, but jobs B and A have respectively higher critical ratios indicating they have some slack time. This gives them respectively lower priorities.

What is Johnson's rule for scheduling N jobs in two production centers?

Johnson's rule provides an optimum prioritization based on minimum processing time when N jobs have to be sequentially processed in two production centers. The net result of utilizing Johnson's rule is a minimization of total idle time at a production center.

The procedure for using Johnson's rule is the following:

1. Show all the processing times for all orders at each respective processing site.
2. Find the job having the shortest processing time. If the job is at the first processing site, schedule it first; however, if it is at the second processing site, schedule it last.
3. Once the job is scheduled, it no longer receives further consideration.
4. The remaining jobs are scheduled using rules 2 and 3.

EXAMPLE 10.39

Five job orders must be sequentially processed through two processing centers. The orders need to be sequenced to achieve minimum idle time.

Processing Time for Jobs in Hours

Job	Processing Center 1	Processing Center 2
A	11	3
B	6	8
C	9	4
D	2	9
E	10	6

Now it is necessary to sequence the jobs starting with the smallest processing time. The smallest job is job D in Processing Center 1. Since it is in Processing Center 1, it is sequenced first and then eliminated from further consideration.

D				

The second smallest processing time is A in Processing Center 2. It is placed last, since it is at Processing Center 2, and eliminated from further consideration.

D				A

The next smallest processing time is job C in Processing Center 2. It is placed next to last.

D			C	A

For the next smallest processing time, there is a tie in job B in Processing Center 1 and Job E in Processing Center 2. B is placed in the next highest sequence after job D and job E is placed directly after B.

D	B	E	C	A

The resulting sequential processing times are:

Processing Center 1	2	6	10	9	11
Processing Center 2	9	8	6	4	3

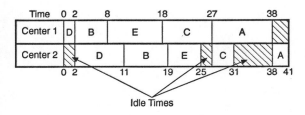

In Processing Center 2 the five jobs are completed in 41 hours, and there are 11 hours of idle time.

10.13 PROJECT MANAGEMENT TECHNIQUES: PERT AND CPM

What is PERT?

The Program Evaluation Review Technique (PERT) was originally developed for the U.S. Navy's Polaris submarine project. The primary purpose of PERT is to plan, schedule, and coordinate the sequential activities required in one time complex project. The PERT model develops a graphical depiction of the sequential activities required to complete a project. It then determines the total anticipated time needed for the project's completion.

PERT is considered a network method of project scheduling since activities are depicted as arrows while intermediate goals, or events, are depicted as circles.

There are four steps necessary in developing a PERT network project schedule:

1. A comprehensive project analysis is performed.
2. All of the required project activities are categorized according to their order of precedence.
3. A PERT chart is drawn where all the activities preceding an event are shown using a lettered arrow and events are numbered using circles.
4. Time and/or cost estimates are assigned to each activity.

EXAMPLE 10.40

It is necessary for a manager to develop a PERT network using the following information listing activities and their respective predecessors.

Activity	Preceding Activity
A	—
B	—
C	B
D	B
E	B
F	C
G	D
H	E

A PERT chart is drawn as in Figure 10.14, where all the activities are lettered using arrows and the events are numbered using circles.

FIGURE 10.14 PERT NETWORK PROJECT SCHEDULE

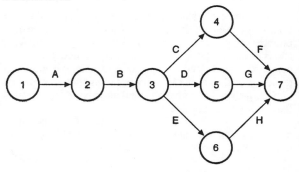

Activities can also be designated by their beginning and ending events. For example:

Beginning Event	Ending Event	Activity
1	2	1-2
2	3	2-3

2	4	2-4
3	4	3-4
4	5	4-5
4	6	4-6
5	7	5-7

What is the critical path method (CPM)?

The critical path method was originally developed to schedule the startup and shutdown of major production plants. It is based on developing three activity time estimates for calculating project completion time with variances. The three time estimates are an optimistic time (a), pessimistic time (b), and most likely time (m).

What are the optimistic, pessimistic, and most likely times?

1. Optimistic time (a). This is an estimate of the least, or minimum, time an activity will take to complete.
2. Pessimistic time (b). This is an estimate of the most, or maximum, time an activity will take to complete.
3. Most Likely time (m). This is an estimate of the average or normal amount of time an activity would take assuming it were to be repeated several times.

In arriving at an expected time (t) for a given project activity, a beta probability distribution is employed in PERT. The three time estimates are combined and averaged to calculate a time estimate. Normally, in PERT applications the most likely time (m) is given a weight of 4 while the optimistic time (a) and pessimistic time (b) are each given a weight of 1. The variance (v) for each activity is also calculated:

$$t = \frac{a + 4m + b}{6}$$

and

$$v = \left[\frac{b - a}{6} \right]^2$$

The expected times (t) and variance (v) are calculated for each activity after the network for the PERT analysis is completed.

EXAMPLE 10.41

There are five activities in a project. It is necessary to compute the expected times and variances for the project:

Activity	Optimistic Time (a)	Most Likely Time (m)	Pessimistic Time (b)	t $\frac{a+4m+b}{6}$	v $\frac{b-a}{6}$
1-2	5	7	9	7	0.67
1-3	1	3	5	3	0.67
2-4	2	3	4	3	0.33
3-4	4	6	8	6	0.67
3-5	3	7	9	6.67	1

What is critical path analysis?

Critical path analysis consists of analyzing the sequence of activities from the beginning event to the ending event. The critical path is the time it takes to finish all the project's activities without any slack time. This is critical to the completion of a project since it controls the project's completion time.

To calculate the critical path, data must be obtained on the earliest start and finish times, the latest start and finish times, and the available slack time:

1. *ES—Earliest activity start time.* The time when all preceding activities are finished; the earliest an activity can commence.

2. *LS—Latest activity start time.* The time when all successor activities have to be finished without delaying the entire project. The latest activity start time is calculated by subtracting the expected time of the activity (t) from the latest finish time (LF) and then subsequently subtracting (t) for the slowest (longest (t) path(s).

3. *EF—Earliest activity finish time.* The earliest activity finish time equals the earliest activity start time (ES) of the activity plus expected time (t) for the activity.

4. *LF—Latest finish time.* The time when the project must be finished. The latest activity finish time equals the latest start time (LS) plus the expected time (t) of the activity.

5. *S—Slack time.* An activity's total slack is the difference between the latest and earliest activity start times (LS – ES) or the latest and earliest activity finish times (LF – EF).

After calculating the preceding data for each activity, the overall project can be analyzed. This includes:

1. *The critical path.* The time it takes to finish all the project's activities without any slack time.

2. *T—total project completion time.* This is the sum of all the project's critical path activities' expected times (*t*).

EXAMPLE 10.42

Using the PERT chart in Figure 10.15, calculate ES and EF for each activity.

FIGURE 10.15 PERT CHART

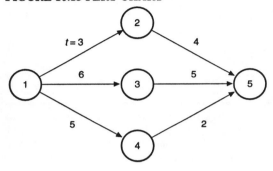

Now the earliest start (ES) and earliest activity finish times (EF) are determined. In order for an activity to begin, all of the preceding activities must be finished. EF is calculated by adding expected time (*t*) to ES for each activity.

Activity	*t*	ES	*EF* (*t* + ES)
1-2	3	0	3
1-3	6	0	6
1-4	5	0	5
2-5	4	3	7
3-5	5	6	11
4-5	2	5	7

The latest activity finish time (LF) of the project is 11 since the earliest activity finish time (EF) for activity 3-5 is 11.

In order to calculate a project's critical path, it is necessary to determine the latest start time (LS) by subtracting the expected time (*t*) of the activity from the latest finish time (LF). It is also necessary to determine the slack time for each activity by subtracting the earliest activity start time (ES) from the latest activity start time (LS).

EXAMPLE 10.43

Using the above data, what is the project's slack time and critical path?

Activity	t	ES	EF (t + ES)	LS	LF (LS + t)	S (LS − ES)
1-2	3	0	3	4	7	4
1-3	6	0	6	0	6	0
1-4	5	0	5	4	9	4
2-5	4	3	7	7	11	4
3-5	5	6	11	6	11	0
4-5	2	5	7	9	11	4

The critical path is the activity with 0 slack time, or activity 3-5. The total completion time of the project is 11 since activity 3-5 is the longest path to completion. Figure 10.16 presents the critical path.

FIGURE 10.16 PERT CHART SHOWING CRITICAL PATH

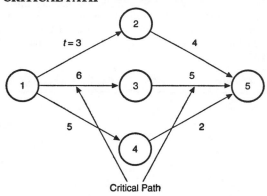

Critical Path

11

Marketing

Marketing is an essential business function. It is the process of planning and distributing the exchange of products and services using the concepts of pricing and promotion. In this sense, marketing is not only an essential function, it is also a creative process.

11.1 THE DEFINITION OF MARKETING

The basic concept of marketing is based on the concept of an exchange of equal market values for the purpose of satisfying human needs or wants. This definition raises several additional questions.

What is an exchange?

A marketing exchange occurs when an individual gives something of value for a sought-after product or service. The vehicle most often used for an exchange transaction is money. Barter is another form of exchange which does not require the use of money. Rather, in a barter system, there is an exchange of property or services. An example is marketing consulting services given in exchange for the purchase of a computer system.

What is market value?

Market value is established by actual or potential buyers and sellers. A marketplace can either be centralized, such as a stock market, or decentralized, as in a national marketplace. In the decentralized marketplace, advertising and mass communication inform the buyers and sellers as to market values.

What is a need?

A need is an unfulfilled desire that an individual has which acts as a strong motivator. The individual seeks to fulfill a need. Needs include physical, social and psychological desires. Marketing can create individual needs.

What is a want?

A want is the process of satisfying an unfulfilled need. Wants are culturally based in the sense that when an individual has a need for shoes, he/she will think of a particular brand name to satisfy the need. Individuals who have a need for a chocolate bar state they want a "Hershey Bar" when any brand chocolate bar will suffice. Wants and needs are often confused. Some computer manufacturers emphasize the speed and power of a computer, when many consumers only need a simple word processor to type a letter. Thus, computer manufacturers who bundle word processing software with the computer can emphasize its simplicity and usefulness for word processing, rather than its technological features, and gain market share.

What is the role of products and services in marketing?

Marketable products and services are used to satisfy the wants and needs of consumers in the marketplace. An individual having a need to appear successful may want to purchase expensive clothing or a luxury car to satisfy the need.

11.2 DEFINING THE MARKET

A market is a group of individuals and/or organizations wanting a particular product or service who have the financial ability to acquire it. This group of people and/or organizations is termed the target market. However, in order to be considered part of the market, the target group must be actively willing to purchase the product or service in question, and have the authority to do so. Otherwise, they are out of the market.

What is mass marketing?

Organizations using mass marketing essentially assume "one size fits all"; *i.e.*, one particular product mix will satisfy everyone in a particular market, and it is not necessary to identify and service different aspects of the overall market. The example that is usually cited to illustrate mass marketing is Henry Ford's marketing of the Model T where he said people could have any color they wanted "as long as it is black." The rationale for mass marketing is that the greatest learning curve and economies of scale result in the lowest unit costs and prices. Increasingly, however, companies are moving away from mass marketing to target marketing.

What is target marketing?

Target marketing consists of breaking a total market into market segments representing smaller homogeneous markets. Once this analysis is performed, it is possible to identify those market segments which can be targeted for a particular product or service based on the conformity of their homogeneous characteristics to the product or service specifications. Using market segmentation, target marketing allows marketing managers to develop more effective marketing strategies.

What is the marketing mix?

The marketing mix consists of four variables—the four Ps—which a marketing manager can control: product (P_1), place (P_2), promotion (P_3), and price (P_4).

TABLE 11.1 THE MARKETING MIX

Product

Quality
Type of features
Brand name
Kind of packaging
Design type
Product-related services (service, warranties, maintenance policies)

Place

Number and type of marketing intermediaries
Market location
Warehouse location
Distribution methods

Promotion

Developing promotion budget
Creating the advertising message

TABLE 11.1 (*cont.*)

Types of advertising media
Developing a sales force
Types of direct marketing
Methods of sales promotion

Price

Choose pricing objective
Estimate product demand
Calculate costs
Maximize product mix pricing
Competitive factors

- *Product.* The most basic element of the marketing mix is a company's product or service. The product component includes quality, features, brand name, types of packaging and design, and product-related services including maintenance and warranties.
- *Place.* Place concerns the processes management uses to make products and services available to the target market. This includes developing marketing intermediaries in order to provide the product or service to market locations. The methods used to distribute products and services are also an essential place component.
- *Promotion.* Promotion involves the methods used to transmit product information to the target market. This involves creating and using advertising, choosing the appropriate media, developing a sales force, utilizing direct marketing where appropriate, and using other promotion methods.
- *Price.* Pricing is an important element of marketing a product or service. Management must choose pricing objectives which are consistent with the target market's expectations as well as the estimated product demand and the costs involved in producing the product or service. Competitive factors also play an important role in achieving product or service pricing.

The marketing mix management chooses at any particular moment, therefore, is a combination of these four Ps. The total marketing mix combinations available at any particular time are the product, place, promotion and pricing alternatives available to management. Thus, marketing mix combinations = $(P_1 \times P_2 \times P_3 \times P_4)$.

EXAMPLE 11.1

A toy manufacturer wants to determine its possible marketing mix combinations available at a particular time. It has the following possible product, place, promotion and price combinations respectively: 5, 10, 8, 7.

marketing mix combinations = $(P_1 \times P_2 \times P_3 \times P_4)$

marketing mix combinations = $(5 \times 10 \times 8 \times 7) = 2800$

What is product positioning?

Product position is the perception consumers have regarding a market offering(s) relative to its competitors. Product positioning is the act of analyzing and managing consumer product position perceptions. Management develops product position maps to analyze how consumers position products relative to the competition. Product position maps can be developed prior to introducing a product or service or subsequent to introduction in order to obtain further market information.

EXAMPLE 11.2

XYZ Food Corporation is considering targeting the retail consumer food market by introducing packaged orange juice. The question the corporation must answer is whether to introduce a high-quality whole orange juice product packed fresh at the citrus grove, a lower quality concentrate also packed at the citrus grove, or a reprocessed concentrate packed locally. Company A has the high-quality whole orange juice medium price market, while company B has the medium-quality and price concentrate market while company C has the low-quality reprocessed concentrate low-price market. Corporation XYZ decides to offer a high-quality whole orange juice premium-priced orange juice product although there is room in the market to offer a low-quality reprocessed concentrate at a high price.

FIGURE 11.1 PRODUCT POSITIONING MAP FOR ORANGE JUICE

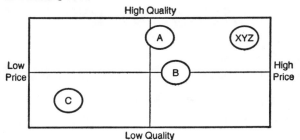

How is market demand determined?

Determining market demand is a critical management concern. Numerous variables ultimately determine market demand. These include demographics (such as age, sex composition, and per capita income of buyers), the state of the economy, past industry sales and others. Thus, market demand is dependent on the current environment. Three methods management can use to project current market demand are total market potential, total industry sales and market shares.

What is total market potential and how is it calculated?

Total market potential is a calculation of the potential market sales for an entire industry assuming a predetermined marketing effort under a given set of market conditions.

The formula for calculating total market potential is:

$$M = nap$$

where:

n = number of buyers in the particular product/market assuming given market conditions
a = average quantity purchased by buyers
p = average unit price

EXAMPLE 11.3

Calculate the total market potential for ballpoint pens in the U.S. in any given year. Out of a population of approximately 250 million, it is necessary to calculate the estimated number of buyers of ballpoint pens. After researching the market, it is determined that the average age of ballpoint pen buyers range from ages 10 to 75. This eliminates approximately 55 million people from the pool. In addition, if another 30 million people are eliminated because they are institutionalized or are illiterate, then a total pool of potential buyers is $(250 - 55 - 30)$ = 165 million. Additionally, market research tells us that annual per capita fountain pen purchases are 8, and that the average price is $1.50 per pen.

The total market potential for ballpoint pens is:

$$M = nap$$
$$M = (165,000,000 \times 8 \times \$1.50) = \$1,980,000,000$$

What is area market potential?

It is necessary for companies to choose the best marketing territories for their products and services. Being able to estimate the market potential of areas including cities and states is essential prior to committing a company's financial resources. The methods primarily used for this are the market-buildup method and the multiple factor method.

How are industry sales and market shares determined?

Trade associations normally provide gross industry sales data. By tracking its own sales against those of the entire industry, a firm can accurately determine its market share and whether it is increasing or decreasing. Additionally, marketing research firms monitor product-category sales in various retail outlets. This data allows a company to compare its own sales with both the overall industry and to particular competitors.

11.3 MANAGING THE MARKETING PROCESS

Marketing management involves marketing analysis, planning, implementing and controlling a marketing strategy. It is involved with product and service development as well as supervising basic marketing functions such as promotion, pricing and distribution.

What is marketing planning?

Marketing planning consists of making decisions about the overall direction of a marketing effort and is a function of effective marketing research. Areas that have to be planned include the company's marketing mix, the marketing budget and the priority allocations, distribution methods, brand names, and packaging.

A marketing plan should have a brief executive summary giving the plan's highlights and major conclusions. It should also discuss the current market, product, competitive and distribution environment. All relevant variables and data are discussed with an analysis of how they impact the marketing plan. Analyses are provided of current opportunities, product market strengths and weaknesses, and of major issues needing attention. Financial and market objectives are also detailed. The marketing plan is used for developing an overall marketing strategy.

What is marketing strategy?

A marketing strategy is a comprehensive marketing methodology that is developed as a result of extensive marketing planning. A marketing strategy details the following factors: target markets, product line, product positioning, price, distribution channels, sales force, service procedures, advertising and promotion methodologies, product research and development expenditure targets. and marketing research.

How are marketing departments organized?

Many types of marketing organizations currently exist. Companies often create various combinations of marketing organizations. The basic types of marketing organizations include the following: functional, geographical, product and brand management, and by markets.

What is a functional marketing organization?

A functional marketing organization consists of marketing personnel typically managed by a marketing vice president. It is the most widely used marketing organization. Since a functional marketing organization is not specialized, it is the simplest to manage. While this is a strength when a firm has relatively few products and services, it can also be a liability as a firm's market offerings become more diversified and specialized. Since a functional marketing organization has broad responsibilities, marketing personnel can compete with each other for specialized product or service resources. Figure 11.1 shows a typical functional marketing organization chart.

FIGURE 11.1 FUNCTIONAL MARKETING ORGANIZATION CHART

What is a geographical marketing organization?

National companies often find it is more effective having regional sales managers reporting to one national sales manager. The regional sales managers usually supervise district sales managers who directly supervise a certain number of sales personnel. This facilitates regional market responses while freeing the national sales manager from excessive responsibility. Figure 11.2 shows a geographical marketing organization.

FIGURE 11.2 GEOGRAPHICAL MARKETING ORGANIZATION

What is a product and brand-directed marketing organization?

Product and brand-oriented marketing structures normally occur when organizations have experienced a large increase in products being offered to the market. Corporate management finds managing individual products and brands to be too time intensive and therefore choose individual managers who specialize in a particular product or brand. Product and brand organizations are essentially separate entities that interface with all elements of the larger organization. Thus, product and brand managers interface with the overall organization's production, promotion, advertising, legal, budgetary, research, purchasing and related functions.

Product and brand managers become deeply knowledgeable about their product areas and can react quickly to market changes. However, product and brand management organizations often multiply to include even minor products. This imposes a large financial cost on the overall organization. Additionally, product and brand managers often compete with each other for organizational resources, creating a highly charged corporate environment.

What is a market organization?

Companies often deal with many different target markets. However, each target market has its own distinctive needs (example, some companies sell products or services to various industrial sectors as well as to federal, state and local governments). Often products are developed just for certain target markets (e.g., a book publisher will produce books for the primary, secondary, college and trade markets). When the market potential is great enough, companies often organize departments to coincide with those specific markets.

The market organization focuses attention on the marketing function. It allows for greater concentration of effort on the markets that are essential to the organization's success. Figure 11.3 shows a market organization for a publisher.

FIGURE 11.3 MARKET ORGANIZATION FOR A PUBLISHER

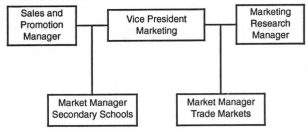

How are marketing plans implemented?

An organizational marketing plan has no value unless it is put into action. A close management interface with all aspects of the organization including production, promotion, marketing, research and design is essential to successfully implement the plan. Successful implementation requires creating a specific management plan to carry out elements of the marketing plan.

11.4 MARKET RESEARCH

Marketing research seeks to answer the question of what market needs exist, where they are located, what purchasing patterns exist, and other factors such as its pattern of growth. Modern marketing research depends on the development of an extensive management information system normally having a large product and consumer database at its core. The research process is ongoing and data about products, manufacturers, customers and competitors is continually being collected and analyzed.

The market research process follows a series of steps which include understanding the problem to be researched, creating a research design for the problem, designating data sources including designing the format in which data is to be collected, designing the data collection methods, implementing the study, analyzing and processing the collected data, and developing the research report. Figure 11.4 illustrates the market research process.

FIGURE 11.4 MARKET RESEARCH PROCESS

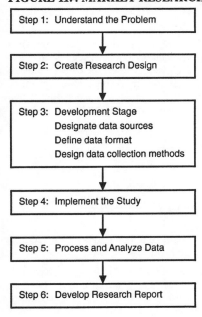

Step 1: Understand the Problem

Step 2: Create Research Design

Step 3: Development Stage
       Designate data sources
       Define data format
       Design data collection methods

Step 4: Implement the Study

Step 5: Process and Analyze Data

Step 6: Develop Research Report

Understanding the problem to be researched

A marketing manager, normally working with a marketing research group, must examine a problem carefully to understand its nature and complexity. A careful definition of the problem's parameters is crucial in developing the research project's goals.

There are various types of research problems. Some research is merely exploratory in nature which allows management to develop a clearer conceptualization of a problem. A more in-depth market study may be concerned with describing a particular problem in detail. A third type of research is interested in understanding the dynamics of a particular situation in terms of what causes it, or related issues, to occur.

The objective of the research is the critical factor in determining the nature of the research design.

How is the research design created?

After developing an understanding of the problem to be researched, the next question to be answered is what potential market value the research has when launching a new product.

EXAMPLE 11.4

Management seeks to determine the market value when launching similar products in a market segment to form the basis for a research budget. It can be determined that other product launches had an average annual profit of $35 million when market research was conducted and only $15 million without market research.

$$\text{market research value} = \frac{\text{average profits with market research}}{- \text{ average profits without market research}}$$

$$\text{market research value} = \frac{\begin{array}{c}\$35 \text{ million} \\ - \$15 \text{ million}\end{array}}{\$20 \text{ million}}$$

In this example it would be possible to justify a $20 million-dollar research budget.

Once a budget can be determined for the research project, it is then necessary to determine what types of data will be used. Two types of research data, primary and secondary, may be used in market research. Primary data such as census data collected by the government is original data which is either collected directly or is provided by a source who collects it directly. Secondary data is data reported on by a secondary source such as another market report or a periodical which provides results of primary data used in preparing the report. For the most part, market research uses primary data, although secondary data can be a useful theoretical source as well as validating results obtained from primary data collection studies.

In the development stage, how is marketing research data collected?

Marketing data is obtained using four basic research approaches: observational, focus group, survey and experimental.

- *Observational.* This is the most unstructured method of collecting data. The data collection method will depend on the context of the situation (for example, if one were to collect data regarding the cruise ship industry, one observational approach would be to book a cruise on one or several selected cruise ships and observe the activities on board, and the food being served, as well as to listen to passengers' before and after comments during embarkation and disembarkation).

- *Focus group.* In the focus-group methodology, a small group of selected individuals are invited to discuss a certain topic. In the cruise ship example, questions would be focused on the group's overall impressions regarding the cruise ship industry, with special attention given to particular cruise lines. Data obtained from a focus group session can be very useful when designing a more in-depth research study.

- *Survey research.* Surveys are the most commonly used form of marketing research. A survey is a systematic research tool used to obtain descriptive data. The three basic types of surveys are mail surveys to specified geographical areas, systematic telephone surveys within a calling area, and one-on-one personal interviews with a single individual or a group.

- *Experimental research.* This type of research has the most methodological accuracy. In experimental research, measures of the affects of variation in independent variables on the subject dependent variable are taken. This is done using as controlled an environment as possible either in a laboratory or field setting. An example of experimental research is testing the impact of various types of advertising on resulting sales. Different types of advertising can be used in different regional markets for the same product to determine if there is any measurable difference in resulting sales. However, controls for inherent regional differences must be predetermined.

How is a sampling plan developed?

A sampling plan is developed for the purpose of ensuring that the data collected is valid and reliable for the selected population. A sampling plan addresses three issues: the sampling unit, the sampling method, and the sample size.

- *Sampling unit.* This is a definition of a particular target population. If a company wants to sample opinions of people using a particular product, then it is necessary to define who that target population actually is.

- *Sampling method.* Researchers can use either a probability or nonprobability sample of the target population. A probability sample is a statistical calculation of the sampling error of a target population. At the 1% level of confidence, there is a 99% probability of being a valid and reliable sample of the target population, while 1% would be inaccurate. In a nonprobability sample, the researcher makes a judgment about what portion of a target population should be included in a sample.

- *Sample size.* Since it usually is impractical to sample opinions of an entire target population, it becomes necessary to develop a representative sample of the target population. Of course, the larger the sample, the more reliable and valid are the results. Sample sizes, either at the 5% or 1% level of confidence, are chosen according to the scope of the study, the resources available, and the criticality of the need for reliability.

How is the market research study implemented?

In the implementation stage, the researcher actually collects the required data. This is the most expensive and error-prone stage of the marketing research process. Data collection methods include mechanical means, computers including bar coding and interactive data input, questionnaires and interviewing. The major concern here is that data collection methods insure valid and reliable data.

How is the data processed and analyzed?

The data processing and analysis stage involves the processes of reviewing, categorizing, and analyzing. First the data must be reviewed for collection errors and omissions to insure that all areas have been completed accurately. Then the data has to be placed in categories where similar data can be compared with each other. The analysis step is crucial for the study's final outcomes. Various statistical analysis methods are utilized for interpreting the results. This can involve using multivariate analysis and frequency distributions.

How is the research report developed?

Final reports should be succinctly written. Results should be interpreted and presented in an understandable format. Management requires report formats that are easily interpreted and conceptually coherent. The appropriate use of graphics can be helpful in explaining outcomes. Oral presentations by researchers often are used to further explain the study.

11.5 MARKET SEGMENTATION

Markets consist of buyers. Buyers have many different characteristics which are important in determining their willingness to purchase products and services. These differences are predicated on geography, demographics, buying power, occupation, education, and buying behavior. Markets can be divided into four clearly defined segments based on these characteristics: geographic, demographic. psychographic, and consumer behavior.

What is geographic segmentation?

Markets can be divided geographically by ZIP Codes, cities, states, regions, or countries. A company having a nationwide distribution system may detect differences in national demand depending on the region of the country. A particular product may sell better in certain regions than in others. The product may be sold, advertised and tailored only for certain designated geographic regions.

What is demographic segmentation?

Demographic segmentation uses various population measures including age, sex, income, nationality, education, and occupation as the basis for dividing people into specific markets. Demographic segmentation is easy to measure and is widely used.

- *Age.* This demographic variable is often used to divide markets (for example, a clothing department store divides departments chronologically: infants, girls, boys, young teens, young women and young men, ladies and men). For a clothing department store, demographic segmentation based on age works well. However, in other areas age may not be so effective, as everyone wants to be perceived as being young.

- *Sex.* Gender is a widely used method of demographic segmentation particularly in the clothing, hairdressing, health, hygiene and print markets. While gender is an easily measured demographic variable, market trends and applications may change quickly. The role of women is evolving rapidly in modern society. Automobile marketing, for one example, is now targeting the large numbers of female automobile owners using options and designs desired by women.

- *Occupation.* Market segmentation by occupations is also effective because of associated lifestyles (e.g., business people are targeted by the travel and clothing industries since they do more traveling and purchase more business clothing).

- *Education.* The level of education is an important demographic segmentation variable primarily because higher levels of education are associated with higher levels of income, and higher proportions of disposable income.

- *Nationality.* Nationality, racial and cultural groupings are important American demographic segmentation variables since the United States has such a diverse population. However, these variables can be difficult since it may be a mistake as well as a misrepresentation to believe that these demographic groupings all have the same desires and purchasing patterns.

What is psychographic segmentation?

Psychographic segmentation divides markets on the basis of social class, personality traits, and/or lifestyles.

- *Social class.* Dividing the population on the basis of social class primarily uses income as a determinant of the buying behavior and lifestyles people exhibit in the various groupings. Social class ranges from the lower class, to middle to the upper class. The classes can be further stratified into upper lower, upper middle and upper upper. Social class is a strong determinant of individual purchasing preferences in consumer goods as well as in services such as education, travel and tourism.

- *Personality traits.* This is a method of segmenting markets based on a perception of how differences in consumer personalities affect buying behavior. Products and services will be marketed in a manner which will appeal to these personality traits (for example, those who are considered more conservative are perceived as desiring products having darker colors and more reserved styles of dress). There is no clear evidence that personality trait market segmentation is successful in accurately identifying target markets and individual personalities.

- *Lifestyle.* A person's lifestyle can best be defined as how that person adapts to and interacts with the environment. Some people may be more artistic or entrepreneurial than others. Segmenting the market according to lifestyle attempts to identify common interests that a group of people has and to target this group for particular products and services (for example, those identified as having an adventurous lifestyle would be perceived as having a greater desire to go on a sailing vacation than to stay at a resort).

- *Consumer behavior.* An additional method of segmenting markets is based on consumer behavior relating to specified products and services. Categories included under consumer behavior would be the amount of usage of a particular product. Here consumers can be classified as heavy, moderate, or light users. Consumer profiles by usage category help determine the characteristics each group displays and how to appeal to them. It is also important to determine who does not use the product in order to determine whether a target marketing program would be justifiable.

  Another market segment area of consumer behavior is brand loyalty. It is important to determine what the nature of consumer brand loyalty is for a specific product or service. By understanding which consumers are extremely loyal and which migrate, it may be possible to develop and implement strategies to increase or maintain consumer loyalty.

  Still another method of segmenting consumer behavior is based on the benefits consumers seek by purchasing particular products and services. Some consumers may seek the speed of service associated with retail fast food. Others may seek hygienic qualities associated with certain consumable products such as toothpaste, household cleaners, paper tissues, etc. After determining the benefits consumers actually seek from specified products, then the characteristics of the consumers must also be examined. Marketing strategies might be developed promoting new or expanded benefits to the consuming groups.

11.6 BRAND MARKETING DECISIONS

The objective of brand marketing is to increase consumer product or service awareness in order to generate increased and predictable demand leading to consumer willingness to buy and display loyalty. Brand marketing decisions involve a wide range of issues.

What is a brand?

A brand is a name, logo, sign or shape which singularly, or in combination, allow the consumer to differentiate the product or service from others in the marketplace.

What is a brand name?

A brand name is either a word or numbers in some combination which can be verbally expressed (for example, 3Com is a brand name).

What is a brand mark?

A brand mark is a symbol, graphic image, or shape, often used as a logo, which describes either a brand manufacturer or product.

What is brand loyalty?

Brand loyalty is repetitive consumer buying behavior resulting from consumer satisfaction with a particular brand.

What is brand recognition?

Brand recognition allows consumers to differentiate a branded product from other brands or those which are not branded.

What is brand acceptance?

At the minimum, marketers hope to generate brand acceptance where the consumer finds the brand meets their expectations. Therefore, they will purchase the product and not resist it.

What is brand preference?

Successful brand marketing causes brand preference where consumers prefer a particular brand over another.

What is brand insistence?

Extremely successful brand marketing may cause brand insistence where consumers insist on having one brand over another. True brand insistence is extremely difficult to generate.

What is brand rejection?

Brand rejection occurs when the consumer is familiar with a particular product but refuses to purchase it because of dissatisfaction with previous purchases. Brand rejection is extremely costly and difficult to reverse since the buyer's bias prevents him or her from considering any more purchases.

What is brand equity?

Brand equity is added value brought to a product by a brand name. This can be enhanced through the use of labels and logos. (Certain clothing and sports accessory manufacturers prominently display their name and/or logo on the product.) Brand equity often will allow the manufacturer to charge a premium price for its products.

How is branding useful?

Branding is an overwhelming market force. It gives the seller numerous advantages:

- Brands divide products into identifiable classes providing the ability to accurately measure sales and provide follow-up.
- Brands provide a methodology for market segmentation.
- Brands can be legally protected and trademarked preventing competitors from usurping products and their respective market share.
- Brands encourage consumer familiarity and loyalty.
- Brands help to create a company image.

How are branding decisions made?

Normally, a firm makes branding decisions only after extensive debate, research and discussion. Occasionally companies even offer a public contest to choose a brand name (for instance, Ford Motor Company offered a national contest when it sought a brand name for the car that later became known as the Edsel).

Companies often use marketing research firms as well as more specialized brand name consultants to choose a brand name.

What is brand strategy?

Brand strategy is the marketing objective sought by giving or associating products or services with a particular brand. There are at least four brand strategies that a firm can pursue: corporate blanket brand, family blanket brand, product range brand, and new product brand.

- *Corporate blanket brand.* A corporate blanket brand occurs when a company uses its name as the primary identifier of its products. The products, such as breakfast cereals, are usually in just one market and the corporation seeks a corporate brand identification.
- *Family blanket brand.* Family blanket brand is used to cover a series of products in a variety of markets. One brand name covers them all.
- *Product range brand.* Product range brands are used to describe a series of products having clear links in one market. An example would be a variety of shampoos having the same brand name but formulated for differing hair conditions.
- *New product brand.* A new product brand is used when

a firm introduces a new product in a totally different market that has no relationship to previous products the firm has on the market. If the firm expects the product will have a long product life cycle, and that it will generate sufficient profits to warrant a separate launch, a new product brand may be justified.

11.7 SERVICE FIRM MARKETING STRATEGIES

As of 1992 over 70% of all U.S. employment was in the service producing sector. Additionally, services account for over 70% of the gross domestic product and will produce 90% of all new jobs in the next ten years.

What are the characteristics of the services industry?

- *Intangibility.* Marketing services are intangible since they cannot be seen, tasted, felt or sensed. Services are unknown until they are performed (for example, a woman seeking a new hairdo from the hairstylist does not know what it will be like until it is actually done). Because of the unknown nature of services, marketers must create an image of quality, reliability and value for the consumer.

- *Immediate production and consumption.* Services are consumed as fast as they are produced. A lawn service leaves a trimmed lawn as soon as it is finished. Therefore, developing a strong relationship with the consumer is critical for the marketer's success.

- *Perishability.* Services cannot be saved or stored. It is difficult for service firms to provide the ideal level of service at all times. During periods of peak demand, resources may be overtaxed, while during periods of low demand, resources are underutilized. Organizations providing mass transit often find that trains or buses are overloaded taking passengers to the urban area during the morning rush while they are empty on the return ride.

- *Inconsistency.* There is no standard in services. The level of quality varies depending on who provides the service as well as when and where it is provided. Résumé writers provide a wide variety of résumés depending on who is writing it, what their industry depth of knowledge is, how well they write and what level of interest they have in the consumer.

How is marketing performed for the service sector?

Marketing for the service sector is more complex than

for tangible products primarily because of the difficulty of defining quality service, and managing productivity.

- *Service market differentiation.* The greatest challenge for service marketers is differentiating between service providers. If consumers perceive that service providers have indistinguishable offerings, then price competition becomes the only differentiating feature. A method of differentiating services from the competition is to add innovative features. Thus, the marketer adds to the primary service package by offering a secondary service package (for instance, an automotive lubrication service provider adds a secondary service package of automotive manufacturer certification, speed of service, and a consumer comfort facility to distinguish its service from the traditional service station or automotive dealership).

- *Service quality.* One of the primary ways to differentiate service providers is on the basis of quality. If the consumer's perceived quality is higher than expected quality, then the service firm will receive a higher evaluation and gain market share. Conversely, if the consumer's perceived quality is lower than the expected quality from the service firm, then the service firm will lose market share. Factors that influence the perception of service include reliability, sensitivity to and interest in consumer needs, courtesy, sincerity, and well-appointed service facilities.

- *Service productivity.* The service industry is experiencing a need to increase its productivity to remain competitive. However, the service industry is highly labor intensive. Increasing productivity, therefore, is extremely challenging. The following methods can be utilized in the service industry to increase productivity.

  Better utilization of labor. Management can research and develop more effective service procedures. Employee skills can be upgraded through training to make their service activities more effective.

  Trade off quality for quantity. In order to improve productivity, organizational procedures are developed whereby less time is spent per service unit. This may require changing the nature of the service as well as how services are delivered (e.g., using an automatic phone router which screens and routes phone calls).

  Automate the provision of services. The implementation of technology often can reduce the need for labor while increasing consumer satisfaction (such as, installing a fax back system which immediately provides consumers with requested information).

Upgrade current employees. Utilizing training and certification programs, it may be possible to upgrade lower paid employees to perform specified services performed by professionals (for example, nurses are now performing many medical services previously performed by doctors).

Allow consumers to perform self-service. Increasingly consumers are substituting their own labor for procedures formerly performed by employees (as in, self-service gas stations).

How can service delivery differentiation be achieved?

Service delivery can be differentiated using the "3 Ps" of service marketing: people, physical environment and process. Having better trained and more competent people can be extremely important in the service delivery process itself. Improving the physical environment of the service delivery environment is also extremely important (for example, having a clean and cheerful waiting room can be crucial in improving the overall image of an organization). Finally, improvements and innovations in the process can also make a critical difference in service market differentiation (e.g., the installation of bar code scanners in a supermarket expedites the check-out process with improved accuracy while enabling management to maintain a real-time management information system).

11.8 PRODUCT LINE DECISIONS

A product line is a group of products related on the basis of similar customers, marketing methods or product characteristics. The range of product lines establishes a product mix. The two types of product lines are those having complementary and substitute products.

What are complementary products?

In a product line, complementary products are those designed to add to the original product. For example, a company producing computers would also manufacture other items such as a mouse, printers, and software.

What are substitute products?

Substitute products are those that appeal to the same basic market segment, but have different specific characteristics. For example, a soup company has a full line of soups including chicken, tomato, turkey, pea, etc. Each soup can easily be substituted for the other.

How long should a product line be?

Product line length is determined by the number of products supported in a particular product line. Companies seeking high market share and growth have longer product lines.

Profitability is also affected by product line length. A product line has too many products if adding to the line reduces profits, while it has too few if profits can be increased by adding products.

Increasing product length tends to increase associated costs including engineering, inventory, ordering and transportation costs. Companies having successful products often tend to increase product line length in order to increase profits. However, overextended product lines can cause diminishing returns.

Lines can be extended by stretching and filling.

What is product line stretching?

Product line stretching develops when a firm adds additional products to a product line. Product lines can be stretched downward, upward, or both.

What is downward product line stretching?

A company producing "high end" products, in the more expensive range of the market segment, stretches downward by offering lower priced products in the market segment. Offering lower priced products will appeal to a wider range of consumers who may upgrade upon seeing the feature differences between the low and high end products. Using the "downward stretch" can be a competitive marketing strategy to challenge competitors either at the high or low end of the market segment.

What is upward product line stretching?

A company producing "low end" products, in the least expensive range of the market segment, stretches upward by offering higher priced products in the market segment. Companies may consider the "upward stretch" for a number of reasons. They may be well entrenched at the lower end of the market segment, but desire greater unit margins by moving upward in the market (for instance, the Japanese automotive companies implemented an "upward stretch" by successfully introducing luxury cars only after becoming well established in the lower end of the market with compact cars). The company may also be interested in experiencing a faster growth rate at the upper end of the market when those conditions exist.

What is two-way market stretching?

Two-way market stretching applies to companies in the middle of a market that want to expand their product line upward and downward. The basic objective is to become competitive in markets it did not previously serve by introducing products into those respective markets.

11.9 NEW-PRODUCT DEVELOPMENT AND MARKETING STRATEGIES

New-product development is essential for a company to remain competitive in today's rapidly changing markets. Marketing plays an important role in new-product development. Analyses of the selected market segments and the targeted consumer groups are performed, and decisions are made regarding the development of appropriate products. Yet, the introduction of new products is extremely risky. New-product failures are estimated to be 80% of all new-product launches in certain markets. There are various levels of failure. A complete product failure is a dead loss and provides no cost recovery. Partial product failures allow the recovery of some variable and fixed costs, while a comparative product failure actually provides some profit, but is relatively less profitable when compared with other products.

Why is there such a high failure rate with new products?

New-product failures occur for a number of reasons:

- *New products may not have significant advantages.* Certain markets may be saturated, and it is very difficult to develop truly innovative product ideas (e.g., the chocolate candy bar market is fairly well saturated, and it is difficult to improve upon the offerings already provided by the chocolate bar market leaders).

- *Divided markets.* Intense international competition is fragmenting markets into smaller segments. Focusing on smaller market segments increases the risks of failure.

- *Increasing product development costs.* As the technology becomes more complex, the cost of developing new products increases.

- *Shorter product life cycles and product development times.* Technological change is occurring at exponentially increasing rates that significantly reduces product life cycles as well as mandating shorter product development times. The risk of failure increases because of the greater likelihood of product development mistakes and misjudgments. Shorter product life cycles also mean a shorter period of time in which to recoup product development costs.

What are the major stages in new-product development?

- *Idea generation.* New-product ideas come from many sources. Customers are one of the best sources of new ideas (software companies rely extensively on their installed user base to provide feedback about how products should be improved). Consumers can be surveyed to identify needs and problems that are otherwise unknown to management. Competitors often introduce new product and service innovations which provide a rich area of product improvement. Employees who work closely with products can also provide significant insight into new product innovations and improvements. Brainstorming can be used by a marketing team where members give ideas in a free flow manner. In the final analysis, new-product ideas are the result of inspiration, imagination and deep experience.

- *Idea screening.* After numerous ideas have been generated, screening is utilized to evaluate the ideas in terms of practicality, cost, profit potential and strategic fit. Not only must new products have significant profit potential, but they must also be consistent with the firm's marketing plan and strategy. Most companies have product evaluation forms where the products are described and rated according to market potential. Subsequently, these forms are screened by a new-product organizational structure.

  There are two significant risks in the idea screening stage. One risk is that a product is rejected because management underestimates its market and profit potential. The other risk is that a firm will approve a product not having good market potential or strategic fit because it received inadequate idea screening.

- *Concept development and testing.* If a product idea survives the idea screening stage, it is developed into a product concept. A product concept is an idea that is developed into an expression of the advantages offered by a new product or service and the target market to which it will be offered. This is termed a product category concept.

EXAMPLE 11.5

A company wants to develop a line of nutritional snacks. It then converts this product idea into several product concepts within the product category. One product concept consists of a candy made out of dried fruit. Another is an all natural cracker using dried fruit to add taste. A third product concept is a dried meat product made out of prepared soy beans.

- *Business analysis.* Having developed the product concept, a preliminary marketing strategy is then developed. This will enable management to evaluate the product concept's business potential. In order to do this, management must perform an extensive cost analysis on product development costs including research and design, marketing and production. Product demand estimates are then combined with cost estimates to develop short- to intermediate-term profit estimates.

- *Product development.* Assuming the business analysis determines the product is worthwhile, it then goes to the product development stage where R&D develops a prototype. Normally, product development represents a substantial financial investment over an extended period of time. Additionally, product development must be sensitive to expressed consumer desires. The use of technology, particularly computer aided design and computer aided manufacturing (CAD/CAM), can help to shorten development time. When the prototype is actually developed, it must be subjected to rigorous functional testing to insure the product is viable, safe, and meets expectations. Assuming the product passes the functional testing stage of the product development process, it must then be subjected to consumer testing to determine whether or not the product would be appropriate for the target market.

- *Market testing.* The market testing process subjects the developed product to actual target market conditions. The product is packaged and branded and introduced using a controlled marketing program. The purpose of market testing is to determine consumer acceptance, the success of various marketing strategies, how large the market actually is, and how competitive it will be. There are several methods used in the market testing process:

  Traditional test marketing. In traditional test marketing, the product is introduced into a selected group of cities. When determining the test market strategy, management must determine in how many and in which cities the test marketing should be performed, the length of the test marketing process, and what factors should be evaluated. Traditional test marketing also allows a variety of promotional methods to be used to introduce the product in order to determine which method works most effectively. The negative side of the traditional test marketing process is that it is costly and time consuming.

Research firm test marketing. The firm introducing a new product may decide to conduct test marketing by contracting with a research firm which directs market research in a group of commercial outlets. Various marketing strategies are carefully controlled and evaluated. Product sales are monitored using scanners and bar codes. Research firm test marketing is performed more quickly and cheaply than traditional test marketing.

Simulated test marketing. In simulated test marketing, a selected group of shoppers is exposed to advertising for the new product as well as advertising for competitive products. They are then given a predetermined amount of money and allowed to shop in a simulated store carrying the new product as well as existing competitive products. Observations and measures are made of the products purchased, and the consumers are then asked why they purchased their chosen products. Follow-up questions are also asked of the selected consumers after a period of time has elapsed. Simulated test marketing can be conducted quickly and much more economically than either traditional test marketing or research firm test marketing.

- *Commercialization.* If the product successfully passes the market testing process, then the marketer is ready to implement a full commercial introduction. The firm now must make its greatest investment in the entire product development process. Manufacturing facilities have to be acquired, a promotional advertising program needs to be developed, sales personnel have to be employed and trained, and administrative support systems have to be put in place. Many activities have to be coordinated. Additionally, evaluations have to be performed concerning the timing, geographical selection of launch sites and the targeting of product launch prospects.

1.10 MARKETING CHANNEL DESIGN DECISIONS

Marketing channel (also termed channels of distribution)

design decisions are critical for successful product distribution. Marketing channels consist of intermediaries who contribute to the product distribution process according to consumer demand. They consist of merchant middlemen, agent middlemen, and facilitators. Companies rely on market intermediaries because of their effectiveness in distributing products as well as their capitalization. A company's chosen channel members develop long-term relationships built on trust, and directly affect the marketing process including price. Marketing channels always have a producer and a final consumer.

Who are merchant middlemen?

Merchant middlemen consist of wholesalers and retailers who actually purchase the product and resell it. Wholesalers buy in large lots and sell in smaller quantities to retailers who in turn sell individual units to the consumer. Wholesalers and retailers assume the risk of ownership in return for a profit markup when selling the merchandise to others.

Who are agent middlemen?

Agent middlemen are sales intermediaries such as brokers, product representatives and sales representatives who seek others to purchase merchandise. They do not actually purchase any merchandise and are compensated on the basis of a percentage of sales and/or salary depending on whether they are independent business people or employees of companies wishing to sell products.

Who are facilitators?

Facilitators are intermediaries who directly assist in the distribution function without taking title to the goods. They consist of a range of organizations including advertising agencies, financial lending organizations, shipping companies, and storage warehouses.

What is channel length?

Channel length describes the number of intermediary levels existing between the producer and the consumer. A direct, or zero, channel is one where there is a direct relationship between the producer and the consumer (e.g., a neighborhood bakery may be considered a direct channel since the retail consumer purchases the finished baked goods directly with no intermediaries). A one-level channel has one intermediary which is usually a retailer (e.g., a regional bakery goods operation utilizes local food stores to distribute the product to the consumer). A two-level channel has two intermediaries to distribute products to the consumer (e.g., a candy manufacturer sells the product to a wholesaler who in turn sells to the retailer). A three-level channel has three intermediaries normally consisting of an agent middleman who sells to a wholesaler who then sells to a retailer.

How are channels developed?

Developing channels of distribution requires many decisions. Channel distribution needs grow and develop as companies grow and markets change. Increased channel utilization increases costs which are passed on to the consumer. The design of channel development begins by studying the buying patterns of the target customers.

What are consumer buying patterns?

Consumer buying patterns affect a channel's characteristics and are classified in the following ways:

* *Units purchased.* Different customers have different purchasing needs. Commercial customers normally purchase larger lot sizes than do the household consumer. Channel modifications have to be made to meet these different needs.

* *Turnaround times.* Some industries, such as fast foods, use rapid turnaround times as an inherent part of the business, while other businesses may have longer turnaround times. Industries having customers needing rapid turnaround times require more direct channels of distribution than those with slower turnaround times.

* *Product assortment.* Industries, particularly retail, offering large product assortments have a need for deeper channels of distribution in order to provide product variety.

* *Services.* High levels of services, including repair, delivery, installation and others, require more intensive channel utilization.

How many intermediaries should be used in a channel?

Determining the number of intermediaries will affect the marketing of a product. Longer channels have more intermediaries and higher costs. On the other hand, intermediary expertise may be essential for successfully marketing a particular product. Thus, a manufacturer may try and limit the number of intermediaries in order to contain costs. The trade-off in having fewer intermediaries is limited distribution.

As manufacturers continue to penetrate markets, greater distribution is desired involving more intermediaries. While this will increase distribution, it will also increase costs while sacrificing some degree of marketing control. This may result in having the product incorrectly positioned.

Finally, not all intermediaries are the same. The marketer wants only those intermediaries who most effectively work with the company to distribute the product.

How do company characteristics affect channel development?

Generally, the companies having the largest array of retail products, particularly product consumables, have the least need for intermediaries. They are well-enough positioned in the market to deal directly with retail outlets. Smaller companies with smaller product lines have a greater need for the market distribution strengths of intermediaries.

How do product characteristics affect channel development?

Products that are perishable, time sensitive (such as fashions), heavy and bulky, or are highly unique in nature (such as those requiring specialized training) generally have short channels of distribution. On the other hand, standardized products often move through several intermediaries in the distribution process.

How are channel alternatives evaluated?

There are several issues in evaluating channel alternatives. One issue is choosing the most economically effective channel alternative. Companies must evaluate channel intermediaries based on those that have the largest level of sales per unit of selling cost. Other issues concern the extent to which marketing management control will be lost by including a sales agency or other sales broker in the marketing channel. A final variable is choosing a channel intermediary that will still allow the producer to maintain maximum marketing flexibility in fast moving markets.

What are the challenges in managing market channel intermediaries?

Several issues are important in channel management.

- *Choosing the most effective channel alternatives.* Management must determine what the characteristics are for the most effective channel intermediaries. Having done this, management must develop strategies for attracting these channel intermediaries to the marketing channel.

- *Maximizing channel member effectiveness.* Management must motivate channel members to create the most cost-effective market distribution system for the company.

- *Evaluating the effectiveness of intermediaries.* Management must develop channel member evaluation systems. While seeking the cooperation of channel members, it is still essential to determine what profit standards must be used as the basis for evaluation.

11.11 DEVELOPING THE PROMOTION BUDGET

One of the most challenging marketing management functions is developing the company's promotion budget. Promotional advertising is extremely expensive, and establishing an acceptable figure is difficult at best. While companies use many different methods, we will describe four widely used methods:

- *Funds available method.* This is the simplest promotion budget allocation method. The marketing manager simply establishes the budget at the amount established by the company's management. It does not require any research and makes long-term planning impractical.

- *Percentage of current sales method.* This method is calculated from last year's or the current year's forecasted sales for various product or service categories. It can be justified in that the promotion budget will increase or decrease proportionally to sales and that it establishes linkage between the sales of a product or service category and the amount budgeted for its promotion. However, it encourages more spending during growth periods when less may be indicated, and spends less during periods of contraction when more may be appropriate.

- *Matching the competition.* A firm allocates an amount to its promotion budget that matches the competition's. This allows a product or service to maintain an amount of advertising equal to that of its competitors. It can also be justified by maintaining that this level of promotion represents an industry consensus. However, it assumes that other companies know the appropriate amount to allocate to the promotion budget when in fact there may be no justification for this assumption.

- *Objective and task method.* The promotion budget is established based on clear marketing goals, defined tasks needed to achieve the stated goals, and defined expenditure estimates. This method depends on estimating the promotional productivity of the resources allocated in each category. However, developing accurate estimates of the effectiveness of promotional expenditures is difficult at best.

11.12 THE PROMOTIONAL MIX

The promotional mix is the blending of five promotional areas of advertising, sales promotion, public relations, direct marketing and personal selling.

- *Advertising.* Advertising is any form of paid public and impersonal communication utilizing the mass media. The purpose of advertising is to emphasize the benefits and characteristics of products or services, often using special effects including graphics, color, sound, music, famous personalities, testimonials and related methods.

- *Sales promotion.* Sales promotions consist of various types of incentives including discounts, rebates, contests, etc., intended to induce a positive response from consumers. Although they are short-term in nature, promotions are designed to induce a rapid increase in sales.

- *Public relations.* Public relations is communication to an organization's publics that extends beyond its immediate target market. The purpose of public relations is to create a positive image of the organization by providing and explaining information. One of the outcomes of public relations is the creation of publicity for all forms of the mass media. Publicity is advantageous since it normally appears as a news story and there is no cost to the organization.

- *Direct marketing.* Direct marketing consists of various types of marketing intended to solicit a direct consumer response. Forms of direct marketing include direct mail, telemarketing, and electronic marketing. Direct marketing is aimed at specific individuals in the target market rather than being broadly disseminated.

- *Personal selling.* Personal selling is the oldest and most successful form of sales promotion. Personal selling is contingent on developing personal long-term one-on-one relationships. Personal selling depends on the development of an organizational sales force.

11.13 ADVERTISING

Advertising is any form of paid nonpersonal communication of messages designed to promote products and services to target markets utilizing the mass media.

What are the objectives of advertising?

The objectives of advertising are to educate, convince, and remind target markets.

- *Educate.* Educational advertising is essential in the early stages of product or service introduction. Education advertising informs the target consumer about the advantages of a particular product or service and how it can be useful.

- *Convince.* In competitive markets it becomes essential to convince consumers about why one product or service is more advantageous than another in terms of features, services, price, or status.

- *Remind.* In mature markets it is necessary to continuously remind consumers to use a particular brand or service. It is also useful for overcoming buyer's remorse, and consumer second thoughts about a purchase, by reminding them of the strengths of a particular product or service.

How is the advertising message developed?

Developing advertising is a creative process. The basic purpose of an advertising message is to stress the positive aspects of a product or service. This is done by collecting and analyzing consumer responses and consumer data. Several advertising variations should be developed and tested; however, the reality is that the costs for doing this are prohibitive.

Nonetheless, an advertisement serves several functions. First, it catches the consumer's attention by using a catchy introduction or headline. Here is where effective headlines make a difference. Once the advertisement has the consumer's attention, the copy should make its message clear.

Which media should be chosen?

The major media markets include newspapers, television, radio, direct response, magazines and outdoor media which include billboards, buildings, buses, and other outside advertising space. The marketing manager seeks to have the best fit between the media and the target market. The basic objective is get the maximum impact for each advertising dollar. This is based on the effectiveness of the ad and the audience size provided by the media for the products and services. Impact can be given a numerical value to rate the specific exposures in a particular medium. Additionally, outcomes have to be continuously evaluated to determine if effectiveness is changing over time.

Other variables include the media's effectiveness in targeting specific geographic areas. The reach of the media is the number of consumers who are exposed to the advertising, while the frequency is the number of times the audience is exposed to the advertising message. The total number of exposures can be calculated as follows:

$$\text{Total Number of Exposures (E)} = \text{Reach (R)} \times \text{Frequency (F)}$$

The total number of exposures is known as the gross rating points (GRP) which is used as a measure for rating the media. This figure is usually calculated for an estimate of the percent of the target market that specific media actually reaches.

EXAMPLE 11.6

A marketing manager wants to know what the gross rating points will be for a television ad when its reach is 75% of the target market with an average frequency of 5.

GRP = 75 × 5
GRP = 375

What is the cost-per-thousand media index?

The cost-per-thousand index is a method of evaluating the cost effectiveness of the media based on its reach in thousands and the cost of an exposure. The formula for calculating the cost-per-thousand index is:

$$\text{Cost Per Thousand (CPM)} = \frac{\text{Exposure Cost} \times 1000}{\text{Reach}}$$

EXAMPLE 11.7

A marketing manager wants to compare the CPM for a 30-second advertisement of instant decaffeinated coffee in two different nonprime TV network shows serving the same target market.

Network Show A has 3,825,000 viewers who regularly drink decaffeinated coffee and charges $45,500 for the advertisement. Network Show B has 2,785,000 viewers who regularly drink decaffeinated coffee and charges $37,500 for the advertisement.

$$\text{Network Show A CPM} = \frac{\$45,500 \times 1000}{3,825,000} = \$11.90$$

$$\text{Network Show B CPM} = \frac{\$37.500 \times 1000}{2,785,000} = \$13.46$$

In this example, Network Show B charges a higher price per thousand viewers for the advertisement.

How is media timing decided?

Marketing managers have to decide between long-term and short-term media timing schedules. In long-term timing the marketer considers such factors as seasonally, competitive factors and product characteristics including repeat buying patterns. Short-term timing considers such factors as the availability of financial resources, the launching of a new product or service, and unique market situations requiring rapid response advertising.

How is advertising impact measured?

Because of its extremely expensive nature, it is essential to measure the impact of advertising to ascertain its effectiveness. Advertising effectiveness is measured using pre- and post-testing methodologies.

What is advertising pretesting?

Pretesting is an extremely cost-effective method to measure the ability of advertising to get its message to the target market group prior to actually launching a full campaign. Direct consumer group evaluations are a pretesting method where consumers rate various types of advertisements. Other types are evaluation scales that measure consumer responses including their ability to recall information from advertisements. Laboratory tests measure physiological responses such as pulse, blood pressure, respiration, etc., as a result of using different types of advertisements.

What is advertising post-testing?

Post-testing is normally used to measure the changes in brand familiarity and preference. Advertisers hope to have a substantial increase in brand awareness as the result of advertising, and post-testing attempts to measure the extent to which the advertiser has been successful. In post-testing the consumer's readership is tested to determine what advertisements were actually read, while recall tests are performed to determine what respondents recall about advertisements they read or saw.

12 _____
Business Law

Business executives need to be familiar with the legal concepts that impact their business operations and decisions. This chapter provides an overview of the areas that managers and owners are most likely to encounter in the business environment. The law as discussed in this chapter consists of basic principles which are generally uniform throughout the states; however, for specific provisions or variations within a particular state, you must consult an attorney.

12.1 CONTRACT LAW

12.1.1 The Importance of Contracts

Contracts are the basis for our commercial activities. A contract is essentially a promise that is enforceable at law, thereby ensuring that society can rely on the promises of others in the conduct of its business.

What constitutes a legally binding contract?

The following are the essential elements of a contract:

- Agreement
- Consideration
- Contractual capacity
- Legality of purpose
- Genuine assent
- Compliance with law as to form

How do we know if there is agreement?

An agreement is manifested by an offer followed by an acceptance which "mirrors" the terms of the offer (prior to revocation). If the acceptance varies any terms of the offer, the acceptance becomes a counter-offer which in turn must be accepted by the original offeror.

EXAMPLE 12.1

X offers to sell Y 400 units of product at $100/unit. To be an acceptance, Y must agree to pay $100/unit. If Y agrees to purchase 400 units at $99/unit, Y has made a counter-offer and there is no agreement unless X accepts Y's counter-offer, agreeing to sell at $99/unit.

Unilateral offers may be accepted by performing in accordance with the terms of the offer prior to its revocation.

What is consideration?

Consideration is the fair exchange of something of value to induce the other party to enter into a legally binding contract. Consideration must be bargained for; that is, it must be sought by the parties to the contract. To be legally sufficient to support an enforceable contract, consideration must be beneficial to the promisor (party making the promise) or detrimental to the promisee (party receiving the promise). If something is beneficial to one party, it is usually detrimental to the other.

EXAMPLE 12.2

X pays Y $400 for Y's promise to deliver goods. The payment of $400 is to X's detriment and to Y's benefit.

What form can consideration take?

Consideration can be:

- money, property or rights
- undertaking to do an act or performance of an act that a party was not previously obligated to undertake
- forbearance: refraining from doing something you are legally entitled to do, such as starting legal action to collect a debt
- creating a legal relationship that did not previously exist, modifying or terminating a legal relationship

Agreeing to comply with a pre-existing duty is not legally sufficient consideration because doing what one is already obligated to do creates no legal benefit received or detriment given.

What if one side thinks the consideration is not fair?

The law requires that the consideration be "adequate," or fair, in order to make a contract enforceable. Courts generally do not question the adequacy of consideration where there is no question of the capacity of the parties or unfair circumstances indicating that one of the parties was not free to bargain.

What if there are disputes as to consideration due?

Sometimes, a party agrees to pay—and the other party agrees to accept—something less than what one of them might have thought the proper consideration should be. This is especially so when the parties settle claims. The following are the most common forms of settling claims or resolving disputes:

- Accord and satisfaction: The parties make an agreement (the accord) where the amount necessary to satisfy an unliquidated debt, that is, one in which the amount due is disputed, is usually less than the amount claimed. There can be no accord and satisfaction if the claim is fixed (liquidated).
- Creditor's composition agreement: A debtor agrees to forego the right to file a bankruptcy petition in return for the agreement of two or more creditors to accept part payment.
- Release: A release is given and obtained in good faith, is in writing, and there is consideration; the releasor cannot recover more than the amount set forth in the release.

Are there any types of agreements that are enforceable without consideration?

The following types of contracts are enforceable even where no consideration is given:

- Promises to pay a debt that has been barred by the Statute of Limitations
- Promises to pay debts that have been legally discharged in bankruptcy
- Detrimental reliance or estoppel: Where one party has reasonably relied on the promise to his detriment, the promisor may not deny the contract

What is legal capacity?

Legal capacity is the ability in the eyes of the law for a party to enter into a binding contract. It is not the same as actual capacity.

Who has legal capacity?

The law generally assumes that the parties to a contract have the capacity to enter into a contract; this includes legal entities such as corporations, partnerships, estates, and trusts as well as individuals. However, certain individuals may have no legal capacity or limited legal capacity to enter into a binding contract. Many cases turn on the ability of the individual to understand the nature and subject matter of the contract and its consequences. This will determine whether the contract is void or voidable. The most common instances are cases of incompetent persons, intoxicated persons, and minors.

What is a void contract?

A void contract is one with no force and effect, and is not enforceable from the outset.

What is a voidable contract?

A voidable contract is one that is valid until voided, usually based upon the inability of one of the contracting parties to actually, or in the eyes of the law, understand the nature, substance, and consequences of a contract.

Generally, a party may be released from a voidable contract that has not been executed, if he is able to make restitution, by restoring or returning the money or goods. A voidable contract may also be ratified under certain circumstances, making the contract accepted and legally binding.

Who is considered incompetent and under what circumstances might a contract be binding on him?

Generally, an individual who is declared incompetent by a Court and for whom a guardian has been appointed is considered without legal capacity to enter into a contract, and the contract is null and void.

If an individual is actually incompetent, but there has been no Court declaration of incompetence, the contract is voidable once it is shown that the individual lacked the ability to comprehend the nature, subject matter, and consequences of the contract at the time he entered into it.

If a contract is voidable, the contract can be ratified, by the appointed guardian of the incompetent, or by the incompetent himself, once he is no longer adjudged incompetent.

Who is considered an intoxicated person and under what circumstances might a contract be binding on him?

A contract entered into by an intoxicated person is generally voidable. The courts generally try to use objective criteria to determine whether the party was intoxicated instead of delving into the subjective question of the ability to comprehend.

What is the law relating to contracts entered into by minors?

Contracts entered into by minors, persons who have not reached legal maturity, are voidable, and can be disaffirmed any time during the party's minority or within a reasonable time after reaching adulthood, provided that the minor can make restitution. However, in the case of "necessaries" (food, clothing), even though the minor may disaffirm the contract, he is obligated to pay the value of the goods received. If parents or a guardian are responsible for providing for the minor, there are states in which the parent or guardian may be liable. This is to encourage parties not to turn away a person who is in need because of the ability to disaffirm the agreement if he is a minor.

What is meant by legality of purpose?

The subject matter or transaction contracted for must not violate any laws (such as the purchase and sale of contraband) or public policy (such as an agreement not to sell based on race, color, or creed).

EXAMPLE 12.3

A contract for the purchase and sale of contraband is void and not enforceable.

What factors establish genuineness of assent?

Genuine assent exists where there has been a true "meeting of the minds." The decision to enter into the agreement cannot be based on mistakes, misrepresentation, undue influence, or duress.

What types of mistakes evidence the lack of genuine assent?

Generally a unilateral mistake as to a material fact will not release the mistaken party from the contract. However, if there is a mutual mistake of fact, then the contract may be rescinded.

Where there is a mistake as to value, there is no ground to rescind the contract. The parties are each deemed to assume the risk that the value will change. This, however, must be distinguished from a mistake in fact that affects the value.

EXAMPLE 12.4

X agrees to sell and Y agrees to pay one million dollars for a painting they both believe to be an authentic Picasso. If the painting is a counterfeit, then the issue is not one of value; it is one of material fact.

When will a misrepresentation result in lack of genuine assent?

Fraudulent misrepresentation, in which there is an intentional misrepresentation of material fact by one party, will allow the innocent party to rescind. If the innocent party has reasonably relied on the misrepresentation and has been injured, he may also elect to enforce the contract and sue for damages.

Can silence constitute misrepresentation?

Generally, silence is not misrepresentation because there is no legal duty to disclose unless there is a fiduciary relationship.

What if the misrepresentation is innocent or made negligently?

The majority of jurisdictions permit rescission of a contract where there is a misrepresentation of a material fact made innocently or negligently (failure to exercise reasonable care).

What is the difference between undue influence and duress?

Undue influence generally involves a fiduciary relationship in which there is trust placed in the other party to the extent that his own free will can be overcome (such as a client executing a contract on his attorney's advice which is not beneficial). Where a contract is entered into because of undue influence, the contract is voidable.

Duress requires coercion based upon threatening of the innocent party with a wrongful or illegal act such as blackmail or physical harm. Threatening to exercise a legal right to sue does not constitute duress because the act threatened is not wrongful. A contract entered into under legal duress is void.

12.1.2 Establishing the Contract

How is a contract formed?

An express contract exists if the terms are set forth either orally or in writing. The Statute of Frauds requires some types of contracts to be in writing in order to be enforceable. A contract can also be implied by the conduct of the parties.

What types of contracts must be in writing?

- Contracts creating or transferring an interest in land including property affixed to the land, e.g., contracts to sell land, or to mortgage
- Contracts which by their terms cannot be performed within one year, such as a contract calling for a two-year shipping contract
- Contracts involving the sale of goods in excess of $500
- Promises to pay the debt of another
- Promises in consideration of marriage

Are there exceptions to the Statute of Frauds?

Yes, even though the subject matter of a contract may fall within the Statute of Frauds, it may still be enforceable, although not in writing in the following situations:

- Goods made specifically to the buyer's order that cannot be easily resold
- Admissions in court that a contract was made
- Where performance is complete; problems arise where there is partial performance

12.1.3 Violation of a Contract

What remedies are available if there is a breach of contract?

A breach of contract occurs when a party fails to perform in accordance with the contract. The nonbreaching party is entitled to damages.

- *Compensatory damages.* Compensation for the amount the nonbreaching party would have made if there was no breach, e.g., the contract price
- *Consequential damages.* Reasonably foreseeable damages which flow directly from the breach (e.g., lost profits from resale of goods)
- *Punitive damages.* Rarely awarded in a breach of contract action; meant as a penalty or deterrent to wrongdoing
- *Nominal damages.* Where there is no significant loss or damage; may be awarded simply to indicate that the breaching party was wrong

- *Specific performance.* A breaching party may be required to specifically perform pursuant to the terms of the contract where money damages would not adequately compensate or substitute (e.g., a contract to sell a Picasso painting)

12.2 SECURED TRANSACTIONS

The area of secured transactions is important because it provides the means by which credit can be extended to businesses by securing the party extending credit of payment. Secured transactions are governed primarily by Article 9 of the Uniform Commercial Code.

12.2.1 Security Interest

What is a security interest?

Under the UCC, it is an interest "in personal property or fixtures which secure payment or performance of an obligation." The property which secures the interest is the collateral (tangible—physical property and non-tangible–non-physical property, i.e., trademarks, copyrights).

How is a security interest created?

- By taking possession of the collateral or an agreement in writing
- The creditor must give something of value to the debtor
- The debtor has to have rights in the collateral

How can a creditor protect against claims of other creditors to the same property?

Generally, a secured creditor takes priority over unsecured creditors and judgment creditors who have not begun to execute on the judgment. To establish priority, a creditor must "perfect" his security interest. The methods of perfection are:

- Filing of a financing statement signed by the debtor, stating the debtor and creditor's names and addresses and describing the collateral, with the secretary of state, a local official (e.g., county clerk) or both, depending on the type of collateral
- A "pledge" whereby the secured creditor takes possession of the collateral
- Automatic perfection that attaches when the secured

interest is created—i.e., purchase money security interest where the creditor provided funds to the debtor to secure the collateral (mortgage) or retains or takes an interest in the collateral to secure the purchase price; assignment of accounts receivable to a collection agent under certain circumstances

What are the secured creditor's rights if the debtor defaults?

A creditor may repossess the collateral if he can do so without a "breach of the peace" (e.g., towing a vehicle without confrontation); otherwise, he must seek a court order. The creditor may retain the collateral in full satisfaction of the debt (upon notice to the debtor) or dispose of it in a reasonable commercial manner (provided notice of time, place and manner of sale is given). The debtor is entitled to notice except where the goods are fungible.

Where consumer goods are the collateral for a purchase money security interest, and the debtor has paid 60% of the cash price or loan, the creditor must dispose of the collateral within 90 days.

What rights, if any, does the debtor have?

The proceeds from the disposition is first applied to expenses incurred in the disposition, then to the balance of the debt. If there is still a surplus, subordinate secured parties who have served written notice before all proceeds are distributed will be paid, and any further surplus will be given to the debtor. If the proceeds are insufficient to pay the costs of disposition and balance due, the creditor may enter and collect a deficiency judgment.

At any time prior to the creditor disposing of the collateral or declaring the debt satisfied by his retention of the collateral, the debtor may "redeem" the collateral by paying the balance due and the reasonable costs of repossession.

12.3 BANKRUPTCY

12.3.1 The Mechanics of Bankruptcy

What is bankruptcy and how does it work?

Bankruptcy is a procedure under federal and state law allowing an honest debtor to "discharge" (to be relieved) of certain debts so that a fresh start can be made. The federal bankruptcy law preempts (takes priority over) state bankruptcy laws. Upon filing the bankruptcy petition in the

United States Bankruptcy Court, an automatic stay is imposed prohibiting the continuation of collection activities by creditors. The stay preserves the status quo until a court-appointed trustee can begin a procedure supervised by the court, or the debtor can devise a plan that attempts to pay as much as possible to the creditors. The rights of creditors often depend on whether they are secured or unsecured.

What debts can be discharged?

The bankruptcy law provides for the release of the debtor from most unpaid portions of debt balances. Some items such as alimony, child support and the taxes that are held by the debtor as a "trustee" (i.e., sales taxes and employment withholding taxes which the debtor has failed to pay to the relevant government entities) may not be discharged.

Among the debts that cannot be discharged are those that may involve fraud or wrongful conduct on the part of the debtor. The law will not allow the debtor to use the law for protection against claims arising from this conduct. Among them are:

- Claims out of money or property obtained by false pretenses
- Claims based on willful or malicious conduct against another
- Claims based on embezzlement, larceny, misappropriation or breach of a fiduciary duty

The debtor must be careful to list all creditors so that they will be notified. A creditor who is not listed on the schedules and receives no notice of the bankruptcy will not have his debt discharged.

How are the creditors paid?

This depends on the specific section of the bankruptcy law under which the debtor seeks protection.

What are the various provisions for protection under the bankruptcy law?

The provisions available to individuals and businesses under the bankruptcy law are:

- *Chapter 7:* Sometimes known as a "liquidation plan." The bankruptcy trustee under this section marshals and liquidates all of the nonexempt assets and pays off the debts. Certain property of the debtor is exempt from liquidation so that the debtor will not be destitute after liquidation.
- *Chapter 11:* Known also as a "reorganization" or

"debtor-in-possession plan." This section is available to a viable business provided that it is given enough breathing room to devise a plan for the payment of the business's debt. This may include renegotiating installments, interest rates, and sale of some assets. The debtor stays in possession of the business and continues its operations; the debts accrued prior to the filing of the bankruptcy petition is generally stayed. Post bankruptcy petition debts must generally be paid as accrued. If the debtor cannot come up with a plan to pay off the pre-petition debt in a manner acceptable to the creditors, and provide for the likelihood that the business will survive, the Court may order that the business be liquidated.

- *Chapter 13:* This section is available for individuals who have a regular source of income, including sole proprietors whose unsecured debts are less than $100,000 and secured debts do not exceed $350,000. The Court will allow the debtor to devise a plan for the full or partial payment of creditors over a three- to five-year period. The plan will normally be approved by the Court if the creditors will get at least what they would if the debtor had filed Chapter 7.

What typically happens in a Chapter 7 bankruptcy?

The first step is usually the filing of a petition by the debtor. The filing triggers the automatic stay against collections by creditors of pre-petition debts. The debtor normally files a list of its creditors and amounts owed, along with a schedule of the debtor's assets. However, the debtor has up to 10 days after the filing of the petition to submit these schedules, along with income and expense information.

The clerk of the Court will mail out notices of the bankruptcy filing to the creditors and the debtor, along with the notice of a Section 341 meeting of creditors. The debtor will generally contact and notify the creditors prior to the Court. Once on notice, a creditor may be held in contempt of Court if it makes an attempt to collect its debt.

An interim trustee is appointed until the Section 341 meeting, when the interim trustee will be confirmed or a new one voted on by the creditors. The debtor must be present at this meeting to answer (under oath) any questions from the creditors and the trustee about assets or recent transfers of assets, and material contained in the petition or schedules.

The creditors have 180 days after the first Section 341 meeting to file their "proof of claim" which states the amount of debt owed by the debtor. Failure to file a proof of claim may result in a waiver of any right to share in the proceeds from the liquidation of the debtor's assets.

How does the treatment of a secured creditor differ from that of an unsecured creditor?

A secured creditor will normally be permitted to apply to the Court for a "lift" of the automatic stay so that it can proceed to liquidate the security (collateral) by, for example, foreclosing on the property securing a mortgage. Any deficiency not covered by the liquidation of the collateral is treated as unsecured debt. Unsecured creditors must generally wait to share in a portion of the proceeds from the liquidation of the debtor's assets.

What if the debtor has transferred assets prior to the filing of his bankruptcy petition?

The bankruptcy laws seek to ensure that creditors are treated equally, and will not allow a debtor to favor a specific creditor. The trustee is vested with the power to void certain transfers. Among them are:

- Preferential transfers made within 90 days of the filing that are in excess of $600

- Preferential liens obtained within 90 days prior to filing based on a pre-petition debt. A lien by an insider (party related to the debtor) within one year can be voided by the trustee

- Fraudulent transfers made within a year prior to the filing of the petition where it can be shown that the transfer was to hinder, delay, hide assets or to defraud creditors, where the transfer was made without adequate consideration, or left the debtor with little or no assets to pay creditors

The creditors and trustee will normally consult on the assets of the debtor. The creditors will assist the trustee by informing him of any known assets of the debtor, and may even go as far as taking action to uncover the assets.

What is the procedure in a Chapter 11 bankruptcy?

After a petition is filed, the Court will appoint one or more committees of unsecured creditors to examine records and financial structure, and to assist the debtor in formulating a plan. The committee is authorized to engage accountants, attorneys and other professionals. A trustee may also be appointed if there are assets to be sold, allegations of gross mismanagement in the operation, or if the court deems it in the best interest of the debtor's estate.

Within 120 days after the court enters an order granting relief, the debtor must submit a plan. The plan will contain the following:

- The classes of claims and interests of the creditors
- How each class is to be treated
- Provisions for the execution of the plan

If the debtor fails to file the plan or get creditor approval within 180 days after the court's order of relief, the creditors may submit a plan.

The plan is submitted *to* each class of creditors and requires the approval of two-thirds of the total claim of each class. The approval of the plan by a class is not necessary where the Court deems the plan not adverse to that class's interests. In fact if one class approves, the Court may "cram-down" the plan and confirm it. Once a plan is confirmed by the Court, all creditors are bound.

How does a Chapter 13 bankruptcy work?

After the debtor files his petition, a trustee is appointed. The automatic stay, however, applies only to consumer debt and not to business debt (of a sole proprietor).

The debtor submits a plan in which he will pay all or part of the debt over not more than three years. The Court in its discretion may extend the period to up to five years. The essential elements of the plan are:

- Statement of the amount of the debtor's future income to be turned over to the trustee at regular intervals
- Provide for the full payment of priority claims in installments
- Provide that all members of each class of creditors be treated the same

The Court will confirm the plan if the secured creditors accept it, creditors' liens are retained, and if the amount creditors receive under the plan at least equals the secured portion of their claim or the debtor surrenders the collateral to the secured creditors.

Prior to the full execution of the plan, the Court may allow it to be modified at the request of the trustee, debtor or creditor.

What happens at the end of these procedures?

When the debtor is discharged in bankruptcy, all pre-petition judgments are voided and all rights to collect those debts are enjoined. In Chapter 7, a debtor may be discharged before all of the distributions are made to the creditors from the liquidated assets. In Chapters 11 and 13, the discharge takes place when the plans are executed.

Can creditors force a debtor into bankruptcy?

Yes. The filing of a petition may be voluntary (by the debtor) or involuntary. Creditors will normally file an involuntary petition to force the debtor into bankruptcy in order to have its assets distributed.

What are the requirements for filing an involuntary petition?

If the debtor has 12 or more creditors, at least 3 having unsecured debt totalling $5,000 must join the petition. In the event that there are less than 12 creditors, then one creditor with a debt of $5,000 may file.

The Court will generally allow the involuntary petition to go forward over the debtor's objection if:

- The debtor is not paying debts when due
- 120 days prior to the filing, a receiver, assignee or a custodian has taken control of substantially all of the debtor's assets

How often can a debtor file for bankruptcy?

In Chapter 7, a debtor may be discharged only once every six years.

12.4 CONSUMER LAWS

There is a great deal of government regulation regarding the protection of consumers who can generally be described as individuals acquiring goods, services, credit or land for personal or family use. There are a number of federal statutes dealing with each of these areas as well as health and safety issues.

12.4.1 Consumer Relationships

What are some of the major laws concerning the purchase and sale of goods to consumers?

There are several major laws concerning advertising, labeling and packaging, sales tactics in general, and sales of specific items such as real estate.

What controls are there on advertising?

The Federal Trade Commission Act prohibits unfair and deceptive advertising that may mislead or deceive a consumer when it goes beyond mere "puffing" (obvious exaggerations or generalizations) about a product.

The law prohibits the practice of "bait and switch" in which a less expensive item is advertised but is not made available to the consumer who is then encouraged to buy another more expensive substitute. This unlawful tactic may be evidenced by the refusal of the seller to make the advertised item available, understocking the item, encouraging employees to sell the more expensive item, or inability to deliver the goods advertised within a reasonable time.

In cases of established deceptive advertising, the Federal Trade Commission may issue a cease and desist order, or require affirmative steps on the part of the advertiser to use accurate advertising, advertise admitting the prior misleading ads, or seek penalties.

What labeling and packaging regulations govern consumer goods?

There are a number of labeling and packaging requirements to inform consumers about contents and safety concerns. The Fair Packaging and Labeling Act requires that labels state specifically the product, quantity, number of servings, and the names of the manufacturer and distributor. This law also gives the agency the right to impose further requirements with respect to claims made by a company, as to nutritional content, packing standards, and the like.

What provisions govern sales tactics to consumers?

Most of the regulations governing sales are supervised by the FTC. In the case of door-to-door sales where the selling entity is not located in the community and there is a greater likelihood of pressure tactics, the law gives consumers the right to rescind their decision to purchase for up to three days ("cooling off period"), and longer if the state law provides for a longer period to reconsider. The seller is required to inform the consumer of this right.

With respect to mail order or telephone sales, the regulation is primarily through the laws against mail and wire fraud.

What laws apply to the sale of land?

There are two major laws governing the sale of land. The Interstate Land Sales Full Disclosure Act requires that sellers or lessors of 100 or more lots of vacant land as part of a common promotion, file a "statement of record" and obtain approval of the Department of Housing and Urban Development before beginning sales or leases. This also applies where land is sold interstate, and imposes civil and criminal penalties for fraud or other violations of the statute. Under the law, the consumer has a right of rescission similar to the "cooling off period."

The other major statute is the Real Estate Settlement Procedures Act (RESPA). This law informs the consumer of the costs of settlement for the purchase of real estate when a lender is involved. Within three days of the application for a loan, the lender must send a copy of a HUD booklet that explains the settlement procedures and the costs involved (e.g., appraisal fees, title insurance, lender's charges, and attorneys' fees). The lender must within those three days provide an estimate of the costs, clearly identify the parties the lender will require the borrower to use, and provide a truth-in-lending statement when the loan is approved.

RESPA expressly prohibits the taking of kickbacks for referrals by the lender, or others in the transaction.

What consumer credit protections are available?

Consumer credit is an area in which the consumer is especially vulnerable to unfair practices. Therefore, the law requires certain disclosures and heavily regulates collection practices both on the federal and state levels.

The Truth-in-Lending Act (TILA) requires disclosure of credit or loan terms by sellers and lenders who arrange or extend credit in the ordinary course of their businesses. Individuals are covered under this act, but corporations are not.

The Fair Credit Billing Act is part of TILA which allows a consumer to refuse payment of a credit card charge where the purchased product is defective, providing that the consumer has tried to resolve the matter with the seller in good faith. The debtor also may challenge an error in billing by the credit card company. The company is required to resolve the matter within 90 days of the complaint without additional finance charges or cancellation of the account.

TILA provides that a consumer is responsible only to extent of $50 for unauthorized credit card purchases on a lost or stolen card prior to notification of the theft or loss.

The Equal Credit Opportunity Act prohibits the denial of credit because of a person's race, religion, color, sex, marital status or age.

Under the Fair Credit Reporting Act, consumers are given the right to correct any information on their credit reports. The law requires that the consumer be notified when a party extending credit will obtain credit reports and they must be given the opportunity to correct any information that might affect their ability to get credit, insurance or employment.

With respect to collection practices, the Fair Debt Collection Practices Act prohibits a collection agency from:

- Contacting the debtor at his place of employment where the employer objects

- Calling the debtor at inconvenient times
- Contacting the debtor directly where he is represented by an attorney
- Contacting third parties about the debt without court authorization (except spouse, parents or financial counsellor)
- Harassing or intimidating the debtor
- Continuing to communicate with the debtor once the debtor has stated his refusal to pay the debt (except to notify debtor of further action being taken)

There are specific provisions regarding the collection of a debt by garnishing wages (based on state law) in which the creditor seizes or attaches part of the debtor's wages. State law dictates the percentage of the wages which may be garnished (usually not more than 25% of after-tax wages) and provides for notice and an opportunity for the debtor to object.

12.5 SALES

Contracts involving the sale of goods is governed by Article 2 of the Uniform Commercial Code (U.C.C.), although common law contracts apply. The rights of the parties in a sale under the U.C.C. is determined by whether either or both are merchants.

12.5.1 Selling Goods or Services

What is a sale?

The U.C.C. defines a sale as "the passing of title from the seller to the buyer for a price." The price may be paid in the form of money, other goods, services or real estate.

What are goods?

Goods are tangible and movable property (e.g., clothing, furniture, appliances). They do not include intangible property (e.g., stocks, bonds, copyrights, trademarks) nor real estate and fixtures.

Who qualifies as a merchant?

Per the U.C.C. a merchant is:

- A person who deals in goods of the kind involved in the contract (e.g., retailer, wholesaler or manufacturer), or
- A person who by occupation holds himself out as hav-

ing skill or knowledge peculiar to the practices or goods involved, or

- A person who employs a merchant, broker, agent or other intermediary who holds himself out as having the skill or knowledge peculiar to the goods.

When does title pass from the seller to the buyer?

Goods must exist and be identified as those covered by the contract before title can pass to the buyer. When title actually passes is determined either by the agreement of the parties or if not specified, then at the time and place that the seller makes delivery.

How do rules under the U.C.C. differ from common law?

There are numerous differences between the rules as set forth under the U.C.C. and common law. Among them are the areas of offer and acceptance, consideration, and the Statute of Frauds. This section will cover only some of the salient points. The reader is referred to U.C.C. Art. 2 for more thorough coverage.

How are offers dealt with under the U.C.C.?

The terms of an offer under common law must be definite and certain at the time of its acceptance. Under the U.C.C., an offer may be accepted and bind the offeror even where certain terms are left out, as long as a court can establish that the parties intended to enter into a contract and that there is a reasonably certain basis for filling in the missing terms. The following are common situations:

- Failure to state a price: The court may set a reasonable price at the time of delivery unless the failure to set the price is the fault of either party in which case the contract may be rescinded or the parties may set the price.
- Failure to state shipping arrangements: The shipper must exercise good faith and use a commercially reasonable manner of shipment.
- Failure to state quantity: A court will generally have no basis to grant relief, and the contract will generally not be viable.

How is an acceptance dealt with under the U.C.C.?

Unlike common law where an acceptance must be by the means specified, or if by an unauthorized method, must be received before the expiration of the offer, the U.C.C. permits any form of acceptance which is "reasonable under the circumstances" if no method of acceptance is specified.

Under common law, delivery of conforming goods to a carrier constitutes acceptance. Under the U.C.C., acceptance is effective if there is prompt shipment of the goods or a promise to ship (sent in a commercially reasonable manner).

Under common law, a unilateral offer may be accepted by performance without notification to the offeror of the acceptance. The U.C.C. provides that if notice of acceptance is not given within a reasonable time, the offeror may treat the offer as expired.

An acceptance must "mirror" the terms of the offer under common law, otherwise it is a counteroffer. The U.C.C. states that if there are different or additional terms in the acceptance, the acceptance is binding unless the acceptance is conditional on the offeror agreeing to the different or additional terms. However, whether the additional or different terms become part of the contract will depend on whether the parties are merchants. If one of the parties is not a merchant, the terms are merely proposals. If both parties are merchants, the terms are included if:

- They do not materially alter the terms (e.g., present hardships), or
- The offer had stated that no terms except those stated in the offer are acceptable, or
- The additional or different terms are objected to within a reasonable time.

How does the U.C.C. differ from common law on consideration?

No consideration is required under the U.C.C. for modification of a contract sought in good faith. However, the parties may provide that no modification may be permitted under the contract unless it is made in writing.

What does the U.C.C. say about the Statute of Frauds?

Sales of goods priced at $500 or more must be in writing to be enforceable, and must be signed by the party against whom enforcement is sought. A written confirmation between merchants is sufficient to enforce a contract against the merchant receiving the confirmation if it contains the terms, he fails to object within 10 days of receipt, and he knew or had reason to know of the contents of the confirmation.

Other exceptions to the Statute of Frauds are included in the section on Contract Law.

What other areas are covered under Article 2 of the U.C.C.?

Article 2 also deals with the issues of: risk of loss, when an interest is created so that a party has an insurable interest in goods, the obligations of the seller and buyer with respect to delivery and payment, remedies in case of breach of contract and warranties related to the goods. The subject matter is too voluminous to cover here, so the reader is referred to Article 2 for more thorough coverage. The following are a few additional concepts which may be helpful to the reader.

What are the rules on risk of loss where there is no specific contract provision?

Risk of loss does not always pass with the title to the goods, but may vary depending on manner of shipment or delivery.

- Free on Board (F.O.B.): The goods are delivered at the seller's expense to a specific location. Once the goods are put into the hands of the carrier or party at the designated location, risk of loss passes to the buyer.
- Free Along Side (F.A.S.): The goods are transported by the seller at his expense and risk until the goods are delivered along side the ship which will carry the goods, at which time the risk of loss passes to the buyer.
- Cost, Insurance & Freight (C.I.F. or C. & F. for Cost and Freight): The risk of loss passes to the buyer once the goods are "put in possession of a carrier."
- Delivery Ex-Ship: Risk of loss passes when the goods leave the carrier or are properly unloaded.

What warranties are made about goods under Article 2?

Under the U.C.C., there are several types of warranties made regarding goods sold; they include warranties of title, express warranties, and implied warranties.

What are the warranties of title?

- Warranty of good title: The seller represents that he has good title to the goods and can rightfully transfer the goods.
- Warranty of no liens: The seller represents that there are no encumbrances (e.g., claims, security interests) at the time of delivery that have not been disclosed to the buyer.
- Warranty of no infringements: This applies to a mer-

chant who represents that the goods sold do not infringe upon any copyrights, trademarks, or patents of third parties. No warranty is made if the goods are manufactured according to specifications provided by the buyer.

A breach of these warranties will result in liability against the seller.

What are express warranties made under Article 2?

Representations about quality, condition, description or performance of goods are express warranties. These warranties are made by specific statements of facts, providing a sample or model, or on the basis of labeling information.

What are implied warranties made under Article 2?

Representations that the goods are "reasonably fit for the ordinary purposes for which such goods are used" are implied warranties. The goods must be of average, fair or medium grade, without objection within the trade or market for said types of goods, be properly and adequately labeled, conform to the representations made on the label or container, and represent an even quality and quantity among all such units.

12.6 NEGOTIABLE INSTRUMENTS

Negotiable instruments are part of commercial paper that allow transactions to be facilitated conveniently by acting as cash substitutes or credit instruments.

Commercial paper can be negotiable (governed by Article 3 of the U.C.C.) or nonnegotiable (governed by contract law on assignments). This section covers negotiable instruments.

12.6.1 Issues Surrounding Negotiable Instruments

What is a negotiable instrument?

A negotiable instrument is commercial paper that can be assigned or negotiated. It is defined as an instrument that is:

- Signed by the maker or drawer
- Contains an unconditional promise or order to pay, a sum certain in money, and no other promise
- Payable on demand or at a time certain
- Payable to order or bearer

Who are the maker and the drawer?

A maker issues a promissory note or a certificate of deposit promising to pay a sum certain to a specific payee or to the bearer of the instrument. To be liable, the maker's signature must appear on the face of the instrument.

The drawer is the one who issues a draft or check, and who writes and signs the instrument.

What does "payable to order" mean?

The instrument specifies a payee (party to receive payment), or as the payee directs (by endorsing and delivering the instrument to another).

Who is a bearer?

A bearer is one in possession of an instrument that does not have a specific payee or one that has been endorsed by a specific payee "in blank" (payee's signature only).

What are the most common negotiable instruments?

The most common instruments are:

- Draft: An order by one person (drawer) to another (drawee) to pay money to a third party (payee) or to the bearer
- Check: A special type of draft drawn on a bank and payable on demand
- Promissory note: A promise by one person (maker) to pay money to another (payee) or to the bearer
- Certificate of deposit: A note made by a bank acknowledging that funds were deposited and made payable to the holder of the note

What is negotiation?

Negotiation is the process in which an instrument is transferred to another (transferee) in such a way that the transferee becomes a "holder."

Order paper on which there is a named payee can be transferred by the payee through endorsement (writing "pay to the order of X" and signing it). Bearer paper on which the payee is "bearer" or which was endorsed by a specific payee without an "order" can be negotiated by delivering the instrument to another party.

What is the significance of being a holder?

Whether a party is a holder and how he became a holder determines his right to collect the payments represented by the instrument even though there may be certain defenses which would defeat the collection efforts of an ordinary "holder." There is a specific category of "holder" who is given special protection by the U.C.C., known as the "holder in due course" (HDC). An HDC is one who acquires an instrument for value (consideration), in good faith and without notice that the instrument is defective or overdue, or that a person may have a claim or defense against the collection under that instrument.

For the specific defenses good against an HDC, see Article 3 of the U.C.C.

12.7 AGENCY LAW

In the operation of a business, one is not able to do all tasks and must have the ability to delegate. The law of agency allows a principal (one who authorizes another) to appoint an agent to act on his behalf. A third party may deal with the agent as if he is dealing with the principal himself and hold the principal liable.

Whether a party is liable for the acts of another often turns on whether the party acting is an agent or an independent contractor.

12.7.1 How Agencies Work

How is an agency created?

An agency is created when a principal authorizes another, called the agent, to act on his behalf, and the agent consents to do so.

What is the extent of the agent's authority?

The scope of the agent's authority is based on express authority (oral or written) given by the principal, or implied in law (e.g., based on the position of the agent, those acts reasonably necessary to carry out the principal's instructions).

The Equal Dignity Rule requires that where the underlying subject matter of the agency is required to be in writing to be enforceable under the Statute of Frauds (e.g., authorizing an agent to transfer an interest in land), the agency agreement must also be in writing.

What are the duties of the agent?

The duties of an agent are to:

• Perform the authorized duties in a reasonable and diligent manner based on the skills and the knowledge he possesses (i.e., the agent can be liable for negligence).

- Notify the principal of all material developments. Since the principal will be bound by the agent's acts, he must be informed as to the points on which he may be liable.

- Act with loyalty by acting solely for the principal's benefit, and not in his own or another party's interest.

- Follow instructions which are lawful and clearly stated.

- Account to the principal for all money or property received or paid on behalf of the principal in carrying out his duties as agent. A constructive trust may be imposed on an agent who retains or takes benefits which belong to the principal.

What are the duties of the principal to the agent?

The principal owes certain duties to the agent provided the agent acts within the scope of the authority granted. The principal may not be obligated to fulfill these duties if the agent has violated one of the duties owed to the principal (breach of contract). Among the duties owed by the principal to the agent are to:

- Cooperate so as to allow the agent to carry out his duties.

- Compensate the agent for work done when the parties have agreed upon compensation.

- Reimburse the agent for authorized expenses or reasonable expenses necessary to carry out his duties as agent.

- Indemnify the agent against claims that arise out of his carrying out his duties as agent.

- Provide a safe work place or to warn the agent of possible dangers.

Distinguishing between an independent contractor and an agent

An independent contractor is one who is asked to perform a task for the "employer," but over whom the employer has no control as to how the contractor physically performs the task (for example, a plumber who is asked to repair a pipe). Among the parameters used to determine whether a party is an independent contractor are:

- The employer does not exercise control over work details.

- The contractor has an occupation, skills, a business operation separate from the employer's.

- The work is not supervised by the employer or is executed based upon the skills and knowledge of the contractor.

- The contractor supplies the tools, facilities or means of accomplishing the work.
- The period of hire is short term or based on the completion of a particular project.
- Method of payment is based on completion.
- The contractor has special skills (is a specialist). The greater the number of parameters, the more likely that the party will be deemed an independent contractor.

What is the significance of being an agent or an independent contractor?

An independent contractor is responsible for his own acts, and the employer will not be held liable in the event of negligence or intentional wrongdoing on the part of the independent contractor. The employer (principal), however, may be liable for the acts of its agents (including that of an employee) within the scope of his employment.

12.8 PROPERTY LAW

Property law deals with the legally protected rights and interests in anything that has an ascertainable value. Property is classified as personal property or real property.

12.8.1 How Property Is Treated

What is personal property?

Personal property is either tangible or intangible. Tangible property has physical substance, such as furniture, equipment, and vehicles. Intangible property has no physical substance but represents rights and interest in property (e.g., stock certificates represent the percentage interest of a shareholder in a corporation and all of the rights flowing from ownership).

How is ownership of personal property acquired?

Ownership in personal property is acquired by:

- Possession: Taking possession of something that is not owned by anyone (e.g., capture of a wild animal not in violation of any laws).
- Purchase: Transfer of title from a seller to a buyer for a price (consideration).

- Production: Made through the labor of a party (e.g., painting or writing or manufacture of furniture from raw materials).
- Gift: Voluntary transfer of title to property by a donor (giver) exhibiting delivery, donative intent, and acceptance by the donee (recipient).
- Will or inheritance: Title to property transferred at the death of another by will or under state law governing estates of decedents.

Can title be acquired in personal property that has not been transferred?

Title can be acquired in some instances where the property is found as set forth below:

- Abandoned property: The owner has intentionally discarded the property (e.g., throwing a chair away). The finder who takes possession with an intent to claim ownership becomes the owner (rights are superior to the original owner).
- Lost property: The owner did not intentionally part with the property (e.g., unbeknownst to the owner, a book falls out of his bag). The true owner can reclaim the property from the finder. If the finder knows the true owner's identity, he must return the property.
- Mislaid property: The true owner intentionally places property in a place and without intent to relinquish title, leaves it. The finder has no rights in the property and is deemed to hold the property for the true owner.

Can there be a transfer of possession without transfer of title?

Transfer of possession of personal property without transfer of title is known as bailment.

Bailments are common in the business world and include such activities as leaving a car at a repair shop or a parking garage, or leaving clothes at the cleaners. A bailment is created when:

- The bailor owns or has possessory right to property (e.g., is the owner of a car).
- The bailor delivers possession of the property to the bailee (e.g., brings his car to the mechanic for repair).
- The bailee accepts the property knowing that he has a duty to return the property at the bailor's direction (e.g., the mechanic must return the car to the owner when the repairs are complete and the bill paid).

What if the property is damaged while in the bailee's possession?

The rights and liabilities of a bailee are determined by the nature of the bailment created:

- Bailment for the sole benefit of the bailor: The bailee receives no benefit (e.g., the bailor is permitted to store goods without charge). The bailee is liable only if he is grossly negligent and has a duty to return the goods at the bailor's direction.

- Bailment for the sole benefit of the bailee: The bailor receives no benefit (e.g., the bailor lends the bailee his book so the bailee can study). The bailee must exercise great care, and must compensate the bailor if the property is lost or damaged.

- Bailment for mutual benefit: Both the bailor and bailee receive benefits (e.g., the bailor's clothing is cleaned and the cleaner is paid for the task). The bailee must exercise reasonable care of the property and return the property as directed. The bailor has a duty to disclose known defects that cannot be easily discovered on inspection).

What is real property?

Real property is land or anything permanently attached to it (called fixtures), which includes crops and minerals. Once the crops are harvested or the minerals are mined, they become personal property. Personal property that becomes affixed to the land becomes a fixture (for example, an unattached sink is personal property, but once it is affixed to the structure on the land, it becomes real property).

What rights does a party have in real property?

Rights in real property can generally be described as possessory and non-possessory. Below is a list of some types of rights in real estate, beginning with the most complete.

- Fee simple absolute: The most comprehensive form of ownership in which the owner may use or transfer all, or part of his rights to the property. Upon the owner's death, the property will pass to his successors by will or by the inheritance laws of the state.

- Fee simple defeasible: Ownership is conditioned upon a state of facts and can be terminated if the facts change (for instance, X continues to own the property "so long as it is used for charity").

- Life estate: The party has ownership of the property for his life. Upon death, the property reverts (returns) to the original owner or passes to another if so directed by the owner.

- Easement: A non-possessory right in which a party has the right to use real property for a specific purpose (for example, the right to drive through part of a neighbor's property in a common driveway).
- Profit: Non-possessory right to enter upon the land of another to remove products of the land (for example, the right to harvest timber).
- License: Non-possessory right to enter another property for a specific purpose that can be revoked (as in the right to enter a theater for a show).
- Leasehold estates: The conveyance by the owner of property (landlord) to another (tenant) of a right to use and possess property for a specified period of time (lease/tenancy). The tenancy may be:
  - "For years": for the time expressly stated in the lease contract
  - Periodic: for a period based on the frequency of rent payments (rent paid on a monthly basis creates a month-to-month tenancy)
  - At will: for as long as both parties agree
  - At sufferance: continued possession of property without the landlord's consent

How are rights in real property acquired?

Except for leasehold estates, all of the rights listed above are generally acquired by deed. The rights under a leasehold estate are acquired by lease (that is, by a contract that may be written or oral, express or implied. See section on Contracts for Statute of Frauds).

Sometimes rights in real property may be acquired without delivery of a deed when a party openly and notoriously occupies or uses land for a period specified by law, without challenge by the real owner (called adverse possession).

What is a deed?

A deed is a document used to transfer possession and title to land. The deed must contain the following:

- Names of the grantor (transferor) and the grantee (transferee)
- Words evidencing intent to transfer
- Legally sufficient description of the land
- The signature of the grantor that has been witnessed and acknowledged before a notary or commissioner of deeds

The deed must be delivered to the grantee. For his protection, the grantee should make sure the deed is recorded.

12.9 INSURANCE

Insurance is a risk-management tool in which an insurance company (insurer) agrees to compensate another (the insured) for a loss or injury. Sometimes the compensation is paid to a third party (beneficiary). The agreement between the insurer and insured is the insurance policy. Insurance covers loss of life, injury, damage to property, liability to others, loss of profits and many other business interests.

12.9.1 Insurance Protection for the Business

Who is entitled to obtain insurance?

Insurance may be obtained by a party who has an insurable interest, which is an interest in the well being or life of a person (including himself) or a substantial interest in real or personal property. Without this insurable interest, the purchase of insurance amounts to wagering and may result in acts which violate public policy or encourage unsavory acts. For example, a spouse may buy insurance on the life of a spouse and is generally interested in the well-being of the spouse. However, one has no interest in the well-being of a stranger, and the desire to collect insurance proceeds may result in acts which endanger the life of the stranger.

To be compensated under a policy for loss or injury of another person, an insurable interest must exist at the time the policy was obtained. Compensation for the loss or damage of property will be paid only if the insured has an insurable interest at the time of the loss or damage.

What is "key person" insurance?

This is a policy covering the life of a person important to the enterprise or organization. The enterprise is usually the beneficiary because it expects to suffer a loss in the event of the death or injury of the key person whose contributions to the business are crucial.

When is the insurance effective?

The effective date of insurance is usually when the "binder" (a temporary contract) is issued, when the actual policy is issued, or when a certain time has passed indicating that the insurer has accepted the offer of the party desiring to obtain the insurance.

For an insurance contract to be valid and binding, there must be:

- An offer to purchase insurance
- An acceptance by the insurer
- Consideration paid for the policy
- Legal purpose for insurance
- Capacity on the part of the parties making the contract

What would allow an insurer to cancel a policy?

Some of the reasons an insurer may cancel a policy are:

- Insurance premiums are not paid after proper notice of intent to cancel is given to the insured.
- Discovery of fraud or misstatements by the insured on an application.
- Gross negligence on the part of the insured.
- The insured no longer has an insurable interest (he has sold the insured property).

In the case of life insurance, certain representations made by an applicant may become incontestable, and the policy may not be canceled after the requisite time has passed.

12.10 LABOR AND EMPLOYMENT LAWS

Businesses must be aware of federal and state laws governing their interactions with and responsibilities toward workers and the work place. Laws in the labor/employment field generally deal with protections against employee injuries, maintenance of income or benefits after employment termination, fair wages, hours and terms of employment, preventing discrimination, employee privacy, and enhancing job security.

12.10.1 Employee Relationships

What legislation governs safety and injury to workers?

Many states have enacted statutes mandating work place safety, and compensation for workers who are injured on the job (Workers' Compensation). The federal government has enacted the Occupational Safety and Health Act of 1970.

What is workers' compensation?

Workers' compensation provides for benefits to be paid to an employee in "work related" injuries, which arise out of and during the course of employment. Adjudication of the claim and administration of payments are handled by the state. Funding is provided by requiring employers to buy private insurance, to self-insure (maintaining an adequate fund), or to contribute to a state insurance fund.

The worker does not have to prove negligence on the part of the employer; the award is based on "strict liability," or liability regardless of fault. However, the workers' compensation award is exclusive and the employee may not seek other tort recovery against the employer. The employee is not limited in seeking recovery against a third party.

What may an employee recover under workers' compensation?

- hospital and medical expenses
- certain vocational rehabilitation
- disability benefits
- set recoveries for loss of body parts
- survivor/dependent death benefits

How does OSHA work?

The Act is administered by the Occupational Safety and Health Administration (OSHA), and mandates that employers provide workers with employment and work places free of conditions likely to cause death or serious physical injury.

OSHA may inspect work places and issue citations for violations. The employer is required to remedy the violation with "reasonable promptness," not to exceed six months. Failure to comply may result in civil, criminal and injunctive relief.

Employers are required to maintain records and submit periodic reports of work-related deaths, serious injuries, and exposure to certain toxic and hazardous substances. Employees are protected against employer retaliation for reporting violations to OSHA.

What rights does an employee have after employment is terminated?

There are a number of state and federal provisions for workers after employment is terminated or after retirement.

What is unemployment compensation?

Where employment is terminated due to layoffs, plant closings and the like, a worker may be entitled to unemployment compensation administered on the federal and state levels. An employee who voluntarily terminates his employment, is terminated for cause (such as bad conduct), refuses to seek new employment or accept new employment may not be entitled to benefits. Funding is provided by subjecting employers to unemployment tax payments. The payments received by the employee are usually based on his salary during employment and are for a limited period.

What about health insurance coverage?

The continuation of health insurance coverage after employment termination is a major concern for employees and their families. Under the Consolidated Omnibus Budget Reconciliation Act (COBRA), employers with 20 or more employees must continue group insurance coverage for terminated employees and their families for 18 to 36 months. However, the employee must now pay the entire premium. Protection is effective when there is a "qualifying event," which makes an employee, spouse or dependent no longer eligible for coverage under the employer's group plan, such as termination of employment, reduction of work hours, death of an employee, Medicare coverage for the employee, divorce or separation from the covered employee, end of a child's dependent status, or bankruptcy of the employer.

COBRA sets up specific requirements for notice to the affected parties and guidelines as to time of payments and rates.

What entitlements are there for retired employees?

Retirees are generally entitled to Social Security which provides income benefits, certain insurance coverage (Medicare), and survivor and death benefits to those who have contributed under the Federal Insurance Contributions Act (FICA) during their working years. Under FICA, a mandatory percentage of an employee's income (up to a maximum set by the regulations) is paid into the system, and matched by the employer.

Under the Employee Retirement Security Act of 1974 (ERISA), employers who voluntarily set up retirement systems for their employees are subject to certain rules in order to protect the plan which the employees have come to rely on as part of their retirement, and which was perhaps an inducement to their employment to begin with.

Under ERISA, stringent requirements are set up to insure the solvency of the plan such as diversification of investments of the pension funds, imposing certain fiduciary duties (loyalty, no self-interest, disclosure) on the pension fund managers, setting time frames for employees' participation, and providing for the enforcement of rights by the participants in the plan.

What protections are there with respect to ongoing employer/employee relationships?

There are a number of provisions that govern the exercise of the rights of workers to organize and negotiate with their employers.

Among the major pieces of legislation are:

- *Norris-LaGuardia Act of 1932* which protects the rights of workers to peacefully strike, boycott and picket; and limits the interference of federal courts in the peaceful exercise of these rights.

- *National Labor Relations Act of 1935* (NLRA) created the National Labor Relations Board (NLRB) whose function is to curb unfair labor practices, such as interfering with the right of workers to organize or participate in a union, controlling or manipulating a labor organization, making contributions to the union, discrimination against union members or members who file charges with the NLRB, and refusing to bargain with the chosen representative of employees ("collective bargaining").

- *Labor Management Relations Act of 1947,* also called the Taft-Hartley Act, curbs certain powers of unions by making it illegal for the offer of employment to be conditioned upon union membership ("closed shop"). Although union membership may be required after the employee has worked for a prescribed period ("union shop"), state laws may make it illegal to do so. The Act permits the President of the United States to seek and obtain an injunction against a strike for 80 days where a strike may cause a national emergency.

- *Labor Management Reporting and Disclosure Act of 1959,* also known as the Landrum-Griffin Act, sets forth the rights of union members to attend meetings, nominate and vote for officers, and regulates the business operations of unions by requiring reports and disclosure. It also provides for accountability by union officials for union funds and property, and makes it illegal for ex-convicts or communists to hold union office. The Act makes it illegal for unions to require that employers deal only with union-produced goods.

What expectations may employees have with respect to privacy?

In the age of concerns over societal problems such as crime and substance abuse in the work force which affect performance and subject the employer to liabilities (e.g., for accidental injuries), monitoring by employers and the expectations of privacy of the employee have become major issues.

There are laws that prohibit certain employers from requiring, suggesting, or causing employees to take lie-detector tests and drawing conclusions from such tests or from the refusal to take them. However, employers are often permitted to use lie-detector tests where a theft has occurred.

Drug testing is generally considered an invasion of privacy except in government positions where there is reason to suspect drug use, or there are health, safety, and welfare issues involved. Drug testing, however, may be permitted or prohibited by union negotiations or agreement.

If an employer is monitoring employees' telephone calls, he may be in violation of a federal or state statute unless the employee is informed that he is subject to monitoring. The law must often balance the employer's need for surveillance against the employee's right to privacy, and will often examine whether less intrusive methods were available to the employer.

What constitutes employment discrimination?

Title VII of the Civil Rights Act of 1964 bans discrimination by employers and unions based on race, color, national origin, religion, nationality, age or sex. The Equal Employment Opportunity Commission (EEOC) is charged with investigating and resolving complaints filed by employees. If the matter cannot be resolved, the EEOC may bring legal action, or if it does not, the employee may do so for reinstatement, back pay, retroactive promotions, and even an injunction to prevent future violations once discrimination is proved.

Among the actions that would constitute discrimination are:

Disparate treatment: An employer continued to seek candidates or filled a position with someone who was not a member of a protected class when the plaintiff/applicant was a qualified member of the protected class. If the employer can show a legitimate reason for not hiring the applicant (such as lack of experience), the employer will not be liable.

Disparate impact: An employer's practices result in a work force that does not reflect the composition of protected classes in the local labor market; proof of intent to discriminate is not needed.

Sexual harassment: Promotions, raises, or assignments are given out for sexual favors, or workers are subjected to sexually offensive conduct or comments in the work place. An employer may be liable for the acts of a worker where the employer knew or should have known of the conduct and failed to correct the action. The act of a supervisory employee may be imputed to the employer and result in liability.

Affirmative action: Preferential treatment is given to minorities and women to make up for past discriminatory actions. This area is presently under intense Court and legislative review, and has been heavily criticized for creating "reverse discrimination" in which otherwise qualified applicants who are not members of minorities or women are effectively excluded from obtaining the positions offered.

Pregnancy discrimination: Pregnant women must be treated in the same manner as others with similar ability to work. Equal treatment is required with respect to disability benefits and leave.

Age discrimination: Individuals who are 40 years or older are protected by the Age Discrimination in Employment Act of 1967 (ADEA) from discrimination on the basis of age where the employer has 20 or more employees and whose businesses have an impact on interstate commerce. Among the provisions is a prohibition of a mandatory retirement age for nonmanagerial workers.

Disabilities: Under the Americans with Disabilities Act of 1990 (ADA) an employer may not discriminate against "differently abled" persons whose physical or mental impairments (including blindness, AIDS, cancer, and learning disabilities) substantially limits "one or more major life activities," if a "reasonable accommodation" (without "undue hardship" as assessed by the size of the company, finances, and the like) could be made to enable the person to do his job (e.g., installing a ramp for wheelchairs).

What right does an employer have to discharge an employee?

Generally, employers can discharge an employee "at will," (i.e., without cause) as long as it is not based upon discrimination or unfair employment practices.

However, there may be protections under state or federal law if the employee is a "whistleblower," who has reported hazardous or illegal practices of the employer to the government or the media. In addition, an implied employment contract may exist where there are employee handbooks, personnel materials or representations made that the employee will be discharged only "for cause."

12.11 BUSINESS TORTS, WHITE-COLLAR CRIMES, AND ETHICS

Substantial civil and criminal liability can arise out of business transactions because of tortious conduct (intentional or unintentional wrongs), criminal acts, or violations of ethical duties.

12.11.1 Criminal Acts and Ethical Violations

What kinds of acts constitute business torts?

Business torts are civil wrongs committed within the business context. They include:

- *Interference with a contractual relationship:* Intentionally and knowingly inducing a party to breach a valid and enforceable contract and entering into a contract with the inducing party (Mr. X induces a buyer to breach a contract to purchase from another supplier, and to purchase from Mr. X instead).

- *Interference with a business relationship:* Soliciting customers who specifically already have a relationship or interest in a competitor's product. This exceeds normal, competitive attempts to attract customers.

- *Appropriation:* Unauthorized use of another's name or likeness for the user's benefit.

- *Defamation:* Making a false statement injuring another's reputation. In business, a defamatory statement is one that injures a party in his credit, professional, business or trade reputation.

- *Disparagement of product:* Making false statements about the quality or nature of another's product.

What are some common white-collar crimes?

Crimes related to business are often referred to as white-collar crimes. Among them are:

- *Bribery:* Tendering something of value to a public official in return for a favor.

- *Money laundering:* Processing illegally earned money through a legitimate business enterprise. In an attempt to prevent this, the law imposes reporting requirements for currency (cash) in excess of $10,000.

- *Insider trading:* Violation of certain Securities and Exchange laws by "insiders" (officers, directors, or parties related to them). This involves making a profit from information not generally available to the public.

- *RICO:* The Racketeer-Influenced and Corrupt

454   MANAGE, MARKET, & LEGAL STRATEGIES

Organizations Act prevents participation by organized crime in legitimate enterprises by prohibiting using funds from racketeering to acquire, maintain, or participate in legitimate businesses.

Why is ethics important in business?

Ethics has to do with fairness, duty owed to others, and honesty in one's business. Ethical conduct generally results in better business in that it promotes good will. However, there are legal mandates in the area of ethics, the violation of which can lead to liability. This is especially so where there is a breach of a fiduciary duty in which there is a relationship based upon trust with another party (for example, a doctor, lawyer or accountant has a relationship based upon trust and confidence of their clients). In a fiduciary relationship, there is a duty to act in the interest of the beneficiary and not for one's own interest, and to perform in a diligent and careful manner in carrying out tasks on behalf of the beneficiary.

PART V

ECONOMICS AND MULTINATIONAL ISSUES

13 _____
Economics

13.1 MAJOR ECONOMIC AREAS:
Microeconomics and Macroeconomics

What is microeconomics?

Microeconomics is the study of the individual units of the economy—individuals, households, companies, and industries. Microeconomics focuses on economic variables such as the prices and outputs of specific firms and industries, the expenditures of consumers or households, wage rates, competition, and markets. Questions that arise in the study of microeconomics include: What determines the price and output of individual goods and services? What factors determine supply and demand of a product? How do government policies such as price controls, subsidies, and excise taxes impact the price and output levels of individual markets?

What is macroeconomics?

Macroeconomics is the study of the whole national economy, or of its major sectors. It takes into account such areas as output, employment, national price, inflation, and exports. It looks at the forest instead of the trees. Questions to consider in macroeconomics include: What may be done to combat recession? What may be done to minimize inflationary effects? Why is the inflation rate so high? What are the important variables to national income and employment?

13.1.1 Importance of Business Economics

The MBA should understand economics and its impact

on the company. He or she should know how to read and interpret economic indices and statistics vital to the success of the business in a dynamic, ever-changing economic environment. This knowledge will provide better financial and investment decisions.

> *How can you keep track of the economy with economic and monetary indicators?*

To sort out the confusing mix of statistics that flow almost daily from the government and to help track what is happening in the economy, we examine various economic and monetary indicators.

Economic and monetary indicators show where the economy is heading and where it's been. Each month government agencies, including the Federal Reserve Board and several economic institutions, publish various indicators. Studying these indicators, described below, gives an overall picture of the economy.

13.2 MEASURES OF OVERALL ECONOMIC PERFORMANCE

Economic indicators measure performance in six major categories. These measures include gross national and domestic products, industrial production, personal income, housing starts, unemployment rate, and retail sales.

Gross National Product (GNP). GNP measures the value of all goods and services produced in the economy and is the nation's broadest gauge of economic health. GNP is usually expressed in annual terms, though data are compiled and released quarterly. GNP measures the economic state. For example, many economists speak of recession when there has been a decline in GNP for two consecutive quarters. WARNING: Unfortunately, there is no way of measuring whether we are in a recession or prosperity based on the GNP statistic. Only after the quarter is over can it be determined if there was growth or decline. Further, an increasing number of economists believe the GNP criteria for a recession are no longer valid. Experts look upon other measures as recession indicators—unemployment rate, industrial production, durable orders, corporate profits, retail sales, and housing starts.

The following diagram shows how GNP usually impacts companies, charting a series of events leading from a declining GNP to lower security prices.

$$\underset{\text{down}}{\text{GNP}} - \underset{\text{profits down}}{\text{Corporate}} - \underset{\text{down}}{\text{Dividends}} - \underset{\text{prices down}}{\text{Security}}$$

Gross Domestic Product (GDP). Unlike GNP, GDP only includes the values of goods and services earned by a nation within its boundaries. Thus, it includes only the income derived from factories within the country (and not without). For example, when General Motor's British unit repatriates dividends, profits, or interest on loans, the money is counted as part of GNP, whereas British GM profits are not included in GDP. NOTE: As of December 1991, the Department of Commerce began focusing on GDP rather than GNP when reporting the nation's economic health.

Industrial Production. This index shows changes in the output of U.S. plants, mines, and utilities. Detailed breakdowns of the index provide a reading on how individual industries are doing. The index is issued monthly by the Federal Reserve Board.

Personal Income. This shows the before-tax income received by individuals and unincorporated businesses such as wages and salaries, rents, and interest and dividends, and other payments such as unemployment and Social Security. They represent consumers' spending power. When personal income increases, it typically means that consumers will increase their purchases, which will in turn affect favorably the economic climate. NOTE: Consumer spending makes a major contribution (67%) to the nation's GNP. Personal income data are released monthly by the Commerce Department.

Housing Starts. Housing starts is a key economic indicator providing an estimate of the number of dwelling units on which construction has begun. The figures are issued monthly by the Bureau of Census. When an economy is going to take a downturn, the housing sector (and companies within it) is the first to decline. This indicates the future strength of the housing sector of the economy. At the same time, it is closely related to interest rates and other basic economic factors.

Unemployment Rate. No one economic indicator is able to point to the direction in which an economy is heading. It is common that many indicators give mixed signals regarding, for example, the likelihood of a recession. When the various leading indicators are mixed, many economists look to the unemployment rate as being the most important.

Retail Sales. Retail sales is the estimate of total sales at the retail level. It includes everything from groceries to durable goods. It is used as a measure of future economic conditions: A long slowdown in sales could mean production cuts. Retail sales are a major factor because they represent about half of overall consumer spending. NOTE: Consumer spending accounts for about two-thirds of the country's GNP. The amount of retail sales depends heavily on consumer confidence. The data are issued each month by the Commerce Department.

3.3 PRICE INDICES

Price indices measure the inflation rate. Various price indices are used to measure living costs, inflation, and price level changes. They are:

Consumer Price Index (CPI). The Consumer Price Index (CPI) is the most well-known inflation measure. It measures the cost of buying a fixed bundle of goods (some 400 consumer goods and services), representative of the purchase of the typical working-class urban family. The fixed basket is broken down into the following categories: housing, medical care, food and beverages, apparel, transportation, and other. Generally termed "cost-of-living index," it is published by the Bureau of Labor Statistics of the U.S. Department of Labor. The CPI is widely used for escalation clauses. The base year for the CPI index was 1982-84 at which time it was assigned 100. The following diagram charts a chain of events leading from higher inflation rates to reduced consumer spending and possibly down security market.

CPI up – Real personal income down – Consumer confidence down – Consumer spending down (Retail sales down + Housing starts down + Auto sales down) – Security market down.

Producer Price Index (PPI). Like the CPI, the PPI is a measure of the cost of a given basket of goods priced in wholesale markets, including raw materials, semifinished goods, and finished goods at the early stage of the distribution system.

The PPI is published monthly by the Bureau of Labor Statistics of the Department of Commerce. The PPI signals changes in the general price level or the CPI, some time before they actually occur. (Since the PPI does not include services, caution should be exercised when the major cause of inflation is service prices.) For this reason, the PPI and particularly some of its subindexes, such as the index of sensitive materials, serve as one of the leading indicators that are closely watched by policy makers.

GNP Deflator (Implicit Price Index). The GNP implicit deflator is the third index of inflation used to separate price changes in GNP calculations from real changes in economic activity. The GNP deflator is a weighted average of the price indexes used to deflate the components of GNP. Thus, it reflects price changes for goods and services purchased by consumers, businesses, and governments. The GNP deflator is computed by dividing current GNP in a given year by constant (real) GNP. Because it covers a broader group of goods and services than the CPI and PPI, the GNP deflator is a widely used price index frequently used to measure inflation. The GNP deflator, unlike the CPI and PPI, is available only quarterly—not monthly. It is published by the U.S. Department of Commerce.

13.4 OTHER IMPORTANT ECONOMIC INDICATORS

13.4.1 Indices of Labor Market Conditions

Indicators covering labor market conditions are average workweek of production workers, hourly wage rates, unemployment rate, and applications for unemployment insurance.

13.4.2 Money and Credit Market Indicators

Most widely reported in the media are consumer credit, Treasury bill rate, money supply, and the Dow Jones Industrial Average (DJIA).

13.4.3 Index of Leading Indicators

This widely publicized signal caller consists of 11 data series. They are vendor performance, new orders, money supply, building permits, consumer confidence, change in sensitive prices, average workweek, stock prices, contracts, inventory change, and change in total liquid assets. They monitor certain business activities that can signal a change in the economy. A more detailed discussion will follow.

13.4.4 Measures for Major Product Markets

These measures are indicators for segments of the economy such as retail sales, steel, automobiles, and housing. Examples are 10-day auto sales, advance retail sales, construction permits, and housing starts.

Indicators are only signals, telling the MBA something about the economic conditions in the country, a specific area, and industry and, over time, the trends that seem to be developing.

13.5 INDICES OF LEADING, COINCIDENT, AND LAGGING ECONOMIC INDICATORS

The Index of Leading Economic Indicators is the economic series of indicators that predict future changes in economic activity. It is officially referred to as the *Composite Index of 11 Leading Indicators*. This index shows the direction of the economy in the next six to nine months.

If the index is increasing, even barely, the economy is chugging along and a setback is unlikely. If the indicator drops for three or more consecutive months, look for an economic slowdown and perhaps a recession in the next year or so.

This series is the government's main barometer for forecasting business trends. Each of the series has shown a tendency to change before the economy makes a major turn—hence the term, "leading indicators." The index forecasts economic activity six to nine months ahead (1982 = 100). The series is published monthly by the U.S. Department of Commerce, and is composed of:

- *Residential building permits for private housing.* Gains in building permits signal business upturns.

- *Contracts and orders for plant and equipment.* Heavier contracting and ordering typically lead economic upswings.

- *Average workweek of production workers in manufacturing.* Employers find it easier to increase the number of hours worked in a week than to hire more employees.

- *Factory backlogs of unfilled durable goods orders.* Backlogs signify business upswings.

- *Money supply.* A rising money supply means easy money that sparks brisk economic activity. This typically leads recoveries by as much as fourteen months.

- *Percent change in prices of sensitive crude materials.* Rises in prices of such critical materials as steel usually mean factory demands are going up, which means factories plan to increase production.

- *Stock index prices.* A rise in the common stock indicates expected profits and lower interest rates. Stock market advances typically precede business upturns by three to eight months.

- *New orders for manufacturers of consumer goods and materials.* New orders mean more employees hired, more materials and supplies bought and increased output. Gains in this series typically lead recoveries by as much as four months.

- *Change in consumer confidence.* It is based on the

University of Michigan's survey of consumer expectations. The index measures consumers' optimism regarding the current and future condition of the economy and is based on an index of 100 in 1966. NOTE: Consumer spending buys two-thirds of GNP (all goods and services produced in the economy), so any sharp change could be an important factor in an overall turnaround.

• *Vendor performance.* Vendor performance represents the percentage of companies reporting slower deliveries. As the economy grows, companies have more trouble filling orders.

These 11 components of the index are adjusted for inflation. Rarely do these components of the index all go in the same direction at once. Each factor is weighted. The composite figure tells only in which direction business will go. It is not intended to forecast the degree of future ups and downs.

What are coincident indicators?

Coincident indicators are the types of economic indicator series that tend to move up and down in line with the aggregate economy and therefore are measures of current economic activity. They are intended to gauge current economic conditions. Examples are Gross National Product (GNP), retail sales, industrial production, and employment.

What are lagging indicators?

Lagging indicators follow or trail behind aggregate economic activity. There are six lagging indicators published by the government, including ratio of consumer installment credit outstanding to personal income, ratio of manufacturing and trade inventories to sales, unemployment rate, average prime interest rate, loans outstanding, and labor cost per unit.

3.6 MISCELLANEOUS ECONOMIC INDICES

There are other important indices with which the MBA should be familiar. Some widely watched indices are discussed below.

What is the Dodge Index?

The Dodge Index prepared by F.W. Dodge Division of McGraw-Hill is a monthly market index that evaluates the building industry in terms of the value of new construction projects.

What is the Forbes Index?

Forbes publishes The Forbes Index. This index (1976 = 100) is a measure of U.S. economic activity composed of 8 equally weighted elements: total consumer installment credit, new claims for unemployment, personal income, total industrial production, retail sales, the level of new orders for durable goods compared with manufacturers' inventories, housing starts, cost of services compared to consumer prices.

What is the Purchasing Index?

The National Association of Purchasing Management releases its monthly Purchasing Index which tells about buying intentions of corporate purchasing agents.

What is the Help-Wanted Index?

The Conference Board of New York, an industry-sponsored, nonprofit economic research institute, publishes two indices: The *Help-Wanted Advertising Index* and *Consumer Confidence Index*. The Help-Wanted Index measures the amount of help-wanted advertising in 51 newspapers and tells about the change in labor market conditions.

What are two major consumer confidence indices?

The *Consumer Confidence Index* measures consumer feelings about general business conditions, jobs, and total family income.

The University of Michigan Survey Research Center is a research organization that compiles its own index called the *Index of Consumer Sentiment*. It measures consumers' personal financial circumstances and their future outlook. The survey is compiled by surveying 500 households. The index is used by the Commerce Department in its monthly *Index of Leading Economic Indicators* and regularly charted in the Department's *Business Conditions Digest*.

What is the Optimism Index?

The National Federation of Independent Business, a Washington-based advocacy group, publishes the *Optimism Index* which is based on small-business owners' expectations for the economy. The benchmark year is 1978.

13.7 MONETARY INDICATORS AND HOW THEY AFFECT THE ECONOMY

What are monetary indices?

Monetary indicators apply to Federal Reserve actions and the demand for credit. They are of importance to MBAs because they affect the companies in terms of the costs of debt and equity financing and security prices. They consider long-term interest rates, which are important because bond yields compete with stock yields. Monetary and credit indicators are often the first signs of market direction. If monetary indicators move favorably, this indicates that a decline in stock price may be over. A stock market top may be ready for a contraction if the Federal Reserve tightens credit, making consumer buying and corporate expansion more costly and difficult.

Monetary indicators regularly monitored are:

- T-Bill yield
- 30-year T-Bond yield
- Dow Jones twenty-bond index
- Dow Jones utility average
- New York Stock Exchange utility average

Bonds and utilities are yield instruments and therefore money-sensitive. They are affected by changing interest rates. If the above monetary indicators are active and pointing higher, it is a sign the stock market will begin to take off. An upward trend in these indicators may occur before a stock market increase.

A brief description of monetary and economic variables that should be carefully watched by MBAs follows.

What is the money supply?

This is the level of funds available at a given time for conducting transactions in an economy, as reported by the Federal Reserve Board. The Federal Reserve System can influence money supply through its monetary policy measures. There are several definitions of the money supply: M1 (currency in circulation, demand deposits, traveler's checks, and those in interest-bearing NOW accounts), M2 (the most widely followed measure, it equals M1 plus savings deposits, money market deposit accounts, and money market funds), and M3 (which is M2 plus large CDs). Moderate growth is considered to have a positive impact on the economy. A rapid growth is deemed inflationary; on the other hand, a sharp drop in the money supply is construed as recessionary.

What are interest rates?

Interest rates represent the costs to borrow money and exist in many forms. There are long-term and short-term interest rates, depending on the length of the loan; there are interest rates on super-safe securities (such as U.S. T-bills) and there are interest rates on "junk bonds" of financially troubled companies; there are nominal (coupon) interest rates, real (inflation-adjusted) or risk adjusted interest rates, and effective interest rates (or yields). Interest rates depend upon the maturity of the security. The longer the period, the higher will be the interest rate because of the greater uncertainty.

Some of the more important interest rates are briefly discussed below.

- *Federal funds rate.* The rate on short-term loans among commercial banks for overnight use. The Fed influences this rate by open market operations and by changing the bank's required reserve.

- *Discount rate.* This is the charge on loans to depository institutions by the Federal Reserve Board. A change in the discount rate is a major economic event and is expected to have an impact on security prices, particularly bonds. A change in the prime rate typically follows the change in the discount rate.

- *Prime rate.* The rate banks charge their best customers for short-term loans. This is a bellwether rate in that it is a sign of rising or falling loan demand and economic activity. When the prime rate is climbing, it means companies are borrowing heavily and the economy is still on an upward swing.

- *90-Day Treasury bills.* This yield represents the direction of short-term rates, a closely watched indicator. When yields on 90-day bills rise sharply, this may signal a resurgence of inflation. Subsequently, the economy could slow down.

- *5-Year and 10-Year Treasury notes.* The yields on these notes give an idea of the "going" interest rates for intermediate-term fixed-income securities.

- *30-Year Treasury bonds.* This yield, also referred to as the long bond yield, is a closely monitored bellwether indicator of long-term interest rates because the entire bond market (and sometimes the stock market) often moves in line with this rate.

Interest rates are controlled by the Fed's monetary policy. The Fed's policy tools involve: (1) changes in the discount rate; (2) open market operations—that is, purchase and sale of government securities; and (3) changes in the required reserve ratio. A reduction in the discount rate aimed at stimulating the economy is good for stocks. A summary of the impact of cutting the discount rate on the economy follows.

13.8 WHAT ARE THE EFFECTS OF LOWERING THE DISCOUNT RATE?

- *The players:* The Federal Reserve Board is the country's central bank. It regulates the flow of money through the economy.
- *The action:* Discount rate is what the Federal Reserve charges on short-term loans to member banks. When the Fed cuts the discount rate, it means banks can get cash cheaper and thus charge less on loans.
- *The initial effect.* Within a couple of days, banks are likely to start passing on the discounts by cutting their prime rate, which is what banks charge on loans to their best corporate customers.
- *Impact.* Businesses are more likely to borrow. Second, adjustable consumer loans are tied to the prime, such as credit card rates. These become cheaper, stimulating spending.
- *The second effect.* Within a few weeks, rates on mortgage, auto and construction loans drop.
- *The third effect.* The lower rates go, the more investors move their cash to stocks, creating new wealth.
- *The goal.* To kick-start the economy. If lower interest rates cause businesses to start growing again, laid-off workers get jobs, retailers start selling, and the economy starts to roll again.

The following diagram summarizes the effect of open market activities on the money supply, loan demand, and level of interest rates.

Easy Money Policy:

Fed buys securities — Bank reserve up — Bank lending up — Money supply up — Interest rates down — Loan demand up

Tight Money Policy:

Fed sells securities — Bank reserve down — Bank lending down — Money supply down — Interest rates up — Loan demand down

13.8.1 Inflation

What is inflation?

Inflation is the general increase in prices of consumer goods and services. The federal government measures inflation by comparing prices today—measured in terms of the CPI, PPI, and/or GNP Deflator—to a two-year period, 1982-84. As prices increase, lenders and investors demand greater returns to offset the decline in purchasing power. Companies may reduce borrowing due to higher interest rates. This leads to less capital expenditures for property, plant and equipment. In consequence, output may decrease, resulting in employee layoffs. During inflation, selling prices may increase to keep pace with rising price levels but the company's sales in real dollars remain the same. Companies still lose out since their tax liability will increase.

Most likely, the Federal Reserve will tighten the money supply and increase interest rates (such as discount rate or federal fund rate). It would be too costly to borrow money. Therefore, there is less demand for products, which in turn pushes prices down. The following diagram shows how inflation impacts the prices of products:

Inflation — Fed raises discount rate — Interest rates up — Demand for money down — Demand for products down — Prices down

Interest rates are no more than a reflection of what expectations are for inflation. Inflation means higher interest rates and thus higher borrowing cost to the company.

13.8.2 Productivity

Of what importance are productivity and unit labor costs?

The Labor Department issues data on productivity and unit labor costs. Increased productivity, or getting more worker output per hour on the job, is considered important to increasing the country's standard of living without inflation. Meanwhile, unit labor cost is a key measure of future price inflation along with the CPI, PPI, and GNP Deflator.

13.8.3 Recession

What is recession?

In recession, there is a sinking economy. Unfortunately, there is no uniform definition and measure of recession. Three or more straight monthly drops of the Index of Leading Economic Indicators are generally deemed a sign of recession. Or, two consecutive quarterly drops of GNP signals recession. Or, consecutive monthly drops of durable goods orders which most likely results in less production and increasing layoffs in the factory sector. Recession tends to dampen the spirits of consumers and thus depress prices of products and services.

To kick-start the economy the Fed will loosen the money supply and lower interest rates such as the discount rate. When the Fed cuts the discount rate, it means banks can get cash cheaper and thus charge less on loans.

The size of the cut is important. For example, a half-point discount rate cut is not strong enough to get the economy moving fast. External political conditions (such as a crisis in Iraq), the federal deficit and problems in the banking industry would make companies reluctant to start expanding again and also make consumers nervous for a longer time than the Fed would expect.

13.8.4 Federal Deficit

What is the federal deficit?

The national debt is the total of all money the government has borrowed to finance budget deficits. The only way for a government to reduce its debt is to run a budget surplus, to obtain more money than it spends. The surplus must then be used to pay off maturing debt (bonds, notes, etc.) instead of replacing them (rolling them over) with more debt. This federal deficit affects the entire economy.

Economists believe that larger federal deficits result in higher interest rates for two reasons. First, increased budget deficits raise the demand for the loanable funds resulting in higher interest rates. Second, larger deficits are likely to lead to higher inflation. This may be true either because the sources of the increased deficits—larger government spending and/or lower taxes—result in greater pressure for loan demand and hence inflation, or because the deficit will induce the Fed to expand the money supply to help finance the deficit, thus causing inflation. In any event, if the increased deficit elevates the public's expectation of inflation, it will tend to raise interest rates. Further, the financing of the deficit by issuing government debt securities will compete for funds raised by companies and will deter economic expansion. It also forces companies to borrow at higher interest rates. This is referred to as the "crowding-out effect."

13.8.5   International Trade

What is international trade?

Foreign trade significantly impacts the economies of the nations involved as well as world conditions. Goods and services are sold and bought to improve the economies of the countries. International trade allows a company to obtain goods not available within the country. For example, an industrialized country may export manufactured products and import raw materials and agricultural items. Third World countries may have problems in receiving certain products from developed countries because of protectionist policies. U.S. foreign trade policy is conducted by the Bureau of Economic and Business Affairs of the U.S. State Department.

13.8.6 Balance of Payments

What is the balance of payments?

A balance of payments is a systematic record of a nation's receipts from, or payments to, other countries. The "balance of trade" typically refers to goods within the goods and services category. It is also known as merchandise or "visible" trade because it includes tangibles such as food, produced goods, and raw materials. "Services" are "invisible" trade and include intangibles such as interest or dividends, technology transfers, and services (such as life insurance, financial, and transportation).

When the net result of both the current account and the capital account yields more credits than debits, the country has a surplus in its balance of payments. When deficits persist, this generally depresses the value of the dollar and can boost inflation. A weak dollar makes foreign goods relatively expensive, often allowing U.S. producers of similar products to raise prices. An MBA must know the condition of a country's balance of payments, because its resulting inflation and value of the dollar will impact the company's product demand.

13.8.7 The Value of the Dollar

What is better, a strong dollar (appreciation in foreign exchange rate) or a weak dollar (depreciation in foreign exchange rate)?

The answer is, it depends. This is of concern especially to managers of multinational companies. A strong dollar makes Americans' cash go further overseas and reduces import prices—typically good for U.S. consumers and for foreign producers. If the dollar is overvalued, U.S. products are more difficult to sell overseas and domestically, where they compete with low-cost imports.

A weak dollar restores competitiveness to American products by making foreign goods comparatively more costly. But too-weak a dollar can spawn inflation, first through higher import prices and then through spiraling prices for all goods. Even worse, a falling dollar can drive foreign investors away from U.S. securities, which lose value along with the dollar. A strong dollar can be induced by interest rates. Relatively higher domestic interest rates than abroad will attract money dollar-denominated investments which will raise the value of the dollar. Figure 13.1 summarizes the impacts of changes in foreign exchange rates on the company's products and services.

FIGURE 13.1 THE IMPACTS OF CHANGES IN FOREIGN EXCHANGE RATES

	Strong Dollar (Appreciation)	Weak Dollar (Depreciation)
Exports	More costly	Cheaper
Imports	Cheaper	More costly
Receivables	More costly	Cheaper
Payables	Cheaper	More costly

14 _____

International Trade

Many businesses are multinational companies (MNCs) that have major foreign activities involving a large percentage of their revenue overseas. Financial managers of MNCs must comprehend the difficulties of international trading to formulate correct decisions. "Key" issues include import/export balance, foreign prices, labor cost, exchange rates, foreign restrictions and limitations, and political uncertainty.

International finance considers managing money, financing the entity, foreign activities, and foreign exchange rates. The financial manager must compare the value of the U.S. dollar to the value of the foreign currency in the country in which the MNC is operating. Currency exchange rates may significantly impact imports and exports of the U.S. business. The stronger foreign competition is, the worse for the domestic company in terms of pricing, sales volume, vulnerability, and profitability.

14.1 MANAGING CASH

International cash management relates to reducing the company's susceptibility to foreign-located funds, to exchange rate risks and reducing governmental constraints on the movement of money from one country to the other. For instance, many countries have restrictions on cash remissions back to the U.S. Examples are India and China. Cash held in a politically unfriendly foreign country involves uncertainty. A determination must be made of the political and economic direction of the foreign country. For example, if relations with a particular foreign country are deteriorating, lower quality is associated with current earnings being derived there because future recurrence may be a problem.

How may cash be hastened?

Cash may be accelerated by having bank accounts in each country. In many foreign lands, customers pay their bills by requesting their bank to reduce the amount owed from their account and to transfer funds to another company's account.

14.2 FINANCING

A business may finance its operations abroad, particularly in countries it has activities in. A successful business in domestic markets is more likely to attract financing for international expansion.

A type of commercial bank financing is using overdrafts. An overdraft allows a customer to draw checks up to a specified maximum amount exceeding the checking account base.

In Europe, commercial banks undertake numerous investment banking operations.

What are Eurobonds?

Eurobonds are long-term debt in the Eurocurrency market. They are offered for sale in more than one country via international underwriting syndicates, often denominated in a strong currency (e.g., British pound). If a Eurobond is not issued to U.S. residents, the issue does not need registration.

Eurobonds may be of different types such as straight, convertible, and with warrants. While most Eurobonds are fixed-rate, there are also variable-rate bonds. Maturities range from 10 to 12 years.

Even though Eurobonds are issued in many currencies, you should opt for a stable, fully convertible, and actively traded currency. In some instances, if a Eurobond is denominated in a weak currency the holder may request payment in a different currency. In some cases, the Eurobond requires repayment in a combination of currencies. An example is the European Unit of Account (EUA).

The U.S. dollar is the prime transaction currency. Eurobonds are sometimes denominated for repayment in multiple currencies. The creditor can require payment of interest and principal in any pre-established currencies at agreed-upon parity.

Convertible Eurobonds have lower interest rates plus possible capital appreciation.

Wholly owned offshore finance subsidiaries are set by large companies. These subsidiaries issue Eurobond debt and the proceeds are given to the parent or to overseas operating subsidiaries. Debt service goes back to bondholders via finance subsidiaries.

If the Eurobond was issued by the parent directly, the U.S. would mandate a withholding tax on interest. There may also be an estate tax when the bondholder dies. These tax problems do not arise when a bond is issued by a finance subsidiary incorporated in a tax haven. Thus, the subsidiary may borrow at less cost than the parent.

14.3 FOREIGN OPERATIONS

If a subsidiary is operating in a high-tax country with a double-tax agreement, dividends are not subject to additional U.S. taxes. One approach to transfer income from high-tax areas to low-tax areas is to levy royalties or management fees on the subsidiaries.

What foreign activities can a multinational company expect?

When keen competition exists in the U.S., a company may enter or expand its foreign activities. However, a company having trouble in the U.S. may also have problems overseas. Additionally, the financial manager must be aware of local customs and risks in international markets.

A large, established business with significant international experience may ultimately have wholly-owned subsidiaries. But a small company with limited foreign experience operating in "risky areas" may be restricted to exports and imports only.

If the company's sales force has limited experience in export sales, it is advised to use foreign brokers having specialized knowledge of foreign markets. When there is adequate volume, the company may establish a foreign branch sales office including sales and technical service staff. As the operation takes hold, manufacturing facilities may be located in the foreign market. However, some foreign countries require licensing before foreign sales and production occur. In this instance, a foreign licensee sells and manufactures the product. A problem with this is that confidential data and expertise are passed on to the licensees who can then become competitors at the termination of the agreement.

A joint venture with a foreign company is another approach to proceed internationally and share risk. Some foreign governments mandate this method in their countries. The foreign company may have local goodwill to foster success. A problem is the reduction in control over activities and a conflict of interest.

In appraising the impact that foreign activities have on the company's financial position, the financial manager should take into account the degree of intercountry transactions, foreign limitations and laws, the foreign country's tax structure, and the political and economic stability of the country. In appraising a company's balance of imports/exports, the manager should consider tariffs, quotas, foreign exchange rates, prices of foreign vs. domestic goods, health of the international economy, and the foreign country's policy regarding international trade.

14.4 MONETARY POSITION

Monetary balance is avoiding either a net receivable or a net payable position. Monetary assets and liabilities do not change in value with devaluation or revaluation in foreign currencies.

What monetary activities does a multinational company engage in?

A company with a long position in a foreign currency will be receiving more funds in the foreign currency. It will have a net monetary position (monetary assets exceed monetary liabilities) in that currency.

A company with net receipts is a net monetary creditor. Its foreign exchange rate risk exposure has a net receipts position in a foreign currency that is vulnerable to a drop in value.

A company with a future net obligation in foreign currency has a net monetary debtor position. It is susceptible to foreign exchange risk of the possibility of an increase in the value of the foreign currency.

14.5 FOREIGN CURRENCY EXCHANGE

An exchange rate relates one unit of currency to another. The translation rate between currencies depends on the demand/supply relationship. Exchange rates may be in dollars per foreign currency unit or units of foreign currency per dollar. An exchange rate is set between the different currencies. Because of the change in exchange rates, businesses are vulnerable to exchange rate risks because of a net asset or net liability position in a foreign currency. A rate of $.30 Italian lira means each lira costs the U.S. company $.30. The U.S. company obtains 1/.3 = 3.3 lira for each dollar.

How do changes in foreign exchange affect the business?

International transactions and investments involve more than one currency. For instance, when a U.S. company sells goods to a French firm, the former desires to be paid in dollars but the French company usually anticipates to receive francs. Because of the foreign exchange market, the buyer may pay in one currency while the seller can receive payment in another currency.

EXAMPLE 14.1

An American company that imports goods from England buys pounds to pay for the purchase. An American company exporting to England receives pounds which it sells in exchange for dollars. Both companies use the foreign exchange market.

14.6 SPOT RATES AND FORWARD RATES

The spot rate is the exchange rate for immediate delivery of currencies exchanged, but the forward rate is the exchange rate for future delivery of currencies exchanged. For example, there may be a 120-day exchange rate. The forward exchange rate of a currency will be slightly different from the spot rate at the current date due to future expectations and uncertainties. Forward rates may be greater than the current spot rate (premium) or less than the current spot rate (discount).

EXAMPLE 14.2

On March 1, 19X4, forward rates on the British pound were at a premium relative to the spot rate, while the forward rates for the Italian lira were at a discount from the spot rate. This means that participants in the foreign exchange market expected that the British pound would appreciate compared with the U.S. dollar in the future but the Italian lira would depreciate relative to the dollar.

The percentage discount or premium is calculated as follows. Forward premium (or discount) equals:

$$\frac{\text{Forward rate} - \text{spot rate}}{\text{Spot rate}} \times \frac{12}{\text{Length of forward contract in months}} \times 100$$

EXAMPLE 14.3

On April 6, 19X2, a 90-day forward contract in British pounds was selling at a 23.952% premium:

$$\frac{1.77 - 1.67}{1.67} \times \frac{12}{3} \times 100 = 23.952\%$$

14.7 LONG VERSUS SHORT POSITION

When a devaluation of the dollar occurs, foreign assets and income in strong currency countries are worth more U.S. dollars provided foreign liabilities do not offset this beneficial effect.

How is foreign exchange risk appraised?

Foreign exchange risk may be evaluated by studying anticipated receipts or obligations in foreign currency units. A company that expects receipts in foreign currency units ("long" position in the foreign currency units) has the risk that the value of the foreign currency units will decline. This causes devaluation of the foreign currency compared with the dollar. If a company anticipates having obligations in foreign currency units ("short" position in the foreign currency units), there is risk that the value of the foreign currency will increase and it will require buying the currency at a higher price.

If net claims are greater than debt in a foreign currency, the business has a "long" position because it will benefit if the value of the foreign currency increases. If net liabilities exceed claims with regard to foreign currencies, the company is in a "short" position because it will gain if the foreign currency declines in value.

14.8 EXCHANGE RATE STABILITY

If the exchange rate is stable, an exchange problem does not exist. Because the exchange rates of some countries are more unstable than that of others, the financial manager should ascertain in which countries the company is operating. The financial manager should also determine if the instability in exchange rates is a short-term or long-term problem.

What impact does a varying exchange rate have?

A fluctuating foreign exchange rate results in instability.

The extent of vacillation of the foreign exchange rate may be measured by its percentage change over time and/or its standard deviation.

Rapid exchange shifts detract from earnings stability. The trend in the ratio of (1) foreign exchange gains and losses to net income and (2) foreign exchange gains and losses to total revenue should be appraised. To what degree do foreign currency gains and losses contribute to variability in the earnings stream?

14.9 FOREIGN EXCHANGE RISK

A company that properly balances its foreign assets and liabilities protects the parent from exchange rates and its ensuing variability effect upon consolidated profit. The financial manager should take into account the exposed position of the firm by each foreign country in which a major operation exists.

What risks are there in foreign exchange?

If a foreign currency is increasing in value, the U.S. company has risk exposure if it has a short position in the foreign currency. If the firm has to make payments in foreign currency units or has liabilities stated in such units, an increase in the value of the foreign currency unit will require more dollars to be used to pay it off. A company with future obligations stated in foreign currency units has risk exposure from the potential change in the value of those units.

A company may be aggressive by being a net monetary debtor in a country in which exchange rates are anticipated to decline and a net monetary creditor in a country in which exchange rates are likely to increase.

Foreign exchange risk exposure may be reduced by hedging in the forward market or borrowing and lending through the money markets.

What is a forward exchange contract?

A forward exchange contract is an agreement to buy or sell specific foreign currency where the actual delivery of the foreign currency is at a later date. It is used to protect or hedge against exchange risks arising from foreign currency transactions. The contract guards against unexpected variability in foreign exchange rates. The cost of forward hedging is like an insurance premium to avoid larger exchange losses. The financial manager should look upon such a contract favorably because the company is minimizing its potential foreign currency exposure. Typically, forward contracts are for 30, 60, or 90 days.

A forward exchange contract can also be used for speculating in the foreign exchange market. The financial manager must be careful when undertaking speculative contracts due to the high risk.

A hedge can still take place even if a forward exchange contract does not exist. A foreign currency transaction can serve as an economic hedge offsetting a parent's net investment in a foreign entity when the transaction is entered into for hedging purposes.

EXAMPLE 14.4

A U.S. parent fully owns a Mexican subsidiary having net assets of $5 million in pesos. The U.S. parent can borrow $5 million pesos to hedge its investment in the Mexican subsidiary. Further, assume the Mexican peso is the functional currency, and the $5 million obligation is denominated in pesos. Fluctuation in the exchange rate for pesos does not have a net impact on the parent's consolidated balance sheet, because increases in the translation adjustments balance emanating from translation of the net investment will be offset against decreases in this balance resulting from the adjustment of the obligation denominated in pesos.

4.10 FINANCIAL STRATEGIES

In nations where currency values are apt to drop, financial management of the subsidiaries should:

- Borrow local currency funds when the interest rate charged does not exceed U.S. rates after considering anticipated devaluation in the foreign country.

- Not have excess idle cash. Excess cash can be used to purchase inventory or other real assets.

- Avoid giving excessive trade credit. If accounts receivable balances are outstanding for an extended time period, interest should be charged to absorb the purchasing power loss.

- Purchase materials and supplies on credit in the country in which the foreign subsidiary operates, extending the final payment date as long as practical.

- Avoid paying advances on purchase orders unless the seller pays interest on the advances adequate to cover the purchasing power loss.

14.11 THE TRANSLATION PROCESS

A major objective of translation is to provide information of anticipated affects of rate changes on cash flow and equity. In translating foreign subsidiaries' financial statements into the U.S. parent's financial statements, the following steps are involved:

1. The foreign financial statements are expressed according to U.S. generally accepted accounting principles.
2. The foreign currency is translated into U.S. dollars.

How are financial statement accounts translated?

Balance sheet accounts are translated using the current exchange rate at the balance sheet date. If a current exchange rate is not available at the balance sheet date, use the first exchange rate available after that date.

Income statement accounts are translated using the weighted-average exchange rate for the period.

The current exchange rate is used to translate the statement of cash flows, except for those items found in the income statement which are translated using the weighted-average rate.

Translation gains and losses are reported as a separate item in the stockholders' equity section of the balance sheet. Translation gains and losses are only included in net income when there is a sale or liquidation of the entire investment in a foreign entity.

14.12 FOREIGN CURRENCY TRANSACTIONS

Foreign currency transactions may result in receivables or payables fixed in terms of the amount of foreign currency to be received or paid. Transaction gains and losses are reported in the income statement.

Foreign currency transactions are denominated in a currency other than the company's functional currency. Foreign currency transactions occur when a business:

- Is a party to an uncompleted forward exchange contract.
- Purchases or sells on credit merchandise or services the price of which is denominated in a foreign currency.
- Buys or sells assets, or incurs or settles debt denominated in foreign currency.
- Borrows or lends funds, and the amounts payable or receivable are denominated in foreign currency.

An exchange gain or loss occurs when the exchange rate changes between the purchase and sale dates.

4.13 CONCLUSION

When a company penetrates a foreign market, it may use foreign brokers, foreign licensees, or joint ventures. Financial instruments to support foreign activities may be issued (e.g., Eurobonds). The tax structure in foreign countries also must be taken into account. An unstable foreign exchange rate may result in earnings variability unless hedging occurs. Foreign currency translations and transactions need to be determined along with their financial impact.

Index

NOTES

NOTES

NOTES

NOTES

NOTES

NOTES

NOTES

NOTES

NOTES

NOTES